Prior Fault Criminalization

OXFORD MONOGRAPHS ON CRIMINAL LAW AND JUSTICE

This series aims to cover all aspects of criminal law and procedure including criminal evidence. The scope of this series is wide, encompassing both practical and theoretical works.

OTHER TITLES IN THIS SERIES

Sentencing Discretion and the Constitution
Due Process of Time
Donald A. Dripps

Victims as Agents of State Accountability
A Comparative and Normative Analysis
Marie Manikis

How Juries Work
And How They Could Work Better
Rebecca K. Helm

Civil Recovery of Criminal Property
Colin King, Jennifer Hendry

The Insanity Defence
International and Comparative Perspectives
Ronnie Mackay, Warren Brookbanks

Justice In-Between
A Study of Intermediate Criminal Verdicts
Federico Picinali

Criminal Fraud and Election Disinformation
Law and Politics
Jeremy Horder

Policing the Borders Within
Ana Aliverti

Criminalizing Sex
A Unified Liberal Theory
Stuart P. Green

Reasons to Doubt
Wrongful Convictions and the Criminal Cases Review Commission
Carolyn Hoyle and Mai Sato

Fitness to Plead
International and Comparative Perspectives
Ronnie Mackay and Warren Brookbanks

Criminal Misconducts in Office
Law and Politics
Jeremy Horder

The Preventive Turn in Criminal Law
Henrique Carvalho

Criminal Justice and Taxation
Peter Alldridge

In Search of Criminal Responsibility
Ideas, Interests, and Institutions
Nicola Lacey

Preventive Justice
Andrew Ashworth and Lucia Zedner

Character in the Criminal Trial
Mike Redmayne

Homicide and the Politics of Law Reform
Jeremy Horder

The Insecurity State
Vulnerable Autonomy and the Right to Security in the Criminal Law
Peter Ramsay

Manifest Madness
Mental Incapacity in the Criminal Law
Arlie Loughnan

The Ethics of Plea Bargaining
Richard L. Lippke

Prosecuting Domestic Violence
A Philosophical Analysis
Michelle Madden Dempsey

Prior Fault Criminalization

JOHN J CHILD
Professor of Criminal Law,
University of Birmingham, UK

ADRIAN HUNT
Honorary Associate Professor, Birmingham Law School,
University of Birmingham, UK

HANS S. CROMBAG
Professor of Behavioural Neuroscience, School of Psychology
and Sussex Neuroscience, The University of Sussex, UK

OXFORD
UNIVERSITY PRESS

OXFORD
UNIVERSITY PRESS

Great Clarendon Street, Oxford, OX2 6DP,
United Kingdom

Oxford University Press is a department of the University of Oxford.
It furthers the University's objective of excellence in research, scholarship,
and education by publishing worldwide. Oxford is a registered trade mark of
Oxford University Press in the UK and in certain other countries.

Published in the United States of America by Oxford University Press
546 Fifth Avenue, New York, NY 10036, United States of America.

British Library Cataloguing in Publication Data
Data available

Library of Congress Control Number: 2026937353

ISBN 9780198838517

DOI: 10.1093/9780191874734.001.0001

Printed and bound by
CPI Group (UK) Ltd., Croydon, CR0 4YY

The manufacturer's authorized representative in the EU for product safety is
Oxford University Press España S.A. of Parque Empresarial San Fernando de Henares,
Avenida de Castilla, 2 – 28830 Madrid (www.oup.es/en or product.safety@oup.com)
OUP España S.A. also acts as importer into Spain of products made by the manufacturer.

FSC
www.fsc.org
MIX
Paper | Supporting responsible forestry
FSC® C013604

FOREWORD

This book undertakes a timely and important task: it re-examines the foundations of prior fault in criminal law and asks whether the doctrines built upon it can be justified in principle. The orthodox approach rests on a familiar but fragile premise. Where a defendant, through earlier conduct, has brought about a state in which they lack the mental state or voluntariness required for liability, the law permits that prior fault to stand in for what is missing. In this way, liability may be imposed—or a defence withheld—notwithstanding the absence of the elements that would ordinarily define wrongdoing.

The authors demonstrate that this apparent simplicity masks underlying conceptual problems. Across a sustained analysis of intoxication, automatism, and mental disorder, they show that current doctrine depends upon a contested assumption of equivalence between fault at T1 and culpability at T2. The consequences of this are varying: the law sometimes attributes liability in the absence of sufficient fault; at other times it fails to respond where responsibility should properly arise. A central contribution of the book is to expose these tensions and to recast the issue in more coherent analytical terms, focusing on conduct that spans two temporal points—the defendant's actions at T1 and their consequences at T2.

A distinctive feature of the work is its integration of doctrinal analysis with original empirical research. The authors designed and conducted their own studies, combining controlled laboratory experiments with real-world field data, to examine how impairment—particularly intoxication—affects perception, threat recognition, and behavioural responses. The results demonstrate that the kinds of mistakes central to prior fault cases, including mistaken beliefs in the need for defensive force, arise in ways that are empirically observable and recurrent from impairment of these mechanisms. At the same time, the findings show that such effects are sensitive to degree and context, challenging simplified categorical approaches. The empirical work therefore both informs and constrains the attribution of responsibility, providing a more reliable foundation for legal analysis.

The book is also notable for its careful use of comparative material. By examining developments in other jurisdictions, including those that have adopted bespoke offences or alternative approaches to incapacity, the authors place the common law within a wider context.

Against this combined doctrinal, empirical, and comparative backdrop, the authors advance clear and structured reform proposals, providing a principled basis on which questions of responsibility, fair labelling, and liability may be addressed. The relevance of this analysis extends beyond academic debate. The issues addressed in this book will contribute to debates over how to reform the law, including the Law Commission's forthcoming work on insanity and automatism. The book's insistence on moving beyond historically contingent distinctions, and towards a more coherent and evidence-based account of incapacity, provides a valuable foundation for future reform in this area. Its emphasis on identifying responsibility through a combination of clear normative criteria and empirical understanding is likely to be of considerable importance. This is, therefore, a work of both intellectual and practical significance. It will be of interest to scholars, judges, and those engaged or interested in law reform alike. Its arguments are carefully developed and enrich our understanding of fault, responsibility, and the circumstances in which criminal liability should properly be imposed.

Professor Penney Lewis
Law Commissioner for Criminal Law
Law Commission of England and Wales

CONTENTS

ACKNOWLEDGEMENTS

We would like to thank all those who helped us in the research and publication of this book. In particular, we acknowledge the intellectual input of a range of colleagues, including James Browning, Antony Duff, Samantha Fairclough, Kim Oorsouw, and Alex Sarch; the research assistance of Reece Nicholls; and with special thanks to Rudi Fortson KC for his support and input throughout. We are grateful to the organizers and participants of research events at the University of Birmingham, University of Sussex, Maastricht University, the University of Glasgow, the University of Edinburgh, Kings College London, and the University of Surrey. We thank series editor Jeremy Horder for his support, as well as his predecessor Andrew Ashworth who accepted our original proposal.

The empirical elements of the project were funded through the British Academy, *Understanding the 'Fault' in Prior-Fault Intoxication: A Pathway to Criminal Law Reform* Knowledge Frontiers Project (KF3/100111, 2019). We thank the funder, as well as project Co-Is Dora Duka and Melanie Sauerland; collaborator Kyriaki Nikolaou; post-docs Paloma Manguele and Nicholas Sinclair-House; research assistants Joey Campaniello, Luiza Ludwig, and Francesca Webster; and project partners at the Australian Law Reform Commission, New South Wales Law Reform Commission, South Australian Law Reform Commission, Tasmania Law Reform Institute, Jersey Law Commission, Hong Kong Law Reform Commission, New Jersey Law Reform Commission, Scottish Law Commission, and the Sentencing Council of England and Wales.

John J Child: I dedicate this work to my wife Scarlett, to my little girl Lyra, and to my 'not so little' boy Leon, who was born at the time we started this book.

Adrian Hunt: I dedicate this work to my mother, Clare; and to the memory of my father Tom, and my brother, Paddy.

Hans S. Crombag: I would like to thank and dedicate this work to my wife, Maria Eugenia Olivas, for her support with everything, always; to my father, Hans FM Crombag; and to the memory of my sweet mother, Wiesje Crombag-Teunissen.

AUTHOR BIOS

John J Child is a Professor of Criminal Law at Birmingham Law School, University of Birmingham, specializing in criminal law theory and doctrine. He co-authors two leading criminal law textbooks: *Simester and Sullivan's Criminal Law* and *Smith, Hogan and Ormerod's Essentials of Criminal Law*. Child is also the founder and co-director of the Criminal Law Reform Now Network.

Adrian Hunt is an Honorary Associate Professor at Birmingham Law School, University of Birmingham, where he previously worked as a member of academic staff. He has worked as a consultant for the Council of Europe and the Organization for Security and Co-Operation in Europe . Hunt continues to publish widely in the field of criminal justice, criminal law, public law, and human rights law.

Hans S. Crombag is a Professor of Behavioural Neuroscience in the School of Psychology and Neuroscience, University of Sussex. He researches and has published numerous articles on the neurobiological and psychological foundations of motivated action, with particular emphasis on the role of associative learning in motivation. Crombag's work also addresses the mechanisms underlying substance use and addiction, broader issues in mental health, and the implications—where any exist—of these findings for criminal law and justice.

1
INTRODUCTION

1.1 Introduction

The term 'prior fault' is used to describe and categorize a collection of rules that allow criminal liability to be established across and between events, making a defendant's earlier blameworthy conduct definitive to their liability for a subsequent act. Intoxication rules provide the best-known example. When a defendant (D) becomes voluntarily intoxicated at time 1 (T1), they are not necessarily committing an offence;[1] when D causes potentially criminal harms at a later point (T2), it may also be that no offence is committed, where D's intoxication leads to a lack of mens rea and/or voluntariness.[2] Analysed as separate events (T1/T2), there is no basis for liability. However, given that D lacked mens rea and/or voluntariness at T2 *because* of a choice to become intoxicated at T1, a 'no liability' outcome may appear overly generous, perhaps even perverse. It is on this basis that intoxication rules have developed in law, linking the T1–T2 events in order to establish liability *as if* all offence elements were present in fact at T2, and allowing D to be labelled and punished on that basis.[3]

Prior fault rules can be identified as operating in multiple areas of the criminal law. Just as the intoxication rules are capable of constructing liability despite an absence of mens rea at T2, we will discuss a similar mechanism that operates in relation to prior fault automatism (where D's T1 conduct leads to involuntariness at T2),[4] as well as current—and potential—rules relating to insanity.[5] In Part I of this book, we discuss the role of prior fault rules which function to replace the elements of a crime for which persons are held liable. This is not, however, the sole function of prior fault. A different body of prior fault rules has developed to disapply or block the application of supervening defences which might otherwise exculpate defendants.[6] For example, where D relies on a mistaken belief to satisfy the elements of a defence at T2, and where that mistaken belief is attributable to a state of

[1] Indeed, most intoxication cases involve alcohol, in circumstances where its consumption is legal and widespread.

[2] This would be the case, e.g., where D's intoxicated delusions result in them not recognizing their victim as human. See *Lipman* [1970] 1 QB 152.

[3] We discuss intoxication rules in Chapter 2.

[4] We discuss prior fault automatism rules in Chapter 3.

[5] We discuss prior fault insanity/mental disorder rules in Chapter 4.

[6] The term 'supervening defence' is used to identify defences properly so-called, which provide potential routes to exculpation only after the elements of an offence have been established.

Prior Fault Criminalization. John J Child, Adrian Hunt, and Hans S. Crombag, Oxford University Press.
 DOI: 10.1093/9780191874734.003.0001

voluntary intoxication induced at T1, D will (typically) be disallowed from relying on that belief.[7] Beyond intoxication, prior fault rules may also apply to block a defence at T2 where D has manufactured its conditions at T1 (such as the blocking of self-defence where D has intentionally provoked their victim (V) into an attack in order to employ defensive force), as well as similar rules related to association (such as the blocking of duress where the threat against D originated from their choice to associate with dangerous individuals at T1). We group the discussion of these rules in Part II of the book, which focuses on the role of prior fault in blocking supervening defences.

Despite the prevalence of prior fault rules, their application remains controversial, particularly where they apply to construct a criminal offence. Specifically, because prior fault rules stretch the criminal event across two points in time (T1–T2), they represent an exception to the contemporality principle, which requires that the elements of a crime should coincide at a single temporal point.[8] There is both a practical and a normative basis for the contemporality principle. Normatively, application of the criminal law is not intended to be an aggregation of all the bad choices people make; offences are designed to identify and deter/punish specific criminal wrongs rather than to provide a broader appraisal of D's character. Maintaining the law's narrow application to individual events is also practically desirable, allowing instruments of the law (the police, the courts, etc) to function with a much greater degree of clarity and finality. It is on this basis that the criminal law paradigmatically applies to single snapshot events that are structured and defined by reference to D's single point of conduct.[9] Prior fault rules provide a notable exception to this principle.

But this is not all. It is important to recognize that prior fault rules are not simply a mechanism for stretching a criminal event across T1–T2; they are not simply an exception to the principle of contemporality. Rather, as we have just explained, prior fault rules also apply to identify and constitute the wrong criminalized. Drawing on our opening intoxication example, it is not necessary that D's voluntary drug taking at T1 was done with the mens rea required for the offence charged at T2;[10] prior fault rules are *not* designed to transport or link existing mens rea at T1 to D's harm causing conduct at T2. Rather, D's blameworthy (though individually non-criminal) conduct at T1 is aggregated with D's harmful (though individually non-criminal) conduct at T2, and on the basis of this D is labelled and

[7] We discuss intoxicated mistakes in defence in Chapter 8.

[8] Supervening *defences* can work differently, taking account of certain T1 events in order to assess D's exculpatory claims at T2: e.g. D only used force at T2 to defend themself from attack at T1, following threats from another, following provocation, etc. However, even here, prior fault rules apply to stretch the defensive event a further step to *D's conduct* at T1. We discuss this in Section 1.3 below, criticizing attempts to justify or normalize inculpatory prior fault rules by analogy to defences.

[9] Offences specify certain circumstances and/or causal outcomes from conduct (actus reus), as well as the requirement for accompanying states of mind or fault (mens rea).

[10] In Chapter 2, Section 2.4.2, we discuss if this would even be possible.

punished *as if* they completed the principal offence charged at T2. D is treated *as if* all elements were satisfied at T2; *as if* there was no absence of mens rea or voluntariness; *as if* there was no issue of contemporality. Thus, prior fault rules create a controversial inculpatory legal fiction.

Given the controversial nature of prior fault, as well as the potential for broad application of prior fault rules across different offences and defences, one might expect its doctrinal construction to be tightly controlled and justified. However, nothing could be further from the truth when it comes to the current law, and references here to a body of prior fault 'rules' should not be assumed to imply principled coherence or consistency. Current prior fault rules have developed and exist not as a coherent whole but as a series of discrete exceptions, often interpreted and applied as if in complete isolation from comparable examples, and with reliance on scientifically problematic determinations of incapacity. For example, in spite of over a century of jurisprudence engaging with intoxication rules, they remain contested at the most foundational level: routinely miscategorized as 'defensive' rules, as 'evidential' rather than substantive, and apparently unable to explain the basis upon which inculpation is achieved within a principled legal framework.[11] Indeed, in relation to both prior fault automatism and insanity, outside of drug cases, it remains controversial to suggest that prior fault rules are in operation at all.[12] The prior fault rules that do exist vary—without clear rationale—in their application to different offences and defences, in their characterization of T1 fault, in whether D must be aware at T1 of future dangers and (if so) what D should be aware of, in the causal link (if any) required between T1 and T2 events, as well as in what T2 harms are sufficient to trigger prior fault analysis. Such inconsistencies are not isolated to the difference between prior fault in offending and prior fault regarding defences, or variations between jurisdictions, but exist between each of the examples we explore in this book (as well as within the evolution of those rules individually).[13]

It is with this context in mind that the current book is conceived. We do not approach the issue by starting with a blank page and articulating first principles *de novo*. Rather, we proceed by considering where we currently are, by undertaking an exploratory analysis of the current law looking to identify and evaluate such principles. Canvassing the major areas of prior fault debate, ours is a legal discussion that encompasses key philosophical questions about the nature of culpability and just criminalization, as well as questions within psychology and neuroscience about our understanding of impaired cognitive function. In the brief sections that follow, we begin by exploring the origin and comparative evolution of prior fault ideas, before seeking to concretize some of the specific challenges that will

[11] See Chapter 2, Section 2.2 on the intoxication rules.

[12] See Chapters 3 and 4 on the current operation of prior fault in these areas.

[13] For discussion and critique of current inconsistencies, see, e.g., P Robinson, 'Causing the Conditions of One's Own Defence' (1985) 71 *Virginia Law Review* 1; JJ Child, 'Prior Fault: Blocking Defences or Constructing Crimes' in A Reed and M Bohlander (eds) *Defences* (Routledge, 2014).

re-emerge throughout the book. These challenges include understanding the nature and identity of prior fault, balancing intuitions of justified blame against principles of criminal justice, as well as addressing related substantive and methodological difficulties regarding how the law expresses and applies prior fault rules in practice.

1.2 The origins and evolution of prior fault

The history of prior fault rules, and particularly those relating to intoxication, has been much discussed in the literature.[14] Our aim here is not to challenge those accounts or to replicate the process, but to highlight some of the major issues most relevant to our current appraisal of them. This includes a recognition of the longevity of prior fault analysis in legal discourse and practice, tracing back over centuries; the consistent appeal to intuitions of 'justice', used to supplement or (more often) simply to avoid engagement with legal principle; as well as the diverging paths of prior fault analysis across different criminal law jurisdictions and traditions.

1.2.1 A brief history of prior fault

The basic intuitive rationale for prior fault has been repeated and applied since at least the sixteenth century,[15] drawing on blameworthy causes of incapacity as a basis for criminalization. On the paradigm of intoxication, despite the potential for lack of mens rea and/or voluntariness at T2 (i.e. the lack of an essential offence element at T2), historical commentaries and case law have consistently weighed in favour of liability. We see this in the current leading case of *DPP v Majewski*:[16]

> If a man of his own volition takes a substance which causes him to cast off the restraints of reason and conscience, no wrong is done to him by holding him answerable criminally for any injury he may do while in that condition.

Similarly, more than a century ago in *Beard*, the House of Lords declared:[17]

[14] We also provide more detail—specific to the intoxication rules—in Chapter 2, Sections 2.2.1 and 2.2.2.

[15] RU Singh, 'History of the Defence of Drunkenness in English Criminal Law' (1933) 49 *Law Quarterly Review* 528.

[16] [1977] AC 443, 474.

[17] [1920] AC 479, 494.

> . . . voluntary drunkenness was never an excuse for criminal misconduct; and indeed the classic authorities broadly assert that voluntary drunkenness must be considered rather an aggravation than a defence . . . [A] man who by his own voluntary act debauches and destroys his will power shall be no better situated in regard to criminal acts than a sober man.

Indeed, similar sentiments can be traced back to the sixteenth century, and beyond:[18]

> And Aristotle says, that such a Man deserves double Punishment, because he has doubly offended, viz. in being drunk to the evil Example of others, and in committing the Crime . . . And this Act is said to be done ignoranter, for that he is the Cause of his own Ignorance.

The consistent position reflected in these statements is that, in circumstances of prior fault, D may be guilty of a crime at T2 despite a lack of essential mens rea and/or voluntariness at that point, and that we should accept that 'no wrong' is done to D as a result. The break that this represents from core criminal law principle is then obfuscated by reference to intoxication as a 'defence' (intoxication is never a defence), that D should not benefit from their intoxication (a variation of the inaccurate defence analysis), and the idea that drunkenness means D has 'doubly offended' (a moral rather than a plausible criminal law claim).[19] But despite obfuscation, or perhaps at least partly because of it, the legal position—providing a route to liability—has remained. Historically, the absence of engagement with prior fault outside of intoxication cases should be noted here; however, as we will discuss in chapters throughout the book, it is from this intoxication paradigm that similar rules in relation to automatism and insanity, as well as to the blocking of defences, have drawn support.

The consistent description and application of prior fault rules across time is remarkable, and particularly so when set in the context of fundamental changes during this time in how criminal law was understood and applied more generally. In particular, during the nineteenth and twentieth centuries, there was a clear shift in the common law towards greater precision in how offences were defined, as well as to the use of subjective forms of mens rea.[20] In this manner, inculpatory prior fault rules (expressed in broad non-specific terms) may have had greater

[18] *Fogossa*, 1 Plowden, 19, 1551 (Cam Scacc). This view has a long-lived pedigree. For example, in the *Penitential of Theodore, Archbishop of Canterbury* (668–690 AD), it was declared: '. . . whosoever shall have killed a man while drunk shall be guilty of homicide; he commits one fault by self-indulgence and another by killing a Christian'. See, in general, RU Singh, 'History of the Defence of Drunkenness in English Criminal Law' (1933) 49 *Law Quarterly Review* 528.

[19] AP Simester, 'Intoxication Is Never a Defence' (2009) *Criminal Law Review* 3.

[20] P Handler, 'Intoxication and Criminal Responsibility in England, 1819–1920' (2013) 33(2) *Oxford Journal of Legal Studies* 243.

compatibility with a premodern criminal law system that was characterized by imprecise requirements of blameworthiness. However, establishing culpability through those same prior fault rules becomes strikingly anomalous within a modernizing (and increasingly codified) criminal law system that requires the terms of liability to be defined clearly and specifically, and expects subjective forms of mens rea that define culpability by reference to D's conscious perceptions in action.[21] The idea of prior fault rules representing some form of 'rough justice' may continue to convince some and is a recurring theme in several later chapters, but is firmly out of step with a modernized system.

To find a place for prior fault within this system, various attempts have been made to reconceptualize and/or rearticulate prior fault rules; and in particular, to do so in a way that does not expressly or implicitly acknowledge the fact that prior fault criminalization involves imposing criminal liability by combining non-specific fault from T1 with conduct and harms from T2 (i.e. the legal fiction). Sometimes this was done by framing the absence of mens rea and/or voluntariness at T2 as an attempt to raise a 'defence' which the prior fault rules did not permit. Thus, for example, D is not allowed to raise their intoxication as a defence because it was their fault that they became intoxicated. The problem with this approach is that where D does not fulfil the elements of a crime at T2 (which absent mens rea and/or voluntariness they do not) it is difficult to see what D requires exculpation from.[22] Another approach involves framing the issue merely as one about rules of evidence concerning the issues D is entitled to raise. So, for example, rather than being presented in terms of constructing liability or exculpating in any substantive sense, intoxication rules were to be understood as exclusionary rules of evidence, preventing D raising evidence of intoxication. The problem here is that we would be excluding potentially relevant and compelling evidence as to lack of mens rea and/or voluntariness, and thereby allowing D to be convicted of a crime that they have not in fact committed.[23]

An alternative approach, which seeks to maintain prior fault rules, is to accept their substantive function (i.e. the legal fiction), but to justify that function through a broad claim of *equivalence* between D's fault at T1 and that absent at T2.[24] The argument here is that becoming intoxicated at T1 is a 'reckless' act which gives rise to the criminal harm at T2, and therefore it may be legally appropriate to trace that T1 recklessness through to replace the equivalent missing element at T2. This approach, however, is highly problematic for a range of different reasons which we explore below and in further chapters. Most obvious is the appropriateness of

[21] Ibid; J Stannard, 'The Demise of Drunkenness' (1982) 2 *Legal Studies* 291; A Loughnan, *Manifest Madness* (OUP, 2012) Chs 5 and 7.

[22] AP Simester, 'Intoxication Is Never a Defence' (2009) *Criminal Law Review* 3.

[23] We discuss this further in Chapter 2, Section 2.2.2.

[24] This represents the current position of the Law Commission. See Law Commission, *Intoxication and Criminal Liability* (LC No 314, 2009); *Insanity and Automatism* (Discussion Paper, 2013) Ch 6.

using D's state of mind at T1 to substitute for the necessary mens rea and/or voluntariness at T2. As a matter of fact and principle, these are not equivalent: D's potential understanding of the future risks associated with intoxication (T1) is importantly different to the subjective recognition of a particular risk unreasonably run in action (T2);[25] and in relation to a lack of voluntariness, the potential for equivalence is even more strained and rarely addressed. Whilst the current law can therefore sensibly be described as entrenched by its history,[26] it is not supported by that history in terms of legal principle or doctrine.

1.2.2 Comparative understandings of prior fault

Given the uncertain and problematic legal basis for prior fault rules, it is informative to see how those rules have evolved and crystallized in different jurisdictions. Indeed, although we take the law of England & Wales as our centre point in this study,[27] the appeal and use of prior fault rules—as well as their problems of conceptualization and application—are shared across criminal jurisdictions internationally. Of particular interest here is how intuitions about prior fault seem to vary between jurisdictions, as well as how comfortable courts and legislators are with rules that appear to conflict with the contemporality principle and other fundamentals of offence/defence application.

We address comparative issues of this kind within each of the topic-specific chapters that follow, but some general framing and introduction is useful here. The most direct comparison and similarities are found in other common law jurisdictions. Intoxication rules, often modelled on the approach in English law from *Majewski*, dominate the field in terms of debate, though a plethora of other prior fault rules exist at the margins (not necessarily labelled as prior fault, but constructed using similar T1–T2 rules of inculpation). A small number of jurisdictions have rejected or dispensed with the application of prior fault, at least in terms of offence construction across T1–T2, meaning that a lack of mens rea at T2 resulting from T1 intoxication (or other prior fault) will simply result in acquittal.[28] However, most common law jurisdictions (like England & Wales) have maintained such rules, and here we focus on their varying struggles in terms of definition and

[25] Discussed in Section 1.3 below. See, regarding the Law Commission proposals, JJ Child, 'Drink, Drugs and Law Reform: A Review of Law Commission Report No. 314' [2009] *Criminal Law Review* 488; R Mackay and D Hughes, 'Insanity and Blaming the Mentally Ill: A Critique of the Prior Fault Principle in the Law Commission's Discussion Paper' [2022] *Criminal Law Review* 21.

[26] Discussed in J Stannard, 'The Demise of Drunkenness' (1982) 2 *Legal Studies* 291, 293.

[27] Any subsequent references to the shortened form 'English law' should be read to denote the law of England & Wales.

[28] E.g. New Zealand and the Australian state of Victoria. See S Gough, 'Surviving without *Majewski*?' (2000) *Criminal Law Review* 719; AP Simester and WJ Brookbanks, *Principles of Criminal Law* (5th Ed, Thomson Reuters, 2019) 492–513.

application.[29] A useful example here is Canada, where we see political intuitions towards criminalization (consolidated through statute) in open and ongoing conflict with judicial protection of broader rights-based legal principles.[30]

The position in 'civil law' jurisdictions provides a useful counterpoint, and one that is often drawn upon by those seeking reform in common law jurisdictions.[31] Questions concerning the appropriateness and application of prior fault rules arise in civil law systems in a manner that is remarkably similar to the common law. They include issues over the construction of missing T2 mens rea, as well as when and how excusatory and justificatory rules (i.e. defences) may be disapplied.[32] Indeed, in civil law systems that place a particular value on certainty and codification (i.e. code-based criminal law systems), the presence of uncodified prior fault-based rules gives rise to particular chagrin.[33]

But there are also important differences, both of substance and procedure, which we discuss in later chapters. Substantively, the application of prior fault rules has been more effectively confined and limited in several civil law jurisdictions: limited by the greater use of objective mens rea standards (so prior fault construction is not necessary),[34] by the removal of strict dividing lines in the potential for prior fault rules between insanity and other forms of dissociation,[35] and

[29] See AP Simester, 'Getting Drunk in Singapore and Malaysia' (2012) *Singapore Journal of Legal Studies* 1. For a useful, though slightly dated, overview of jurisdictions, see Law Commission, *Intoxication and Criminal Liability* (LC No 314, 2009) Appendix C.

[30] See *Brown* [2022] SCC 18: the Supreme Court of Canada found s33.1 of the Criminal Code to be incompatible with the Canadian Charter of Rights and Freedoms, meaning that (contra s33.1) intoxication rules may not apply to construct liability where D is involuntary through drug use at T2. It is notable that this limit to the use of intoxication rules was previously recognized in *Daviault* [1994] 3 SCR 63, and that s33.1 was an amendment to the Criminal Code designed specifically to reverse its effect. See further P Leahy, 'Legislative Revision of Extreme Intoxication in Canada' [2022] *Criminal Law Review* 957.

[31] This is so despite structural differences between common law and civil law approaches to required elements for criminalization. Whereas the common law applies a two-element approach—actus reus and mens rea—civil law tends to require three elements: namely, rules relating to offence definition, wrongfulness, and blameworthiness.

[32] See, generally, A Goldberg et al, 'Prior Fault Blame in England and Wales, Germany and the Netherlands' (2021) 8(1) *Journal of International and Comparative Law* 53; J Herrmann, 'Causing the Conditions of One's Own Defence: The Multifaceted Approach of German Law' (1986) 3 *Brigham Young University Law Review* 747; AÖ Atalay, 'The Formulation of Voluntary Intoxication in Continental Law' (2020) 64(13–14) *International Journal of Offender Therapy and Comparative Criminology* 1398.

[33] On the controversial use of such doctrines in German law, see HU Paeffgen, 'Actio Libera in Causa und 323a StGB' ('Actio Libera in Causa and provision 323a GCC') [1985] *Zeitschrift für die gesamte Strafrechtswissenschaft* 513; cf I Stassen-Rapp, *Die Behandlung von Selbstverschuldeten Rauschzuständen im Angloamerikanischen Strafrecht—Vorbild für eine Gesetzliche Regelung in Deutschland* ('The Handling of Selfintoxication in Anglo-American Criminal Law—A Model for Legal Regulation in Germany') (Tectum, 2011), 304–07.

[34] The Netherlands provides a particular example of this. See A Goldberg et al, 'Prior Fault Blame in England and Wales, Germany and the Netherlands' (2021) 8(1) *Journal of International and Comparative Law* 53. See also RA Duff, 'Two Models of Criminal Fault' (2019) 13(4) *Criminal Law and Philosophy* 643. Discussed in Chapter 11, Section 11.3.1.

[35] The absence of a strict provision excluding prior fault analysis from insanity cases avoids much of the complex and problematic line drawing we see in English law, discussed in Chapter 4.

by the alternative availability of special part prior fault-based offences—a topic of perennial debate within common law jurisdictions.[36] In procedural terms as well, many of the practical obstacles associated with the reform of prior fault rules appear ameliorated within inquisitorial systems. This includes issues around expert evidence, the potential for prior fault offences to work alongside traditional forms of liability, for the staged discussion of prior fault within a trial, and so on. Such issues remain of vital importance and appear to have been instrumental in the Law Commission's decision to abandon its 1993 proposal for thc creation of an English prior fault intoxication offence.[37]

1.3 Theoretical and practical challenges

The study of prior fault is challenging, perhaps uniquely so as a collection of disparate rules existing in apparent open conflict with established legal principle in circumstances of philosophical and scientific uncertainty. To engage appropriately with this challenge, it is necessary to analyse the specific functions and applications of the rules as we do in the chapters that follow. But this is not to say that each set of rules—intoxication, automatism, insanity, and beyond—is entirely unique and self-contained. Indeed, several first principles debates will cut across the discussion of each: debates about the nature, justification, and function of prior fault rules in general.

In the subsections below, we introduce some of the most important debates of this kind. Although in doing so we provide some foreshadowing of our later conclusions, our aim at this juncture is not to resolve such debates, but rather to alert the reader to a collection of first principle issues that will be revisited throughout the book.

1.3.1 One problem or many?

Raising this issue helps us shed light on some of the conceptual issues relevant to understanding and evaluating prior fault rules. It is a question that may usefully be teased apart here as a set of associated questions. First, should we conceptualize prior fault as a single set of related issues that are or should be capable of expression within a single set of doctrinal rules? Second, what is the appropriate status of intoxication within an analysis of prior fault? And finally, by way of introduction

[36] E.g. the German offence of dangerous intoxication (§323a GCC). Discussed in Chapter 5, Section 5.3.1.

[37] See proposal in Law Commission, *Intoxication and Criminal Liability* (LC No 229, 1993) Part 6; later rejected in Law Commission, *Intoxication and Criminal Liability* (Consultation 127, 1995) Part 5. See G Dingwall, *Alcohol and Crime* (Routledge, 2006) Ch 5. Discussed in Chapter 5, Section 5.2.4.

at least, does an evaluation of prior fault require us to consider legal constructions that have not traditionally been presented as prior fault based? We outline each in turn.

1.3.1.1 Is prior fault a single set of rules?

The question here is whether prior fault presents one set of related issues, requiring and capable of a single set of doctrinal responses? Although prior fault rules are typically applied in a disconnected case-specific fashion, academic commentators have attempted various overarching conceptualizations seeking to link them together within a single doctrine.[38] Robinson, in particular, has contended that prior fault rules may be understood as the mirror image of supervening defences.[39] His argument is that despite the paradigm of single-event crimes in line with the contemporality principle, criminal law does accept the application of a series of supervening defences that look back to a previous (T1) event in order to provide potential exculpation for a crime committed at T2. When assessing D's claim to the defence of duress, for example, it is necessary to examine the threats made to D at T1; when assessing loss of control, it is necessary to assess things said or done at T1 that might have triggered D's response; and so on with other defences. It is from these more familiar T1–T2 defence constructions that—for Robinson—we should move to analyse and evaluate prior fault rules operating on offences, looking to identify a common rationale or pattern of use.

However, despite similarities, the characterization of prior fault as a mirror of defences is potentially misleading. It is a characterization that underplays the breadth of prior fault rules: such rules apply to offences to construct or substitute for missing elements, but they also apply to *defences*, blocking the application of a defence that would otherwise be available on the basis of prior fault a *further* step back from other defence elements. An example of the latter is contrived self-defence, where D provokes V to attack them in order to respond with defensive force.[40] Focusing on V's attack (T1) and D's defensive force (T2) alone may satisfy the elements of self-defence, but the prior fault rule allows us to look back to *D's* provocation (pre-T1) as a basis for denying the defence.[41] Presenting prior fault as a mirror of defences also risks underplaying the significance of rules that inculpate (as opposed to exculpate) a defendant. Although we may accept general rules of exculpation that take account of the context of D's conduct, this is quite

[38] This seems to have been most common in the 1980s and 1990s, and is exemplified by the discussion of prior fault doctrine in M Gur-Arye, *Actio Libera in Causa in Criminal Law* (Jerusalem, 1984); P Robinson, 'Causing the Conditions of One's Own Defence' (1985) 71 *Virginia Law Review* 1; A Ashworth, *Principles of Criminal Law* (2nd Ed, Clarendon Press, 1995); P Robinson, *Structure and Function in Criminal Law* (Clarendon Press, 1997) Ch 4. See also Law Commission, *Insanity and Automatism* (Discussion Paper, 2013) Ch 6.

[39] P Robinson, *Structure and Function in Criminal Law* (Clarendon Press, 1997) Ch 4.

[40] Discussed in Chapter 8, Section 8.3 and Chapter 10 in general.

[41] *Rashford* [2005] EWCA Crim 3377.

different from the aggregation of multiple non-criminal events being recast in label and punishment into a standard T2 offence (i.e. the acceptance of an inculpatory legal fiction).

Our critique of Robinson's approach is not, however, to suggest that a broader conceptualization of prior fault (i.e. beyond the atomized approach of the current law) is undesirable or impossible. Rather, we simply doubt that prior fault can effectively be conceptualized as a single doctrine or single set of rules, whether presented as a mirror of defences or otherwise.[42]

Our approach within this book, drawing on previous work,[43] begins with the recognition that prior fault rules are theoretically and functionally distinct from other rules within the criminal law: prior fault rules do not mirror supervening defences, they do not represent defences in their own right, they are not a form of constructive liability,[44] and any analogy with complicity is more likely to confuse than to enlighten.[45] Our contention that prior fault rules should be the subject of distinct study does not, however, tell us anything about the internal structure of the object of that study. Indeed, as we have already indicated, we contend that the study of prior fault rules should distinguish between, first, prior fault criminalization that operates so as to construct an otherwise incomplete offence and, second, prior fault rules that operate so as to block an otherwise available defence. We do so because—despite family resemblances in stretching across criminal events—these two categories of prior fault are distinct in function, and therefore require distinct rationalization and critique. In the context of *defences*, our task is to understand rules that deny D's claim to legitimate exculpation, asking when and how claims of excuse or justification may be undermined by D's previous conduct. However, the construction of *offences* (rather than blocking defences) is quite different, and in many ways more challenging. Here, uniquely, prior fault analysis requires us to consider when D's previous conduct may be aggregated with later conduct to substitute for absent mens rea and/or voluntariness; it is here that prior fault rules currently operate as a legal fiction.

We reflect this function-focused distinction in our separation of the discussion of prior fault rules which operate so as to construct offences, which we address in Part I of the book, and prior fault rules which operate to block the availability of a defence, which we address in Part II of the book. Additionally, alongside the

[42] Singular accounts of this kind are often misdirected by the inaccurate discussion of intoxication as a defence. Where intoxication is conceived as a 'defence', blocked in application by D's prior fault, then it becomes enticingly similar in function to the prior fault blocking of other defences such as self-defence and duress.

[43] JJ Child, 'Prior Fault: Blocking Defences or Constructing Crimes' in A Reed and M Bohlander (eds) *Defences* (Routledge, 2014); S Dimock, 'Actio Libera in Causa' (2013) 7 *Criminal Law and Philosophy* 549.

[44] A point of discussion for intoxication rules in particular is set out in Chapter 2, Section 2.3.

[45] This is a point of discussion for intoxication rules in particular, which is set out in Chapter 2, Section 2.3.

collective term 'prior fault', we employ a notation device to distinguish between both sets of rules. Prior fault rules used to substitute for the missing elements of an offence will be referred to as 'prior fault^{OFF}', and prior fault in the context of blocking otherwise available defences will be referred to as 'prior fault^{DEF}'.

1.3.1.2 What is the status of intoxication in prior fault rules?

At a minimum, it is clear that intoxication rules—both in the construction of crimes and the blocking of defences—provide the *paradigm* example of prior fault rules within the current law. We see this in the historical analysis of prior fault outlined in the previous section, which may be more accurately described as a history of intoxication rules and intuitions. This is also the case within contemporary debate, where all examples of prior fault are typically discussed by analogy to the intoxication rules.[46]

It is certainly the case that an analogy with intoxication can be useful in considering other areas of prior fault, drawing out similar intuitions towards criminalization where D's T1 conduct has led to T2 harms. But the paradigm status of intoxication can also be problematic: there is a clear underdevelopment of rules relating to T1 fault where drug taking is not involved, and a similar lack of clarity where T1 drug taking arises in circumstances of addiction or other comorbidity.[47] There is also a danger (which we have discussed elsewhere[48]) that intoxication as a paradigm for prior fault becomes intoxication as a *proxy* for prior fault. Our concern here is that because the analysis of intoxication rules has become overly fixated on the definition of 'intoxication', this has led to the assumption of culpability as soon as whatever definitional threshold agreed is arrived at, without any discussion of whether in fact or morally it is actually appropriate to attach criminal blame to persons who are 'intoxicated' in that sense. In such a situation the establishment of 'intoxication' becomes a *proxy* for the establishment of 'culpability'. In addition, the focus on 'intoxication' gives rise to unnecessary problems of application (e.g. courts drawn into scientific analysis of the boundaries of intoxication rather than questions of legitimate blame),[49] as well as unprincipled limitations within reform debate (e.g. discussion of intoxication offences rather than prior fault offences).[50] We explore these and related criticisms throughout the book, whilst building an articulation of prior fault that does not rely on proxy states such as intoxication.

[46] We see this, e.g., in the leading criminal law textbooks.

[47] This is part of the reason why, in this book, we have separated the discussion of prior fault across chapters focusing on different T1 causes. These causes include, but are not limited to, intoxication.

[48] H Crombag, JJ Child, and R Fortson, 'Understanding the "Fault" in Prior-Fault Intoxication' in A Reed and M Bohlander (eds) *Fault* (Routledge, 2022) Ch 5.

[49] See, e.g., *Taj* [2018] EWCA Crim 1743, discussed in JJ Child, HS Crombag, and GR Sullivan, 'Criminalising the Mistakes of the Delusional, the Irrational, and the Dangerous' [2020] *Criminal Law Review* 302.

[50] Discussed in Chapter 5.

1.3.1.3 How to deal with prior fault beyond the label?

The third of our questions relates to legal constructions that are not typically labelled as prior fault, and this also provides a further important dimension to any first principles discussion. The point here is that, if we are to look behind the labels/proxies within the current law to provide a better understanding of T1–T2 culpability, then this analysis should carry through to an evaluation of rules that avoid as well as those that engage with the label prior fault.

We discuss some specific examples of this in different chapters, such as the so-called trigger-slip cases which have been traditionally analysed (we contend, incorrectly) outside the realms of prior fault.[51] Beyond this, we discuss whether internal conditions leading to insanity (or otherwise) should be caught within prior fault rules,[52] doctrines of wilful ignorance,[53] the so-called grand-schemer cases,[54] and so on. Indeed, more broadly in the concluding chapter, we discuss this in relation to the use of objective fault standards (i.e. fault derived from a comparison of D's conduct and/or mental state to that of a reasonable person).[55] Objective fault standards, whether used in the definition of offences or defences, will invariably employ a 'reasonable person' construction that does not include states of intoxication or other dissociation (and will often not include characteristics of mental disorder). In this way, the use of objective fault standards can avoid questions of prior fault.[56]

1.3.2 Legal challenges

There is a considerable degree of legal uncertainty in relation to prior fault, both in its doctrinal and theoretical constructions. In this subsection, we set out some of these, moving from more familiar first principles debates to those that have previously received insufficient attention.

1.3.2.1 Legal and conceptual justifications

At its foundation, prior fault lacks an agreed conceptual justification, though a number of alternatives are canvased in the literature (and courts). The first, and perhaps longest serving justification, presents the prior fault rules as mechanisms for preventing abuse of the law. Historically, this may be understood in non-specific

[51] Trigger-slip cases will typically involve a physical confrontation between D and V in which D accidentally kills V (e.g. due to slipping and pulling the trigger of a gun). We discuss such cases as an example of prior fault analysis in Chapter 3, Section 3.4.

[52] Discussed in Chapter 4.

[53] Discussed in Chapter 3, Section 3.5.1.

[54] Discussed in Chapter 3, Section 3.3.

[55] Discussed in Chapter 11, Section 11.3.1.

[56] It has been claimed that the greater use of objective fault in the criminal law can remove the need for prior fault rules. See J Stannard, 'The Demise of Drunkenness' (1982) 2 *Legal Studies* 291.

terms, related to the demonization of drugs and drug taking;[57] but in modern times, the argument focuses more specifically on the punishment of defendants who seek to manipulate the law through their T1 acts in an attempt to unfairly avoid liability at T2.[58] There is much to be said for this justification, and concerns about the conscious manipulation of legal rules may have some traction in cases where D intentionally provokes an attack to justify defensive force, for example (i.e. contrived defence cases).[59] However, cases of *intentional* manipulation are vanishingly rare in practice, and the idea that individuals might become incompetent through drugs in the hope that they will cause certain harms when unable to control their conduct is barely plausible.[60] The problem, then, is that conscious abuse of law provides only a narrow justification for a subset of prior fault rules; it does not provide a justification capable of generalization.

An alternative, typically presented in combination with others, is to justify prior fault by a simple appeal to intuition. We see this in legal pronouncements that explicitly set aside issues of 'logic' and 'legal principle' in favour of appeals to 'necessity', 'common sense', and 'order'. As Lord Salmond states in *Majewski*, for example, responding to a critique of the intoxication rules as illogical:[61]

> The answer is that in strict logic this view cannot be justified. But this is the view that has been adopted by the common law of England, which is founded on common sense and experience rather than strict logic.

Appeals to common sense over principle are almost always problematic since they fail to clearly articulate what the basis for the 'common sense' position is, and this lack of clarity is magnified in relation to prior fault rules that arise inconsistently across different criminal offences and defences.[62] Certainly, where intuition is used to justify criminalization in apparent contradiction to established legal principles, more work is required to explain and justify that position.

Arguably better (though flawed) attempts at justification have sought to articulate intuitions of prior fault^{OFF} inculpation by focusing on claims of culpability equivalence (referred to throughout this book as the 'equivalence thesis'). Since prior fault^{OFF} rules are used to construct or substitute for missing T2 offence

[57] Discussed in C Mitchell, 'The Intoxicated Offender—Refuting the Legal and Medical Myths' (1988) 11(1) *International Journal of Law and Psychiatry* 77, 80–83.

[58] See, e.g., J Hall, 'Intoxication and Criminal Responsibility' (1944) 57(7) *Harvard Law Review* 1045. We discuss the historic origins of prior fault further in Section 1.2 below.

[59] Discussed in Chapter 8, Section 8.3 and Chapter 10 in general.

[60] A criticism that has been long recognized: see, e.g., G Williams, *Criminal Law: The General Part* (2nd Ed, Stevens, 1961) 559. Such cases may also be resolved through standard causation rules, without recourse to prior fault, as we discuss in Chapter 3, Section 3.3.

[61] *DPP v Majewski* [1977] AC 443, 482. There are similar statements throughout the judgments.

[62] On the problematic appeal to intuition, see also M Shain and G Higgins, 'The Intoxication Defence and Theories of Criminal Liability: A Praxeological Approach' (1997) 24(4) *Contemporary Drug Problems* 731.

elements, the claim is that D's prior fault at T1 provides an equivalent basis for D to be labelled and punished as if the full offence had been completed at T2. The need to demonstrate such equivalence may be challenged, or avoided—as it is within the current law—by the presentation of intoxication, and other prior fault^{OFF} rules, as 'defences'.[63] However, once it is accepted that such framings are simply inaccurate, the need for some form of equivalence thesis becomes clear.[64] There are several variations of the equivalence thesis that we will discuss in the chapters that follow, with particular attention given to leading accounts based on T1–T2 causation,[65] as well as the aggregation of fault across T1–T2.[66]

It is our view that accounts of this kind can be highly beneficial in understanding T1–T2 culpability, but that each falls short of demonstrating *equivalence* with the elements missing at T2.[67] It is on this basis that we reject the use of prior fault^{OFF} rules to construct the missing elements of offences, and from here that we pivot to a discussion of special part offences that might replace current prior fault^{OFF} rules.[68] The potential for a bespoke offence allows us to set aside the futile search for equivalence and refocus our discussion on markers of legitimate blame, including the endangering effects of incapacity (mistake making) and D's awareness and behaviour in relation to those effects.

In contrast, where prior fault^{DEF} rules are alternatively used to block the application of a defence, no such issues of culpability equivalence arise to begin with. Accounts of blame across T1–T2 will still be necessary and informative, but there is no need here to demonstrate specific equivalence to a missing offence element. In the context of defences, therefore, we are able to move more quickly to the analysis of alternative potential justifications.

1.3.2.2 Associated legal uncertainties

Discussion of the equivalence thesis has understandably dominated much of the legal theorizing around prior fault^{OFF}, but it is useful to highlight other important associated areas of legal uncertainty. We discuss two examples in this subsection.

The first relates to uncertainties within the descriptive general part. As we have discussed elsewhere,[69] although standard mens rea terms are often used in the description of T1–T2 crimes such as inchoate offences and complicity (e.g. specifying

[63] If prior fault rules acted as true supervening defences, with the implication being that D had already committed a crime and was seeking exculpation, then the only question would be whether D's conduct warrants such exculpation.

[64] D has not completed the elements of the T2 crime and so, logically, requires no defence. Prior fault rules are not concerned with exculpation, but with the construction of offending.

[65] See, e.g., P Robinson, 'Imputed Criminal Liability' (1984) 93 *Yale Law Journal* 609.

[66] See, e.g., G Yaffe, 'Intoxication, Recklessness and Negligence' (2012) 9(2) *Ohio State Journal of Criminal Law* 545.

[67] Discussed in Chapters 2–4.

[68] Discussed in Chapters 5–7.

[69] JJ Child and A Hunt, 'Beyond the Present-Fault Paradigm: Expanding Mens rea Definitions in the General Part' (2021) 42(2) *Oxford Journal of Legal Studies* 438.

what D must 'intend' or 'know' at T1 in relation to offences taking place at T2), the definition of those mens rea terms cannot be interpreted and applied in the same way as they are for standard T2 crimes. For example, the mens rea term 'intention' is typically defined in relation to D's reasons for action: D intends a result where they act in order to cause that result, or when they know that their action is virtually certain to cause that result.[70] But where an offence requires D to intend a future action (by themselves or another), the same definition cannot apply: D is not acting at T1 to cause future action at T2, or with virtual certainty that it will be caused. Thus, although the same mens rea *term* may be used in the description of standard T2 crimes and T1–T2 crimes, the definition of that term must adapt to the circumstances of its use. We have previously written about this and its implications for the legal treatment of inchoate offences and complicity, but the same point applies when considering the T1–T2 structure of prior fault rules.[71] Thus, where commentators highlight the role of T1 mens rea in the discussion of prior fault (most often in the context of reform), it is necessary to interrogate how they are defining those mens rea terms, and whether they recognize and have engaged with the definitional challenges described here.[72]

The second associated area of legal uncertainty relates to challenges of practical application. Understanding the T1–T2 structure of prior fault analysis is almost unavoidably complex. We say 'almost' here because, in the current law, we have a system of rules that is quite effective at hiding that complexity: the fact that a claim of intoxication would effectively relieve the prosecution of part of its burden in proving T2 mens rea means that intoxication will rarely be raised in evidence by the defendant, and even where it is, the labelling of prior fault^{OFF} rules as 'defences' has avoided deeper consideration of equivalent fault beyond appeals to intuition. However, as soon as we begin to unpack the realities of the current law, to move beyond the repetition of legal fictions, the resulting complexity can appear equally (indeed, even more) unattractive.

The response from various quarters is often that any reform would create complications in the law that would be unwelcome given that the current legal position is well understood. This happens even where the aim is simply to rationalize and codify the rules that already apply, as with the Law Commission's ill-fated intoxication project in 2009,[73] where its recommendations were formally rejected

[70] See, e.g., definitions in the US MPC 1962, §2.02(2) and the Law Commission's Draft Criminal Code for England and Wales Bill 1989, s8.

[71] JJ Child and A Hunt, 'Beyond the Present-Fault Paradigm: Expanding Mens rea Definitions in the General Part' (2021) 42(2) *Oxford Journal of Legal Studies* 438. See also, making the extension to prior fault, JJ Child, 'Wrong on Many Levels: Understanding Crimes Across and Between Events' [2024] *Criminal Law Review* 378.

[72] See discussion in Chapter 2, Section 2.4.2.

[73] Law Commission, *Intoxication and Criminal Liability* (LC No 314, 2009). Critiqued in JJ Child, 'Drink, Drugs and Law Reform: A Review of Law Commission Report No.314' [2009] *Criminal Law Review* 488.

by the Ministry of Justice.[74] The same issues of complexity (both in doctrine and court-based application) have also been principal considerations in the rejection of proposals for reform, most often based around the potential for an intoxication offence to replace current prior fault^{OFF} rules.[75] The burden for those seeking reform in this area—and the burden for this book—is therefore to better unpack and explain the hidden complexities and unfairness of the current law, as well as to offer proposals for reform that provide a practical (as well as a principled) response to the problem.

1.3.3 Scientific uncertainties

Scientific uncertainty represents a further challenge for the law, and one that gains particular prominence in the area of prior fault. In order to understand and evaluate current prior fault rules and intuitions, as well as potential reform options, it is necessary to engage with some scientific/empirical questions. Examples of these scientific/empirical question are: what are the effects of intoxication and other forms of incapacitation on D at T2, what level or type of awareness or foresight of risk and dangerousness is D likely to possess at T1, what (if at all) are the impacts of addiction and other mental disorders on choices made at T1, and so on. These and related questions are far from straightforward, and the scientific evidence available is often uncertain and always nuanced in its detail. There can therefore be a temptation to ignore such scientific complexity when debating and applying legal rules, and we have previously been critical of this approach to prior fault in the courts.[76] The appropriate challenge is how to construct criminal rules, and how to apply them in practice, in light of scientific uncertainty and complexity, whilst engaging with whatever scientific insight is available.

We therefore take significant time throughout this book to engage with and evaluate the scientific evidence and challenges. These scientific challenges to the law of prior fault involve fundamental questions about the necessity of such rules in the first place. Mitchell contends, for example, that prior fault rules exist in 'vein to fight a phantom enemy',[77] claiming that states of complete dissociation due to drug or alcohol intoxication (sufficient to undermine mens rea and/or voluntariness at T2) are legally accepted medical 'myths'. While we may agree to an extent

[74] Ministry of Justice, *Report on the Implementation of Law Commission Proposals* (HC 1900, 2012) [49–50].

[75] See Law Commission, *Intoxication and Criminal Liability* (LC No 229, 1995), in which the Commission rejects its own previous proposal for an intoxication offence.

[76] See JJ Child, H Crombag, and GR Sullivan, 'Defending the Delusional, the Irrational, and the Dangerous' [2020] *Criminal Law Review* 306, highlighting and critiquing scientific claims made in Court of Appeal case *Taj* [2018] EWCA Crim 1743.

[77] C Mitchell, 'The Intoxicated Offender—Refuting the Legal and Medical Myths' (1988) 11(1) *International Journal of Law and Psychiatry* 77, 77.

with Mitchell's point about the rarity of such profound acute dissociative states produced by drugs or alcohol, we find Mitchell's argument overstated in other ways, not least because it fails to adequately engage with the issue of intoxicated mistake making, which may also undermine mens rea at T2.

Other scientific challenges are less direct in their critique of the law, but nevertheless represent crucial points of engagement, particularly when considering reform options. Notable here, for example, is the legal preference for identifying, separating, and quantifying the causes of D's absent T2 mens rea or mistake in defence.[78] The question is whether, and to what extent, such questions can be grounded in the science: is it possible to separate causes in circumstances of co-morbidity, for example? And even where the separation of causes can be achieved, or assumed, it may be necessary to question the scientific nature of those causes. For example, where D is addicted to a certain dissociative drug, scientific debates about the nature of addiction—the interplay between disease and choice—become an essential point of reference in any sensible assessment of D's culpability.[79]

1.3.3.1 Empirical studies

As part of this work, we engaged with the scientific literature bearing upon the questions raised above, as well as designing and carrying out a series of empirical studies ourselves (funded by the British Academy[80]). This work is explained in detail in Chapter 6 and Chapter 9, Section 9.4, and the data from these studies inform reform proposals which are explained in Chapter 7 and Chapter 9, Section 9.5. The studies tested a range of intoxicated (and control) participants in the human psychopharmacology laboratory, as well as in-the-field in pubs/bars, to better understand the effects of different levels of alcohol on mistake making and related perceptions. We will see that studies of this kind—of which more are needed[81]—provide valuable empirical evaluation of prior fault intuitions and alternative constructions of the law.

[78] Discussed in JJ Child, H Crombag, and GR Sullivan, 'Defending the Delusional, the Irrational, and the Dangerous' [2020] *Criminal Law Review* 306. For an example of use in reform, see Law Commission, *Insanity and Automatism* (Discussion Paper, 2013) [6.87].

[79] If we blame an intoxicated D for their choice to become intoxicated at T1, then it becomes necessary to interrogate addiction as a condition that challenges the freedom of that choice. See N Levy, *Addiction and Self-Control* (OUP, 2013); N Heather and G Segal, *Addiction and Choice* (OUP, 2017).

[80] Knowledge Frontiers (KF3/100111).

[81] Discussed in H Crombag, JJ Child, and R Fortson, 'Understanding the "Fault" in Prior-Fault Intoxication' in A Reed and M Bohlander (eds) *Fault* (Routledge, 2022) Ch 5; U Maoz and G Yaffe, 'What Does Recent Neuroscience Tell Us About Criminal Responsibility?' (2015) 3(1) *Journal of Law and the Biosciences* 120; G Yaffe, 'Intoxication, Recklessness and Negligence' (2012) 9(2) *Ohio State Journal of Criminal Law* 545.

1.4 Mapping our analysis

The book is divided into two parts and eleven chapters. Part I explores prior fault^{OFF} rules that operate to construct or substitute for the missing elements of T2 crimes. This includes intoxication rules (Chapter 2), non-intoxication prior fault rules (Chapter 3), and prior fault rules relating to mental health disorder and irresponsibility (Chapter 4). Our focus in each will be to understand and evaluate the current rules and to interrogate the potential routes for reform. We conclude that reform is required, and that this would be best achieved through a new bespoke offence (allowing for the abolition of current prior fault^{OFF} rules). Chapter 5 explores the option for a new bespoke offence, identifying comparative lessons and those that might be learned from previous failed attempts at reform in English law. Chapter 6 provides a layer of empirical analysis and critique, including original data from our own studies. Finally, in Chapter 7, we set out and justify our proposal for a new bespoke offence of culpable incapacity.

Part II of the book switches to consider prior fault^{DEF} rules that apply to block defences. Chapter 8 introduces and conceptualizes prior fault in the context of supervening defences, distinguishing two categories of prior fault^{DEF} rules (incapacity- and contriving-based) to be explored in the subsequent chapters. Incapacity-based prior fault^{DEF} rules, our focus in Chapter 9, share a number of features with the prior fault^{OFF} rules discussed in Part I: D is blamed for their incapacity at T2 (e.g. due to intoxication), and so they are prevented from relying on their (exculpating) mistaken beliefs or status. Prior fault^{DEF} rules applicable to contriving, our focus in Chapter 10, are quite different. Here, D's T1 blame is based on their manufacturing of exculpating circumstances (e.g. provocation leading to self-defence), such that D is prevented from relying on those circumstances in defence at T2. Across each chapter, our aim is to understand and evaluate the current law with a view to potential rationalization and reform.

Chapter 11 concludes the book. We summarize the central arguments from each part, as well as engage with related concerns about the use and construction of objective fault and of prior fault equivalences at sentencing. In doing so, we identify areas for fruitful future research.

PART I

PRIOR FAULT IN THE CONSTRUCTION OF OFFENCES

Part 1 engages with cases where D causes certain harms at T2, but does not complete the elements of an offence due to absent mens rea and/or voluntariness. We explore prior $\text{fault}_{\text{OFF}}$ rules as a legal mechanism for constructing liability, drawing upon D's prior conduct at T1 to establish T1-T2 criminalisation.

2
INTOXICATION PRIOR FAULT OFFENDING

2.1 Introduction

There is a robust empirical connection between alcohol/drug intoxication and criminally harmful events, evidenced at both individual and societal levels.[1] However, as we begin to assess prior fault^{OFF} intoxication rules,[2] it is important to recognize that explanations for the connection between intoxication and crime are not simple or singular, and that the vast majority of intoxicated crimes will not engage with prior fault rules. For example, where D's intoxication and/or desire to become intoxicated provides the motivation for offending (e.g. where D offends to maintain a drug habit) or results in disinhibition (e.g. where D's intoxication leads them to discount or diminish reasons against offending), D will satisfy the elements of an offence, and liability can be established without recourse to separate intoxication rules.

Prior fault^{OFF} rules, of the kind relevant to this chapter, are engaged within a subset of intoxicated harmful events, where D's intoxication explains the *absence* of an offence element. This will arise where D causes potentially criminal harm(s) but lacks mens rea for an offence because of a mistake induced by intoxication: such as where D causes damage to another's property but denies criminal damage on the basis that they did not foresee a risk of causing damage, and/or mistakenly believed that the property was their own, due to their intoxicated state.[3] Beyond this, in more extreme cases, intoxication rules may also be engaged where drug taking leads to a lack of voluntariness: such as cases where D harms a person but claims to have lacked any voluntary control over the relevant movements due to intoxication.[4] It is only in these cases, where single-event analysis of T2 might

[1] We see this within the Crime Survey data (crimesurvey.co.uk), suggesting that consistently high proportions of crime—and particularly violent crimes—are committed when a perpetrator is intoxicated with alcohol or other drugs. See also Law Commission, *Intoxication and Criminal Liability* (LC No 314, 2009) [1.1]. For wider context and discussion, see G Dingwall, *Alcohol and Crime* (Routledge, 2006); J Herring et al, *Intoxication and Society* (Palgrave, 2013).

[2] As introduced in Chapter 1, we are adopting the notation 'prior fault^{OFF}' and 'prior fault^{DEF}' to distinguish between prior fault rules relevant to the construction of a crime and prior fault rules relevant to the blocking of a defence.

[3] See *Caldwell* [1981] 1 All ER 961.

[4] See *Lipman* [1970] 1 QB 152.

Prior Fault Criminalization. John J Child, Adrian Hunt, and Hans S. Crombag, Oxford University Press.
 DOI: 10.1093/9780191874734.003.0003

otherwise result in D's acquittal, that intoxication prior fault^{OFF} rules have developed to provide a multi-event route to liability, allowing the absence of mens rea and/or voluntariness at T2 to be substituted with D's prior fault in becoming intoxicated at T1. Where such rules apply, D will be labelled and punished *as if* all offence elements were present at T2.

As we saw in the previous chapter, the intoxication rules provide the paradigm example of prior fault^{OFF}, having been recognized (in some form) since at least the sixteenth century,[5] and across most common law and civil law jurisdictions.[6] But the theoretical basis for intoxicated prior fault^{OFF}, and its practical application, remains uncertain and contested. Indeed, it is telling that despite their longevity, the intoxication rules continue to operate at common law largely through appeal to intuitions of 'order' and 'justice' rather than being expressed or justified by reference to clearly articulated legal and moral principles.[7]

It is because of the lack of structural and functional clarity within the current law that, in Section 2.2 below, we spend some time unpacking and critiquing the different ways in which the intoxication rules have been described and rationalized. We conclude that the current intoxication rules are best understood as an inculpatory mechanism, using T1 fault to substitute for missing offence elements at T2. A critique of the intoxication rules on these terms is then provided in Section 2.3. Having identified the major theoretical and practical challenges for a theory of prior fault^{OFF} for intoxication, Section 2.4 questions whether the current structure of those rules can be maintained and concludes that this is not possible if we want to meet the challenges identified. Section 2.5 highlights options for reform outside of current prior fault^{OFF} structures, highlighting our preference for a new bespoke offence. We discuss the potential for such an offence further in Chapters 5–7.

It should be noted that in this chapter we will not discuss the so-called grand schemer or Dutch courage cases, where D becomes intoxicated to the point of involuntariness with the purpose of causing a criminal harm whilst in that state.[8] Although such cases are commonly discussed under the heading of prior fault^{OFF} intoxication, we do not agree with this categorization, and deal with such cases (to the extent that they might exist at all, outside of hypotheticals) through standard rules of causation. We explain this position in Chapter 3, Section 3.3, within a broader review of involuntariness cases.

[5] Discussed in Chapter 1, Section 1.2. See also RU Singh, 'History of the Defence of Drunkenness in English Criminal Law' (1933) 49 *Law Quarterly Review* 528.

[6] Discussed in Chapter 1, Section 1.2.

[7] See *DPP v Majewski* [1977] AC 443. Discussed in Sections 2.2 and 2.3 below.

[8] See discussion in *AG for Northern Ireland v Gallagher* [1963] AC 349.

2.2 The structure and function of prior fault^{OFF} intoxication rules

Intoxication rules apply to construct liability, taking D's T1 objective fault in becoming intoxicated and using that fault to substitute for certain missing offence elements at T2. This basic mechanism is simple enough to state,[9] but it poses considerable challenges within a system of law that would not typically allow objective fault exhibited at one point in time to satisfy subjective mens rea requirements at another. Obvious questions arise. Why, for example, should the law equate a T1 choice to become intoxicated with an absent T2 choice to offend; why does the law target non-criminal T1 choices at all; and in doing so, is D inappropriately criminalized and/or labelled as a T2 offender? These questions are challenging to answer. However, whether engaging descriptively and/or normatively, it is difficult to make sense of the law without providing a response, and this difficulty becomes a real-time challenge for the courts as a consequence. And it is a challenge that is not being met. As Stannard remarks, 'the rule is too well established to be overturned, and the courts have struggled in vain to find some logical justification for it'.[10]

In this first section, we do not engage with the challenge of justifying intoxication-based prior fault^{OFF}. Rather, we identify and evaluate attempts to avoid that challenge. We evaluate alternative *descriptions* of the intoxication rules that avoid portraying those rules as a mechanism to construct liability (i.e. that avoid explanations to the effect that D's T1 fault in becoming intoxicated is used to substitute for certain missing offence elements at T2). As we will show below, we do not believe that any of these alternative descriptions provide a viable explanation for the current law. But each, to a varying extent, provides a basis for courts and commentators to avoid engaging with the difficult questions that underlie the intoxication rules, and thereby continue to undermine and obfuscate necessary debates. Indeed, it is noteworthy that alternative examples of the different descriptions below have routinely featured within the same cases (and even the same judgments), making it difficult to determine the basis upon which the law is applied.[11] It is only after we have cleared the ground muddied by these alternative (and inaccurate) descriptions of the intoxication rules that we can, in Section 2.3, properly engage with the challenges presented for the current law.

[9] It is also not novel or controversial to state, having been set in these terms for some time in leading textbooks such as *Simester and Sullivan's Criminal Law* and *Smith, Hogan and Ormerod's Criminal Law*.

[10] See J Stannard, 'The Demise of Drunkenness' (1982) 2 *Legal Studies* 291, 294.

[11] See A Dashwood, 'Logic and the Lords in *Majewski*' [1977] *Criminal Law Review* 532.

2.2.1 Framing intoxication rules as a defence

The most common and long-standing 'alternative' description of the intoxication rules is that they represent an intoxication defence.[12] Essentially, where D denies certain offence elements at T2 on the basis of their intoxicated state (i.e. denial of mens rea and/or voluntariness), such denials are recast as if D were raising a supervening defence. From here, in circumstances where intoxication rules apply to construct T2 liability, the preferred description is simply that D's liability ensues because 'D is not permitted to raise the intoxication defence'. As expressed by the then Lord Chancellor, Lord Elwyn-Jones, in the leading case of *Majewski*:[13]

> ... it is no excuse in law that, because of drink or drugs which the accused himself had taken knowingly and willingly, he had deprived himself of the ability to exercise self-control, to realise the possible consequences of what he was doing, or even to be conscious that he was doing it. As in the instant case, the jury may be properly instructed that they 'can ignore the subject of drink or drugs as being in any way a defence' to charges of this character.

Describing the intoxication rules in this way—as an intoxication defence that is denied in certain cases—remains commonplace both in English courts[14] and courts across other common law jurisdictions.[15]

Describing the intoxication rules in terms of a 'defence' has an obvious appeal for those wishing to justify its use (as well as for those who would rather avoid having to make such justifications). Where intoxication is presented as an inculpatory tool, as we set out above, it becomes necessary to demonstrate the basis for D's criminalization; to show that, despite not completing the elements of the offence at T2, D should still be labelled and punished as if they did. However, employing the language of defences recasts that debate. When discussing if D should be permitted to rely on the defence of intoxication, there is an implication that D has already committed an offence. The debate is no longer about the grounds for criminalization, but the legitimate basis for D to be claiming an exculpatory excuse for their behaviour, and voluntary intoxication does not look like a very compelling ground for excuse. In this way, even allowing the intoxication defence to apply in *some* cases can be presented plausibly as a 'merciful relaxation' of its complete refusal.[16]

[12] We use scare quotes here because, although this is an *alternative* description to our opening presentation of the law, it remains arguably the dominant description of intoxication rules in case law.

[13] *DPP v Majewski* [1977] AC 443, 476.

[14] See, e.g., important appeal cases such as *Bratty v AG for Northern Ireland* [1963] AC 386; *Lipman* [1970] 1 QB 152; *Heard* [2007] EWCA Crim 125; *Taj* [2018] EWCA Crim 1743.

[15] Discussed in AP Simester, 'Getting Drunk in Singapore and Malaysia' (2012) *Singapore Journal of Legal Studies* 1.

[16] *DPP v Majewski* [1977] AC 443. The phrase, employed by Lawton LJ in the Court of Appeal (411), is repeated with approval several times by the Lords.

Describing intoxication as a defence, however, has always been (and remains) a misleading mischaracterization. Intoxication is never a defence. Supervening defences, properly so-called, apply to excuse or justify criminal acts; they engage only after an offence (all elements of an offence) has been completed. Where D completes an offence at T2, intoxication is irrelevant. There is no basis upon which D, satisfying the elements of the T2 offence, can draw upon their intoxicated state as any form of substantive excuse.[17] However, intoxication is relevant where it results in the absence of an offence element: but this is not a defence, it is an explanation for the lack of an offence.

Thus, what is happening here is that D's denial of the offence on the basis of intoxication is being mischaracterized. Lawyers might refer to D's denial of the offence in the language of defences, in the same way we might (mis)refer to an alibi as a defence, saying that D is 'defending themselves by raising evidence of intoxication'. But the use of the term 'defence' here is imprecise, and to the extent that it implies a supervening defence, it is misleading.[18] In reality, whenever D denies the elements of a crime, D is simply denying the prosecution case against them: D is denying the essential elements of inculpation. Thus, where intoxication rules apply to find liability despite the successful denial of offence elements, this is not about the denial of a defence, this is *logically* about the construction of a crime.[19]

A popular variation of the intoxication defence description is for courts and commentators to acknowledge that the intoxication rules are not really a 'defence' properly so-called, and perhaps to acknowledge their inculpatory function, but to say that the term 'defence' will be used in discussion nonetheless.[20] The motivation here is to preserve consistency in language with older cases, allowing the rules to be better understood across time, whilst acknowledging the functional inculpatory reality. The problem with this approach, however, is that the functional acknowledgement rarely survives to the critical analysis and application of the law. Such acknowledgements are repeated frequently in *Majewski*, for example, and yet Lord Elwyn-Jones still finds it appropriate (in the extract quoted above) for juries to be directed in terms of a 'defence'. Similarly, in the more recent case of *Taj*,[21] the 'incremental extension' of *Majewski* to the 'proximate consequences' of drug use (i.e. intoxication induced states of psychosis) is discussed and approved without reference to expanding terms of inculpation.[22] Instead, the Court of Appeal repeat

[17] *Kingston* [1994] 3 All ER 353. Intoxication may be relevant at sentencing, but not as an excusatory defence.

[18] See AP Simester, 'Intoxication Is Never a Defence' (2009) *Criminal Law Review* 3.

[19] See A Dashwood, 'Logic and the Lords in *Majewski*' [1977] *Criminal Law Review* 532.

[20] See, e.g., the House of Lords in *DPP v Majewski* [1977] AC 443; the Canadian Supreme Court in *Brown* [2022] SCC 18. See also the project papers from the Law Commission in 1993, 1995, and 2009: Law Commission, *Intoxication and Criminal Liability* (Consultation 127, 1993); *Intoxication and Criminal Liability* (LC No 229, 1995); *Intoxication and Criminal Liability* (LC No 314, 2009).

[21] [2018] EWCA Crim 1743.

[22] Ibid [56–57].

oft-quoted passages that intoxication rules should ensure intoxicated defendants are 'no better situated in regard to criminal acts than a sober man'.[23] The problem, of course, is that intoxication rules do not ensure equality between intoxicated and sober defendants, they apply—as they have for at least the last century—to provide additional routes to criminalization for intoxicated harm causers that are not applicable to others. These examples of analytical dissonance can only be avoided when we recognize that intoxication is never a defence, and no longer describe it as such.

2.2.2 Framing intoxication rules as evidential

As an alternative to presenting intoxication rules as a 'defence', they have at times been framed instead as rules of evidence. Here, where D lacks mens rea and/or voluntariness at T2 due to becoming intoxicated at T1, rather than presenting intoxication rules as a *substantive* legal mechanism of inculpation (or exculpation), we are told that D may not raise *evidence* of intoxication. As Lord Salmon states in *Majewski*:[24]

> According to our law as it has stood for about 150 years, in such cases evidence that the injuries were inflicted by a man not knowing what he was doing because he was intoxicated by drinks or drugs which he has voluntarily taken is wholly irrelevant.

The logic here provides that, where D's T2 conduct appears voluntary and intentional, excluding evidence of intoxication (that might otherwise establish doubt) will allow the prosecution to prove that the offence was committed. As stated in *Richardson and Irwin*,[25] 'in considering what the defendant actually foresaw the jury must disregard the fact that the appellants had been drinking'.[26]

However, as Simester notes, this approach produces an absurdity.[27] It is an oxymoron to talk of *actual* foresight if the evidential rule at issue is designed to produce a counterfactual picture of what D's foresight would have been if sober. The rule is not (as sometimes claimed) seeking to exclude 'irrelevant' evidence, at least with any standard legal definition of that term.[28] Evidence of D's intoxication will often be relevant to their foresight of contested facts, perhaps irresistibly

[23] Ibid [50], quoting from *Beard* (1920) 14 Cr App R 159.
[24] [1977] AC 443, 484.
[25] [1999] 1 Cr App R 392, 395.
[26] See also the Criminal Code Act 1995 (Aus), s8(1): 'Evidence of self-induced intoxication cannot be considered in determining whether a fault element of basic intent existed.'
[27] AP Simester, 'Intoxication Is Never a Defence' (2009) *Criminal Law Review* 3, 6.
[28] I.e. *A (No2)* [2001] UKHL 25, 31: 'to be relevant the evidence need merely have some tendency in logic and common sense to advance the proposition in issue'.

so where it demonstrates an extreme lack of capacity. It is precisely because of this relevance (i.e. potentially establishing doubt regarding D's offence) that the intoxication rules exist. This is very far from a standard example of evidential exclusion. Describing the intoxication rules in evidential terms involves excluding evidence which is potentially highly relevant to demonstrating D's innocence, and conceives of 'proving' factual guilt on the basis of a counterfactual fiction.

The evidential description of the intoxication rules strains credulity, and must be rejected. D's substantive legal position is being altered by the application of these rules; the basis for D's guilt is being transformed. Presenting this as an exclusion of evidence is, at best, misleading. However, in truth, it is more accurately described as intellectually dishonest.

2.2.3 Framing intoxication at T1 as recklessness at T2

The final approach explored in this section differs from the others just discussed because it concedes that the intoxication rules operate as an inculpatory mechanism of prior fault^{OFF} between T1 and T2 events. However, rather than accepting that intoxication rules are used to construct T2 fault on the basis of quite different prior fault at T1, this approach presents D's prior fault at T1 as a species of recklessness directly capable of satisfying the T2 mens rea requirements of an offence. As stated by Lord Elwyn-Jones in *Majewski*:[29]

> If a man of his own volition takes a substance which causes him to cast off the restraints of reason and conscience . . . in reducing himself by drugs and drink to that condition in my view supplies the evidence of mens rea, of guilty mind certainly sufficient for crimes of basic intent. It is a reckless course of conduct and recklessness is enough to constitute the necessary mens rea . . . The drunkenness is itself an intrinsic, an integral part of the crime, the other part being the evidence of the unlawful use of force against the victim. Together they add up to criminal recklessness.

This explanation of the intoxication rules provides another appealingly simple route to criminalization. This argument goes as follows: D is liable for a recklessness-based offence because D was reckless at T1. D may appear to lack mens rea at T2, but if we accept the linking of T1 and T2, and if we accept that D possessed the requisite mens rea at T1, then the offence will be complete. This involves saying that 'recklessness' at T1 meets the requirement of 'recklessness' at T2.[30]

[29] [1977] AC 443, 474–75.

[30] See S Gardner, 'The Importance of Majewski' (1994) 14 *Oxford Journal of Legal Studies* 279.

The steps necessary to produce this definitional result however—(i) linking T1–T2 and (ii) identifying recklessness at T1 as the required recklessness at T2—are both highly contestable. It is the second definitional claim about T1 that is most important to our rejection of this approach which frames the recklessness at T1 as the recklessness required at T2. Simply put, even if we concede that D's actions at T1 are wrongful, their description as satisfying T2 recklessness is only possible through an 'abuse'[31] or a misunderstanding[32] of that term. Recklessness at T2 requires the subjective foresight of a specific risk in action, a risk relevant to the definition of a specific offence, where D continues unreasonably to run that risk.[33] The intoxication rules do not require D to foresee any specific risk when becoming intoxicated at T1, and it is not therefore a risk that D chooses to run through their action; rather, D's only choice is to consume a drug that they should (objectively) understand as posing dangers regarding their future behaviour. Definitional problems arise, therefore, both in the shift from objective to subjective fault,[34] as well as the specificity of the target object of that fault (the culpability link between D and the T2 harm).[35]

Presented with this critique, defenders of the intoxication rules have not typically persisted with the definitional claim. Rather, even within cases such as *Majewski*, we see the recklessness description is morphed into one of *equivalence*: D's T1 fault may not be the same as the absent mens rea at T2, but it is claimed it is broadly equivalent in terms of culpability, and so it is not necessarily objectionable to treat it functionally in the same way.[36] This broadly represents the position of most modern defenders of the intoxication rules.[37] It recognizes something of a fiction within the current law—D is treated as if they satisfied offence elements that were in fact missing at T2—but presents this as a morally defensible form of rough justice, providing an unconventional route to the 'correct' outcome. Arguing in terms of equivalence also helps explain the potential for intoxication

[31] F Stark, *Culpable Carelessness* (CUP, 2016) 33.

[32] Statements such as that quoted above from Lord Elwyn-Jones suggest a conflation of 'recklessness' as a mens rea term and 'recklessness' as a description of behaviour. See A Dashwood, 'Logic and the Lords in Majewski' [1977] *Criminal Law Review* 532.

[33] *Cunningham* [1957] 2 QB 396; *G* [2003] UKHL 50.

[34] This challenge was less pronounced, of course, during times when objective fault was sufficient to satisfy a recklessness requirement: *Caldwell* [1982] AC 341. See J Stannard, 'The Demise of Drunkenness' (1982) 2 *Legal Studies* 291.

[35] See E Macdonald, 'Reckless Language and *Majewski*' (1986) 6(3) *Legal Studies* 239.

[36] See, e.g., Lord Simon at 479: 'there is nothing unreasonable or illogical in the law holding that a mind rendered self-inducedly insensible (short of M'Naghten insanity), through drink or drugs, to the nature of a prohibited act or to its probable consequences is as wrongful a mind as one which consciously contemplates the prohibited act and foresees its probable consequences (or is reckless as to whether they ensue). The latter is all that is required by way of mens rea in a crime of basic intent.'

[37] See G Yaffe, 'Intoxication, Recklessness and Negligence' (2012) 9(2) *Ohio State Journal of Criminal Law* 545; Law Commission, *Intoxication and Criminal Liability* (LC No 314, 2009); J Horder, 'Sobering Up? The Law Commission on Criminal Intoxication' (1995) 58 *Modern Law Review* 534.

rules to substitute for missing voluntariness at T2, something that is by no means self-evident if T1 intoxication is definitionally equated with T2 recklessness.

Having reached the most plausible description of the intoxication rules—the *equivalence* description—we have effectively circled back to where we began this section. The equivalence description is logical in its own terms, but it begs a series of normative challenges to that claim of equivalence.

2.3 Framing intoxication rules in terms of equivalence

The intoxication rules represent an extraordinary mechanism of criminalization, and it is only once that structure and function is recognized (as we have done in Section 2.2) that we can engage in sensible critique. It is useful to begin doing so by emphasizing that *extraordinary* nature.

It is often highlighted that the intoxication rules (and prior fault^{OFF} rules in general) provide an exception to the contemporality principle, in that the mens rea and actus reus of D's offence do not coincide in time. But more should be said. First, even as an exception to the contemporality principle, the intoxication rules are unique: unlike other legal mechanisms designed to link actus reus and mens rea within a single transaction or course of events,[38] the intoxication rules apply in circumstances where D does not actually hold the relevant mens rea at T2, T1, or any other point in the transaction. The intoxication rules provide for a legal fiction of T2 mens rea, constructed upon quite different fault at T1.

Intoxication rules are also quite different from other offence constructions, and so justification (or critique) by analogy is generally unhelpful. For example, certain offences also exhibit a T1–T2 structure, such as the two-event construction common to many inchoate offences and to complicity. In these cases, D's liability for conduct at T1 is at least partially derived from ulterior fault in relation to a T2 principal offence, and/or the completion of that T2 offence in fact. But these are not typically described as prior fault^{OFF} offences, and we agree that they should not be so described. The reason is not structural, but functional. Prior fault^{OFF} rules do not simply apply across T1–T2 events, they apply to identify fault at T1 that is then reconstructed to substitute for absent fault at T2; D is not labelled and punished for a T1–T2 offence; D is labelled and punished *as if* all offence elements were present at T2. It is this functional reconstruction (the legal fiction) that separates prior fault^{OFF} from other forms of T1–T2 liability (i.e. including inchoates, complicity, etc), and it is this functional role that has proven so difficult to justify in terms of culpability equivalence.

[38] E.g. *Thabo Meli* [1954] 1 All ER 373.

Similarly, *contra* Simester, we argue it is misleading to categorize—and thereby potentially normalize—the intoxication rules as a species of constructive liability (i.e. offence constructions that operate through an initial gateway wrong which is aggravated by subsequent resulting harms, such as unlawful act manslaughter, assault occasioning actual bodily harm, and so on).[39] As Simester acknowledges, constructive liability typically requires a gateway *crime* at T1, where D's choice to commit that offence changes their normative position and provides the basis for constructing liability that includes additional resulting harms.[40] This is not true of the intoxication rules of course, where there is no need to demonstrate a crime at T1 (and, typically, no crime is committed at T1). Thus, to the extent that any comparison with constructive liability helps, intoxication rules are more akin to a subset of constructive strict liability offences.[41] But this comparison only serves to demonstrate (again) the extraordinary nature of the intoxication rules: intoxication rules are not limited to strict liability crimes; rather, where prior fault^{OFF} rules apply, D may be convicted, labelled, and punished for a variety of offences ostensibly requiring mens rea. Finally, and not insignificantly, whereas constructive liability offences involve a single point of conduct and potentially unforeseen aggravating harms that result *from that conduct*, the structure of the intoxication rules is fundamentally different. D's conduct at T1 does not cause the harms at T2 in any standard mechanical sense, and can only be tied to D's T2 harm-causing conduct on the basis of D's impaired capacity. This provides a potential basis for linking blame, but one that is nonstandard, and much further removed.

The overarching question is whether this extraordinary inculpatory mechanism can be justified on its own terms? This is not a criminalization question per se; we are not asking whether mistaken harms caused by intoxicated defendants should *ever* attract criminal sanction.[42] We may even accept, for the sake of argument, dicta from *Majewski* which declared 'there is no juristic reason why mental incapacity . . . brought about by self-induced intoxication . . . should not be such a state of mind stigmatised as wrongful by the criminal law'.[43] Rather, our focus in Section 2.3.1 below is a critique of the explanation and operation of the current intoxication rules, and in particular the use of T1 fault to substitute for missing offence elements at T2, resulting in D being labelled and punished as if the T2 offence were complete. This is a critique of the equivalence description (or 'equivalence thesis') since the necessary contention of those defending a version of the current law is

[39] See AP Simester, 'Intoxication Is Never a Defence' (2009) *Criminal Law Review* 3, 7–9.

[40] On constructive liability and the change of normative position justification, see J Gardner, 'Rationality and the Rule of Law in Offences Against the Person' (1994) 53 *Cambridge Law Journal* 502; cf A Ashworth, 'A Change of Normative Position' (2008) 11(2) *New Criminal Law Review* 232.

[41] See AP Simester, *Appraising Strict Liability* (OUP, 2005) 46–48.

[42] We discuss this in Section 2.5 below.

[43] [1977] AC 443, per Lord Simon: 478.

that D's T1 fault is not only deserving of criminal blame (normatively speaking), but that it is also *functionally equivalent* to the missing offence elements at T2.

2.3.1 Doctrinal moves towards equivalence

Historic references to intoxication-based criminalization imply a wide-ranging mechanism whereby T1 intoxication simply replaced missing fault elements at T2.[44] However, over the last 150 years at least, likely influenced by a growing recognition of intoxication rules as inculpatory, courts have gradually refined the law to require additional markers of culpability at T1, and to narrow the potential for substitution at T2. In essence, courts have recognized the need for greater T1–T2 fault equivalence, and taken doctrinal steps in that direction.

There are two main tokens of fault required by the current law at T1, establishing D's blameworthy choice. First, establishing *choice*, the intoxication rules will only apply in cases of voluntary intoxication.[45] Where D was unaware of the drug (e.g. due to spiking) or forced to take it under duress, D's involuntary intoxication will not substitute for missing offence elements at T2.[46] Second, establishing *blame*, the drug taken at T1 must be 'dangerous'. The classification of a drug as dangerous/non-dangerous is a legal designation by the court, based on common understanding of a drug's destabilizing effects and its potential contribution to future harms. In this manner, dangerousness is not confined to illicit drugs, and, as we have highlighted already, legally consumed alcohol is the paradigm example.[47]

It is notable that other possible T1 requirements have not developed. There are no stipulations on the quantity of the drug consumed for example,[48] or the circumstances of its consumption (e.g. whether D becomes intoxicated at home or whilst in public). Indeed, although the drug must be viewed by the court as objectively dangerous, there is no subjective requirement for D to be aware personally of the potentially dangerous effects of the drug.

Having established fault at T1 (i.e. through the voluntary taking of a dangerous drug), the next question is when (and how) this fault may be employed to construct liability at T2. The principal restriction here is that T1 fault will only be able to substitute for missing elements at T2 (mens rea and/or voluntariness) where the

[44] Discussed in Chapter 1, Section 1.2.

[45] Discussed in *Kingston* [1994] 3 All ER 353.

[46] I.e. intoxication becomes irrelevant in a substantive legal sense. Involuntary intoxication is also irrelevant as a potential defence, even in cases where D might plausibly claim that they would not have offended but for the disinhibiting effect of the drugs. *Kingston* [1994] 3 All ER 353; discussed in GR Sullivan, 'Making Excuses' in AP Simester and A Smith (eds) *Harm and Culpability* (OUP, 1996) 131.

[47] Discussed in A Loughnan and N Wake, 'Of Blurred Boundaries and Prior Fault' in A Reed and M Bohlander (eds) *General Defences in Criminal Law* (Routledge, 2014) 113.

[48] D's intoxication must explain their lack of mens rea at T2 however, which becomes more likely at higher levels.

offence charged is one of 'basic intent' as opposed to 'specific intent'.[49] We discuss the problematic nature of this distinction in the following subsection, but for now it is useful to observe that the elements of a basic intent offence typically require a mens rea of 'recklessness' at most, and so the challenge for the equivalence thesis may be narrowed to this target.[50] A further restriction, qualifying the T1–T2 link, is that D's missing fault at T2 must have resulted from their intoxication at T1.[51] Where, for example, D would have made the same mistake at T2 (negativing mens rea) had they been sober, the intoxication rules will not apply. The court will direct the jury to consider a counterfactual, where they must be satisfied that D would have recognized the relevant risk absent the effects of intoxication.[52]

There are no other major restrictions. Unlike Canada, for example, the intoxication rules in English law (as typical elsewhere) will replace a lack of voluntariness at T2 as well as other mens rea for basic intent offences,[53] and beyond the foresight counterfactual, there are no causal requirements between T1 and T2.

2.3.2 Problems with the equivalence thesis

The equivalence thesis represents a significant improvement from the alternative framings discussed in Section 2.2, in that, unlike those alternatives, the equivalence thesis at least attempts to engage with the reality of the inculpatory intoxication rules. However, for a thesis of this kind to be accepted as a justified route to criminalization, even as a form of rough justice, we require a level of precision in its construction, and an explanation for how fault is appropriately substituted. These are basic rule of law concerns.

In the subsections below, we evaluate these concerns in relation to the current legal position, and we find claims of equivalence to be wholly inadequate. First, to claim equivalence between T1 and T2 fault, it is logically necessary to understand and provide a stable definition of what those fault standards entail: we must understand what at T1 is claiming equivalence with what at T2. As we explain below, answers within the current law remain imprecise and confused. Second, to justify the

[49] See *Beard* (1920) 14 Cr App R 159; and discussion in *Majewski* [1977] AC 443. Cf the position in Scottish criminal law, *Ross v HM Advocate* 1991 JC 210.

[50] It is notable that the target (recklessness) has shifted in the years following *Majewski*, and was broadly capable of being satisfied by objective fault for over twenty years following *Caldwell* [1981] 1 All ER 961. In what follows, we focus on potential equivalence of T1 intoxication and the current subjective understanding of recklessness established in *G* [2003] UKHL 50. We discuss the role of objective mens rea in Chapter 11, Section 11.3.1.

[51] See *Richardson and Irwin* [1999] 1 Cr App R 392.

[52] On the use of counterfactual questions, see K Simons, 'Does Punishment for "Culpable Indifference" Simply Punish for "Bad Character"?' (2002) 6(1) *Buffalo Criminal Law Review* 219, 255–57.

[53] On the position in Canada, see *Brown* [2022] SCC 18; P Leahy, 'Legislative Revision of Extreme Intoxication in Canada' [2022] *Criminal Law Review* 957.

substitution of equivalent states from T1 to T2 (or what is often termed 'tracing'), it is necessary to demonstrate that the substituted mens rea can perform the same role within the T2 offence in terms of culpability, linking D to the harms caused. Again, as we explain below, there are significant problems with culpability tracing claims of this kind.

2.3.2.1 Imprecision at T1

We have talked about the status of 'being intoxicated' as a paradigm of prior fault^{OFF}. However, the way the current law operates means that it is perhaps more accurate to refer to it as a proxy for prior fault^{OFF}.[54] We say this because, when identifying fault at T1, the courts are not looking for generalized markers of blame that happen to apply most often to intoxication cases: the identification of T1 blame does not take account of the context in which D was acting, does not engage with wider factors indicating greater/lesser risk creation (what one might call problematic verses unproblematic intoxication), does not explore D's awareness of risks and/or types of risks, and so on. These matters are not examined or evaluated. Rather, where the courts have engaged in an examination of conduct at T1, such engagement begins and ends with whether D became voluntarily intoxicated with a dangerous drug, and the blaming of that state.[55]

We can appreciate why the courts have progressed in this way. There is safety and familiarity in applying an intoxication threshold test, rather than looking to markers of prior fault blame, having to select and justify which markers (or combinations) should be preferred, how they should be measured, and where thresholds should be set. However, without more, the intoxication proxy approach represents very rough justice. And may not even provide this much. This is because, despite the familiarity and apparent simplicity of the intoxication proxy, the lack of a normative underpinning leads to almost inevitable mismatches of fault and liability, and therefore pressure on (at least) the boundaries of the proxy definition. These problems are best expressed in terms of the potential for under- and over-inclusivity.

Most obviously, the intoxication rules are under-inclusive because of their inability to apply to fault-based incapacity outside of intoxication. We explore the existence of prior fault^{OFF} rules outside of intoxication in depth in Chapters 3 and 4, but it suffices to say here that such examples are piecemeal and inconsistent. The problem is that, if we accept the intuitive appeal of intoxication-based

[54] For an extended defence of this claim, see H Crombag, JJ Child, and R Fortson, 'Understanding the "Fault" in Prior-Fault Intoxication' in A Reed and M Bohlander (eds) *Fault* (Routledge, 2022) Ch 5.

[55] We see this clearly in leading cases such as *Beard* (1920) 14 Cr App R 159 and *Majewski* [1977] AC 443, where the courts explain the blameworthiness of intoxication rather than the blameworthiness which intoxication exemplifies. See S Gough, 'Intoxication and Criminal Liability' (1996) 112 *Law Quarterly Review* 335.

criminalization, it is difficult to see why other blameworthy states (e.g. voluntary sleep deprivation, negligent management of medication, etc) are not likewise included.

An associated problem emerges at the edges of the intoxication status: where D's state appears to sit just outside the definition of 'intoxication', but shares the markers of blame. This arose, for example, in the case of *Taj*,[56] which involved a defendant who caused harm in an apparent state of alcohol-induced psychosis.[57] Crucially, it could not be proven that Taj had drugs in his system at the time of his offence. However, for the Court of Appeal, the fact that Taj's state was induced by his previous intoxication meant that the intoxication rules continued to apply:[58]

> The fact is that medical science has advanced such that, in the modern age, the longer term sequelae of abusing alcohol or drugs are better known and understood; and, as in the present case, it was agreed that Taj's episode . . . was a direct result of his earlier drink and drug-taking in the previous days and weeks.

The claim, therefore, is that medical science (now) enables us to distinguish between the various conditions associated with intoxication, and that some may be appropriately captured within intoxication rules even where drugs or alcohol are no longer present (in pharmacological terms) in D's system.

Two points should be stressed here. First, we firmly disagree with the court's assessment of the science. The kind of causal clarity relied upon by the Court of Appeal is simply not supported by the clinical and preclinical academic data (and is not even supported in *Taj*[59]). Second, and more important for present purposes, we can see how a focus on the nature of 'intoxication' has led the court into fine-grained scientific debates that will further complicate the law. The case did not focus on the extent to which D was to blame at T1. Rather the focus was a binary question of categorization: was D intoxicated? This is a consequence of the under-inclusive potential of a proxy state that does not speak to wider assessments of blame. Generalized tokens of blame connected with a normative evaluation of D's conduct—such as engaging in incapacity inducing conduct or creating the circumstances of risk—are not expressly engaged with. Rather, the court is left with

[56] [2018] EWCA Crim 1743.

[57] We talk of an 'apparent' state here because there was evidence on appeal that D's state was alternatively caused by an independent mental disorder. See JJ Child, H Crombag, and GR Sullivan, 'Defending the Delusional, the Irrational, and the Dangerous' [2020] *Criminal Law Review* 306.

[58] *Taj* [2018] EWCA Crim 1743, [57].

[59] By the time *Taj* went to appeal, following months of observation, new expert evidence acknowledged that his psychosis may not have been induced by intoxication. Discussed in H Crombag, JJ Child, and GR Sullivan, 'Drunk, Dangerous and Delusional: How Legal Concept-Creep Risks Overcriminalization' (2020) 115(12) *Addiction* 2200. On similar problems in Australian courts, see J Quilter and L McNamara, 'The Meaning of "Intoxication" in Australian Criminal Cases: Origins and Operation' (2018) 21(1) *New Criminal Law Review* 170.

a choice of not imposing criminal liability in circumstances of apparent blame, or expanding the definition of intoxication to include those cases.

The lack of critical engagement at T1 also leads current intoxication rules to apply in an over-inclusive manner, giving rise to potentially inappropriate criminalization. This is the case, for example, if we think it is ever *reasonable* to become voluntarily intoxicated with a dangerous drug.[60] Whilst we might accept a route to criminalization where D causes harm in a state of acute intoxication—or does so having foreseen the potential for dangers at T1 or does so when out of control in a public place—none of these restrictions (i.e. quantity, foresight, place, etc) are relevant to the current law.[61] Again, where we look beyond the status of intoxication to identify markers of T1 blame, factors of this kind are evidently more important.[62]

Associated with this broader point is the more specific problem of addiction. Where D is intoxicated in circumstances of severe clinical drug addiction or alcoholism, it is prudent to question whether that disorder affects their blameworthiness. For example, should the fact of addiction change our assessment of D's voluntariness in taking the drug at T1?[63] And if so, can we still blame D on the basis that an addiction necessarily involves (repeated) *prior* voluntary intoxications?[64] And so on. The current law—focused on the status of intoxication—struggles to engage with these issues, only allowing D to escape liability through vanishingly small gateways of involuntariness and insanity, and requiring courts to draw strict causal distinctions between intoxication and ongoing comorbid mental disorder.[65]

2.3.2.2 Imprecision at T2

Problems for the intoxication rules at T1 are compounded by uncertainty and imprecision at T2. This further diminishes any coherent basis for the equivalence thesis.

[60] See A Lynch, 'The Scope of Intoxication' (1982) *Criminal Law Review* 139. We should also note here, more generally, that attitudes to drug consumption, and particularly alcohol consumption, are complex and changeable over time. See, G Dingwall, *Alcohol and Crime* (Routledge, 2006); A Loughnan, *Manifest Madness* (OUP, 2012) Ch 7.

[61] Simester makes a similar point when he says that there may be an insufficient general empirical link between intoxication and future harms to justify its role as a gateway wrong to constructive liability: 'Intoxication Is Never a Defence' (2009) *Crim LR* 3, 8–9. See also C Mitchell, 'The Intoxicated Offender—Refuting the Legal and Medical Myths' (1988) 11(1) *International Journal of Law and Psychiatry* 77.

[62] The T1 critique here has prompted several of the alternative approaches to equivalence, discussed in Section 2.4 below.

[63] See J Hall, 'Intoxication and Criminal Responsibility' (1944) 57(7) *Harvard Law Review* 1045; N Levy, *Addiction and Self-Control* (OUP, 2013).

[64] This is Robinson's preferred approach in 'A Brief Summary and Critique of Criminal Liability Rules for Intoxicated Conduct' (2018) 82(5) *Journal of Criminal Law* 381. Cf N Sinclair-House, JJ Child, and H Crombag, 'Addiction Is a Brain Disease, and It Doesn't Matter' (2019) 26(1) *Psychology, Public Policy, and Law* 36.

[65] See, generally, A Goldberg and P Manguele (eds), *Criminal Law and Prior Fault: Comparative Perspectives on Addiction and Intoxication* (Hart, 2025).

The T2 criticism is best illustrated by the uncertain distinction between basic and specific intent offences, both at common law and within the theoretical literature. The basic/specific intent distinction plays a crucial role in narrowing the range of offence elements capable of being substituted for or constructed from T1 fault. By limiting the substitution to basic intent offences only, focused on absent T2 mens rea and voluntariness, the challenge for the equivalence thesis is similarly narrowed. However, this only helps us (in theory and in practice) where the distinction between basic and specific intent offences is clear and reasoned, and this is absent from the current law. How the rule should be interpreted and applied continues to be debated.[66]

Probably, the best explanation for the current basic/specific intent offence distinction sees it as a product of its time, being recognized by the courts in a period where only certain offences required proof of a particular (i.e. specific) mens rea standard beyond typical (i.e. general/basic) markers of fault.[67] The criminal law has changed considerably from this point however, requiring particular (though varied) mens rea for *all* offences.[68] The challenge for those applying or defending the current law has therefore been either to justify the broad imprecise terms of the intoxication rules within the modern legal system,[69] or to reinterpret those rules as precise claims of mens rea equivalence to try and make them compatible with that system.[70] Both approaches have been attempted. However, with both options (and variations within them) remaining in play, case law has proceeded to categorize offences one way or the other on an ad hoc basis without the articulation of a comprehensive test.[71]

Having said that, some points of functional agreement are discernible. Most importantly, specific intent offences are typically marked by requirements of 'intention', or 'ulterior mens rea'.[72] Thus, for example, where D is charged with an offence that requires D to have intended to cause a certain result, it is likely the offence will be classified as a specific intent offence and any absence of mens rea at T2 will

[66] See, e.g., J Hall, 'Intoxication and Criminal Responsibility' (1944) 57(7) *Harvard Law Review* 1045; G Fletcher, *Rethinking Criminal Law* (OUP, 2000) 846–52. See also the most recent Law Commission analysis of the topic in *Intoxication and Criminal Liability* (LC No 314, 2009) [2.3–2.28].

[67] P Handler, 'Intoxication and Criminal Responsibility in England, 1819–1920' (2013) 33(2) *Oxford Journal of Legal Studies* 243; J Stannard, 'The Demise of Drunkenness' (1982) 2 *LS* 291.

[68] This typically includes a presumption of mens rea (recklessness) where statutory offences do not specify a culpability requirement. On the presumption in English law, see *K* [2002] 1 AC 462.

[69] See, e.g., S Gough, 'Intoxication and Criminal Liability' (1996) 112 *Law Quarterly Review* 335; S Gardner, 'The Importance of Majewski' (1994) 14 *Oxford Journal of Legal Studies* 279.

[70] See, e.g., E Colvin, 'A Theory of the Intoxication Defence' (1981) 59(4) *Canadian Bar Review* 750, focused on the role of ulterior mens rea; cf T Quigley, 'Specific and General Nonsense' (1987) 11(1) *The Dalhousie Law Journal* 75. See also the Law Commission, *Intoxication and Criminal Liability* (LC No 314, 2009), focused on recklessness.

[71] Multiple editions of the textbook *Smith and Hogan's Criminal Law*, e.g., advise readers to learn the basic/specific classification of each offence as a matter of individual offence precedent.

[72] Discussed within the leading cases of *DPP v Majewski* [1977] AC 443 and *Heard* [2007] EWCA Crim 125.

not be susceptible to prior fault^{OFF}–based substitution. Problems remain with the practical application of these rules, such as how the courts have distinguished intention as to conduct (compatible with basic intent) from intention as to results (not compatible with basic intent),[73] and in the classification of ulterior mental states short of ulterior intention.[74] However, these developments reflect the possibility of a more comprehensive overarching set of rules for distinguishing between basic and specific intent offences, and it is telling that they do so by attempting to map the intoxication rules onto specific mens rea states at T2 (as opposed to general conceptions of blame).

But even assuming we could rely on these functional indicators as an overarching basis for the classification of crimes as basic or specific intent, this only raises further fundamental questions and problems. This is because the current basic/specific distinction is one which separates offences in a manner that for prior fault^{OFF} purposes either allows mens rea in respect of all or none of the relevant offence elements (i.e. conduct, circumstances, results, etc) to be constructed from T1 fault. If we accept, for the sake of argument, that T1 intoxicated fault is equivalent to absent T2 recklessness and voluntariness, then why distinguish between categories of *offence* along the basic/specific lines at all? Even the so-called specific intent offences may well include requirements of recklessness as to certain elements (and will certainly require voluntariness), so it would seem that the current rules are inconsistent in not allowing these elements at least to be constructed from T1. The better analysis, it seems, would be that only those offence *elements* requiring intention or ulterior mens rea would have to be proven in fact at T2.[75] This analysis was a driving force behind the Law Commission's move to the adoption of element level analysis in its 2009 report.[76] The Law Commission's recommendations were not accepted by government however,[77] and the current law has maintained an offence level analysis that continues thereby to resist claims of direct or coherent mens rea equivalence.

2.3.2.3 Difficulty linking fault between T1 and T2

Uncertain legal requirements at both T1 and T2 make precise assessments of equivalence challenging. But problems for the current law are not limited to lack of precision at these two points in time. For the current law and the equivalence thesis

[73] E.g. are intentional sexual offences such as rape and sexual assault correctly classified as basic intent? Discussed in R Williams, 'Voluntary Intoxication—A Lost Cause?' (2013) 129 *Law Quarterly Review* 264, 271–74.

[74] See Law Commission, *Intoxication and Criminal Liability* (LC No 314, 2009) [2.8].

[75] See P Robinson, 'Causing the Conditions of One's Own Defence' (1985) 71 *Virginia Law Review* 1, 19.

[76] Law Commission, *Intoxication and Criminal Liability* (LC No 314, 2009). Discussed further at Section 2.4 below.

[77] Ministry of Justice, *Report on the Implementation of Law Commission Proposals* (HC 1900, 2012) [49–50].

to function as a coherent explanation, it also needs to demonstrate that 'equivalent' T1 fault can perform the culpability role of the T2 fault for which it is substituting. In other words, we need to understand how D's fault is linked or traced from T1 to T2.

Understanding this issue may usefully be examined by considering what we might call 'equivalence criteria' which are derived from Greenberg's discussion of criminal negligence and in particular his examination of the connection[78] between negligent behaviour at T1 (e.g. failure to perform adequate medical checks) and T2 harms (i.e. death). Greenberg posited two criteria which might usefully be applied to deciding whether it was appropriate to criminalize D in such situations. The first focuses on the relative culpability of D's conduct at T1 and the offence requirements (missing elements) at T2; the second 'culpability connection' criterion asks whether the fault from T1 is capable of tying D to the harms of the offence in the same way as if fault were present at T2.[79] We discuss each of these 'equivalence criteria' in turn.

The first 'equivalence' criterion requires a balancing of culpability weight between T1 and T2. For example, for Greenberg, in the context of medical negligence, given that D's negligence at T1 amounts to a 'failure to gather evidence, where one is culpable to a relatively minor degree', it would be unjustified to use this fault to substitute for (absent at T2) 'a more egregious error to fail to recognize what that evidence indicates'.[80] Similarly, we would argue that the potential culpability mismatch highlighted here, and the inappropriate criminalization that can flow from it, is equally apparent within the intoxication rules. Indeed, as emphasized across much of the critical literature,[81] the potential mismatch is considerably greater where the intoxication rules are employed: D's conduct at T1—becoming intoxicated with a dangerous drug—need not involve a criminal act and does not need to be unreasonable or negligent, and yet it is employed to substitute for missing mens rea states at T2 that include the specific foresight and choice to run risks in action. Where D is convicted of such crimes (e.g. criminal damage, reckless non-fatal or fatal offences, and so on), offences where demonstrating negligence at T2 would not be sufficient for liability, the apparent mismatch of culpability in terms of its gravity based on D's T1 choices is even greater.

[78] A Greenberg, 'Why Criminal Responsibility for Negligence Cannot be Indirect' (2021) 80(3) *Cambridge Law Journal* 489, 490. Curiously, Greenberg specifically exempts prior fault rules from his thesis (514), though he provides little justification for the exemption that would appear to conflict with his more general thesis. We believe the exemption is a mistake.

[79] Similar principles of culpability equivalence are explored in A Sarch, *Criminally Ignorant: Why the Law Pretends We Know What We Don't* (OUP, 2019) 155–61.

[80] A Greenberg, 'Why Criminal Responsibility for Negligence Cannot be Indirect' (2021) 80(3) *Cambridge Law Journal* 489, 501.

[81] See P Robinson, 'Causing the Conditions of One's Own Defence' (1985) 71 *Virginia Law Review* 1, 2–27; S Dimock, 'What Are Intoxicated Defendants Responsible for? The "Intoxication Defence" Re-examined' (2011) 5 *Criminal Law and Philosophy* 1, 10–16; D Husak, 'Intoxication and Culpability' (2012) 6 *Criminal Law and Philosophy* 363, 368.

The second 'culpability connection' criterion is equally informative. Greenberg uses it to show that even where D's culpability at T1 is significant (e.g. in the medical context, where it was extremely poor practice not to perform certain obvious tests), it would still be unjust to trace that fault through to substitute for missing fault at T2.[82] This is because, although we might have identified a similar *level* of culpability at T1, that culpability does not tie D to the physical harms at T2 in the same way as their missing T2 culpability necessarily would have: it is still not equivalent fault. T1 demonstrates D's culpability in failing to perform a test that leads to a lack of information, but the absent negligence at T2 focuses on failing to observe clear risks of injury that materialize in fact. The latter provides a much clearer link between D and the harms at T2, establishing the necessary culpability connection.

Again, we can observe the same equivalence deficit in the context of the intoxication rules. The culpability exhibited by D at T1, even in cases of extreme intoxication, may demonstrate a broad disregard for the rights of others, but the objective risks associated with impaired capacity are fundamentally different from the subjective foresight of specific risks that occur in fact.[83] And the use of counterfactuals within the current law does not repair that deficit. Even if we could be sure that D would have foreseen the relevant risk if sober at T2 (potentially a big 'if'[84]), T2 recklessness in action is not simply about foresight, as it includes the decision to continue acting unreasonably to run that risk.[85] It is typically this combination of foresight and intentional conduct at T2 that ties D to the resulting harms.

2.3.3 Retreat from the equivalence thesis

It should be clear at this point that having accepted the T1–T2 structure and inculpatory function of the intoxication rules, that an appeal to the equivalence thesis struggles to provide adequate justification for the current law. There is insufficient clarity and explanation for the definition of fault at T1; the definition of the target at T2 is also uncertain, not least because of the tension between mens rea equivalence and offence level analysis; and our examination of the tracing from T1 to T2 exposes a culpability mismatch in both gravity and function. D's conduct at T1 may be deserving of blame, perhaps even criminal blame, but it is not equivalent

[82] A Greenberg, 'Why Criminal Responsibility for Negligence Cannot be Indirect' (2021) 80(3) *Cambridge Law Journal* 489, 504–11.

[83] See P Robinson, 'Causing the Conditions of One's Own Defence' (1985) 71 *Virginia Law Review* 1, 2–27.

[84] See R Williams, 'Voluntary Intoxication—A Lost Cause?' (2013) 129 *Law Quarterly Review* 264, 266–71.

[85] See E Paton, 'Reformulating the Intoxication Rules' [1995] *Criminal Law Review* 382, 384, highlighting the Law Commission's inconsistent treatment of this point.

to D's absent mens rea and/or voluntariness at T2, and so the substitution of fault within the current law is unsupported.

The responses to these and similar critiques have varied. For some, the equivalence thesis remains an achievable goal, prompting reform recommendations remaining within the broad structure of the current law (discussed in Section 2.4 below); whilst for others, ourselves included, the equivalence thesis is not salvageable, and should lead us to consider alternatives outside of that mechanism (discussed in Section 2.5 below). Each of these accepts the problems outlined above as fundamental, and requires us to reconceptualize and significantly reform the law.

Alongside these responses, however, a third approach is discernible; coming particularly from the courts that are charged with interpreting and applying the law as it stands rather than with the discussion of potential reform. This response has been the maintenance of the current law through an appeal to intuitions of 'order' and 'justice', challenging and even doubting the necessity of the equivalence thesis. We see this in *Majewski*, for example, where Lord Salmon acknowledges certain principled critiques of prior fault^{OFF}, stating in response:[86]

> But this is the view that has been adopted by the common law of England, which is founded on common sense and experience rather than strict logic.

A similar line is employed by Lord Edmund-Davies:[87]

> Illogical though the present law may be, it represents a compromise between the imposition of liability upon inebriates in complete disregard of their condition (on the alleged ground that it was brought on voluntarily), and the total exculpation required by the defendant's actual state of mind at the time he committed the harm in issue.

It is also a position adopted in later cases, such as the appeal to '*broadly* equivalent culpability' in *Heard*.[88]

We can understand the appeal of this approach without accepting it. We contend that it concedes too much to say the law need not be logical or that it need not support the equivalence thesis. Without T1–T2 equivalence, we are left with an inculpatory mechanism of legal fiction that risks inappropriate criminalization (i.e. where an *ex-post* assessment of D's conduct suggests it is not deserving of criminalization), and will always result in inappropriate labelling (i.e. for an offence the

[86] [1977] AC 443, 482. And later, at 484: 'I am satisfied that this rule accords with justice, ethics and common sense, and I would leave it alone even if it does not comply with strict logic.'

[87] Ibid 494.

[88] [2007] EWCA Crim 125, [30] (emphasis added).

elements of which D has not satisfied either directly or through indirect equivalence). This is not a tenable position.

Does it make a difference that intoxication rules are not often applied in practice? We do not have empirical evidence to inform this question, but it is certainly an anecdotal response offered by some, thereby diminishing, perhaps, the case for reform. The problem with this view, however, and any potential empirical support for it, is that the current law provides a significant disincentive for defendants to raise evidence of intoxication even if it provides the best explanation for D's lack of mens rea. Where D is charged with a basic intent offence, raising evidence of intoxication to deny mens rea in practice operates so as to relieve the prosecution of their burden, since by virtue of the prior fault^{OFF} rules at that point D is treated as if they had mens rea. The claim that defendants are understandably reluctant to make such concessions is supported by empirical work from the Netherlands, from (albeit small scale) practitioner interviews.[89] Of course, inappropriate criminalization and labelling should be unacceptable on any scale within the criminal law, but it is worth emphasizing that the true scale of this injustice is currently unknowable because of the supressing effects of the law itself.

It is on this basis that we move to consider the reform-focused responses. First, we discuss alternatives within the current structure of prior fault^{OFF} intoxication rules, and second, alternatives outside of that structure.

2.4 Reforming the equivalence thesis

This section explores whether the equivalence thesis can be salvaged through legal reform, looking to maintain broadly the same structure and function of the current law (i.e. using T1 fault to substitute for missing offence elements at T2). We begin by discussing approaches focused on narrowing the elements that can be substituted for at T2, before going on to more comprehensive reform proposals. As will be seen, we do not believe that any of these accounts provide an adequate response to the problems identified in Section 2.3.

2.4.1 Doctrinal narrowing to core cases

The approach here would be to accept the broad tenants of the equivalence thesis (implicitly at least), but make the task of finding equivalence easier by narrowing the target at T2 (i.e. narrowing the range of elements that can be substituted for). The distinction between crimes of basic intent (that can be constructed from T1

[89] A Goldberg, *Blaming the Addicted Brain* (Eleven, 2022) Ch 7.

fault) and specific intent (that cannot be constructed from T1 fault) is an early example of this, but other jurisdictions and reform proposals have gone further.

Looking to other jurisdictions, a notable variation of this kind has developed in Canada. Here, although a *Majewski*-type rule allowing for the construction of T2 mens rea remains at common law,[90] the legal position of intoxicated automatism has been subject to considerable flux. Supported by the academic literature,[91] focus has been placed on whether T1 intoxication should *ever* be able to replace a lack of voluntariness at T2 (whether D is charged with a specific or basic/general intent offence); most recently leading the Supreme Court to declare legislation allowing for substitution of this kind unconstitutional.[92] This is influenced by provisions of the Canadian Charter of Rights and Freedoms, and sections 7 and 11(d) in particular, which guarantee core presumptions of innocence and security against unjust punishment. But behind this, of course, is an anti-equivalence critique: D would be unjustly punished in these circumstances because their conduct at T1 is not equivalent to the absence of voluntariness at T2.[93]

Narrowing the potential for T2 substitution in this way (i.e. allowing intoxication to substitute for certain mens rea states, but *not* for involuntariness) certainly has potential to aid the case for equivalence. The position of involuntariness at T2 has remained a particular problem for those defending the intoxication rules, because even if we accept a broad equivalence with T2 recklessness (which we do not), this does not provide an obvious justification for constructing absent voluntariness as well; additionally, allowing for the construction of T2 intentional conduct but not for T2 intentional results means having to identify a clear distinction between those elements.

The Canadian example only engages with a small subset of the problems introduced in the previous section however, and even as an answer to concerns around T2, it leaves intact the offence level analysis and the distinction between basic and specific intent offences that has been so problematic. A more comprehensive response can be seen in the work of the Law Commission for England & Wales, which in its most recent report (2009) focused on establishing equivalence through a redefinition of T2 targets in particular.[94] Recognizing the need for and implications of the equivalence thesis, the Commission defended the position that D's fault at T1 is 'morally equivalent' to absent recklessness at T2,[95] and recommended codification and reform of the intoxication rules to thereby allow such prior fault^{OFF} to construct absent mens rea of this kind regardless of the offence charged. Crucially,

[90] See *Brown* [2022] SCC 18, where the Supreme Court 'specifically leave intact the common law rule' [4].

[91] See, e.g., S Dimock, 'What Are Intoxicated Defendants Responsible for? The "Intoxication Defence" Re-examined' (2011) 5 *Criminal Law and Philosophy* 1.

[92] *Brown* 2022 SCC 18.

[93] Ibid [49].

[94] Law Commission, *Intoxication and Criminal Liability* (LC No 314, 2009).

[95] Ibid [2.17].

this would have shifted the analysis and application of intoxication rules from offences (basic/specific) to individual elements within offences: distinguishing the so-called non-integral elements (that can be constructed from T1 fault, e.g. recklessness) from integral elements (that cannot be constructed from T1 fault, e.g. intention).[96]

The Commission's recommendations in 2009 were rejected however, with implications for the potential viability of the equivalence thesis.[97] First, despite the depth and detail of the Commission's work, the element level analysis recommended was not possible (or was found to be inappropriate) in several areas. This included intentional conduct, that was not included in the list of integral elements:[98] leading to principled questions of equivalence (i.e. on what basis is D's T1 fault equivalent to missing T2 voluntariness?), as well as practical questions about the separation of conduct and results.[99] It also included the treatment of complicity and inchoate assisting and encouraging, where the Commission's recommendations would retain an offence level analysis (i.e. allowing T2 mens rea to be constructed or not across a full offence, rather than focusing on individual elements).[100] This was done to avoid undue complexity in the application of intoxication rules to offences with multiple parties, but involves a significant concession to the internal logic of the Commission's scheme, with integral elements now susceptible to prior fault^{OFF} construction in the application of these offences.[101] Second, despite the Commission's criticism of the current law as overly complex, and its aim for greater simplicity as well as clarity, the scheme recommended falls some way short from that ideal. The reality of the Commission's scheme, if implemented, would have been the necessary separation of offence elements within each case (far from straightforward legally) and jury directions on the relevance or irrelevance of intoxication to different elements within single offences. Indeed, it was this concern about *additional* complexity that was highlighted in the government's rejection of the Commission's recommendations.[102]

Each of these examples demonstrates positive steps taken in an attempt to rationalize the operation of the equivalence thesis. However, they also demonstrate the inadequacy of reform that does not engage with the range of criticisms

[96] Ibid [3.46]. See also draft Bill cl.3(5).

[97] See JJ Child, 'Drink, Drugs and Law Reform: A Review of Law Commission Report No.314' [2009] *Criminal Law Review* 488.

[98] Law Commission, *Intoxication and Criminal Liability* (LC No314, 2009) [3.46] and fn 53; draft Bill cl.3(5)(a).

[99] JJ Child, 'Drink, Drugs and Law Reform: A Review of Law Commission Report No.314' [2009] *Criminal Law Review* 488, 492–95.

[100] Law Commission, *Intoxication and Criminal Liability* (LC No 314, 2009) draft Bill cl.3(5)(e) and (6) and cl.4.

[101] JJ Child, 'Drink, Drugs and Law Reform: A Review of Law Commission Report No.314' [2009] *Criminal Law Review* 488, 494–500.

[102] Ministry of Justice, *Report on the Implementation of Law Commission Proposals* (HC 1900, 2012) [49–50].

identified in Section 2.3, as well as the potential for new problems to arise (e.g. additional complexity). We move now to consider more comprehensive reform options.

2.4.2 New theories of equivalence

In a final effort to salvage the equivalence thesis, and with it the basic structure of current prior fault^{OFF} intoxication rules, new focus has been placed on understanding (and better defining) fault at T1. This engages with our primary critique of the current law, in its problematic transition from objective and unrelated fault at T1 to the substitution of subjective and specific mental states at T2, and with potential to engage with several other of our concerns as well.[103] We explore leading accounts from Robinson, Dimock, and Yaffe, whilst explaining our continued reservations about each of their proposals.

The accounts offered by Robinson and Dimock may usefully be considered together. Each has provided an excellent critique of the current law, and particularly the claims of the equivalence thesis.[104] However, in both cases, they also contend that some version of the equivalence thesis may be reformed to allow for the T1–T2 imputation of fault (refocused, in Robinson's case, around the language of causation).[105] And for both, the primary target for reform is identified as the T1 point of intoxication, with greater and better-targeted T1 fault offering the route to legitimate substitution of mens rea. It is perhaps unsurprising, at this point in the argument, that both are prone to drift into the discussion of the so-called grand schemer cases (i.e. cases where D becomes intoxicated at T1 *in order* to lose voluntary control *in order* to cause a particular harm).[106] Grand schemer scenarios provide a compelling case for criminalization, with D's fault at T1 demonstrating a clear and targeted culpability link to the harms at T2. However, as we have mentioned already, to the extent that grand schemer cases are ever likely to arise, it is questionable whether intoxication rules are required to find liability: D's conduct

[103] E.g. the treatment of addiction and other mental disorders at T1.

[104] See, in particular, P Robinson, 'Causing the Conditions of One's Own Defence' (1985) 71 *Virginia Law Review* 1; 'Imputed Criminal Liability' (1984) 93 *Yale Law Journal* 609; S Dimock, 'What Are Intoxicated Defendants Responsible for? The "Intoxication Defence" Re-examined' (2011) 5 *Crim L Phil* 1.

[105] See P Robinson, 'Causing the Conditions of One's Own Defence' (1985) 71 *Virginia Law Review* 1, 50–51; S Dimock, 'What Are Intoxicated Defendants Responsible for? The "Intoxication Defence" Re-examined' (2011) 5 *Crim L Phil* 1, 17–18.

[106] This is particularly true of Robinson. See P Robinson, 'Imputed Criminal Liability' (1984) 93 *Yale Law Journal* 609, 639–42; 'Causing the Conditions of One's Own Defence' (1985) 71 *Virginia Law Review* 1, 30–37; 'A Brief Summary and Critique of Criminal Liability Rules for Intoxicated Conduct' (2018) 82(5) *J Crim L* 381, 384–85. But also see S Dimock, 'Actio Libera in Causa' (2013) 7 *Criminal Law and Philosophy* 549, 560–66.

at T1 is accompanied by mens rea, and this conduct can be causally linked to the harms at T2 without having to consider separate rules of imputation.[107]

Standard prior fault^{OFF} cases are more difficult, where D's intoxication at T1 is not consciously directed at future harms. Both Dimock and Robinson want increased culpability at T1 to justify T2 substitution, but employ quite different approaches to achieve it. Robinson focuses on the mens rea required for the T2 offence, asking the deceptively simple question:[108]

> Ask: at T1 (the time of becoming intoxicated) did the defendant have the culpability required for the offence? If so, then she will be liable . . .

The approach here—requiring the mens rea of the offence to exist at T1—has an obvious attraction and is endorsed by others in the field,[109] as well as other jurisdictions.[110] These are not grand schemer cases, as an intoxication rule is required to link T1–T2. But in common with grand schemers, and attractive to Robinson, the fact that D possesses the mens rea for the offence at T1 means that the rule need only transfer that mens rea rather than construct it from unrelated fault.

There are at least two major problems with this approach, however. The first is that D is extremely unlikely to subjectively foresee the future elements of a particular crime when becoming intoxicated at T1, making the potential application of the intoxication rules (unduly[111]) narrow—a critique recognized by Robinson[112] (and others[113]). Robinson has suggested remedying this with a 'rebuttable presumption' that D possessed the required mens rea at T1.[114] However, he recognizes the problems with this as well, including the inappropriate (and potentially unconstitutional in the US context) nature of presuming guilt, the fact that the presumption may be easily rebutted anyway, and so on;[115] and it is perhaps telling

[107] We discuss these cases further in Chapter 3, Section 3.3.

[108] P Robinson, 'A Brief Summary and Critique of Criminal Liability Rules for Intoxicated Conduct' (2018) 82(5) *Journal of Criminal Law* 381, 385.

[109] E.g. Yaffe (discussed below); F Stark, 'Prior Fault' (2014) 73(1) *Cambridge Law Journal* 8; A Greenberg, 'Why Criminal Responsibility for Negligence Cannot be Indirect' (2021) 80(3) *Cambridge Law Journal* 489, 495.

[110] The approach here is similar to the construction of *actio libera in causa* in German law. See A Goldberg, JJ Child, H Crombag, and D Roef, 'Prior Fault Blame in England and Wales, Germany and the Netherlands' (2021) 8(1) *Journal of International and Comparative Law* 53.

[111] Intuitions will pull in either direction here, but it certainly leaves the T1–T2 route to liability extremely narrow in practical terms.

[112] P Robinson, 'Causing the Conditions of One's Own Defence' (1985) 71 *Virginia Law Review* 1, 58.

[113] E Macdonald, e.g., claims it would render the intoxication rules 'useless': 'Reckless Language and Majewski' (1986) 6(3) *Legal Studies* 239, 254–55.

[114] P Robinson, 'Causing the Conditions of One's Own Defence' (1985) 71 *Virginia Law Review* 1, 58–61.

[115] Ibid. Robinson discusses the potential for recasting the presumption of mens rea as a defence, 'circumventing the constitutional burden-of-persuasion problems' (Ibid 61). A similar argument is made in F Stark, 'Prior Fault' (2014) 73(1) *Cambridge Law Journal* 8. With respect, this approach disguises rather than resolves such problems—a perennial issue with the analysis of intoxication rules.

that he does not include reference to a presumption in a more recent paper on the topic.[116]

The second problem with Robinson's approach, which has not been generally recognized, is that (outside of grand schemer cases) D's fault at T1 can never be exactly the same as the mens rea required for the offence at T2. This is because, even if at T1 D were to foresee potential T2 harms, this would be foresight of future harms arising from subsequent conduct. Such foresight may be culpable, but it does not satisfy the definition of recklessness in English law[117] (or elsewhere[118]) that requires D to foresee a risk of certain harms or circumstances in action, and to continue unreasonably to run such risks. The point here, as we have argued elsewhere,[119] is that there is an important culpability difference between (i) foreseeing that my conduct may cause certain harms *and choosing to run that risk* and (ii) foreseeing that my future conduct may cause certain harms *if I decide to act in that way*. The difference between (i) and (ii) is mitigated in the context of the intoxication rules because D's initial conduct (T1 intoxication) gives them less control over their choice at T2, but the core difference between 'taking a risk' and 'foreseeing a risk' remains. Thus, *contra* Robinson and others, intoxication rules that look for T2 mens rea at T1 will either never find it (by definition) or will involve an imputation of different mens rea states from T1 to T2.

Dimock recognizes at least the first of these criticisms—that D is unlikely to foresee T2 offence elements when becoming intoxicated at T1—and opts for an alternative approach. Although only sketched lightly at the end of a paper focused on critique of the current law, Dimock suggests that requiring T1 'recklessness with respect to impairment' would lead to a situation where 'for all practical purposes the concerns raised in this paper would dissolve'.[120] With respect, we believe that she is selling her critique short. It is certainly true that the current law requires very little at T1 in terms of culpability and that requiring foresight of impairment would help to engage with this problem, and would do so in a way that does not suffer the same defects of Robinson's alternative. However, having set out the inappropriate claims of the equivalence thesis, it is difficult to understand the basis upon which foresight of incapacity (T1) can be equated with absent subjective mens rea states concerning the running of specific foreseen risks in action (T2). Drawing back to our discussion of T1–T2 links in Section 2.3, there seems to be a mismatch here both in terms of the gravity and target of D's fault.

[116] P Robinson, 'A Brief Summary and Critique of Criminal Liability Rules for Intoxicated Conduct' (2018) 82(5) *Journal of Criminal Law* 381.

[117] *G* [2003] UKHL 50.

[118] See, e.g., US Model Penal Code, §2.02.

[119] JJ Child and A Hunt, 'Beyond the Present-Fault Paradigm: Expanding Mens rea Definitions in the General Part' (2021) 42(2) *Oxford Journal of Legal Studies* 438.

[120] S Dimock, 'What Are Intoxicated Defendants Responsible for? The "Intoxication Defence" Re-examined' (2011) 5 *Criminal Law and Philosophy* 1, 17.

Probably the most complete account of how the equivalence thesis might be reformed has come from Yaffe.[121] Moving quickly from a critique of the current law, Yaffe aims to provide a theoretical justification for a reformed equivalence thesis (according, at least, to our current empirical understanding of the states involved[122]). Yaffe contends that missing T2 states of subjective recklessness may be constructed from T1 fault according to what he terms the 'intoxication recklessness principle'. He outlines two separate routes to such construction, distinguishing (i) unjustified T1 intoxication and (ii) non-justified T1 intoxication.

D's intoxication will be 'unjustified' under Yaffe's scheme if, when becoming intoxicated at T1, D 'is aware of the relevant risked harms' that later arise at T2.[123] In such cases, Yaffe would allow a finding of T2 recklessness, on the condition that a sober reasonable person would have been aware of the relevant risk at T2. At this point, the approach is very similar to that advocated by Robinson. And in line with Robinson, Yaffe also claims that D is effectively reckless at T1 in these cases, and so the intoxication rules are simply transferring that mental state to T2 rather than constructing fault. Yaffe also pre-empts the critique that D will rarely possess reckless foresight at T1, highlighting first that there is an alternative route to equivalence (i.e. non-justified intoxication, discussed below), and also mitigating the critique by saying that we should interpret T1 recklessness more broadly in line with what Ferzan calls 'opaque recklessness'.[124] Essentially, his claim here is that T1 recklessness need not be as precisely targeted at specific harms as that typically required at T2, and that as with areas of civil law, foresight of a more general set of harms (within which the actual T2 harm is located) can still provide sufficient culpability for a defensible equivalence thesis.

We do not believe that Yaffe goes far enough, however, to avoid the critique outlined with regard to Robinson. We might again question how many cases will be caught within Yaffe's (extended) definition of T1 recklessness. But more importantly, as above, we challenge the idea that foresight at T1 can be accurately described as recklessness at all: even bracketing the shift to opaque recklessness, the fundamental difference remains between running a foreseen risk in action (whether specific or opaque) and simple foresight of risks associated with future action. There is a culpability deficit in the latter that undermines Yaffe's equivalence claim.

The second route identified by Yaffe is more complex, requiring a construction of culpability upon 'non-justified' T1 intoxication. Here Yaffe is dealing with more typical intoxication cases, where D demonstrates some negligence at T1 in becoming intoxicated (something that is usefully distinguished from *justified*

[121] G Yaffe, 'Intoxication, Recklessness and Negligence' (2012) 9(2) *Ohio State Journal of Criminal Law* 545.
[122] Yaffe rightly highlights the need for greater empirical testing of theories of prior fault. Ibid 549.
[123] Ibid 573.
[124] Ibid 578–81.

intoxication[125]) and goes on to cause mistaken harms at T2. Yaffe—correctly in our view—criticizes the potential imputation of T2 recklessness within the current law, recognizing that *at this stage* all we can say is that D has been negligent. In order to substitute for absent T2 recklessness, Yaffe explains that D must demonstrate additional disregard for the interests of others. He locates this potential 'addition' at T2, asking whether an 'intoxicated reasonable person would have been aware of the risked harms'.[126] The focus here on an intoxicated reasonable person is crucial: where D fails to see the risks at T2 as a result of the intoxication *simpliciter* then we can say no more than D is negligent, it is only where D is negligent at T1 (becoming intoxicated) and again at T2 (falling below an intoxicated reasonable standard) that we have the multiple required by Yaffe to transform negligence into recklessness.

There is much to be said for Yaffe's approach to non-justified intoxication cases, providing a novel analysis of the potential accumulation and translation of culpability. But, ultimately, it does not convince us. On the level of principle, we do not agree that two occasions of negligence should be equated so freely with absent T2 recklessness: subjective recklessness is not simply an aggregation of fault credits, but it involves blaming someone for their choice to run a foreseen risk (i.e. something that does not occur in this category of cases). Whilst we might sensibly blame D for an increased or sustained negligence, the route to equivalence with subjective awareness remains obscure.[127]

We are also confronted with very tangible problems in terms of process and outcome. On process, it will be difficult for courts to articulate and apply the standard of a 'reasonable intoxicated person' (i.e. a misnomer in the current law), and even more difficult to apply that standard to acutely intoxicated individuals, even leaving aside clinical uncertainties about the specific effects of different drugs on different individuals at different times. Indeed, it is here we locate the problems of outcome, as Yaffe's requirement for two separate negligent events means that the more intoxicated (*the more negligent*) D is at T1, the less likely that we will be able to locate a second independent negligent event at T2, and so the less likely D will be caught within the intoxication rules. In contrast, the less intoxicated (*the less negligent*) D is at T1, the more likely that we will be able to locate a second independent negligent event, and so the more likely D will be caught within the intoxication rules. *Contra* Yaffe, this approach does not underpin the current law, but would mark a

125 Ibid 572–73. The potential for and appropriate legal consequences of reasonable intoxication are discussed further in Chapters 5–7.

126 Ibid 577–78.

127 One response would be to narrow the fault required to 'advertent negligence' which—in the US context—requires foresight of a risk, but a lack of awareness that the risk is substantial. This would come closer to an equivalence standard in requiring advertence, but remains susceptible to our other lines of critique.

volte-face to punishing carelessness in those with lower levels of intoxication.[128] We do not believe that such a shift would improve the law.

2.5 Conclusion

Our conclusion from the preceding sections is that the equivalence thesis is not salvageable, and that any version of the intoxication rules relying on its validity will produce culpability mismatch and injustice (in terms of conviction and/or labelling). In this final section, we consider where that conclusion should take us. Should we follow those common law jurisdictions that have simply abolished the intoxication rules without replacement, preventing the substitution of mens rea on the basis of T1 intoxication in all cases? Or, if we still think liability is appropriate in certain cases, what alternative mechanisms are there for the criminalization of this group of intoxicated mistaken offenders?

2.5.1 Abolition without replacement

The simplest response to the injustice occasioned by current prior fault^{OFF} intoxication rules is to abolish them without replacement. And there may be much to be said for this approach. Abolition of the intoxication rules would not provide impunity for the intoxicated: as we discussed in Section 2.1 of this chapter, but is worth repeating, where D completes all elements of the offence charged at T2 they will be liable for that offence regardless of intoxication, including cases where D may plausibly claim that they would not have offended but for the disinhibiting effects of the drug.[129] The only cases impacted by abolition of prior fault^{OFF} intoxication rules would be those where D lacks mens rea/voluntariness at T2, and we rely on their intoxicated state at T1 to substitute for those missing elements. The scale of this category is difficult to gauge, but several commentators have argued that it may be very small, such that abolition would not lead to problems of under-criminalization in fact.[130] This view may be supported by the experience of jurisdictions that have abolished the intoxication rules, such as New Zealand, South Africa, and (albeit not universally[131])

[128] The focus of the current law (and associated intuitions) with acute intoxication and the dangers of targeting lower levels of intoxication are usefully discussed in A Lynch, 'The Scope of Intoxication' (1982) *Criminal Law Review* 139.

[129] *Kingston* [1994] 3 All ER 353.

[130] See, e.g., C Mitchell, 'The Intoxicated Offender—Refuting the Legal and Medical Myths' (1988) 11(1) *International Journal of Law and Psychiatry* 77; R Shiner, 'Intoxication and Responsibility' (1990) 13(9) *International Journal of Law and Psychiatry* 9.

[131] Despite the abolition of *Majewski*-style intoxication rules at common law (*O'Connor* (1980) 146 CLR 64), a majority of states have legislated to allow for a similar mechanism of inculpation.

Australia,[132] and has led to calls for abolition in other jurisdictions in the literature.[133]

We agree with much of the position outlined here, and it is plainly correct to emphasize that intoxication leading to involuntariness (as currently defined) will be extremely rare in practice.[134] However, we *do* remain concerned about the potential for under-criminalization if prior fault^{OFF} intoxication rules were to be abolished without any replacement, in both its direct and indirect effects. Whilst intoxicated involuntariness may be rare (at least in terms of involuntariness leading to harms rather than simple unconsciousness[135]), by focusing on incapacity in that sense, advocates of simple abolition have often underplayed or even ignored the potential for intoxicated mistake making (i.e. mistakes that undermine a claim of mens rea, but do not entail involuntariness).[136] The denial of an offence on the basis of an intoxicated mistake is entirely plausible, be it a mistake about circumstances (e.g. a victim's age, their consent, the ownership of property, etc) or about results (e.g. the potential harm to a person or property). It remains difficult to know the scale of such mistakes empirically,[137] but where they arise it will often be the case that no liability can be established in the absence of recklessness,[138] and so abolition of the prior fault^{OFF} intoxication rules without replacement would result in acquittal. This would also be the case, for example, where an acutely intoxicated individual fails to see the risks associated with walking in that state through a public place and stumbles, causing damage to others property and/or non-fatal harm to other persons. The direct effects of this approach are therefore to risk under-criminalization in blameworthy circumstances.[139]

[132] See *Kampeli* [1975] 2 NZLR 610 (NZ); *S v Chretien* 1981 (1) SA 1097 (SA); *O'Connor* (1980) 146 CLR 64 (Aus).

[133] See, e.g., Law Commission, *Intoxication and Criminal Liability* (Consultation 127, 1993) Part 5; G Williams, *The General Part* (2nd Ed, Stevens, 1961) 571; AP Simester, 'Getting Drunk in Singapore and Malaysia' (2012) *Singapore Journal of Legal Studies* 1, 15; C Mitchell, 'The Intoxicated Offender—Refuting the Legal and Medical Myths' (1988) 11(1) *International Journal of Law and Psychiatry* 77; G Dingwall, *Alcohol and Crime* (Routledge, 2006) 111; R Shiner, 'Intoxication and Responsibility' (1990) 13(9) *International Journal of Law and Psychiatry* 9.

[134] Under the current English law, e.g., even irrational and uncontrolled movement may still satisfy the legal requirement of voluntariness. See *Coley* [2013] EWCA Crim 223; JJ Child, 'Defence of a Basic Voluntary Act Requirement in Criminal Law from Philosophies of Action' (2020) 23(4) *New Criminal Law Review* 437.

[135] Unconsciousness can result in serious harms of course, e.g., where D is driving.

[136] See, e.g., discussion in G Dingwall, *Alcohol and Crime* (Routledge, 2006) 111; R Shiner, 'Intoxication and Responsibility' (1990) *International Journal of Law and Psychiatry* 9.

[137] Not least, as we discussed, because the current law provides a significant disincentive for the defence to raise evidence of intoxication.

[138] This is because, in English law, typical offences against the person and against property are not broadly underpinned by negligence or strict liability equivalents.

[139] See S Gough, 'Surviving without Majewski?' (2000) *Criminal Law Review* 719, 721–26; R Williams, 'Voluntary Intoxication—A Lost Cause?' (2013) 129 *Law Quarterly Review* 264; M Shain and G Higgins, 'The Intoxication Defence and Theories of Criminal Liability: A Praxeological Approach' (1997) 24(4) *Contemporary Drug Problems* 731, 753–54; S Dimock, 'What Are Intoxicated Defendants Responsible for? The "Intoxication Defence" Re-examined' (2011) 5 *Criminal Law and Philosophy* 1, 6–7.

One might respond that intuitions of blame here are misplaced, and that an acquittal is the correct outcome in cases of this kind. But this too requires justification. Where we can locate fault at T1 through unreasonable intoxication, and where this can be linked to serious harms at T2 through causal or other means, there appears (at the very least) to be a basis for potential criminalization.[140]

In circumstances of apparent T1–T2 blame, abolition of prior fault^{OFF} intoxication rules without replacement also raises the potential for a mismatch between public expectations and the substantive law. There are several examples of this. In South Africa, for example, abolition at common law was followed quite swiftly with the creation of an intoxication offence.[141] Similarly, whilst the Australian state of Victoria has maintained its position on the use of intoxication rules (i.e. abolition without replacement), state authorities have come under significant pressure to find a route to liability,[142] and so we see an inconsistent approach taken on this issue between different states. Even within the single criminal jurisdiction of New Zealand, a curious anomaly exists to allow intoxication rules to substitute missing T2 mens rea for the circumstance elements of an offence but not for the result elements,[143] showing an internal conflict of policy leading to complexity with a lack of principled justification. Finally, at least some commentators within jurisdictions who have abolished the intoxication rules claim that they continue to exist informally, where prosecutions are achieved despite plausible claims by a defendant that they lacked mens rea due to intoxication (a type of reverse jury equity).[144]

2.5.2 Abolition with replacement

Outside of the current intoxication rules and reformed iterations of the equivalence thesis, two mechanisms in particular have been advanced as providing an alternative route to liability in cases of intoxicated harm causing. The first relies on the greater use of objective mens rea in the definition of offences against the person and property, such that intoxicated harm causers are more likely to satisfy the elements of the offence at T2. The second alternative requires the creation of a

[140] We explore this further below and in Chapters 5–7.

[141] South African Criminal Law Amendment Act 1988, s1.

[142] Especially following high profile cases such as *Nadruku*, where a professional rugby player was acquitted following an intoxicated incident in which he inflicted significant injury upon two female victims. See S Gough, 'Surviving without Majewski?' (2000) *Criminal Law Review* 719, 720–26; 'Intoxication and Criminal Liability' (1996) 112 *Law Quarterly Review* 335.

[143] Discussed in AP Simester and WJ Brookbanks, *Principles of Criminal Law* (5th Ed, Thomson Reuters, 2019) 501.

[144] Discussed in A Ashworth, *Principles of Criminal Law* (2nd Ed, OUP, 1995), 213.

bespoke offence, defined specifically to apply to those who become intoxicated and later cause harms. Both alternatives reject the premise that intoxicated harming may be equivalent to current subjectively defined offences, but still allow for the possibility that it may cross the culpability threshold for justified criminalization. More complete analysis will follow in later chapters, but we introduce and explain both below.

First, taking the option of greater use of objective mens rea. In certain jurisdictions, including the Netherlands for example,[145] a broad range of negligence offences (or variations within offences) exist to criminalize harms caused to persons and property. As a result, when assessing T2 liability, there is much less call for prior fault^{OFF} intoxication rules: if we define a reasonable person as non-intoxicated, and such a reasonable person would have acted and/or foreseen events differently at T2, then an intoxicated harm causer is likely to be liable at this point without the need to impute mens rea states from T1. Indeed, during the period where English law allowed for an objective definition of recklessness, similar arguments were made here about the lack of a need for a *Majewski*-style approach.[146] Therefore, one solution to our current debate would be to abolish current intoxication rules, but to replace them through the much greater use of objective mens rea, ensuring that liability can still be found.[147] We discuss this approach in Chapter 11, Section 11.3.1, delayed to that point because the arguments about the appropriate use of objective standards (and the role of intoxication within such standards) cut across the definition of both offences and defences. Suffice it to say here, however, that we do not endorse this approach as a response to the potential under-criminalization of intoxicated harm causers, both because of its implications outside of intoxication cases (i.e. the broadening of criminal law more generally to target objective fault) as well as its inability (currently at least) to separate reasonable and unreasonable episodes of voluntary intoxication.

Turning then to the second alternative, this would involve finding liability for intoxicated harm causers outside of current offence definitions through the creation of a new and bespoke offence. Intoxication offences already exist in certain jurisdictions,[148] and have been debated and endorsed across a wide range of common law and civil law jurisdictions.[149] Despite obvious advantages however,

[145] Discussed in A Goldberg, JJ Child, H Crombag, and D Roef, 'Prior Fault Blame in England and Wales, Germany and the Netherlands' (2021) 8(1) *Journal of International and Comparative Law* 53.

[146] E.g. J Stannard, 'The Demise of Drunkenness' (1982) 2 *Legal Studies* 291.

[147] A more sophisticated version of this argument is provided in D Husak, 'Intoxication and Culpability' (2012) 6 *Criminal Law and Philosophy* 363.

[148] Notably in South Africa and Germany.

[149] See discussion in Law Commission, *Intoxication and Criminal Liability* (Consultation 127, 1993) Part 6, where the Commission propose the creation of an intoxication offence in English law.

including the potential to criminalize and label offenders more precisely, significant problems have been raised about the definition of such offences and their ability to operate practically alongside other offences.[150] We discuss these challenges in Chapter 5, before outlining our preferred approach to a new bespoke offence that includes (but is not limited to) prior fault^{OFF} intoxication in Chapter 7.

[150] See discussion in Law Commission, *Intoxication and Criminal Liability* (LC No 229, 1995), where the Commission opts not to adopt its previous proposal for an intoxication offence following consultation.

3
NON-INTOXICATION PRIOR FAULT OFFENDING: EXTERNAL CAUSES

3.1 Introduction

This chapter explores examples of prior fault^{OFF} that apply in situations outside of the paradigmatic case of intoxication.[1] The characterization of such rules as examples of prior fault^{OFF} is open to debate. Indeed, it is a debate that returns us to our discussion in the introductory chapter about whether prior fault should be considered as a 'doctrine', or simply as a label for a loose collection of similar legal rules applied in cognate but different circumstances.[2] Any *systematic* approach to the topic of prior fault would suggest that other circumstances (i.e. alongside voluntary intoxication) should also qualify, and perhaps already do, when giving rise to comparable intuitions of blame where D's conduct at T1 leads to harms at T2.[3] The consumption of alcohol or other drugs at T1 may provide evidential assistance, but there is little difference in theoretical terms between this and the reckless or negligent mismanagement of medication, or chronic lack of sleep, or any other T1 choice that might provide a logical explanation for decreased awareness and mistake making at T2. The problem is that prior fault rules have not developed systematically, and examples of prior fault^{OFF} are invariably obfuscated by illogical legal framing (e.g. intoxication as a defence) and a lack of principled scrutiny. Such problems, as we will see, are only exacerbated further outside of the paradigmatic intoxication context.

Despite the potential for prior fault^{OFF} outside of intoxication cases, there is no single set of 'non-intoxication' prior fault^{OFF} rules to cover all cases of this kind.

[1] As introduced in Chapter 1, we are adopting the notation 'prior fault^{OFF}' and 'prior fault^{DEF}' to distinguish between prior fault rules relevant to the construction of a crime and prior fault rules relevant to the blocking of a defence.

[2] Discussed in Chapter 1, Section 1.3.1. One view holds that prior fault^{OFF} rules do not exist outside of the intoxication paradigm, with the only exception being certain non-dangerous drugs: JC Smith, *Smith and Hogan's Criminal Law* (8th Ed, OUP, 1996) 39 and 234.

[3] See, e.g., Law Commission, *Insanity and Automatism* (Discussion Paper, 2013) [5.1] and Part 6; M Gur-Arye, *Actio Libera in Causa in Criminal Law* (Jerusalem, 1984); Child JJ, 'Prior Fault: Blocking Defences or Constructing Crimes' in A Reed and M Bohlander (eds) *Defences* (Routledge, 2014).

Prior Fault Criminalization. John J Child, Adrian Hunt, and Hans S. Crombag, Oxford University Press.
 DOI: 10.1093/9780191874734.003.0004

Rather, in this chapter (and in Chapter 4[4]), we explore a series of rules that *appear* to share both the structural and functional characteristics of prior fault^{OFF}. We begin (Section 3.2) by analysing *core* cases of prior fault^{OFF} automatism, where D's conduct at T1 leads to a lack of voluntariness and mens rea when causing harms at T2. We follow this—still focused on prior fault^{OFF} automatism—with a discussion of two sets of cases that have given rise to particular debate in the literature: 'grand schemer' cases (Section 3.3) where D acts at T1 to cause harm at T2 without voluntary control, and 'trigger slip' cases (Section 3.4) where D accidentally causes harm during the course of a criminal enterprise. Finally, in Section 3.5, we discuss the potential for prior fault^{OFF} where D's blameworthy conduct at T1 results in a lack of mens rea at T2, but where D remains voluntary (i.e. where automatism does not feature).

The discussion within each topic section mirrors our Chapter 2 methodology and analysis of prior fault^{OFF} intoxication in several important ways. Our aim across each section is to identify the structural and functional characteristics of prior fault^{OFF}, examining whether the particular rules are or are not framed in a way which reflects prior fault^{OFF} methodology. The question is whether liability is established at T2 despite a factual absence of voluntariness or mens rea, on the basis of D's prior blameworthy conduct at T1. Where prior fault^{OFF} construction of this kind is found, the discussion then moves to questions of justification and the application of the equivalence thesis. As with prior fault^{OFF} intoxication, justification for the use of prior fault will be shown to rest on the claim that D's fault at T1 is culpably equivalent to the offence elements missing at T2, and from there, we will again demonstrate that this claim (the equivalence thesis) is false. Finally, to the extent that *some form* of liability may be appropriate, we contend that this is best achieved through the abolition of current prior fault^{OFF} rules and the creation of a new bespoke offence.

Although we employ the same pattern of analysis as in Chapter 2, our findings in this chapter vary considerably from those in that chapter. When discussing prior fault^{OFF} intoxication, we identified and evaluated a number of alternative framings that sought to explain the law, but it was ultimately possible to reduce these alternatives to a single approach based on claims of culpability equivalence. In this chapter, beyond similar inconsistencies in framing, we find new and significant problems in the structure and function of the rules being framed.

There are two main examples of these (new) problems not found in our prior fault^{OFF} intoxication discussion which will be explored across the sections of this chapter. First, we identify rules that have been incorrectly analysed (in courts and/or academic debate) as examples of prior fault^{OFF}. We argue that this arises in situations where liability can alternatively and preferably be found through single

[4] The potential for prior fault^{OFF} based on mental disorder and/or the mismanagement of related medication is discussed in Chapter 4, as they raise important stand-alone issues.

event analysis, without the need to engage the inculpatory fictions of prior fault^{OFF} (i.e. cases where current framings cannot and should not be reduced to claims of culpability equivalence). Where this is found, we seek to clarify the appropriate route to liability, and urge courts and commentators to avoid the unnecessary complexity and principled unfairness of locating D's culpability by reference to prior fault^{OFF} mechanisms. We term this problem 'locating liability'.

The second 'new' set of problems we identify here arise where there is an *absence* of prior fault^{OFF} rules in current explanations/analyses. In contrast to prior fault^{OFF} intoxication—where the courts have identified routes to liability in cases where D lacks mens rea and/or voluntariness at T2—there is no equivalent set of rules covering all non-intoxication prior fault^{OFF} cases. Rather, prior fault^{OFF} has been grafted onto existing rules, most importantly those relating to automatism (i.e. claims of involuntariness). This creates a familiar framing problem, relating to the error of characterizing automatism as a 'defence'. But beyond this, it also creates a problem of criminalization: automatism rules are only engaged where D is involuntary at T2, and so we will see there is no obvious mechanism for prior fault^{OFF} to construct liability where non-intoxicated D, who is incapacitated by some other means, lacks mens rea at T2 *but is not involuntary*. Where some form of liability may be justified in these circumstances—whether via prior fault^{OFF} or (more appropriately) via a new bespoke offence—the current prior fault^{OFF} rules only provide for it where D is voluntarily intoxicated. We term this problem 'under-criminalization'.

3.2 Prior fault^{OFF} automatism

Cases within this category appear where D acts at T1 to risk future incapacity, and then goes on to cause harms at T2 when 'unconscious'. This will arise, for example, where D (who is diabetic) takes insulin at T1, fails properly to regulate their blood sugar levels with food/drink, and then goes on (at T2) to cause harm to V (e.g. 'assault' them) when suffering from a diabetic coma.[5] Examples of this kind do not fit within the intoxication rules, because D has not taken a 'dangerous' drug.[6] However, in common with intoxication, the courts have developed legal rules that allow for liability: D may be involuntary at T2 (and therefore also lacking all mens rea), but this is because of their culpable choices at T1, and so some versions of T1 fault are allowed effectively to substitute for the missing elements at T2. As with the current intoxication rules, D is labelled and punished as if all offence elements were completed at T2 (i.e. on the basis of an inculpatory legal fiction).

[5] See, e.g., *Quick* [1973] 3 WLR 26; *Bailey* [1983] 1 WLR 760.

[6] Where T2 involuntariness is caused by D taking a dangerous drug at T1, then the intoxication rules should be applied. Discussed in Chapter 2.

In the subsections below, we discuss the structure and function of current prior fault^{OFF} automatism rules, such as the examples just discussed, including important doctrinal differences from the intoxication rules. We question whether and how prior fault^{OFF} automatism rules may be justified, before considering options for reform. We highlight problems with locating liability (i.e. cases where prior fault^{OFF} analysis is not necessary), as well as problems of potential under-criminalization.

3.2.1 Structure and function of prior fault^{OFF} automatism rules

The prior fault^{OFF} automatism rules share the same basic structure and function as the intoxication rules discussed in Chapter 2. This is the basis for our categorization of such rules within the umbrella of prior fault^{OFF}. If we take the unconscious 'assault' example above, traditional analysis focusing on the point at which harm is caused to V (T2) would suggest that no offence has taken place: at this point, D is acting involuntarily and will also lack the mens rea required for an offence against the person.[7] In order to establish liability, it becomes necessary to construct D's missing T2 culpability from their conduct and fault at T1.

The structural and functional similarity with intoxication rules has led some to present prior fault^{OFF} automatism as a species of intoxication, rather than as a distinct set of prior fault^{OFF} rules.[8] It is an association that may help to organize thinking around prior fault^{OFF} automatism, particularly given the paradigm status of the intoxication rules,[9] but it is not one that we endorse for two reasons.

First, as we discuss further below, there are several doctrinal differences between establishing prior fault^{OFF} through the intoxication rules and the prior fault^{OFF} automatism rules. The most significant of which (for prior fault^{OFF} automatism) are requirements of *subjective* foresight at T1 of incapacity and complete involuntariness at T2. The requirement of foresight and its subjective construction both substantially narrow the potential for prior fault^{OFF} criminalization in this category.[10] In this way, they also (arguably) recast debates around culpability equivalence.[11]

The second reason why we do not believe prior fault^{OFF} automatism should be treated as a straightforward species of intoxication is because although most cases analysing prior fault^{OFF} automatism have involved drugs (albeit 'non-dangerous' drugs), there is no reason in principle why prior fault^{OFF} automatism should be

[7] Even offences of assault or battery require D to foresee a risk (in action) of unlawful contact with V or causing V to apprehend imminent violence: *Venna* [1976] QB 421.

[8] As Smith noted in *Smith and Hogan's Criminal Law* (8th Ed, OUP, 1996) 39: 'There is . . . no case which does not involve the use or misuse of drink or drugs and it is thought that this anomalous rule is properly confined to such cases.'

[9] Discussed in Chapter 2.

[10] See the interpretation of involuntariness in *Coley* [2013] EWCA Crim 223, [23]; usefully discussed in R Mackay, '*R v Coley*; *R v McGhee*; *R v Harris*' [2013] *Criminal Law Review* 923.

[11] Discussed in Section 3.2.2.

limited to cases of this kind. For example, were D to become automatic through some other culpable act at T1, such as failing to wear required head protection at work leading to head trauma and involuntariness, presumably the same rules could be applied if D causes harms when in that state at T2. This is why we present intoxication and prior fault^{OFF} automatism as belonging to the same broad category of prior fault^{OFF}, but not forming parts of a single doctrine.[12]

It is on this basis therefore that we proceed to discuss the structure and function of prior fault^{OFF} automatism, certainly by reference to the intoxication paradigm, but at the same time as a stand-alone legal mechanism for the cases it encompasses. First, we demonstrate how, like intoxication, the inculpatory function of prior fault^{OFF} automatism is disguised by inappropriate framing of automatism as a defence. Second, we unpack the framing of prior fault^{OFF} automatism in terms of culpability equivalence, which is ostensibly the implicit functional claim essential to justify the application of these rules. Finally, we highlight the first example of mistaken categorization, where an apparent subset of prior fault^{OFF} automatism cases would, we argue, be more appropriately explained through the relocation of liability via an alternative route (i.e. without the use of prior fault^{OFF} construction).

3.2.1.1 Inaccurate framing of automatism as a defence

Automatism—like intoxication—is never a defence, not even exceptionally.[13] To qualify within the automatism rules D must be involuntary, and if D is involuntary then D has not committed an offence. Automatism may therefore be employed as a shorthand for D's *lack of offending*, but without a crime having been committed, there can be no logical role for the same involuntariness to operate as a supervening defence. This basic logic is occasionally recognized by the courts, as we see from Lord Denning in *Bratty*:[14]

> No act is punishable if it is done involuntarily: and an involuntary act in this context—some people nowadays prefer to speak of it as 'automatism'—means an act which is done by the muscles without any control by the mind, such as a spasm, a reflex action or a convulsion . . .

[12] Similarly, see R Mackay, *Mental Condition Defences in the Criminal Law* (OUP, 1995) 153; Law Commission, *Insanity and Automatism* (Discussion Paper, 2013) [5.1] and [5.107].

[13] See JJ Child and A Reed, 'Automatism Is Never a Defence' (2014) 65(2) *Northern Ireland Legal Quarterly* 167. Cf KJM Smith and W Wilson, 'Impaired Voluntariness and Criminal Responsibility' (1993) 13(1) *Oxford Journal of Legal Studies* 69, who present the peculiar application of prior fault^{OFF} rules as suggesting automatism is a defence.

[14] [1963] AC 386, 409. The point is neatly captured by Fletcher: 'Excuses arise in cases in which the actor's freedom of choice is constricted. His conduct is not strictly involuntary as if he suffered a seizure or if someone pushed his knife-holding hand down on the victim's throat. In these cases there is no act at all, no wrongdoing and therefore no need for an excuse.' G Fletcher, *Rethinking Criminal Law* (OUP, 2000) 10.3.2.

However, express recognition of this kind is uncommon, and rarely enduring. It is notable, for example, that Denning continues his judgment in *Bratty* using the language of defences. In most cases, the presentation of automatism as an exculpatory 'defence', which D holds the burden for raising in evidence, is left unquestioned.[15]

To the extent that the term 'automatism' implies anything other than involuntariness (i.e. the absence of an *offence* element[16]), it may be preferable to remove it from the legal lexicon.[17] This is because—just as we argued regarding intoxication—the consistent misrepresentation of an absent offence element as a defence can have significant and negative effects on the law. In the case of automatism, alongside other concerns,[18] we see problematic skewing of legal analysis and application in the direction of both over- and under-criminalization.

As for over-criminalization and the potential for inappropriate criminalization, we see this in two areas in particular. The first concerns the threshold at which the courts are willing to find involuntariness/automatism. The issue here is that having displaced discussion of involuntariness to the 'defence' of automatism, the common law has interpreted and evolved the rules as if they apply to exculpate a defendant from wrongdoing (i.e. as if they define a defence); and alongside many common law defences, automatism rules have been narrowed considerably in recent decades. This is best illustrated in (then) Lord Justice Hughes' leading judgment in *Coley*,[19] where a potential defence of automatism was rejected on the facts. In *Coley*, D physically assaulted his neighbour whilst experiencing what doctors described as a 'brief psychotic episode', meaning that at the point of attack D had no conscious or rational control over his movement. However, reflecting upon the complex movements performed by D during this episode, the court rejected the potential application of automatism, and rejected an involuntariness description:[20]

[15] The same position is taken in other common law jurisdictions. See, e.g., *Ross v HM Advocate* (1991) JC 210 (Scotland); *Parks* (1992) 95 DLR 27 (Canada); *Bannin* [1991] 2 NZLR 237 (New Zealand); Draft Criminal Code for England & Wales (1989) cl.33. On evidential burdens, see T Jones, 'Insanity, Automatism, and the Burden of Proof on the Accused' (1995) 111 *Law Quarterly Review* 475.

[16] A separate question is whether automatism amounts to a denial of action (both actus reus and mens rea) or whether involuntariness can be isolated as a denial of mens rea alone. Nothing in the current discussion turns on the answer to this question, though we prefer the latter interpretation. See JJ Child and A Reed, 'Automatism Is Never a Defence' (2014) 65(2) *Northern Ireland Legal Quarterly* 167, 172–73.

[17] This argument is set out more fully in JJ Child, 'Defence of a Basic Voluntary Act Requirement in Criminal Law from Philosophies of Action' (2020) 23(4) *New Criminal Law Review* 437. On the broader history of automatism, see A Loughnan, *Manifest Madness* (OUP, 2012) Ch 5.

[18] When automatism is incorrectly labelled, we can forget the basics of criminalization. E.g. in its most recent paper on automatism (*Insanity and Automatism* (Discussion Paper, 2013)), the Law Commission recognizes that it is not, strictly speaking, a supervening defence, but it continues to employ that label for 'convenience' [A.116]. Later, however, it outlines proposals for disallowing the defence for certain groups, even where no alternative defence is available [5.120]. This would allow for the criminalization of individuals who do not satisfy the elements of an offence, in the absence of prior fault; it is difficult to believe that this would have been proposed if automatism were appropriately and consistently labelled as the denial of an offence element.

[19] [2013] EWCA Crim 223.

[20] Ibid [24].

> [D's] mind may well, if the doctors were right, have been affected by delusions or hallucinations and in that sense his detachment from reality might be described by some as an absence of conscious action. Such condition, however, clearly falls short of involuntary, as distinct from irrational, action. . . . The doctor said 'He is conscious in a way but it is conscious in the belief that he is a character [in a computer game]. He does not have an awareness of what he is doing.' That is a description of irrational behaviour, with a deluded or disordered mind, but it is not a description of wholly involuntary action.

The decision and analysis in *Coley* can only be understood as the court analysing automatism/involuntariness as a defence, asking itself what conditions D must satisfy to avoid liability for the crime they have committed (i.e. was D's conduct justified or excusable?). However, once we recognize voluntariness as a core requirement of criminal responsibility, then we must also recognize that what is at play is not a defence, but rather an *offence* element. This recasts the question to one of inculpation: was D responsible for the movement of their body, and was D in sufficient deliberative control to be held responsible for the harms that occurred? Recasting the question in this manner, we argue it would be extraordinary for a court to find irrational conduct performed without awareness as sufficient grounding for liability.[21] Therefore, it transpires that (incorrectly) analysing 'automatism' as a defence leads to the application of a much lower threshold for criminal liability than would be the case if automatism was correctly analysed as the correlation of the 'voluntary' act requirement.

Our second concern about potential over-criminalization relates more specifically to the analysis and application of the prior fault^{OFF} automatism rules. With the characterization of automatism as a defence so entrenched in the courts,[22] it is unsurprising that this becomes the analytical and normative backdrop for their engagement with prior fault^{OFF} automatism as well. Where the potential for prior fault^{OFF} automatism arises, it is presented by the courts as a mechanism for denying a defence, with the implication that D has already offended and so such denial or blocking of the defence should naturally result in liability. In *Quick*,[23] for example, Lawton LJ quotes with approval:

> Automatism is a defence to a charge . . . provided that a person takes reasonable steps to prevent himself from acting involuntarily in a manner dangerous to the

[21] Compare the US case of *People v Newton* (87 Cal Rprt 394 (1970)), where similar complex movement to that in *Coley* was nevertheless held to be involuntary, with the court focusing on the minimum requirements for responsibility. Discussed in G Yaffe, 'The Voluntary Act Requirement' in A Marmor (ed) *The Routledge Companion to Philosophy of Law* (Routledge, 2012) 174.

[22] We would argue even more so than the intoxication rules.

[23] [1973] QB 910.

> public. It must be caused by some factor which he could not reasonably foresee and not by a self-induced incapacity.

Similarly in *Coley*,[24] Lord Justice Hughes states that:

> . . . the defence of automatism is not available to a defendant who has induced an acute state of involuntary behaviour by his own fault.

The problem here—mirroring our discussion of intoxication in Chapter 2—is that D's prior fault in these cases is not simply used to deny or block a defence. Where liability is found despite automatism/involuntariness at T2, D's T1 fault is being used to substitute for that missing voluntariness (and any other absent mens rea) as an inculpatory legal fiction. It is not enough therefore that D acts with fault at T1; justification for the current law requires equivalence of culpability between D's T1 fault and the absent elements at T2 and this includes quite obviously absent voluntariness at T2 (as well as absent mens rea). This requirement is confused and obfuscated within the current law, thereby risking over-criminalization.[25]

Alongside risks of over-criminalization, we also highlighted above that the mischaracterization of automatism and prior fault^{OFF} automatism can skew debates in the other direction as well, risking under-criminalization. The most obvious example of this is the limitation on the use of prior fault^{OFF} reasoning in automatism to cases where D is automatic/involuntary (rather than when D is voluntary but lacks mens rea). Such a limitation may seem obvious if we think of automatism as a defence, and prior fault as a mechanism for denying that defence. But, as we have explained, that is a mischaracterization. If we accept that prior fault^{OFF} is being used to substitute for missing elements at T2, based on D's conduct at T1, then we should question why prior fault^{OFF} is tethered to automatism in this limited way. Indeed, the tethering of prior fault^{OFF} to automatism creates an absurdity where prior fault^{OFF} rules can provide a route to liability where D is least to blame at T2 (i.e. situations where they lack both mens rea *and* voluntariness), but not in cases where D lacks mens rea but retains voluntariness at T2. In the vast majority of prior fault^{OFF} intoxication cases, D will not be involuntary, but prior fault^{OFF} may still operate to substitute for a lack of mens rea. Why should the same not be possible for non-intoxication cases where D is acting voluntarily but lacks mens rea? Indeed, the more narrowly automatism is defined by the courts, the greater the potential for prior fault^{OFF} to lack a mechanism for application, and the greater the potential for a simple acquittal (due to a lack of mens rea) despite blameworthy conduct at T1.

[24] [2013] EWCA Crim 223, [24].

[25] We discuss claims of culpability equivalence further in Section 3.2.1.2.

3.2.1.2 Accurately framing prior fault^{OFF} automatism in terms of equivalence

It may be thought from the above analysis that since prior fault^{OFF} automatism cannot and should not be framed in terms of a 'defence' that—in like manner to the position we saw with intoxication—this must mean that the only coherent explanation is one which presents the current legal position as framing prior fault^{OFF} automatism in terms of equivalence between T1 fault and missing T2 offence elements. This would be the obvious and coherent thing to be done on the courts part. After all, if the application of prior fault^{OFF} automatism rules are to be justified at all, one might think that this would proceed on the basis that the fault that D does demonstrate at T1 must surely be commensurate with that required for the offence. However, we should warn the reader at this point that there is what we might call a general explanatory incoherence in the authorities. That is to say, they do not all speak with the one voice, and rarely expressly articulate a clear or consistent equivalence rationale, let alone clearly explain what it is. Thus, even though below we look more closely at the doctrinal requirements for prior fault^{OFF} automatism in order to try to identify the current basis for a claim of equivalence in English law, we are to some extent engaged in a process of reading between the lines, and trying to provide the best-case argument/rationale which the courts might make in this regard, even though they scarcely do that themselves.

Turning to the law, and its apparent grounding and rationale, when D's conduct at T1 create involuntariness at T2, it is now reasonably clear that the law requires that for criminal liability to arise, they must be subjectively reckless at T1 as to their future involuntariness as a consequence of their actions. This is the interpretation most recently endorsed by the Law Commission, taken from the limited pool of cases that have engaged with the issue.[26] Although there has been some judicial support for an objective test,[27] akin to the intoxication rules, this has not been adopted. Most interestingly, for present purposes, is the reasoning employed by subsequent cases (and the Law Commission) for preferring a subjective approach, since this comes very close to accepting an equivalence-based framing of the prior fault^{OFF} rules. The Court of Appeal in *Bailey*, for example, states:[28]

> Automatism resulting from intoxication as a result of a voluntary ingestion of alcohol or dangerous drugs does not negative the mens rea necessary for crimes of basic intent, because the conduct of the accused is reckless and recklessness is enough to constitute the necessary mens rea . . .

[26] Law Commission, *Insanity and Automatism* (Discussion Paper, 2013) [6.12–6.28].

[27] See *Quick* [1973] QB 910, suggesting that the automatism 'defence' would be defeated where D 'could have *reasonably* foreseen [the criminal harms] as a result of either doing, or omitting to do, something', per Lawton LJ (emphasis added).

[28] *Bailey* [1983] 1 WLR 760, 764–65, per Griffiths LJ. For academic support of this position, see J Horder, 'Sobering Up? The Law Commission on Criminal Intoxication' (1995) 58(4) *Modern Law Review* 534, 544–45.

> . . . it seems to us that there may be material distinctions between a man who consumes alcohol or takes dangerous drugs [prior fault intoxication] and one who fails to take sufficient food after insulin to avert hypoglaecemia [prior fault automatism]. It is common knowledge that those who take alcohol to excess or certain sorts of drugs may become aggressive or do dangerous or unpredictable things, they may be able to foresee the risks of causing harm to others but nevertheless persist in their conduct. But the same cannot be said without more of a man who fails to take food after an insulin injection.

Indeed, for the court in *Bailey*, prior fault^{OFF} automatism should only be found where 'the prosecution have proved the necessary element of recklessness', demonstrating that (at T1) D 'knows that his actions or inaction are likely to make him aggressive, unpredictable or uncontrolled'.[29] However, where D foresees *both* involuntariness and the associated risks of committing the actus reus of the offence, it may well be that prior fault^{OFF} analysis is unnecessary: liability may be found by relocating D's liability to the event at T1 alone, asking whether D's conduct and mens rea at this point are sufficient to satisfy the offence.[30] This is recognized by the Law Commission, which is why the Commission interprets the current law to include a broader category of cases where D foresees involuntariness but not necessarily the future harms at T2.[31]

Requirements at T2 have followed a similar pattern, and are now likely to mirror those of the intoxication rules, so that T1 fault will replace the missing elements of a basic intent offence but not a specific intent offence. This was also clarified in *Bailey*,[32] following dicta in *Quick* that suggested prior fault^{OFF} automatism could replace the elements of any offence.[33] As above, the narrowing of the T2 target provides (at least implicit) recognition of the need for T1–T2 culpability equivalence.

3.2.1.3 Framing prior fault^{OFF} automatism: Relocating liability

Framing prior fault^{OFF} automatism in terms of denying a defence is always inaccurate, but it may also be inaccurate to frame *all* such cases in terms of culpability equivalence. Indeed, as we will demonstrate, a significant proportion of cases that are currently discussed by courts and academic commentators in terms of prior fault^{OFF} automatism have been incorrectly categorized. These are cases where liability can be found and explained by focusing on D's conduct and mens rea at T1 alone (i.e. by relocating liability), rendering the application of prior fault^{OFF}

[29] *Bailey* [1983] 1 WLR 760, 765.

[30] We discuss this approach in more detail in Section 3.2.1.3, focused on categories of cases that do not require prior fault^{OFF} analysis.

[31] Law Commission, *Insanity and Automatism* (Discussion Paper, 2013) [6.12–6.28]. The Commission reference *Hardie* [1985] 1 WLR 64 as support for its preferred interpretation.

[32] *Bailey* [1983] 1 WLR 760, 763.

[33] *Quick* [1973] QB 910, 922. See critique of this position in R Mackay, 'Intoxication as a Factor in Automatism' (1982) *Criminal Law Review* 146.

mechanisms an unnecessary and potentially unjust complexity. Not all cases can be resolved by relocating liability to T1—there remains a category of prior fault^{OFF} automatism cases that require framing in terms of culpability equivalence[34]—but where alternatives are available outside the problematic fictions of prior fault^{OFF}, we contend they should always be preferred.

When discussing prior fault^{OFF} automatism, it is typical for courts and commentators to refer to driving cases, where D's insulin and lack of blood sugar regulation (T1) leads to unconsciousness and harms when driving (T2).[35] Fact scenarios of this kind are much more common than our unconscious 'assault' example, as involuntariness will typically result in a lack of movement rather than a physical attack, and a lack of movement is much more likely to result in third-party harms where D is meant to be controlling a moving vehicle.[36] When being analysed as examples of prior fault^{OFF} automatism, it is common to refer to D's liability for causing T2 harms (e.g. death to another road user) as being established through the tracing of fault from D's T1 decision to drive despite foresight of potential unconsciousness (i.e. undermining any potential 'defence' of automatism). However, we contend that prior fault^{OFF} analysis is neither necessary nor useful in these cases, and courts would be better served by focusing on a single point of conduct, locating liability at T1 alone.

Where an unconscious D causes death at T2, and is charged with causing death by dangerous driving,[37] the offence they are charged with does not require mens rea for causing death. All the offence requires is for D to be driving dangerously and for this to cause V's death, and this can be established from traditional single-event analysis alone. As long as D begins their drive with some control (i.e. is not automatic throughout), our focal point becomes D's actions just before losing consciousness and causing harms. At this point, D is driving voluntarily, the driving is dangerous, and this conduct makes a material contribution to V's death (i.e. there is no reason why D's subsequent unconsciousness should break the chain of

[34] We would not find liability in the case of the unconscious assault, e.g., by refocusing on the conduct that led to D's unconsciousness (T1): whilst we *could* make a case that taking insulin and failing to regulate blood sugar levels had a causal impact on the subsequent harms to V (subject to foreseeability constraints), D does not perform that conduct at T1 with foresight or the intention of *thereby* causing harms to V (i.e. D lacks mens rea).

[35] See, e.g., J Rumbold and M Wasik, 'Diabetic Drivers, Hypoglycaemic Unawareness and Automatism' [2011] *Criminal Law Review* 863, 866: 'Usually the diabetic driver has been at fault in the management of their condition, and so any defence of automatism fails . . . [T]he condition of hypoglycaemic unawareness is highly relevant to this issue of fault, and is a factor to which lawyers involved in such cases should be alert.' We have also previously made the same category error: see JJ Child and A Reed, 'Automatism Is Never a Defence' (2014) 65(2) *Northern Ireland Legal Quarterly* 167; JJ Child, 'Prior Fault: Blocking Defences or Constructing Crimes' in A Reed and M Bohlander (eds) *Defences* (Routledge, 2014).

[36] See, e.g., *Treadwell* [2022] EWCA Crim 1513; *C* [2007] EWCA Crim 1862; *JG* [2006] EWCA Crim 3276; *Marison* [1997] RTR 457.

[37] Road Traffic Act 1988, s1.

causation[38]). It is on this basis that we endorse the view of Lord Justice McCowan and the Court of Appeal in *Marison*:[39]

> It was argued before this court . . . that [D] was driving as an automaton and therefore cannot be guilty of the offence. In our judgment, automatism does not come into this case at all . . . Even if the appellant was in an automatic state for the last few seconds, he had already committed the offence by driving to that point, in circumstances which he knew were such that he might have a hypoglycaemic attack at any moment.

It is unfortunate that McCowan L.J. follows this passage directly with a reference to *Quick*[40] and prior fault^{OFF} automatism, which obfuscates the analysis. Rather, we contend, the law would be better served by approaching these cases through traditional single-event analysis alone.

It follows—generalizing from the above driving example—that we may be left with a smaller category of cases here where prior fault^{OFF} analysis is required under the current law to find liability.[41] However, other cases do and will exist. The structure of prior fault^{OFF} analysis is clearly at issue in cases such as the unconscious 'assault', and, of course, the narrowness of the current law may expand if involuntariness is interpreted more broadly.[42] Thus, principled justification is required.

[38] D's conduct here can be interpreted as both the act of driving and the omission to stop doing so in view of the danger created. The resulting death is factually caused by this conduct, and is foreseeable.

[39] [1997] RTR 457, 461. See also R Mackay and D Hughes, 'Insanity and Blaming the Mentally Ill: A Critique of the Prior Fault Principle in the Law Commission's Discussion Paper' [2022] *Criminal Law Review* 21, 34–35.

[40] [1997] RTR 457, 461. Referencing *Quick* [1973] QB 910.

[41] Whether single-event analysis is possible will depend upon the facts of each case, and the offence charged. We see this, e.g., in *Commonwealth v Fain* 79 Ky 183 (1879), where D fell asleep in a public place with a loaded weapon (T1), knowing he had a sleep-pattern disorder that made him involuntarily violent when woken, and subsequently (T2) causing death when involuntary. Robinson accurately highlights here that—rather than a prior fault^{OFF} approach—the court could have found liability for reckless homicide based on D's conduct at T1 alone: P Robinson, 'Causing the Conditions of One's Own Defense' (1985) 71 *Virginia Law Review* 1, 33. See also R Mackay and D Hughes, 'Insanity and Blaming the Mentally Ill: A Critique of the Prior Fault Principle in the Law Commission's Discussion Paper' [2022] *Criminal Law Review* 21, 34–35.

[42] I.e. as many academics have advocated: see J Horder, 'Pleading Involuntary Lack of Capacity' (1993) 52(2) *Cambridge Law Journal* 298; JJ Child, 'Defence of a Basic Voluntary Act Requirement in Criminal Law from Philosophies of Action' (2020) 23(4) *New Criminal Law Review* 437. A parallel debate, with similar potential to broaden this category of prior fault^{OFF}, involves the legal treatment of impaired (as opposed to absent) capacity: see, e.g., A Reed, 'Quasi-Involuntary Actions and Moral Capacity' in B Livings et al (eds) *Mental Condition Defences and the Criminal Justice System* (Cambridge Scholars, 2015) 178.

3.2.2 Justification of prior fault^{OFF} automatism rules

Prior fault^{OFF} automatism arises where D's absent voluntariness and mens rea at T2 is substituted for by their prior fault at T1, where D subjectively foresees the potential for involuntariness arising from their conduct at T1. In order to assess whether the current rules of prior fault^{OFF} automatism can be justified, it is useful to separate three areas for discussion, arising from our analysis above.

First, we consider the justification for applying prior fault^{OFF} automatism to construct liability within the framing of 'culpability equivalence' (i.e. is D's fault at T1 sufficient to substitute for the offence elements missing at T2?). Second, we consider the justification for tethering prior fault to the automatism rules in such a way that prior fault^{OFF} analysis is not possible without T2 involuntariness. Finally, we consider the justification for current doctrinal inconsistencies between prior fault^{OFF} intoxication and prior fault^{OFF} automatism (and insanity).

3.2.2.1 The application of prior fault^{OFF} automatism and culpability equivalence

Where prior fault^{OFF} automatism is being used as the basis for criminal liability, the equivalence thesis demands that D's fault at T1 is sufficient to substitute for the offence elements missing at T2. As we did in Chapter 2, it is useful to consider equivalence across two limbs: the gravity of culpability manifested and the link provided by that culpability between D and the harms at T2.[43]

The potential for equivalence across both limbs is arguably greater in the context of prior fault^{OFF} automatism than with the intoxication rules, because prior fault^{OFF} automatism already requires subjective fault at T1. In the case of prior fault^{OFF} intoxication rules, the substitution of *subjective* offence elements (at T2) with *objective* prior fault (from T1) represents one of the more obvious culpability mismatches associated with those rules,[44] and is an area where reform recommendations have focused.[45] However, as we discussed in Section 3.2.1, it is likely that the subjective fault required at T1 for prior fault^{OFF} automatism does not extend beyond foresight of unconsciousness at T2, and does not necessarily include foresight of the particular harms or species of harms at T2. In this manner, although subjective fault may be identified at T1, it does not provide sufficient culpability to meet the demands of the two limbs of the equivalence thesis. On gravity, there remains a magnitude of difference between foresight at T1 of future potential incapacity (where this may—is likely even to—pose no risk of harm to others[46]) and

[43] We introduce and discuss this approach more fully in Chapter 2, Section 2.3.

[44] Discussed in Chapter 2, Section 2.3.

[45] Discussed in Chapter 2, Section 2.4. Macdonald provides specific comment on how the approach taken in prior fault^{OFF} automatism cases may be used to model the reform of intoxication rules: E Macdonald, 'Reckless Language and Majewski' (1986) 6(3) *Legal Studies* 239.

[46] This is recognized in the extract from *Bailey* quoted above.

foreseeing a specific risk of harm at T2 and continuing unreasonably to run that risk. Equally, when establishing a culpability link to the harms at T2, foresight of incapacity remains a significant step removed from the specific foresight potentially required within even a basic intent offence.[47] Absent such equivalence, the only rational conclusion is to accept that the current law risks over-criminalization of defendants who would otherwise commit no offence, and will always mislabel them for the crime constructed at T2.

3.2.2.2 The non-application of prior fault^{OFF} automatism in cases where D's T2 actions are voluntary but they lack mens rea

Assuming one has a set of prior fault^{OFF} rules associated with automatism, one then encounters a difficulty in justifying the current law in situations which are excluded from that regime. This is particularly true of non-intoxicated prior fault^{OFF} automatism cases. Where automatism is simply a synonym for involuntariness, it is entirely unclear why the law requires involuntariness as a prerequisite for prior fault^{OFF} automatism, preventing the same acts of prior fault substituting for absent mens rea where D remains voluntary at T2. The irony here is that the narrowing of the definition of automatism—incorrectly framed as a 'defence'—results in the narrowing of the potential for prior fault^{OFF} inculpation, making acquittal, despite circumstances of prior fault, more likely. This is a problem for those who may seek to defend the use of prior fault^{OFF} rules. It is also a problem for those—like us—who are critical of prior fault^{OFF} rules, but recognize that some of the conduct in this area may nevertheless be deserving of criminalization via an alternative route.

3.2.2.3 The inconsistent application of prior fault^{OFF} rules

Our final concern relates to the inconsistency of prior fault^{OFF} rules between intoxication, automatism, and insanity.[48] The difficulty of distinguishing between alternative causes of incapacity at T1 are well known.[49] Therefore, where prior fault^{OFF} rules are used to construct liability in spite of such incapacity, there is an obvious case for making those rules consistent so they can be applied without causal distinction. The current law however, as we have outlined, has recognized significant doctrinal differences between each set of prior fault^{OFF} rules, making causal distinctions *essential*.

From the practical perspective, requiring the courts to isolate the cause of D's incapacity, distinguishing between intoxication, sane automatism, and insanity

[47] See T Quigley, 'Specific and General Nonsense' (1987) 11(1) *The Dalhousie Law Journal* 75, 102–14.

[48] We will discuss prior fault insanity in Chapter 4.

[49] See, e.g., A Loughnan and N Wake, 'Of Blurred Boundaries and Prior Fault: Insanity, Automatism and Intoxication' in A Reed and M Bohlander (eds) *General Defences in Criminal Law* (Routledge, 2014) 113; N Padfield, 'Exploring a Quagmire: Insanity and Automatism' (1989) 48(3) *Cambridge Law Journal* 354.

resulting from a 'disease of the mind', before then continuing to consider prior fault, creates a formidable factual (and scientific) challenge. From a normative perspective, it is also not clear what the principled reason for distinction is, nor is it clear what justifies the particular differences in the way the rules work in the different situations.

3.2.3 Reform of prior fault^{OFF} automatism rules

Reform debates on the topic of prior fault^{OFF} automatism have been extremely limited. One of the few comprehensive reviews has come from the Law Commission in its 2013 Discussion Paper, where prior fault is discussed across automatism and insanity.[50] However, although the Commission provides very useful clarificatory analysis on how current prior fault rules may be defined and codified, the Discussion Paper does not engage with the broader justificatory challenges outlined in the previous subsection, and does not consider the case for more comprehensive reform. The Commission's project has also stalled at the Discussion Paper stage, and so there has not (yet) been an opportunity to engage with the Commission on these more fundamental questions.

Beyond this, there has been very little specific academic attention.[51] This is understandable given the limited application of prior fault^{OFF} automatism in practice, though the potential problem of its non-application (discussed in the previous subsection) should not be forgotten.[52] The potential for reform here—like the rules themselves—can borrow from debates applicable to the intoxication rules. So, as we look to construct a reform debate, it is likely to focus on the potential for salvaging the equivalence thesis, asking what changes are required at T1 and T2 to justify the substitution of fault elements. Indeed, looking back to the theories of equivalence explored in Chapter 2, Section 2.4, the approaches adopted there have clear potential to apply outside of intoxication situations, and in some cases this is an explicit aim of the authors.[53]

However, as discussed in Chapter 2, Section 2.5, we do not believe that the equivalence thesis can be salvaged, and instead support the abolition of current prior fault^{OFF} rules. To the extent that liability is appropriate, we prefer the option of a specific new offence that can be tailored to target the specific wrongs at issue, and provide appropriate labelling and punishment for those wrongs. This position

[50] Law Commission, *Insanity and Automatism* (Discussion Paper, 2013) Part 6.

[51] See JJ Child and A Reed, 'Automatism Is Never a Defence' (2014) 65(2) *Northern Ireland Legal Quarterly* 167, 182–85; C Finkelstein, 'Involuntary Crimes, Voluntarily Committed' in S Shute and AP Simester (eds) *Criminal Law Theory: Doctrines of the General Part* (OUP, 2005) 143.

[52] I.e. the potential for under-criminalization in circumstances where liability appears justified.

[53] See, e.g., S Dimock, 'Actio Libera in Causa' (2013) 7 *Criminal Law and Philosophy* 549, Part 2; P Robinson, 'Imputed Criminal Liability' (1984) 93 *Yale Law Journal* 609.

applies as much to prior fault^{OFF} automatism as it does to intoxication. As we move to discuss the potential for a new offence in Chapter 5 therefore, we do not limit this discussion (as others do) to the development of an 'intoxication offence', but rather look beyond this to the potential for an offence that can apply consistently across circumstances of prior fault^{OFF}.

3.3 Prior fault^{OFF} automatism and grand schemers

In contrast with the situations discussed thus far, the so-called grand schemer cases are characterized by D's conscious decision at T1 to perform certain conduct that will lead to incapacity at T2, *with the intention* (at T1) that they will perform certain harmful acts when in that state (at T2). For example, at D's request, D is hypnotized at T1 to kill V, and does so when acting involuntarily at T2 under a hypnotic trance.[54] Other common examples in the literature include D becoming acutely intoxicated at T1, consuming alcohol or other drugs, again *with intention* of losing control and causing certain harms. In all cases of this kind, if the law were to focus narrowly on the T2 event alone, we would be likely to conclude that D has not committed an offence. As all offences require voluntary conduct (whether we analyse this in terms of voluntariness or the 'defence' of automatism), so D's involuntary state at T2 undermines potential criminal liability. A 'no liability' outcome here, however, would be wholly inappropriate: the harms D causes can be traced back to their intentional conduct, and any legal problems are due to D's intentional manipulation of the legal position. The challenge, then, is to provide an account that explains and justifies liability.[55]

Establishing criminal liability in grand schemer cases is forcefully endorsed in *obiter* comments from Lord Denning in *Gallagher* (though the legal route to liability remains imprecise):[56]

[54] We use hypnotism as a convenient example of an involuntary state typically recognized across legal systems. It should be noted, however, that the legal acceptance of hypnotism causing involuntariness is not reflected in the scientific literature, especially where D is hypnotized to commit an offence. See, e.g., G Wagstaff, 'Hypnosis and the Law: Examining the Stereotypes' (2008) 35(10) *Criminal Justice and Behaviour* 1277; Z Dienes et al, 'The Role of Phenomenological Control in Experience' (2023) 32(2) *Current Directions in Psychological Science* 145; WC Coe et al, 'Experimental and Ethical Problems of Evaluating the Influence of Hypnosis in Antisocial Conduct' (1973) 82(3) *Journal of Abnormal Psychology* 476.

[55] It should be acknowledged that the factual make-up of grand schemer cases can sound rather fanciful—where D renders themselves unconscious to evade liability—and indeed they are. The only UK case authority on the matter arises through *obiter* discussion in *A-G for Northern Ireland v Gallagher* [1963] AC 349. However, cases of this kind remain possible in practice, and have become a focal point for much theorizing on prior fault^{OFF}, and so warrant our specific attention.

[56] Ibid 382.

> I think the law on this point should take a clear stand. If a man, whilst sane and sober, forms an intention to kill and makes preparation for it . . . and then gets himself drunk so as to give himself Dutch courage to do the killing, and whilst drunk carries out his intention, he cannot rely on this self-induced drunkenness as a defence to a charge of murder, nor even as reducing it to manslaughter. He cannot say that he got himself into such a stupid state that he was incapable of an intent to kill . . . The wickedness of his mind before he got drunk is enough to condemn him, coupled with the act which he intended to do and did do.

Responding to hypothetical examples of this kind, a near consensus of academic opinion suggests that grand schemer cases should be dealt with using prior fault^{OFF} rules.[57] D may not be acting voluntarily at T2 (and therefore lacking all mens rea), but they are to blame for putting themselves in that state at T1, and so D's T1 fault can/should be used to substitute for those missing elements at T2, allowing D to be treated as if all offence elements were present at T2. Indeed, as per Lord Denning, it is generally accepted that D's intention at T1 may provide the basis for construction of specific intent offences as well as basic intent offences.[58] Detailed variations of this approach are usefully explored by Robinson and Dimock,[59] both of whom recognize the same approach should be applied to intoxication and non-intoxication cases.[60]

Although grand schemer cases are probably very rare in practice, academic discussions of them occupy a key role in the wider debate about prior fault^{OFF}. Where D is consciously attempting to manipulate the law's single event focus to evade liability, there is perhaps the strongest intuitive appeal for prior fault^{OFF} rules that can hold D accountable across T1–T2. Though complex, intention-based examples of this kind also provide the most straightforward comparisons with other legal rules that construct liability across T1–T2, allowing scholars to re-inforce prior fault^{OFF} rules by analogy to a conspiracy with one's later self, or using oneself as an innocent agent.[61] And it is from this basis that wider approaches to prior fault^{OFF} are then constructed (i.e. where D at T1 is not intending the future

[57] Cf C Finkelstein, 'Involuntary Crimes, Voluntarily Committed' in S Shute and AP Simester (eds) *Criminal Law Theory: Doctrines of the General Part* (OUP, 2005) 143, 163–69, who offers an alternative approach based on more or less complex act descriptions.

[58] On the basic/specific intent distinction, see Chapter 2, Section 2.3.

[59] P Robinson, 'Causing the Conditions of One's Own Defence' (1985) 71 *Virginia Law Review* 1; S Dimock, 'Actio Libera in Causa' (2013) 7 *Criminal Law and Philosophy* 549.

[60] See also R Mackay, 'Intoxication as a Factor in Automatism' (1982) *Criminal Law Review* 146; EW Mitchell, 'Culpability for Inducing Mental States: The Insanity Defence of Dr Jekyll' (2004) 32(1) *Journal of the American Academy of Psychiatry and Law* 63.

[61] See P Robinson, 'Causing the Conditions of One's Own Defence' (1985) 71 *Virginia Law Review* 1, 34; S Dimock, 'Actio Libera in Causa' (2013) 7 *Criminal Law and Philosophy* 549, 565–67; L Katz, 'Entrapment Through the Lens of the Actio Libera in Causa' (2013) 7(3) *Criminal Law and Philosophy* 587, 591. Similar logic has also appeared in successive editions of JC Smith, *Smith and Hogan's Criminal Law* (8th Ed, OUP, 1996).

circumstances); typically argued from the premise that since imposition of criminal liability in prior fault^{OFF} grand schemer cases is acceptable, the question is how far we can depart from that model (in terms of T1 mens rea in particular) before we encounter problems of culpability inequivalence.

We do not agree with this analysis of grand schemer cases, however, and therefore we also depart from the dominant theorizing of prior fault^{OFF} more generally. Whilst we accept that liability is appropriate in grand schemer examples, we reject the claim that prior fault^{OFF} rules are a necessary or appropriate mechanism for such liability to be found. This is not a situation where it is necessary for T1 fault to substitute for absent T2 mens rea/voluntariness. Rather, we contend that traditional approaches to criminal liability can be applied, such that liability would arise in any event. In other words, the problem can be resolved (again) through relocating liability.

The key to our analysis is to relocate liability to D's conduct and mens rea at T1 *alone*, with any subsequent involuntary conduct relevant only to questions of causation. For example, where D engages a hypnotist at T1 to allow them to kill V at T2 in a hypnotic trance, rather than focusing on D's involuntary conduct at T2, we should focus instead on D's engagement with the hypnotist at T1. D's conduct *at this point* is voluntary, and D is acting in order for this conduct (working with the hypnotist) to result in V's death. Thus, D appears to hold the relevant mens rea for murder of an intention to kill or to cause serious harm. In terms of causation, from T1, there is no reason why subsequent involuntary movements should interrupt the causal chain leading to V's death.[62] Much like a defendant who shoots a gun, or releases a herd of cattle with the intent they should trample V, causation in law can be achieved without the need to show that D is in control of the full causal mechanism (i.e. the bullet in flight, the stampeding cattle, the involuntary movement, etc); it is enough that D begins (or contributes to) the causal chain with the requisite mens rea. As Williams once remarked:[63]

> Suppose . . . that a man sets a time-bomb to kill people, and is asleep when it goes off; obviously he is guilty of murder. Similarly, if he fuddles himself with drink in order to commit murder, he turns himself into a kind of human time-bomb.

Thus, we contend, prior fault^{OFF} analysis of grand schemer cases is unnecessary, and criminal liability can be found simply by relocating our traditional lens onto T1.

[62] Cf C Finkelstein, 'Involuntary Crimes, Voluntarily Committed' in S Shute and AP Simester (eds) *Criminal Law Theory: Doctrines of the General Part* (OUP, 2005) 143, 146–53.
[63] G Williams, *Textbook of Criminal Law* (Sweet & Maxwell, 1978) 422.

But does relocating analysis to T1 create the potential for over-inclusivity, as critics of this approach have claimed?[64] We believe not. On a descriptive level, it is certainly true that 'working with a hypnotist' or 'consuming drugs' can seem like odd descriptions of the conduct element for murder,[65] and that such descriptive problems may be more pronounced in the context of conduct crimes (e.g. where D is hypnotized in order to have non-consensual sex with V).[66] But we reject the implication that descriptive oddities of this kind should lead to a substantive change of approach: such descriptions provide for *unusual*, as opposed to *invalid*, conduct descriptions.[67]

Additionally, on a substantive level, finding liability from T1 conduct does not lead to unchecked causation and over-criminalization.[68] This is because D's liability is also contingent on proof of mens rea at T1: proof that D (in our example) acted with the intention to kill or cause serious harm, not just in general terms, but specifically *through that conduct*. Thus, for example, if D loses control through intoxication whilst considering or even intending to kill V in the future, and then causes death whilst out of control, D will not commit murder. Simply, D did not possess mens rea at T1.

Therefore, whilst grand schemer cases *can* be approached through some version of prior fault^{OFF}, we do not believe that such an approach is necessary or useful. Rather than attempting to use D's fault at T1 to substitute for missing elements at T2—raising issues of culpability equivalence and unnecessary complexity[69]—the law is better served by simply relocating our analysis to D's conduct at T1, asking whether D commits the offence through that conduct alone. In doing so, we should remove grand schemer cases from the discussion of prior fault^{OFF}, and ask new questions of those theorists who have highlighted grand schemer cases as an anchor point for their theories of prior fault^{OFF} and culpability equivalence.

[64] See, in particular, C Finkelstein, 'Involuntary Crimes, Voluntarily Committed' in S Shute and AP Simester (eds) *Criminal Law Theory: Doctrines of the General Part* (OUP, 2005) 143.

[65] See L Katz, 'Entrapment Through the Lens of the Actio Libera in Causa' (2013) 7(3) *Criminal Law and Philosophy* 587, 594; J Herrmann, 'Causing the Conditions of One's Own Defence: The Multifaceted Approach of German Law' (1986) 3 *Brigham Young University Law Review* 747.

[66] See L Katz, 'Entrapment Through the Lens of the Actio Libera in Causa' (2013) 7(3) *Criminal Law and Philosophy* 587, 529; C Finkelstein, 'Involuntary Crimes, Voluntarily Committed' in S Shute and AP Simester (eds) *Criminal Law Theory: Doctrines of the General Part* (OUP, 2005) 143, 145, 153–56.

[67] See further JJ Child, 'Prior Fault: Blocking Defences or Constructing Crimes' in A Reed and M Bohlander (eds) *Defences* (Routledge, 2014).

[68] See critique in C Finkelstein, 'Involuntary Crimes, Voluntarily Committed' in S Shute and AP Simester (eds) *Criminal Law Theory: Doctrines of the General Part* (OUP, 2005) 143.

[69] Other potential problems for the prior fault^{OFF} analysis of grand schemer cases include their uncertain reach beyond intoxication cases, as well as in situations where D *wrongly* believes that they have no control at T2.

3.4 Prior fault^{OFF} automatism and trigger slips

Another category of cases requiring specific consideration are those commonly referred to as 'trigger slip cases'. These involve situations where D causes harm by an accidental movement in the course of a criminal venture. The Australian case *Ryan v R* provides a useful example:[70] in the course of a robbery, D held a loaded shotgun (with safety catch removed) to V's head with one hand as he attempted to tie him up with the other, D was 'startled' by a sudden movement from V, D pulled the trigger as a 'reflex action', and killed V instantly. Upon arrest, and subsequently at trial, D maintained that 'I did not mean to kill him; it was an accident'.[71] Nevertheless, D was convicted of murder, which was upheld on appeal. The question here, as previously, is *whether* and *how* liability can properly be found in these circumstances.

It is generally accepted that D must act voluntarily for liability to be found, even in trigger slip cases.[72] However, in finding voluntariness, two different mechanisms are often unhelpfully conflated. The first relocates liability to D's voluntary acts at T1 *before* pulling the trigger at T2, which in *Ryan* would include preparing, using, and particularly holding the gun against V's head; as we explain below, this is not a case of prior fault^{OFF}. The second approach treats D's T2 act (pulling the trigger) as voluntary because of their voluntary acts at T1. The second of these approaches, we contend, is an example of the application of prior fault^{OFF} rules. We consider both in turn.[73]

3.4.1 Relocating liability to T1

Relocating liability to previous voluntary acts at T1 represents a traditional form of analysis, discussed already in relation to grand schemer cases and certain unconscious driver cases.[74] Focusing on T1 allows us to accept that D's acts at T2—pulling the trigger in a reflex action—was (or at least might have been) involuntary, focusing instead on whether D's voluntary acts at T1 are capable of constituting the offence. For Barwick CJ in *Ryan*:[75]

70 (1967) 121 CLR 205, High Court of Australia. See also the English civil case *Gray v Barr* [1971] 2 QB 554, involving the accidental shooting of a gun during a physical altercation. It is noted that—anecdotally from practicing lawyers at least—cases of this kind are not uncommon.

71 (1967) 121 CLR 205, High Court of Australia.

72 Ibid. Cf Menzies J, at para 5, who contends that liability should be found even where D's acts in causing death are involuntary.

73 A third approach is also present in the literature, claiming that D's conduct was voluntary in the sense that D was conscious and 'his reaction was like the sudden movement of a tennis player retrieving a difficult shot'. ID Elliot, 'Responsibility for Involuntary Acts: Ryan v The Queen' (1968) 41 *Australian Law Journal* 497, 500. With respect, however, the analogy is inapt, since the pulling of the trigger was an entirely unwanted physical reaction, and in that sense more akin to a spasm or reflex.

74 I.e. in both of the previous sections of this chapter.

75 (1967) 121 CLR 205, [31].

> ... the jury, having concluded that the discharge of the gun was involuntary could have concluded that the act causing death was the presentation of the cocked, loaded gun with a safety catch unapplied and that its involuntary discharge was a likelihood which ought to have been in the contemplation of the applicant when presenting the gun in the circumstances.

This approach has been endorsed as the reason why prior fault^{OFF} analysis is not necessary for the resolution of such cases.[76]

However, not all trigger slip cases can be resolved in this way (i.e. through the relocation of liability), meaning that prior fault^{OFF} analysis cannot be entirely excluded from trigger slip scenarios. The first problem is causation: if we accept that the immediate cause of V's death (i.e. pulling the trigger) is involuntary, can we present D's earlier conduct at T1 as still causal in effect? Barwick CJ, in the quoted passage, focuses on the most immediate conduct leading up to the shooting, contending that causation could be found here provided D had the requisite foresight. Taylor and Owen JJ, in their combined judgment, were willing to go further, stating that D's conduct in 'loading and cocking ... the rifle, the failure to apply the safety catch, the presentation of the rifle ... were done deliberately and were as much part of the act causing death as was the pressure of the trigger which fired the rifle'.[77] Whether acts of this kind provide a sufficient causal link to resulting harms and how they might be brought together within a single transaction remain crucial points of uncertainty, remembering also that causal foreseeability will be required at the point of voluntary action.

The second problem did not arise in *Ryan*, but is arguably more significant. This is the problem of mens rea. Relocating liability to T1 allows for coincidence of mens rea with a voluntary act, but it will often be difficult to identify mens rea for all offence elements at this earlier point. In *Ryan*, section 18 of the Crimes Act 1900—defining murder—allowed for liability in circumstances of 'reckless indifference to human life' *or* causing death in the commission of another serious crime, both of which could be satisfied at T1 on the facts. However, this would not be the case if D were charged with murder under current English law, since the required mens rea is an intention to kill or to cause grievous bodily harm. In this case, D could rationally contend that he had no such intention from his T1 actions, even if he intended to cause such harms in the immediate future. In the absence of mens rea for murder at T1, it would be necessary to identify an alternative offence that may have been completed, such as gross negligence manslaughter. However, even this solution will not always be available, such as in cases where D causes non-fatal harm to V and lacks (at T1) intention or recklessness as to causing harm.

[76] This is the approach taken consistently across editions of *Smith and Hogan's Criminal Law* (now *Smith, Hogan and Ormerod's Criminal Law*) when discussing automatism and trigger slip cases.

[77] (1967) 121 CLR 205, [8].

3.4.2 The need for prior fault^{OFF}

Where relocating liability to T1 does not provide a viable route to a conviction, an alternative is provided via prior fault^{OFF}. This arises where D's blameworthy conduct at T1 is used to transform apparently involuntary conduct at T2 into voluntary conduct. Although not essential for the particular case, we see this approach outlined in the judgment of Windeyer J in *Ryan*:[78]

> ... 'reflex action' and 'automatic reaction' ... seem to me to have no real application to the case of a fully conscious man who has put himself in a situation in which he has his finger on the trigger of a loaded rifle levelled at another man. If he then presses the trigger in immediate response to a sudden threat or apprehension of danger, as is said to have occurred in this case, his doing so is, it seems to me, a consequence probable and foreseeable of a conscious apprehension of danger, and in that sense a *voluntary act.*

Responsibility is located at T2, with apparently involuntary action transformed into voluntary action by the legal fiction of prior fault^{OFF}. Fischer and Ravizza argue that the rule here can also be understood in terms of guidance control:[79]

> When one acts from a reasons-responsiveness mechanism at T1, and one can reasonably be expected to know that so acting will (or may) lead to acting from an unresponsive mechanism at some later time T2, one can be held responsible for so acting at T2.

The basic structure and function of the prior fault^{OFF} rule here is familiar, using blameworthy conduct from T1 to substitute for missing elements at T2; as is the implicit justification, that D's conduct across T1–T2 is just as bad—D is equally culpable—as if they had committed the offence in full at T2 (i.e. the equivalence thesis).

Employing prior fault^{OFF} rules allows for voluntariness to be constructed at T2, as well as (necessarily) other missing mens rea elements. In this way, compared to the relocation of liability to T1, the prior fault^{OFF} route provides additional certainty about the conduct element of the offence (i.e. we can focus on T2 as the most obvious point of mechanical causation), as well as providing an opportunity to avoid the mens rea problem, by allowing mens rea to be constructed at T2 in the same way as we see with prior fault^{OFF} rules elsewhere. This allows the prior fault^{OFF} route to apply more broadly than would be possible through a relocation of liability to T1 alone.

78 Ibid [20] (emphasis added).

79 JM Fischer and M Ravizza, *Responsibility and Control* (CUP, 1988) 50.

However, the use of prior fault^{OFF} in this way remains deeply problematic, for the reasons already well-rehearsed in Chapter 2 and the earlier sections of this chapter. Most importantly, prior fault^{OFF} relies on the equivalence of T1 fault with missing offence elements at T2, an equivalence claim that we do not believe can be justified.[80] As we have seen in other areas, the analysis of trigger slip cases will often be accompanied by broad claims of equivalence (exemplified in the quoted passages above), but the doctrinal reality does not bear it out. There is a lack of clarity here in the case law, but it seems that D's T1 fault may be established even in the absence of subjective foresight, requiring merely that D objectively *should* have foreseen the risk of involuntariness at T2 (and potentially circumstances of danger). This objective fault at T1 will then be used to replace a lack of voluntariness at T2, and a lack of subjective mens rea at T2 as well (though there is a lack of clarity here, including whether we should distinguish basic and specific intent offences at T2). We are left with a culpability mismatch, both in terms of gravity and the link provided to the harms at T2, as well as an unexplained inconsistency between the requirements for prior fault^{OFF} in trigger slip cases and the core prior fault^{OFF} automatism cases discussed in Section 3.2.

We recognize that where D causes involuntary harms in the course of another criminal venture, the risk of over-criminalization through prior fault^{OFF} is very low because D is already committing an offence. However, the risk of inappropriate labelling and punishment for a crime, the elements of which D has not committed in fact, remains extremely high, and so, again, we reject a prior fault^{OFF} analysis. In Chapters 5–7, we discuss the extent to which conduct of this kind should be captured within any new bespoke free-standing prior fault offence.

3.5 Prior fault^{OFF} and lack of mens rea

In this final section, we consider the potential for prior fault^{OFF} where D is *not* automatic at T2, but does lack mens rea as a result of non-intoxicated prior fault at T1. This could arise in several of the situations already raised in the sections above. It could arise in the unconscious assault scenario discussed in Section 3.2, for example, where D's hypoglycaemic state results in a lack of awareness (i.e. absence of intention or foresight of harms) but not complete involuntariness. It could also arise in trigger slip cases where D's slip is found to be reflexive rather than involuntary, but where D still lacks mens rea corresponding to the harms caused. Indeed, it has the potential to apply more broadly, to any blameworthy conduct leading to a lack of awareness short of involuntariness, such as sleep deprivation,[81] avoidable

[80] See discussion in Chapter 2, Section 2.4 and Section 3.2.

[81] We are thinking here of D who is voluntary in their lack of sleep, leading to foreseeable impairment.

concussion,[82] and so on. The potential breadth of this category (i.e. beyond prior fault^{OFF} automatism) is only increased by the progressively narrow interpretation given to 'voluntariness' within the current law.[83]

Where D's prior fault is attributed to voluntary intoxication, missing T2 mens rea (for basic intent offences) can be replaced regardless of whether D was also involuntary at T2; indeed, cases of intoxicated involuntariness remain rare.[84] However, in the category of cases currently under discussion, where prior fault is *not* attributable to voluntary intoxication, it seems that the law lacks any prior fault^{OFF}–based route to criminalization in the absence of T2 involuntariness. This position is absurd. As discussed previously, it may be explicable on the basis that prior fault^{OFF} has become doctrinally tethered to rules of automatism, which have been framed in terms of a defence. But once we recognize such framing as a misconception, that prior fault^{OFF} is being used to substitute for missing offence elements (i.e. as a mechanism for inculpation), there is no principled basis for restricting its application to circumstances of involuntariness. All things being equal, how can we consider D's prior fault^{OFF} at T1 capable of replacing absent voluntariness and mens rea at T2, but not a simple lack of mens rea?

For those who defend the use of prior fault^{OFF} outside of the intoxication rules, it seems that the current law should be criticized as under-criminalizing. Indeed, even for those critical of prior fault^{OFF}, such as ourselves, recognition that *some form* of criminalization may be appropriate in circumstances of prior fault will lead to the same conclusion. The difference, of course, is that we do not propose to remedy this potential under-criminalization through the expansion of prior fault^{OFF} rules, but rather—to the extent necessary—through a new bespoke offence that is able to better capture, label, and punish D's culpable conduct across T1–T2. We discuss thc potential for reform of this kind in Chapters 5–7.

3.5.1 Wilful ignorance and prior fault^{OFF}

The final matter to be considered in the context of non-intoxication prior fault^{OFF} is the doctrine of 'wilful ignorance'. The doctrine, as we will explain, shares several common features with prior fault^{OFF} rules, including the potential for a T1–T2 structure. It also applies to construct mens rea—a state of knowledge—in circumstances where D is neither intoxicated nor involuntary. Therefore, if wilful ignorance is a species of prior fault^{OFF}, it represents a counter-example to the general lack of prior fault^{OFF} rules (and associated risk of under-criminalization) discussed

[82] We are thinking here of D who suffers concussion through their own negligence, such as a failure to wear appropriate protective equipment, leading to foreseeable impairment.

[83] Discussed in Section 3.2.

[84] See Chapter 2. On intoxication leading to involuntariness, see *Lipman* [1970] 1 QB 152.

in this section. As we will explain, however, despite sharing certain features with prior fault^{OFF} rules, we contend that wilful ignorance should not be identified as a species of prior fault^{OFF}.

The so-called doctrine of wilful ignorance is recognized in several jurisdictions,[85] and applies to construct a state of legal 'knowledge' where D foresees a risk of certain existing circumstances at T1, but intentionally fails to investigate further despite a duty to do so, and continues to run the risk of those circumstances in action at T2.[86] For example, D buys a new state-of-the-art laptop from a friend (P) for a nominal fee, knowing that P has been involved in the trade of stolen goods. By not asking P where the laptop comes from, D can avoid *knowing* (in the standard sense) that it is stolen, and thereby hope to avoid liability for knowingly handling stolen goods.[87] However, in such situations, the doctrine of wilful ignorance may apply so that D is criminally liable by allowing knowledge-based criminal liability to be manufactured from D's choice not to self-inform.

The operation of the doctrine of wilful ignorance appears to bear a strong family resemblance to prior fault^{OFF}. D does not have knowledge at T2 in the standard sense, as D does not correctly believe that a certain circumstance is factually present. Rather, at both T1 and T2, D simply foresees a risk that the circumstance is present. Knowledge is therefore constructed from an accumulation of fault across T1 and T2, including D's culpable failure to investigate. This seems both to reflect the structure and function of prior fault^{OFF} rules, and has been similarly justified. For Sarch,[88] and others,[89] defending different versions of wilful ignorance, the debate typically focuses on questions of equivalence: whether D's culpability across T1–T2 is or can be made equivalent to a state of knowledge at T2. In making this argument, commentators often draw directly on models of prior fault^{OFF} for support, and, in the other direction, present their models of wilful ignorance as a basis for the understanding and reform of 'other' prior fault^{OFF} rules.[90] Indeed, in previous work, we too have identified wilful ignorance as a species of prior fault^{OFF} in our critique of these equivalence claims.[91]

Why, then, do we now say that wilful ignorance should *not* be categorized as an example of prior fault^{OFF}? The answer lies in our very detailed and deeper consideration in this study of the structure and function of those rules. The core function

[85] The leading English authority is *Westminster CC v Croyalgrange Ltd* (1986) 83 Cr App R 155.

[86] See, generally, A Sarch, *Criminally Ignorant: Why the Law Pretends We Know What We Don't* (OUP, 2019).

[87] Theft Act 1968, s22.

[88] A Sarch, *Criminally Ignorant: Why the Law Pretends We Know What We Don't* (OUP, 2019).

[89] E.g. G Yaffe, 'The Point of Mens Rea: The Case of Willful Ignorance' (2018) 12 *Criminal Law and Philosophy* 19.

[90] E.g. A Sarch, *Criminally Ignorant: Why the Law Pretends We Know What We Don't* (OUP, 2019) Ch 8; G Yaffe, 'Intoxication, Recklessness and Negligence' (2012) 9(2) *Ohio State Journal of Criminal Law* 545, 551.

[91] JJ Child, 'Knowledge by Any Other Name: Alexander Sarch on Wilful Ignorance' (2021) 12(2) *Jurisprudence* 236.

of the prior fault^{OFF} rules is to provide for the substitution of voluntariness and/or mens rea absent at T2, constructed from a different kind of fault located at T1.[92] It is true that wilful ignorance is also typically expressed across two temporal stages, including recklessness and a failure to investigate at T1, and a later point (T2) where D is reckless and runs that risk in action. However, it is quite possible for these stages to be collapsed into a single point in time where D foresees a risk they could investigate, but D chooses instead to run that risk in action.[93] In a case of this kind, wilful ignorance would apply in the same way, and we would have to conclude that D is acting with 'knowledge' of the risk foreseen.[94]

Unlike the situation with prior fault^{OFF} rules, this means that the wilful ignorance doctrine functions to provide something more akin to a parallel definition of 'knowledge' in law. And so, where wilful ignorance is identified across T1–T2, the law is not constructing 'knowledge' from different fault at T1. Rather, in common with other temporal transaction rules,[95] the law is allowing for offence elements to be grouped into a single transaction across events, and thereby allowing for coincidence. These rules remain controversial, but they are distinct from prior fault^{OFF}.

It is of course still essential for advocates of wilful ignorance to demonstrate culpability equivalence between wilful ignorance and the standard definition of knowledge (i.e. acting with a true belief), and relevant for critics to highlight any absence of equivalence.[96] However, that discussion of equivalence is not the same exercise as arises when using prior fault^{OFF} at T1 to substitute for offence elements at T2. Rather, it is essentially a debate about the definition of the mens rea term 'knowledge', in a similar vein to debates about other mens rea terms such as the 'equivalence' of indirect or oblique intention with more standard definitions of direct intention.[97]

In contrast, prior fault^{OFF} rules (properly explained and understood) are different: they will never collapse into a single point in time to provide an alternative definition of a mens rea term, but rather will always function across T1–T2

[92] In this manner, we are not simply dealing with a T1–T2 structure (common to other forms of liability), and, crucially, we are not simply dealing with the same mens rea required at T2 being found at T1. E.g. where recklessness as to a circumstance is required at T2, but it can only be found at T1, our best approach is to see if liability can be relocated to T1 (as discussed in the previous sections of this chapter) or coincidence can be found through a single transaction analysis. We are not looking to construct *absent* mens rea here through prior fault^{OFF}, but to analyse the offence in such a way that allows coincidence between existing elements.

[93] See JJ Child, 'Knowledge by Any Other Name: Alexander Sarch on Wilful Ignorance' (2021) 12(2) *Jurisprudence* 236. An example would be D who sets fire to a building, reckless as to whether anybody is inside, where D knows they could investigate: D would be held to have knowledge of any occupant.

[94] A point accepted by Sarch in 'Reply to Commentators' (2021) 12 *Jurisprudence* 291, 293–94.

[95] See, e.g., *Thabo Meli* [1954] 1 All ER 373; K Arenson, 'Thabo Meli Revisited: The Pernicious Effects of Result-Driven Decisions' (2013) 77 *Journal of Criminal Law* 41.

[96] See JJ Child, 'Knowledge by Any Other Name: Alexander Sarch on Wilful Ignorance' (2021) 12(2) *Jurisprudence* 236; D Husak and C Callender, 'Wilful Ignorance, Knowledge, and the "Equal Culpability" Thesis' (1994) 29 *Wisconsin Law Review* 40.

[97] See RA Duff, *Intention, Agency and Criminal Liability* (Wiley-Blackwell, 1990).

in a manner that constructs liability from different fault at T1. In part, this is because prior fault^{OFF} rules are characterized by D's impaired capacity at T2, where D's impairment means that fault from an earlier point (i.e. when D was competent) becomes essential. For this reason, we contend that wilful ignorance is not an example of prior fault^{OFF}. It serves quite a different function from prior fault^{OFF} properly so-called and analysed.

3.6 Conclusion

In this chapter, we have sought both to analyse and critique examples of non-intoxication-based prior fault^{OFF}, whilst at the same time using that exercise as a vehicle for analysing and critiquing prior fault^{OFF} as a species of criminal liability. In the course of that discussion, we have identified three groups of cases that should be carefully distinguished in analysis, application, and evaluation.

The first is a group of cases where prior fault^{OFF} analysis is *not* required, either because we are really discussing the definition of mens rea terms (as with wilful ignorance) or because we are better off relocating traditional forms of analysis from T2 to T1 (as with *all* grand schemer cases, and several examples within our discussion of automatism and trigger slip cases). Everything within this group does not (or should not) rely on prior fault^{OFF} rules, as we are not constructing absent voluntariness and/or mens rea with tokens of different previous blameworthy behaviour.

The second group of cases requires prior fault^{OFF} analysis within the current law to find liability, and is exemplified by prior fault^{OFF} automatism (e.g. the unconscious 'assault') and trigger slip cases where liability cannot be found by relocating the offence to T1. Our focus has been to understand the structure and function of prior fault^{OFF} rules in these cases, including their doctrinal inconsistencies, before scrutinizing how they are (and how they might best be) justified. Our conclusion, following our analysis of intoxication rules in Chapter 2, is that these rules cannot be justified in their present form, and that—where liability is warranted—it would be better achieved through a new bespoke offence.

The third group of cases also requires prior fault^{OFF} analysis as the basis for finding liability, but such analysis is not available within the current law. We identified cases of this kind where D's prior fault at T1 leads to a lack of mens rea at T2, but where D remains voluntary in their conduct. For these cases, the concern is one of under-inclusivity, and potentially one of under-criminalization. This should not prompt an expansion of existing prior fault^{OFF} rules, since this would merely extend the problems in the second group of cases just mentioned. Rather, we contend that these cases should be considered when analysing the potential for new bespoke offences.

4
NON-INTOXICATION PRIOR FAULT OFFENDING: INTERNAL CAUSES

4.1 Introduction

This chapter is concerned with the potential application of prior fault^{OFF} rules where D lacks the mens rea (and/or voluntariness) for an offence due to an *internal* cause (e.g. a mental disorder) at T2, where that state or disorder is itself caused or exacerbated by D's prior blameworthy conduct at T1.[1] This might include, for example, the failure to take prescribed medication, the failure to seek medical assistance following symptoms of disorder, and other conduct leading to disorder, such as drug taking resulting in a state of psychosis or more persistent/longer-term sequalae associated with chronic drug use including addiction. In this manner, the discussion builds upon the previous two chapters, which focused on absent mens rea and/or voluntariness resulting from *external* causes.[2]

Our starting point in this chapter, however, is quite different. That is because, in England & Wales at least, there are no prior fault rules applicable where D's lack of mens rea and/or voluntariness is due to an internal cause. Unlike external causes, missing offence elements at T2 will not be substituted or replaced by prior fault^{OFF} regardless of D's conduct at T1 in creating or exacerbating the internal cause.[3] Our task is not therefore to critique an existing mechanism for prior fault^{OFF}, but to analyse the basis for its specific exclusion in this context, as well as to discuss the potential for prior fault^{OFF} rules and alternative routes to criminalization in the future. Furthermore, since in other chapters we have mooted the creation of a new bespoke offence, facilitating the abolition of existing prior fault^{OFF} rules, in this chapter we will consider whether that offence should include or exclude internal cause conditions from its scope.

[1] As introduced in Chapter 1, we are adopting the notation 'prior fault^{OFF}' and 'prior fault^{DEF}' to distinguish between prior fault rules relevant to the construction of a crime and prior fault rules relevant to the blocking of a defence.

[2] In Chapter 2, where D lacks mens rea and/or voluntariness due to self-induced intoxication, and in Chapter 3, where D lacks voluntariness (and associated mens rea) due to external circumstances other than intoxication.

[3] Exclusion of prior fault^{OFF} in this context is reflected across common law jurisdictions, but is not reflected (in the substantive law at least) within the civil law tradition. See A Goldberg, JJ Child, H Crombag, and D Roef, 'Prior Fault Blame in England and Wales, Germany and the Netherlands' (2021) 8(1) *Journal of International and Comparative Law* 53.

Prior Fault Criminalization. John J Child, Adrian Hunt, and Hans S. Crombag, Oxford University Press.
 DOI: 10.1093/9780191874734.003.0005

The chapter is structured to engage with both tasks in turn, beginning with the central debate about whether prior fault^{OFF} rules should include internal causes (Sections 4.2 and 4.3), before moving to consider future reforms outside of current prior fault^{OFF} rules (Sections 4.4 and 4.5). On the current law debate (i.e. prior fault^{OFF} and internal causes of impairment), Section 4.2 begins with some essential context, introducing two fundamental points of confusion within the current literature. In Section 4.3, we are then able to focus on the core arguments on both sides of the debate, exploring the reasons for the current exclusion of internal cause conditions, as well as the counter-arguments made by those minded to extend the reach of prior fault^{OFF} to such conditions. Much of this debate will be familiar from previous chapters, focusing on the potential for T1 prior fault^{OFF} to provide culpability equivalence with those elements missing at T2. But there are also important considerations that are unique, or uniquely impactful, in the context of internal causes. We conclude Sections 4.2 and 4.3 with the view that the current exclusion of prior fault^{OFF} rules is appropriate for all internal cause conditions.

In Sections 4.4 and 4.5 we change tack, looking to the future of prior fault^{OFF} debates in the context of potential reform. Crucially, although we are principally concerned with reform to the prior fault^{OFF} rules themselves (i.e. the potential for a bespoke offence to replace current rules), we highlight and discuss the relevance of potential parallel reform to legal understandings of insanity as crucial to that endeavour. Section 4.4 considers prior fault^{OFF} and internal cause conditions in the context of reform to expand the application of insanity, and Section 4.5 considers internal cause conditions and prior fault^{OFF} if certain insanity rules were abolished. In each case, we highlight and explore significant implications for the potential inclusion of internal cause conditions within any future prior fault^{OFF} or alternative regulation.

4.2 Understanding the internal cause prior fault^{OFF} debate

As explained above, current prior fault^{OFF} rules do not apply to cases where D's T2 impairment was internally caused. This makes the starting point for debate about prior fault^{OFF} within this chapter very different to previous chapters; however, the basic structure of debate will be familiar. We are concerned with a scenario in which D causes potentially criminal harms at T2, but does so without the mens rea and/or voluntariness required for liability. The question—again—is whether D's conduct at T1 may be used to substitute for the missing offence elements at T2. In this case, D's lack of capacity at T2 is caused by an internal condition such as a mental disorder, and any potentially blameworthy conduct at T1 is understood in terms of D having caused or exacerbated that internal condition.

Just as the structure of this debate should be familiar, we also observe familiar problems within that debate which continue to (unnecessarily) complicate and confuse the literature. Two foundational problems will be unpacked in this section. The first is the siloing of internal cause prior fault^{OFF} debates within discussions of insanity rules alone, a similar problem to that discussed in Chapter 3 in the context of automatism in particular. The second is the characterization of internal cause prior fault^{OFF} in terms of blocking a defence, which is—again—both inaccurate and misleading. If we are to make sense of existing debates (discussed in Section 4.3 below), it is essential in the first instance to distinguish legitimate arguments in favour of or against criminalization from the products of entrenched mischaracterization and misunderstanding.

4.2.1 Siloing internal cause prior fault^{OFF} debate to insanity

Prior fault^{OFF} rules operate to substitute for missing mens rea and/or voluntariness at T2, but they do not do so in all cases. Even in the context of *external* causes of absent culpability, discussed in previous chapters, the current law will only engage in prior fault^{OFF} substitution where D's T2 state results from (i) voluntary intoxication or (ii) amounts to complete involuntariness (automatism). Thus, where D lacks mens rea at T2 from an external cause other than voluntary intoxication, even where this has resulted from D's blameworthy conduct at T1, prior fault^{OFF} substitution is not permitted. There is no principled reason for this confinement (i.e. the siloing of prior fault^{OFF} to intoxication and automatism alone), rather than considering prior fault^{OFF} in relation to any external cause of absent culpability at T2. And doing so creates a risk of under-criminalization, at least for those who support the application of prior fault^{OFF} on grounds of culpability.[4]

So why does the law silo the application of prior fault^{OFF} in this way? In simple terms, it seems to be the product of misunderstanding. Prior fault rules have traditionally been framed in terms of blocking defences, preventing D from relying on a defence where they are deemed culpably responsible for the circumstances leading to that defence. This framing, as we have discussed, is always inaccurate where prior fault^{OFF} is used to replace missing offence elements.[5] However, it remains the dominant framing of the law, and it is one that leads to our current problem. If prior fault can only operate to block a defence, then we must always identify a defence to be blocked. In the context of *external* causes of absent culpability, this feeds into the inaccurate framing of intoxication and automatism as defences (to be blocked by prior fault), and in turn prevents the application of prior fault^{OFF} rules outside of those 'defences'.

[4] We discuss this in relation to automatism in Chapter 3, Section 3.2, and further for insanity in Sections 4.3 and 4.5 below.

[5] Discussed across Chapters 2 and 3.

The same problem is apparent within debates about the potential for prior fault^{OFF} and *internal* causes of absent culpability. Logically, there is no reason to distinguish between categories of internal cause at T2, the focus should simply be on whether there is a blameworthy route of those causes at T1.[6] However, within the dominant framing of defence blocking, the analysis of prior fault^{OFF} has—again—gone in search of defences to block. The only candidate here, which is again mischaracterized as a defence, is insanity. In the context of mental disorders (and more general internal causes of absent culpability), this manifests in a debate almost universally confined to the potential for 'prior fault^{OFF} insanity'.[7] There is no principled basis for this confinement. Where D lacks mens rea and/or voluntariness at T2 due to an internal condition such as a mental disorder, and where that disorder is caused or exacerbated by prior fault at T1, whether D's T2 state also satisfies the narrow terms of insanity provides no obvious basis for criminalization. It is simply a product of misunderstanding: if prior fault operates to block a 'defence', we need a relevant defence to be blocked.

4.2.2 Framing insanity as a defence

A second point of confusion relates to, and rather complicates, the first. This is the discussion of insanity rules without explicit recognition of the two functions performed by those rules. In this chapter, we are concerned with cases where D lacks mens rea and/or voluntariness at T2 as a result of an internal cause, where the insanity rules might otherwise apply to divert D to the special verdict of 'not guilty by reason of insanity', and where prior fault^{OFF} rules *could* apply ahead of this diversion as a route to liability. In these cases, insanity is not applied as a defence, and prior fault^{OFF} rules represent a potential mechanism for the substitution of missing culpability elements.

However, insanity rules can also apply (uniquely) as a supervening defence, where all elements of the T2 offence are completed, and where prior fault^{DEF} rules (i.e. prior fault rules relevant to the blocking of a defence) could apply to block D's claim of exculpation. This represents an *alternative* application of insanity rules, and an *alternative* potential application of prior fault rules. We discuss this in Chapter 8, in the context of prior fault^{DEF} blocking defences. In this way, whilst it is sometimes accurate for courts and commentators to refer to insanity as a defence, nevertheless, it is always inaccurate to do so where insanity rules are applied to those lacking mens rea and/or voluntariness at T2 (i.e. our focus in this chapter).

[6] Indeed, there is no principled reason for distinguishing any internal or external causes of T2 absent culpability.

[7] This is apparent in the courts, academic debate, and materials from reform institutions such as the Law Commission.

It is necessary to separate the two functions of the insanity rules to avoid conflating discussion of prior fault^{OFF} and prior fault^{DEF}. Conceptual clarity is crucial to our understanding of the prior fault^{OFF} debate in this chapter. This is because—as we have seen in previous chapters—misrepresenting insanity as a defence (in application to cases where D lacks mens rea and/or voluntariness) disguises a core culpability challenge for prior fault^{OFF} rules, to demonstrate equivalence between D's fault at T1 and the offence elements missing at T2. This is a headline issue of framing, which shapes the prior fault^{OFF} discussion in the next section. However, the need for clarity goes beyond headline framing alone, and must be kept in mind throughout our evaluation of specific arguments within the prior fault^{OFF} debate. This is because, where existing debates about prior fault insanity have failed to separate the two functions of insanity, they are essentially treating two conceptually distinct debates, with two quite different sets of issues, as one and the same debate.[8] In what follows, therefore, we undertake the important process of scrutinizing arguments as they relate to the issues in this chapter *alone* (i.e. to issues of prior fault^{OFF} criminalization).

4.3 The current exclusion of internal cause prior fault^{OFF}

There are no prior fault^{OFF} rules within English law where D lacks mens rea and/or voluntariness from an *internal* cause condition. However, as we have stated, entrenched confusions within the law mean that this general exclusion has been expressed and debated in terms of insanity rules alone (i.e. as an exclusion of prior fault from the 'defence' of insanity). This characterization is unfortunate, creating unnecessary complication and disguising the substance of a debate that should be about criminalization. But despite these shortcomings, the debate is still instructive, and so will be reviewed here to inform our discussion of prior fault^{OFF} in the context of internal causes of impairment.

The exclusion of prior fault^{OFF} from insanity cases was clearly articulated in the case of *Davies* in 1881,[9] quoted with approval by the House of Lords in the seminal case of *Beard* in 1920:[10]

> . . . drunkenness is one thing and the diseases to which drunkenness leads are different things; and if a man by drunkenness brings on a state of disease which causes such a degree of madness, even for a time, which would have relieved him

[8] See discussion in Chapter 1, Section 1.3. The conflation warned against here is observed throughout the existing literature on prior fault^{OFF} and insanity, contributing to many of the confusions unpacked in this chapter.

[9] *Davies* (1881) 14 Cox CC 563.

[10] *Beard* [1990] AC 479, 500.

> from responsibility if it had been caused in any other way, then he will not be criminally responsible.

Indeed, speaking categorically, the Lords state that 'the law takes no notice of the cause of insanity'.[11]

Dismissing the (potentially blameworthy) causal route of insanity however, whilst examining the causal route of *externally* caused incapacities, creates a strict internal/external cause distinction. Essentially, there may be no consideration of prior fault^{OFF} for internal cause conditions, but there is potential for prior fault^{OFF} (as discussed in Chapters 2 and 3) for many external cause conditions. This is a causal distinction that can be extremely difficult to draw, in both scientific and legal terms, particularly in cases of concurrent or overlapping causes (e.g. where D is experiencing the effects of mental health disorder and drug- or alcohol-induced intoxication).[12] However, despite such difficulties, and even in cases where such difficulties arise, courts have treated the exclusion of prior fault^{OFF} from insanity cases as clear and binding authority.[13] Thus, regardless of D's blameworthy conduct at T1, there are only two possible outcomes in cases where D lacks mens rea and/or voluntariness due to an *internal* condition: where the insanity rules apply at T2, D will be diverted to the special verdict of 'not guilty by reason of insanity', and where the insanity rules do not apply, absent *alternative* prior fault^{OFF} rules, D will receive an unqualified acquittal.[14]

Despite the long-standing exclusion of prior fault^{OFF} from insanity cases, the continued appropriateness of that exclusion remains contested. This arises in part because of the practical difficulties—just described—of separating internal and external cause conditions. But beyond this, and more fundamentally, internal cause cases can evoke the same policy and culpability considerations that underpin the application of prior fault^{OFF} rules elsewhere. If D chooses to not take medication at T1 for example, and then—in the resulting state of psychological confusion—causes harm absent mens rea and/or voluntariness at T2, an acquittal on that basis may strike us as inappropriate. D may not be fully responsible at T2, but their choices at T1 provide a form of meta-responsibility that—arguably—should

[11] Ibid.

[12] See A Loughnan and N Wake, 'Of Blurred Boundaries and Prior Fault: Insanity, Automatism and Intoxication' in A Reed and M Bohlander (eds) *General Defences in Criminal Law* (Routledge, 2014) 113; N Padfield, 'Exploring a Quagmire: Insanity and Automatism' (1989) 48(3) *Cambridge Law Journal* 354.

[13] See, e.g., *Taj* [2018] EWCA Crim 1743.

[14] We note here—and explore further in the chapter—the prevalence of comorbidity in cases of potential prior fault^{OFF}, including cases where D's lack of capacity is caused by a combination of mental health disorder and the voluntary consumption of dangerous drugs. Where D's intoxication is found to be the primary cause of incapacity, the prior fault^{OFF} intoxication rules may be applied as a route to criminalization. See, e.g., discussion across the combined cases *McGee, Harris, Coley* [2013] EWCA Crim 223.

extend to T2 as a route to criminalization.[15] Indeed, outside of English law, several jurisdictions are already willing to engage with prior fault^{OFF} rules in cases of this kind.[16]

In what follows, we separate the three main themes of the debate, analysing the arguments both in favour and against the continued exclusion of prior fault^{OFF} from insanity (and more broadly from all internal cause conditions). We explore public policy considerations, claims of culpability and 'meta-responsibility', as well as issues of coherence and consistency with existing prior fault^{OFF} rules.

4.3.1 Public policy

We begin with issues of public policy (i.e. concerns about public safety and dangerousness) in recognition of the central role played by such concerns within the wider prior fault^{OFF} debates. We have seen, particularly in relation to voluntary intoxication, the striking willingness of courts and commentators to prioritize some version of perceived public policy concern ahead of 'strict logic'.[17] Partially disguised by the (inaccurate) language of defences, we are repeatedly assured that 'no wrong is done' when labelling and punishing a defendant for an offence the elements of which they have not completed (i.e. due to absent mens rea and/or voluntariness),[18] and that this is warranted by 'criminal recklessness' [19] and by intuitions of 'order' and 'justice'.[20] It becomes important to ask, therefore, what role, if any, these same policy arguments have played in debates about prior fault^{OFF} insanity?

In answering this question, it is clear that internal cause conditions are not uniquely immune from intuitions about prior fault and dangerousness. Quite the opposite in fact. In the context of insanity and mental disorder, criminal law rules have developed to engage explicitly with forward-looking questions of dangerousness, applicable where D causes harm in the absence of mens rea and/or voluntariness (i.e. despite a lack of offending). However, this has not involved seeking to identify a subset of cases involving prior fault^{OFF} facilitating criminal conviction and consequent criminal punishment of persons whose behaviour evinces a concern about their future dangerousness. Rather, it has involved the application

[15] On a conception of meta-responsibility, and on prior fault^{OFF} insanity in general, see E Mitchell, *Self-Made Madness* (Ashgate, 2003). The intuition is shared by the Law Commission, *Insanity and Automatism* (Discussion Paper, 2013).

[16] Within many civil law jurisdictions (including, e.g., Germany and the Netherlands), the insanity rules are actually the *primary* vehicle for the application of prior fault rules, though these are principally focused on the role of voluntary intoxication.

[17] *DPP v Majewski* [1977] AC 443, 482. Discussed in Chapter 2, Section 2.3.

[18] Ibid 474.

[19] Ibid 475.

[20] On the problematic appeal to intuition, see also M Shain and G Higgins, 'The Intoxication Defence and Theories of Criminal Liability: A Praxeological Approach' (1997) 24(4) *Contemporary Drug Problems* 731.

of a different set of rules known as the *M'Naghten* rules,[21] dealing with insanity in criminal cases. The effect of these rules is that even where D lacks culpability and would otherwise receive an unqualified acquittal, if D's conduct is caught within the insanity rules, their case is diverted to the 'special verdict' of 'not guilty by reason of insanity'. This is a finding that has previously resulted in indefinite hospitalization, and still now gives rise to a host of disposal options including compulsory treatment and/or supervision.[22] Formally speaking, this is an acquittal. However, one that can give rise to significant restriction of liberty in the interests of public policy. As stated in *Bratty*:[23]

> Suppose a crime is committed by a man in a state of automatism or clouded consciousness due to a recurrent disease of the mind. Such an act is no doubt involuntary, but it does not give rise to an unqualified acquittal, for that would mean that he would be left at large to do it again. The only proper verdict is one which ensures that the person who suffers from the disease is kept secure in a hospital so as not to be a danger to himself or others. That is, a verdict of guilty but insane.

The role for insanity rules here in 'clutching' and restraining a potentially dangerous person—explicitly focused on issues of public policy—has been consistently reiterated by the appellate courts, including in the now leading case of *Sullivan*.[24]

The application of insanity rules here, and subsequent diversion of the case to the special verdict, has clear implications for the prior fault^{OFF} debate. Although the special verdict represents an acquittal, it is a technical acquittal that provides the court with powers of compulsory restraint, and so public policy aims of societal protection can be achieved without recourse to prior fault^{OFF}. This represents a major point of distinction from cases where D lacks culpability due to an *external* cause, where the choice is simply between criminalization (via prior fault^{OFF} rules) or an unqualified acquittal.

Since, arguably, relevant public policy objectives can be achieved through other means, there is a much weaker public policy case for criminalizing persons whose internal conditions lead them to cause harm, than is the case for those who do so as a consequence of externally caused incapacity discussed in previous chapters.

[21] Emanating from debate in the House of Lords following the case of *M'Naghten* (1843) 10 Cl & Fin 200.

[22] Criminal Procedure (Insanity and Unfitness to Plead) Act 1991, s5, as amended by the Domestic Violence, Crime and Victims Act 2004.

[23] *Bratty v Attorney-General for Northern Ireland* [1963] AC 386, 410. Note that the old terminology of the special verdict is employed within this statement ('guilty but insane'). The contemporary formulation of this is 'not guilty by reason of insanity', better reflecting the finding of a technical acquittal.

[24] *Sullivan* [1984] AC 156: 'The purpose of the legislation relating to the defence of insanity, ever since its origin in 1800, has been to protect society against recurrence of the dangerous conduct', per Lord Diplock at 182. On the concept of 'clutching', see J Feinberg, *Doing and Deserving* (Princeton University Press, 1970) Ch 10.

Therefore, our debate moves onto the related but distinct issue of culpability. This asks whether the law should *blame* Ds with internal conditions through prior fault^{OFF} where their action/inaction exacerbated that condition leading them to cause harm. Assuming it were made possible in law, would criminalization on these terms be appropriate?

However, before we turn to that debate in Section 4.3.2 below, it is useful to interrogate the public policy assumptions underlying the diversion of insanity cases to the special verdict of 'not guilty by reason of insanity'. The question is whether current insanity rules meet the public policy objective of protecting the public from dangerous people in all appropriate internal cause cases. We think not. Although public policy objectives *may* be served by the diversion of insanity cases to the special verdict, only cases which meet the current narrow requirements of the insanity rules are dealt with in this way. Those rules require that D either does not understand the nature or purpose of their actions, or their legal and moral wrongfulness. These requirements have been applied in (progressively) restrictive terms,[25] thus leading to consistent calls for reform.[26] The reality of the current law is that D may lack mens rea as a result of an internal cause condition, but this remains squarely outside the insanity rules.[27] Such defendants will not be 'clutched' by the insanity rules and will not be diverted to the special verdict, and, crucially, this will be the case even if there are circumstances of *potential* prior fault. In these cases, therefore, public policy objectives may not be achieved at all.[28]

4.3.2 Culpability and meta-responsibility

Separate from issues of public policy protection is a core question of culpability: although D may have lacked mens rea and/or voluntariness at T2, would it be *fair* to use their prior fault^{OFF} at T1 to substitute for those missing elements in order to

[25] See JJ Child and GR Sullivan, 'When Does the Insanity Defence Apply? Some Recent Cases' [2014] *Criminal Law Review* 787; R Mackay, '"Nature", "Quality" and Mens rea—Some Observations on "Defect of Reason" and the First Limb of M'Naghten Rules' [2020] *Criminal Law Review* 588.

[26] The need to expand current insanity rules (alongside other reforms) is set out clearly within the stalled Law Commission project on insanity. See Law Commission, *Insanity and Automatism* (Discussion Paper, 2013). The Commission has announced that it will continue the insanity project as part of its Fourteenth Programme: Law Commission, *Fourteenth Programme of Law Reform* (2025) Ch 2.

[27] The case of *Harris* [2013] EWCA Crim 223 provides a useful illustration, where D was held to be outside the insanity rules despite significant evidence of mental disorder and delusional beliefs.

[28] Even cases that are currently caught within the insanity rules (i.e. allowing for diversion to the special verdict) raise concerns. This is because, as we discuss in Section 4.5 below, we believe that it is inappropriate for insanity rules to apply to *any* cases where D has not first committed an offence (i.e. that insanity rules should be redefined to apply as a supervening defence only). If this argument is accepted, then insanity rules will no longer function to divert defendants to the special verdict where an internal cause has led to a lack of mens rea, and the public policy ends served by such diversion will be lost entirely.

establish liability? This is a question concerning culpability equivalence that will be familiar from the previous chapters. However, in the context of insanity, where the public policy concerns are (at least partly) ameliorated by the availability of the special verdict, culpability questions are perhaps even more important. With forward-looking questions of dangerousness to one side, we can focus on backward-looking questions of blame and appropriate criminalization.

The claim of culpability equivalence, essential for prior fault^{OFF}, is *again* obfuscated by the inaccurate language of defences. Courts and commentators discuss insanity as a defence, and the potential for D's prior fault at T1 to undermine that defence. For example, in framing the prior fault^{OFF} debate, Mitchell states:[29]

> This study proposes a new motion to the debate: the mentally disordered should only enjoy their privileged position within the criminal justice system if the incapacity which grants them exemption from the rules of the game is not of their own making.

The 'motion' set out here is misleading. If prior fault^{OFF} were to operate in this context, it would not be restricting a privilege (i.e. a defence), but rather constructing a crime. Removing the exemption provided by insanity rules because of circumstances of prior fault—as Mitchell advocates—would not achieve liability by returning the individual to the standard system of criminalization. It cannot, because D lacks mens rea/voluntariness. Rather, it would serve as a mechanism of prior fault^{OFF}: preventing diversion to the special verdict, and then substituting absent T2 culpability elements with fault established at T1.

The case for prior fault^{OFF} rules here, as elsewhere, requires an equivalency between absent culpability elements at T2 and D's prior fault^{OFF} at T1. And, indeed, we can see arguments of this kind being made—either implicitly or explicitly—within the literature. Historically, culpability claims have been constructed upon the crude (mis)association of 'madness' and 'badness', on the premise that suffering a mental health disorder represents (or is even punishment for) moral failing.[30] Demonization of this kind, of course, has no place within an informed modern debate. But the opposite premise—that mental disorder is *always* absent of fault—may also be resisted. Certainly, it seems plausible to argue that, where D intentionally (or even recklessly) fails to take medication, knowing that this is likely to lead to incapacity and potential harms at T2, D ought to be blamed where those harms are caused in fact. In doing so, D is not blamed for causing harms involuntarily

[29] E Mitchell, *Self-Made Madness* (Ashgate, 2003) 4.

[30] See discussion in, e.g., E Mitchell, *Self-Made Madness* (Ashgate, 2003) 20–23; A Loughnan, *Manifest Madness* (OUP, 2012); TS Szasz, *The Myth of Mental Illness* (Hoeber-Harper, 1961).

(i.e. singling D out for punishment because of their disorder), but rather for their choice to avoid treatment at T1 leading to those harms. Mitchell refers to this phenomenon—blaming D across T1 and T2—in terms of meta-responsibility,[31] and provides some useful clinical insights into its appearance in practice.[32] Where this is most forceful, it challenges the appropriateness of the special verdict, which may provide a form of public protection, but may be insufficient or inappropriate because it fails to *blame* D.

Claims that culpability is being ignored here—and a consequent potential move to criminalization to address this—have not been entirely lost on the courts, even whilst maintaining the headline exclusion of prior fault^{OFF} insanity. We see this, for example, where the potential for prior fault^{OFF} is accepted by lower courts, only to be reversed on appeal.[33] Such cases, however, are extremely rare. Much more common, in the context of comorbidity, are examples of courts emphasizing prior fault^{OFF} blame, and then foregrounding intoxication-related causes (which provide a route to liability) and backgrounding alternative causes based on mental disorder (which, of course, do not currently provide a route to liability).[34] Indeed, where alternative routes to prior fault^{OFF} liability are not available,[35] or may be contested,[36] we see the appeal courts increasingly willing to criticize the exclusion of prior fault^{OFF} from insanity (and/or to marginalize it, through the expansion of intoxication rules[37]). As Hughes LJ stated in *Harris*, for example, having concluded that the intoxication rules were not applicable:[38]

> We agree that there is scope for the argument that an illness caused by his own fault ought as a matter of policy to be treated in the same way as is drunkenness at the time of the offence . . . But in the present state of the law, *Majewski* applies to offences committed by persons who are then voluntarily intoxicated but not to those who are suffering mental illness.

31 E Mitchell, *Self-Made Madness* (Ashgate, 2003).

32 Ibid Ch 3.

33 See, e.g., the US case *State v McCleary* No CR49471 (Ohio 1979); No CR42116 (Ohio Ct App 1980): D had been taking medication for schizophrenia for eleven years, but stopped doing so days before the incident. The lower court sought to distinguish 'insanity and insanity that can be controlled' (at 44). And, more recently, *State v Eager*, 398 P3d 756 (Haw 2017), discussed in C Caveney and C Cooper-Lehki, 'Improper Application of Self-Induced Intoxication' (2019) 47(1) *Legal Digest* 105.

34 See, e.g., *Oye* [2013] EWCA Crim 1725. Discussed in JJ Child and GR Sullivan, 'When Does the Insanity Defence Apply? Some Recent Cases' [2014] *Criminal Law Review* 787. We see a similar approach being taken across common law jurisdictions: see, e.g., recent Australian cases *Stefanski v Western Australia* [2022] WASCA 5; *R v Scott (No 3)* [2021] NSWSC 164.

35 See, e.g., *Harris* [2013] EWCA Crim 223.

36 See, e.g., *Taj* [2018] EWCA Crim 1743.

37 Discussed in JJ Child, H Crombag, and GR Sullivan, 'Defending the Delusional, the Irrational, and the Dangerous' [2020] *Criminal Law Review* 306.

38 *Harris* [2013] EWCA Crim 223, [25].

Beyond this, in the context of sentencing, where judges have considerably more discretion, we see evidence that blameworthy conduct at T1 leading to a mental health disorder is likely to have an aggravating effect.[39]

Culpability claims have also triggered academic and reform debates, suggesting the recognition of prior fault^{OFF} for insanity alongside prior fault^{OFF} intoxication and automatism. However, it is notable that such debates have not progressed much beyond familiar appeals to intuition, highlighting compelling examples rather than setting out a principled basis for equivalence. Mitchell's case for prior fault^{OFF} based liability, for example, focuses on medication non-compliance only.[40] In this context, he distinguishes T1 blame in terms of 'consensual meta-responsibility', where D avoids medication in pursuit of other ends (e.g. avoiding unwanted side effects), and 'purposive meta-responsibility', where D avoids medication in preference for a disordered state.[41] He argues that each may warrant criminalization, though he does little to explain the move from meta-responsibility to crime, beyond a simple analogy to intoxication rules and appeals to 'common sense notions of justice'.[42] Indeed, Mitchell's accompanying empirical work—which does not establish a clear preference for criminalization in such cases—rather exposes the omission.[43]

A similar approach is adopted by the Law Commission when discussing the potential expansion of prior fault^{OFF} to insanity cases. The following example is illustrative:[44]

> N has a recognized medical condition and has a total loss of capacity but that total loss of capacity is caused by his own culpable fault. The only significant difference between N and L (who has unreasonably ingested a substance when he was aware, or ought to have been aware, of the likely consequences) is that N failed to do something he ought to have done and L did something he ought not to have done. *We believe that the culpability is the same in this context and therefore the outcome should be the same.*

Like Mitchell, rather than making the case for criminalization directly (i.e. setting out a principled basis for equivalence between prior fault^{OFF} and absent culpability elements), the Commission constructs an indirect claim of equivalence through broad allusions to the intoxication rules.

39 See discussion in Chapter 11; N Sinclair-House, JJ Child, and H Crombag, 'Addiction Is a Brain Disease, and It Doesn't Matter: Prior Choice in Drug Use Blocks Leniency in Criminal Punishment' (2019) 26(1) *Psychology, Public Policy, and Law* 36.
40 E Mitchell, *Self-Made Madness* (Ashgate, 2003).
41 Ibid Ch 3.
42 Ibid 49. See also ibid 30, for a general appeal to 'common sense'.
43 Ibid Part II: Mock Juror Study.
44 Law Commission, *Insanity and Automatism* (Discussion Paper, 2013) [6.77] (emphasis added).

However, as previous chapters demonstrate, we do not believe that the case for culpability equivalence has been convincingly made in the context of prior fault^{OFF} intoxication or prior fault^{OFF} automatism,[45] and so—by extension—we contend that simple referral to those rules cannot provide for equivalence here. Specific case examples may demonstrate blameworthiness, and perhaps to the point that criminalization becomes appropriate, but this is not the same as principled equivalence. Following the criteria for equivalence discussed in previous chapters, it does not demonstrate that D's T1 culpability is of the same 'gravity' as that missing at T2 (i.e. foresight of risks in action vs foresight of potential future harms), nor that it is similarly 'connected' to the harms caused at T2 (i.e. as identified specific risks vs unidentified non-specific risks).[46] Therefore, although we may continue to debate the criminalization of certain behaviours, there is no basis for the systematic application of prior fault^{OFF} across the category of cases.

Additionally, as we have found elsewhere, some of the more convincing examples used to make the case for liability—presented in terms of prior fault^{OFF}—may be more appropriately resolved within standard criminal rules. We refer here *again* to the so-called grand schemer cases, where D's conduct at T1 is specifically targeted at causing harm without consciousness at T2.[47] Where this is the case, whether D brings about unconsciousness through intoxication, hypnosis, medical non-compliance, or any other means, it will be possible to target D for their conduct and associated mens rea at T1 alone, relying only on a causal-based connection to the harms at T2 to establish liability.[48] Once grand schemer examples are (appropriately) removed from debate through this relocation of liability, the case for culpability equivalence becomes weaker still.

It is also important to acknowledge specific concerns about assessments of culpability in the context of insanity (and by extension, other internal cause conditions). To establish prior fault, it is necessary to scrutinize the *causal route* of D's internal condition at T1: we must distinguish blameworthy causes of internal conditions from non-blameworthy causes, as we do (however imperfectly) when distinguishing externally relevant factors such as voluntary/involuntary intoxication and dangerous/non-dangerous drugs. It is here that we encounter a dual critique, questioning the moral appropriateness of scrutinizing the causal routes of

[45] Discussed in Chapter 2, Sections 2.3–2.4 and Chapter 3, Section 3.2.

[46] We discuss these criteria, in the context of intoxication, at Chapter 2, Section 2.3.2. Unlike in the context of intoxication, it is notable regarding insanity that we do not see academics or others engaged in the kind of work necessary to provide a basis for equivalence. See, e.g., G Yaffe's work on how culpability equivalence might be established for intoxication in 'Intoxication, Recklessness and Negligence' (2012) 9(2) *Ohio St J Crim L* 545; and our critique in Chapter 2, Section 2.4.2.

[47] See, e.g., discussion of grand schemers in E Mitchell, *Self-Made Madness* (Ashgate, 2003) Ch 3.3; 'Culpability for Inducing Mental States: The Insanity Defence of Dr Jekyll' (2004) 32(1) *JAAPL* 63, 64.

[48] We discuss grand schemer cases generally at Chapter 3, Section 3.3. See also, on internal cause cases specifically, R Mackay and D Hughes, 'Insanity and Blaming the Mentally Ill: A Critique of the Prior Fault Principle in the Law Commission's Discussion Paper' [2022] *Criminal Law Review* 21, 34–35.

mental health disorder in general (i.e. a dignity critique), as well as the clinical uncertainty of such causal route distinctions in practice (i.e. a scientific and diagnostic critique).[49]

Criticisms of this kind are most prevalent in debates about 'addiction', where questions concerning the fault of individuals in becoming addicted require us to trace back over several/many years, and are likely to be complicated by factors such as comorbid mental health disorders.[50] However, even with the most 'simple' and/or one-off cases of failure to take medication, important questions arise about the many and varied factors that contribute to such a failure (i.e. only some of which may be legitimate targets of blame).[51] This is not to say that certain *specific* cases may not be identified where T1 blame is tolerably clear,[52] but we should be mindful of a change that is likely—outside of isolated examples—to engage courts with significant factual, scientific, and diagnostic uncertainty. Indeed, in civil law jurisdictions, even where internal cause prior fault^{OFF} routes are available, the same dignity and scientific critiques mean that such routes are rarely availed upon in practice.[53]

In summary, we are left with a mixed picture regarding culpability, demonstrating some basis for prior fault^{OFF}, but exposing associated dangers of inappropriate criminalization. We return to this in terms of potential reform below, after engaging the final set of debates regarding consistency and coherence.

4.3.3 The consistency and coherence debate

More recent academic and policy debates, arguments in favour of expanding prior fault^{OFF} to insanity, have tended to focus upon issues of consistency and coherence. The argument here is enticingly simple: if we accept the application of prior

[49] See, e.g., M Wondemaghen, 'Evaluating Predominant Causes of Insanity in Cases of Drug-Induced Psychoses' (2015) 14(1) *International Journal of Forensic Mental Health* 76; H Crombag, JJ Child, and GR Sullivan, 'Drunk, Dangerous and Delusional: How Legal Concept-Creep Risks Overcriminalization' (2020) 115(12) *Addiction* 2200 (including responses).

[50] See, e.g., N Heather and G Segal, *Addiction and Choice: Rethinking the Relationship* (OUP, 2017); DA Regier et al, 'Comorbidity of Mental Disorders with Alcohol and Other Drug Abuse: Results From the Epidemiologic Catchment Area (ECA) Study' (1990) 264 *Journal of the American Medical Association* 2511; and a useful discussion of causal routes and disposition to addiction in S Nemerson, 'Alcoholism, Intoxication and the Criminal Law' (1988) 10 *Cardozo Law Review* 393, 411–19.

[51] See, e.g., R Mackay and D Hughes, 'Insanity and Blaming the Mentally Ill: A Critique of the Prior Fault Principle in the Law Commission's Discussion Paper' [2022] *Criminal Law Review* 21, 29–32; R Mackay, 'The Insanity Defence in English Law' in R Mackay and W Brookbanks (eds) *The Insanity Defence* (OUP, 2022) 21, 37; A Loughnan and N Wake, 'Of Blurred Boundaries and Prior Fault: Insanity, Automatism and Intoxication' in A Reed and M Bohlander (eds) *General Defences in Criminal Law* (Routledge, 2014) 113, 127–32.

[52] A point emphasized in E Mitchell, *Self-Made Madness* (Ashgate, 2003) 57–62, and accepted in principle by the Law Commission when proposing the expansion of prior fault^{OFF}.

[53] See, e.g., A Goldberg, JJ Child, H Crombag, and D Roef, 'Prior Fault Blame in England and Wales, Germany and the Netherlands' (2021) 8(1) *Journal of International and Comparative Law* 53.

fault^{OFF} for intoxication and automatism, then it is incoherent to exclude their similar application to insanity cases, and removing this exclusion (creating consistency) will also remove the need to distinguish internal and external causes for the purpose of prior fault^{OFF} assessments. It is an argument that features prominently in the Law Commission's most recent Discussion Paper on insanity and automatism, where the Commission sets out proposals for extending prior fault^{OFF} rules to insanity,[54] as well as within associated academic writing.[55]

It might be thought that this argument would and should appeal to us, not least because it appears—on the surface at least—to accept our view that prior fault should not be understood as synonymous with intoxication.[56] Having accepted that prior fault can arise outside of intoxication cases however, we would expect considerably more from the Commission (and others) to interrogate what such T1 fault should entail (i.e. leading to discussions of culpability equivalence with the offence elements substituted for at T2). But we do not see this in the literature. Rather, the use of intoxication as a proxy for prior fault is essentially maintained (or at least left unchallenged), and the case for expanding prior fault^{OFF} rests on broad analogies between intoxication and prior fault^{OFF} automatism, and from here to prior fault^{OFF} insanity. Coherence and consistency are foregrounded, but the arguments remain theoretically shallow.

As such, each argument becomes relatively easy to rebut. Claims of current incoherence may be effective in burden shifting, asking those who support the exclusion of prior fault^{OFF} insanity to justify that position, but the special features of internal cause conditions discussed above (i.e. in terms of public policy and culpability) provide a coherent response. Arguments concerning inconsistency are perhaps more effective, particularly where current inconsistencies create an artificial legal distinction between internal and external cause conditions. However, proposals for prior fault^{OFF} insanity do not represent a panacea, even in terms of consistency. Prior fault^{OFF} insanity is still likely to operate with different substantive requirements from other prior fault^{OFF} rules, and will therefore likely maintain the requirement of a distinction between rules,[57] and, as discussed above, the application of prior fault^{OFF} insanity will require new points of distinction to be made in the assessment of D's blameworthy/non-blameworthy causal route to insanity. Indeed, as Mackay and Hughes rightly observe,[58] the pursuit of consistency could also take us in the other direction, abolishing prior fault^{OFF} rules across

[54] Law Commission, *Insanity and Automatism* (Discussion Paper, 2013) Ch 6.

[55] See, e.g., D Ormerod and M Dsouza, 'Reforming the Insanity Defence in England and Wales' in R Mackay and W Brookbanks (eds) *The Insanity Defence* (OUP, 2022) 45.

[56] See discussion in Chapter 2, Section 2.3.2.

[57] The Law Commission seeks to limit inconsistencies in its proposals, within a broader 'recognised medical condition' set of rules, but it will still be necessary to distinguish intoxication cases for example. See, Law Commission, *Insanity and Automatism* (Discussion Paper, 2013) Ch 6.

[58] R Mackay and D Hughes, 'Insanity and Blaming the Mentally Ill: A Critique of the Prior Fault Principle in the Law Commission's Discussion Paper' [2022] *Criminal Law Review* 21.

cause conditions. Abolition of prior fault^{OFF} rules would also remove the need to distinguish internal and external causes for the purpose of fault attribution, and, additionally, would do so without introducing new points of scrutiny in the causal route to insanity.

The problem with this particular debate—concerning surface level (in) consistencies—is that it does little to engage with important underlying concerns. For example, for those in favour of extending prior fault^{OFF} to insanity cases, why not extend it to *all* cases where D lacks culpability and/or voluntariness at T2 due to blameworthy conduct at T1? This question is not engaged—within this debate—because the debate has focused on categorical consistency (i.e. between pre-identified sets of rules) rather than principled consistency across the piste. Equally, in their rebuttal of the Commission, Mackay and Hughes focus simply on their preference for 'consistency' in the other direction (i.e. abolition of prior fault^{OFF}).[59] But in so doing, they leave largely uninterrogated their preference for maintaining prior fault^{OFF} in the context of intoxication alone,[60] as well as their willingness to reform current insanity rules to provide additional ancillary orders (e.g. driving bans) that they accept would sit poorly with a 'not guilty' verdict.[61]

4.3.4 Conclusions about current prior fault^{OFF} insanity debates

We do not see a convincing case for extending prior fault^{OFF} rules to insanity within the current law. The debate, analysed above, is confused by several dubious attempts at burden shifting: presenting insanity (inaccurately) as a defence, to avoid the challenge of demonstrating culpability equivalence; presenting the lack of prior fault^{OFF} insanity as an unjustified inconsistency, in an attempt to shift the persuasive burden for change; and more generally, through simple appeals to common sense and analogy. These devices merely serve to mask the absence of principled argument. Simply put, the case for prior fault^{OFF} insanity requires good reasons for focusing on insanity alone (as opposed to other cause conditions), requires clarity on the meaning of prior fault, and requires culpability equivalence between D's prior fault at T1 and the culpability elements substituted for at T2. Each of these are lacking, as are many of the public policy drivers that have directed the debate (in absence of legal principle) elsewhere.

[59] Ibid.
[60] Ibid 38–40.
[61] As per Mackay and Hughes: 'We point to the change in nomenclature of the new [Recognized Medical Condition] special verdict which rather than one of "not guilty by reason of insanity" will be "not criminally responsible by reason of recognised medical condition". This is an important alteration in the nature of the verdict in that it signifies that D is "would not be to blame" rather than "not guilty".' Ibid 40.

Our conclusions regarding the potential application of prior fault^{OFF} do not, of course, rule out the broader case for criminalization. We can agree with the proponents of prior fault^{OFF} insanity that certain examples may warrant criminalization, and yet look to an alternative mechanism (i.e. criminalization outside of prior fault^{OFF} rules) to achieve that end. We note, for example, that even those explicitly opposed to prior fault^{OFF} insanity have occasionally recognized a discrete case for liability, engaging with wrongs across T1 and T2.[62] The challenge here—which we address in Chapters 5–7—is to design a new bespoke offence capable of isolating and punishing only those cases where liability is warranted, and to provide an effective answer to the dignity and scientific threshold critiques discussed above.

Before moving onto a series of chapters connected with the construction of a new bespoke offence, the final sections of this chapter will provide an account of two related areas of debate in the context of prior fault^{OFF} insanity (and internal cause conditions more generally). We first consider the potential expansion of insanity rules, before turning to debates about the partial abolition of insanity, in cases where D has not committed an offence. We do not aim to provide a complete account of each. Rather, we seek first to demonstrate the importance of these debates to core issues connected with prior fault^{OFF} insanity, despite their absence (in large part) from current discussions; and second to demonstrate their importance to any alternative approach to criminalization, leading into our discussion of a new potential bespoke offence.

4.4 Widening the interpretation of insanity rules

There is a well-developed and ongoing debate about whether and to what extent insanity rules should be reformed to apply more broadly, either within or outside the *M'Naghten* structure.[63] As we have noted above, current insanity rules are exceptionally narrow in their application, averaging only around thirty successful pleas in England & Wales each year.[64] This is in the context of a justice system that continues to convict and incarcerate large numbers of people with serious mental health conditions.[65] The Law Commission provided an important Discussion Paper scoping the potential reform of insanity (and automatism) in 2013.[66]

[62] See, e.g., R Mackay, 'The Insanity Defence in English Law' in R Mackay and W Brookbanks (eds) *The Insanity Defence* (OUP, 2022) 21, 37–38: allowing for liability where medication non-compliance is linked to the breach of a hospital order.

[63] See discussion in JJ Child et al, *Simester and Sullivan's Criminal Law* (8th Ed, Hart, 2022) Ch 19.2. For an excellent comparative resource, see R Mackay and W Brookbanks (eds), *The Insanity Defence* (OUP, 2022).

[64] In context of around 25,000 Crown Court trials per annum. See discussion in R Mackay, 'Ten More Years of the Insanity Defence' [2012] *Criminal Law Review* 946.

[65] See, e.g., Justice Committee, *Mental Health in Prison* (Fifth Report of Session 2021–22, 2021). See also J Senior et al, 'The Management of Mental Health Problems among Prisoners in England and Wales' (2014) 11(3) *International Psychiatry* 56.

[66] Law Commission, *Insanity and Automatism* (Discussion Paper, 2013).

Although the project stalled at that point, the paper remains a useful touchpoint in terms of potential reform, setting out a series of proposals that would significantly extend the reach of insanity (reconceived as a 'recognised medical condition defence') beyond its current limits.[67] This is particularly important given the Law Commission's more recent commitment to resume its examination of the law on insanity as part of its Fourteenth Programme of Law Reform.[68]

Our concern here then is how a potential expansion of insanity rules might impact the prior fault^{OFF} insanity debates just discussed in Section 4.3. It is a concern highlighted in the Law Commission's 2013 paper, prompting a full chapter on the application of prior fault.[69] It is not one that has otherwise featured in academic and policy work, however. Essentially, expanding the scope of insanity rules is unlikely to create *new* problems for the exclusion of prior fault^{OFF}, but it is likely to exacerbate those already highlighted in Section 4.3.

This is most clearly illustrated in relation to culpability questions, and the operation of legal thresholds. In terms of culpability, we explained above that certain defendants may demonstrate significant culpability at T1, such that intuitions in favour of criminalization (and associated public policy concerns) are particularly strong. Within the current law, the total number of individuals is limited by the narrow application of insanity, and alternative prior fault^{OFF} rules are likely to apply in common circumstances of intoxication comorbidity (i.e. providing a route to prior fault^{OFF} criminalization). It is a simple matter of logic to see that—where insanity rules are expanded—the number of culpable individuals covered by the insanity rules (and diverted to the special verdict) will increase, thus adding further weight to the case for addressing underlying normative issues associated with the exclusion of prior fault^{OFF}. The same is true for the problematic application of thresholds—particularly the internal/external cause threshold—necessary when excluding prior fault^{OFF} insanity. The currently narrow reach of insanity rules creates fewer 'mixed cases' where distinctions of this kind are required, but that would change if insanity is given greater breadth: more cases will hold the potential for an insanity outcome, and so the courts will more frequently be faced with complex (and often scientifically and diagnostically uncertain) questions of causation to identify which set of criminal rules to apply.

The Law Commission was clearly cognizant of these increased problems when proposing that prior fault^{OFF} should be extended to insanity cases (i.e. within its expanded 'recognised medical condition defence').[70] By extending prior fault^{OFF} rules to apply consistently between insanity and automatism cases, and broadly

[67] See discussion in D Ormerod and M Dsouza, 'Reforming the Insanity Defence in England and Wales' in R Mackay and W Brookbanks (eds) *The Insanity Defence* (OUP, 2022) 45; B Livings et al (eds), *Mental Condition Defences and the Criminal Justice System* (Cambridge Scholars, 2015).
[68] Law Commission, *Fourteenth Programme of Law Reform* (2025) Ch 2.
[69] Law Commission, *Insanity and Automatism* (Discussion Paper, 2013) Ch 6.
[70] Ibid.

in line with intoxication rules, both problem areas are engaged: the most culpable defendants caught within the insanity rules might still be subject to prior fault^{OFF}–based liability, and distinctions in terms of prior fault^{OFF} would be removed as a factor requiring strict causal thresholds between internally and externally caused incapacity.[71] Indeed, although this is not identified by the Commission, we should also highlight that the recognition of prior fault^{OFF} within expanded insanity rules would mitigate our criticism of tethering prior fault^{OFF} to insanity in the first place. This is because, simply, there will be a reduced potential for prior fault–induced internal causes to undermine mens rea and/or voluntariness without also coming within the (expanded) insanity rules.

However, a difficulty for those advocating the extension of prior fault^{OFF} within an expanded set of insanity rules is that, as well as exacerbating problems with the current *exclusion* of prior fault^{OFF}, expanding the application of insanity would also exacerbate the problems identified in Section 4.3 regarding the potential *application* of prior fault^{OFF} as well. Most importantly, expanding the application of insanity rules does not resolve the lack of culpability equivalence between prior fault^{OFF} insanity and missing T2 offence elements: where criminalization in the face of inequivalence gives rise to injustice, the effects of this are simply magnified. Equally, where prior fault^{OFF} insanity requires scrutiny of the causal route to insanity (i.e. to establish prior fault), associated criticisms in terms of dignity and factual/scientific uncertainty are, again, magnified. The Commission plays down the significance of both problems in its Discussion Paper,[72] but as we concluded in Section 4.3, we do not agree that any extension of prior fault^{OFF} is appropriate on this basis.

We are left with the issue of prior fault^{OFF} representing a significant obstacle to the expansion of insanity rules, whether prior fault^{OFF} is applied to insanity or whether the current exclusion is maintained. It is an issue that is rarely acknowledged within broader insanity debates outside of the Commission's Discussion Paper,[73] but one with very real negative implications for insanity reform. More positively, however, the potential for a new bespoke offence provides a possible solution. This is because the new offence allows us to abolish all *current* prior fault^{OFF} rules, decoupling the issue of prior fault^{OFF} from the potential expansion of insanity rules. The challenge remains to provide an appropriate mechanism for the

[71] Though retained, substantive differences between intoxication and other prior fault^{OFF} rules would, under the Commission's scheme at least, preserve the need for some distinction. See A Loughnan and N Wake, 'Of Blurred Boundaries and Prior Fault: Insanity, Automatism and Intoxication' in A Reed and M Bohlander (eds) *General Defences in Criminal Law* (Routledge, 2014) 113, 120–22.

[72] Law Commission, *Insanity and Automatism* (Discussion Paper, 2013) Ch 6. Cf R Mackay and D Hughes, 'Insanity and Blaming the Mentally Ill: A Critique of the Prior Fault Principle in the Law Commission's Discussion Paper' [2022] *Criminal Law Review* 21.

[73] See also C Hogg and JJ Child, 'Not Guilty by Reasons Other than Insanity' in AP Simester (ed) *Modern Criminal Law* (Hart, 2024) 155.

criminalization of those individuals demonstrating culpability across T1–T2, but this challenge is (correctly in our view) taken outside of the insanity rules.

4.5 Partial abolition of insanity rules

It was explained in the introduction to this chapter that the *M'Naghten* rules are unique in their dual potential application, being either a denial of offending (i.e. as an explanation for D's not satisfying the definitional elements of the offence charged) or acting as a supervening defence (i.e. as a defence where D has satisfied the definitional elements of the relevant offence). In both cases, if D has satisfied the physical elements specified in the actus reus of an offence, and where D is proved to come within the insanity rules, their case will be diverted to the special insanity verdict.[74] The issue in this section concerns an argument that current insanity rules should be *partially* abolished, such that they would no longer apply where D lacks mens rea and/or voluntariness (i.e. where D does not commit an offence).[75]

We have seen that the rationales for the dual functions of insanity are quite different. As a denial of offending, insanity is playing an essentially forward-looking role, diverting the case outcome from an unqualified acquittal (otherwise available where D is not proved to have had the relevant mens rea) in order to maintain the court's control over the disposal of D. Where insanity is applied in this manner, we can readily understand why defendants may want to resist its application, and why courts rationalize its application on grounds of public policy and social protection. Where insanity is applied as a supervening defence, in contrast, its role is much more clearly exculpatory. Here D has committed an offence and would otherwise be liable to conviction, with insanity offering a route to a qualified acquittal. The narrow terms of the current defence may restrict its availability to D in practice, but (in this function) it is likely to represent their preferred outcome.

The partial abolition of insanity rules would mean they would only continue to apply in the second supervening defence role. Any detailed discussion of this recommendation lies outside of our current focus,[76] though two points in favour of the reform may be usefully highlighted. The first is a concern about the fairness of diverting the cases of those who have not committed a crime to the special verdict. The application of insanity rules here may be described as *in*culpatory in effect: the insanity rules apply to divert D's case from the unqualified acquittal that would

[74] See JJ Child and GR Sullivan, 'When Does the Insanity Defence Apply? Some Recent Cases' [2014] *Criminal Law Review* 788.

[75] C Hogg and JJ Child, 'Not Guilty by Reasons Other than Insanity' in AP Simester (ed) *Modern Criminal Law* (Hart, 2024) 155.

[76] Ibid.

otherwise be available,[77] and forces them instead to prove their insanity with a reversed burden of proof.[78] Where D successfully discharges this burden, the special verdict will result in the potential for disposal orders restricting their freedom.[79] And where D fails to prove insanity, there is a significant risk of inappropriate criminalization.[80] The second point focuses on how partial abolition of insanity rules can facilitate their expansion elsewhere (i.e. when applied as a supervening defence).[81] The argument here, essentially, is that the insanity rules functioning as a denial of offending, and the insanity rules functioning as an exculpating defence, rest on quite different rationales, and that reform focused on one is not necessarily likely to be appropriate for the other. When arguing for the expansion of insanity rules, for example, commentators (including the Law Commission) will invariably focus on insanity as a supervening defence, where expansion provides greater potential for the exculpation of offenders with mental illness. However, so long as the other dimension of the insanity jurisprudence exists, any attempt to broaden the application of *M'Naghten* as a defence will also broaden the catchment of defendants who lack mens rea and/or voluntariness.

Were partial abolition accepted, and insanity rules applied only as a supervening defence, it would have a profound effect on the prior fault^{OFF} debate set out in Section 4.3 above. In terms of the current law's approach to prior fault^{OFF}, the absence of insanity rules (i.e. the abolition of insanity rules applying where D lacks mens rea and/or voluntariness) would effectively rule out prior fault^{OFF} analysis. Where prior fault^{OFF} only operates in the application of established rules (i.e. intoxication, automatism, insanity, etc), the abolition of prior fault^{OFF} insanity rules would create a vacuum, just as we see in external cause cases of non-intoxication where D lacks mens rea but does not come within the automatism rules.[82] The result is that, for those in support of prior fault^{OFF} insanity, the partial abolition of insanity rules would not be a welcome reform.

Things would be quite different in the context of a new bespoke offence. Having decoupled prior fault^{OFF} from existing rules (including insanity), prior fault^{OFF} concerns would be removed as an obstacle to wider reform of the insanity rules.

[77] I.e. would be available if D's denial of offending was not predicated on circumstances that engage the insanity defence.

[78] See T Jones, 'Insanity, Automatism, and the Burden of Proof on the Accused' (1995) 111 *Law Quarterly Review* 475.

[79] Note also how the language of the special verdict—'not guilty by reason of insanity'—incorrectly labels and inculpates defendants in the second category, implying that D would otherwise be guilty of an offence that (where, e.g., mens rea is absent) D has simply not committed.

[80] D may, e.g., choose to avoid the special verdict by pleading guilty. Or the jury may reject D's plea of insanity. With regards to the latter, where D denies voluntariness or mens rea, there is a danger that the rejection of insanity will be treated in practice as if voluntariness or mens rea were proven. See, e.g., *Bratty v Attorney General for Northern Ireland* [1963] AC 386.

[81] Discussed in C Hogg and JJ Child, 'Not Guilty by Reasons Other than Insanity' in AP Simester (ed) *Modern Criminal Law* (Hart, 2024) 155.

[82] See Chapter 3, Section 3.5.

Our focus at the liability stage would be on potential offences alone, including the new bespoke offence to be discussed in the next chapters. It is only after an offence is found that defences, including the supervening insanity defence, would be considered. It may be that—in the application of insanity *as a defence*—we should also take account of D's culpability at T1, as a possible reason to block the application of that defence. We discuss this possibility, and the blocking of defences on grounds of prior fault^{DEF} more generally, in Chapters 8–10.

Simply put therefore, the point here is that a new bespoke offence, and the abolition of current prior fault^{OFF} rules, would have the advantage of clearing the ground of various impediments to wider reform of insanity rules.

4.6 Conclusion

Across this chapter, two major points have been established. The first is that, *in the context of the current law*, the case for extending prior fault^{OFF} rules to insanity (and across internal cause conditions) is extremely weak, and should continue to be resisted. Arguments of public policy, of culpability equivalence, and of coherence and consistency do not hold up under analysis, and wider account of reform debates (i.e. reform of the insanity rules in general) make the case for prior fault^{OFF} weaker still. The second point, however, is more positive. When considering *the case for a new bespoke offence*, many of the problems that undermine the case for prior fault^{OFF} insanity are avoided, including those associated with the future reform of insanity rules. This does not establish a settled position in favour of including internal conditions within a new offence, not least because certain criticisms remain (in particular, we still have major concerns around scrutinizing the causal route of mental health disorder). However, the transition to a new bespoke offence offers a unique opportunity to address remaining concerns of this kind, which will be taken forward into the next chapters.

5

REFORM THROUGH A BESPOKE OFFENCE

5.1 Introduction

This is the first of three chapters exploring our preferred option for reform, which involves abandoning the current law's approach to prior fault^{OFF} and replacing it with a free-standing T1–T2 bespoke offence.[1] In this manner, we are moving on from the use of prior fault^{OFF} as a mechanism for creating liability within existing T2-focused offences in the various ways discussed in previous chapters (i.e. moving away from the current legal fictions). Rather, the 'bespoke offence' approach involves defining a new particular offence, which blames individuals criminally for their culpable actions in becoming incapacitated at T1 and going on to cause harms at T2.

This is not a wholly novel idea. The bespoke offence approach has been considered in one form or another in different jurisdictions for several decades. However, reform of this kind has only been achieved in a small minority of jurisdictions (such as Germany and South Africa), and even here it has been limited to intoxication prior fault only,[2] typically applicable to a subset of cases often alongside a broader regime of prior fault^{OFF}. This is the case despite apparent consensus in many different jurisdictions about the weaknesses of current prior fault^{OFF} rules,[3] and even though a bespoke offence option has been considered and endorsed (academically and judicially) for such a long period.[4] The bespoke offence option has remained an unlikely route to reform in England & Wales,[5] notwithstanding the one-time backing from the Law Commission, and active support of leading criminal law theorists, notably Professors Glanville Williams and JC Smith.

This chapter explores the context of those reform discussions and debates, highlighting the key decisions that must be made in the construction of a new bespoke offence, and evaluating examples of such offences within the current law

[1] As introduced in Chapter 1, we are adopting the notation 'prior fault^{OFF}' and 'prior fault^{DEF}' to distinguish between prior fault rules relevant to the construction of a crime and prior fault rules relevant to the blocking of a defence.
[2] See Section 5.3.
[3] See Chapters 1–4.
[4] See Sections 5.3 and 5.4.
[5] See Section 5.4.

Prior Fault Criminalization. John J Child, Adrian Hunt, and Hans S. Crombag, Oxford University Press.
© Oxford University Press 2026. DOI: 10.1093/9780191874734.003.0006

and literature. The following chapter provides further context, focusing on the scientific and empirical basis for reform—including our own studies—which will be used to inform the doctrinal questions raised in this chapter. Both feed into the final chapter of Part I, Chapter 7, where we set out, explain, and justify our proposed version of a bespoke offence built around the concept of 'culpable incapacity'.

5.2 The context for reform and the bespoke offence

The headline case for reform should be clear from our discussion in the preceding chapters of Part I. We have identified problems of over-criminalization within the current law. This occurs in the application of prior fault^{OFF} for intoxication and automatism, resulting in (i) the inappropriate labelling of defendants *in all cases*, where D has not completed certain offence elements and in the absence of equivalent fault and (ii) the inappropriate criminalization of defendants *in certain cases*, where there is insufficient fault to justify liability of any kind. We have also analysed problems of under-criminalization within the current law. This occurs in the non-application of prior fault^{OFF} where some form of T1–T2 criminalization is considered appropriate, across both external (including intoxication and automatism) and internal (including insanity) conditions. In this manner, we have accepted the case for T1–T2 criminalization but have rejected current prior fault^{OFF} approaches as the mechanism for this to be achieved.

In light of this critique, the bespoke offence option becomes our obvious (perhaps inevitable[6]) destination. The construction of a bespoke offence allows us freedom to consider the basis and acceptable limits of T1–T2 criminalization, and to do so, unlike current prior fault^{OFF} rules, without the encumbrance of demonstrating direct equivalence with existing offences.[7] Indeed, we have argued that such equivalence is not achievable within current prior fault^{OFF} models, and so departing from that mechanism provides the *only* way to engage sensibly with the question of criminalization. And from here, we are also freed to consider and debate associated questions of fair labelling and of sentencing—again, questions that are foreclosed within the current mechanisms of prior fault^{OFF}. In short, through the abolition of prior fault^{OFF} as a legal fiction, the vague notions of rough justice underpinning it can be unpacked, analysed, and remodelled into a principled route to liability.

Why, then, do we *not* see bespoke offences of this kind in England & Wales already, or within most other jurisdictions? It is necessary to engage with at least two major obstacles to reform to answer this question. The first relates to the stubborn, yet obfuscatory, framing of current prior fault^{OFF} rules in terms of defences (i.e. if

6 See G Dingwall, *Alcohol and Crime* (Routledge, 2006) Ch 5.
7 We discuss this, in particular, in Chapter 2.

prior fault rules are defences, then the idea of replacing them with an offence of any kind seems wrongheaded). The challenge here is to reset the legal understanding of prior fault^{OFF}: to break down the beguilingly simple framing of the current rules, and to expose the complex and flawed mechanisms of culpability equivalence that underlie them. There is a long-standing literature engaging with this issue, across jurisdictions internationally, which we have sought to clarify and add to in the preceding chapters of Part I. However, without a readymade policy alternative, we can understand why the legal fiction of simplicity and rough justice remains attractive for both judicial and policy audiences.

The absence of a readymade alternative engages the second obstacle. This concerns decisions to be made about the content of any bespoke offence itself, and the lack of common ground on how such an offence should be constructed. In practice, this second obstacle has been impacted by the first, since complex critique of current prior fault^{OFF} rules in academic and policy publications often leaves little space for detailed analysis of the specifics of a new offence. This in turn has resulted in the under-theorizing of the bespoke offence option.[8] Proper theoretical consideration of that option is seriously warranted. This requires a solution which is conceptually coherent, while also paying rigorous attention to the specific elements of the detailed nuts and bolts of any such offence.

Having stepped away from current models of/approaches to prior fault^{OFF}, the benefits of normative freedom must be balanced against challenges in offence construction: fundamental questions must be answered and justified about the T1–T2 target, and about the construction of actus reus and mens rea elements. This raises questions of legal theory and doctrine, as well as associated scientific questions of psychology and the neurosciences, to understand D's (in)capacity and the basis for associated blame. Defining and justifying a bespoke offence of this kind is difficult, and inevitably complex. As we will see, attempts to avoid this complexity (e.g. by modelling the offence on existing crimes) have so far led to unsatisfactory outcomes. The result has been a combination of stagnation and incoherence, with some commentators abandoning the project of reform for fear of making things worse, and others moving to support abolition without a new offence (i.e. a position that remains politically unviable in most jurisdictions,[9] and that is—we believe—normatively undesirable).[10]

Context is therefore important, and the latter sections of this chapter are dedicated to the evaluation of bespoke T1–T2 offences in the current law and literature, both international (Section 5.3) and domestic (Section 5.4). To make this evaluation meaningful, however, it is necessary first to map out and explain the major

[8] See Section 5.4.
[9] Discussed in JC Smith, 'Intoxication and the Mental Element in Crime' in P Wallington and R Merkin (eds) *Essays in Memory of FH Lawson* (Butterworths, 1986) 119, 129.
[10] See Section 5.4.

doctrinal questions with which any T1–T2 bespoke offence must engage. These range from the target and scope of criminalization (discussed in Section 5.2.2)), associated issues of labelling and sentencing (discussed in Section 5.2.3), and issues of practical application (discussed in Section 5.2.4). In doing so, we stress the positive opportunities provided by a bespoke offence, but also the challenges and alternative routes that need to be considered. We begin by examining the need for criminalization.

5.2.1 The need for criminalization

If current prior fault^{OFF} rules are abolished, we will be left with a series of open questions on criminalization. These include whether *any* new bespoke offence is necessary or desirable. Which is where we will begin, examining (and rejecting) the minority position in favour of 'simple abolition'. From there, we consider the potential for a new bespoke offence, exploring questions about the scope and focus of any such offence.

It is possible to abolish current prior fault^{OFF} rules without replacement, defaulting to standard rules of criminalization and existing offences; what we refer to as 'simple abolition'. Two principal arguments are advanced by proponents of this position, neither of which we find convincing. The first is a concern—often stated without elaboration—that the difficulty of creating a new offence might cause more problems than it resolves.[11] This argument must be taken seriously, but will depend on the specific offence proposal at issue, and so will be something we come back to in the evaluation our proposed offence in Chapter 7.

The second, in contrast, requires some immediate discussion. It is the claim that prior fault^{OFF} rules are unnecessary because blameworthy incapacity will rarely (if ever) undermine mens rea and/or voluntariness in practice.[12] Thus, the argument goes, there is no *need* to replace prior fault^{OFF} rules because they serve no practical purpose. This argument may be thought to have particular merit in jurisdictions that set a low threshold for voluntary conduct (such as England & Wales),[13] and/or in jurisdictions that make extensive use of objective negligence standards in offence definitions (as we see within many civil law jurisdictions).[14] In circumstances

[11] See, e.g., R Shiner, 'Intoxication and Responsibility' (1990) 13(9) *International Journal of Law and Psychiatry* 9, 11; S Gough, 'Intoxication and Criminal Liability' (1996) 112 *Law Quarterly Review* 335, 349. Each author also engages with the second argument discussed below.

[12] See, e.g., C Mitchell, 'The Intoxicated Offender—Refuting the Legal and Medical Myths' (1988) 11(1) *International Journal of Law and Psychiatry* 77. The same argument is also apparent in AP Simester's transition from supporting the creation of a new offence in 2009 (AP Simester, 'Intoxication Is Never a Defence' (2009) *Crim LR* 3) to a simple abolition position in 2012 (AP Simester, 'Getting Drunk in Singapore and Malaysia' (2012) *Singapore Journal of Legal Studies* 1).

[13] Discussed in Chapter 3, Section 3.2.

[14] Discussed in A Goldberg, JJ Child, H Crombag, and D Roef, 'Prior Fault Blame in England and Wales, Germany and the Netherlands' (2021) 8(1) *Journal of International and Comparative Law* 53.

of this kind, D's relative state of incapacity is much less likely to take them outside the scope of existing offences, and so alternatives (i.e. whether prior fault^{OFF} or a bespoke offence) are redundant. The claim that prior fault^{OFF} rules are unnecessary can also be supported by the experience of jurisdictions which have pursued the solution of 'simple abolition', such as New Zealand and the Australian state of Victoria, where floodgate concerns about intoxicated impunity have proven unfounded.[15]

However, we have several worries about the apparent merits of this approach, even in the contexts mentioned above. In terms of thresholds, we would highlight that many (ourselves included) are critical of the low bar set for voluntariness,[16] and that whilst there may be an expansion in objective forms of liability, this remains far from universal (particularly for serious offences against the person). We would also argue that the theoretical understanding of negligence in terms of culpable indifference (i.e. when causing harms at T2) translates poorly to circumstances of culpable incapacity. The worry here is that, even where the current law allows for a negligence finding in circumstances of incapacity (i.e. a reasonable *sober* person in D's position might well have foreseen relevant risks), we have serious concerns whether it should always do so. If D is at fault at all in these circumstances, it is not because of a culpable indifference at T2, it is because of their conduct at T1. Thus—akin to current prior fault^{OFF} rules—the use of negligence disguises a claim of culpability equivalence between T1 and T2, which is not tested.[17]

Similarly, regarding the experience of simple abolition jurisdictions, whilst we welcome the fact that apparently they have not experienced a flood of intoxicated 'offenders' benefiting from impunity, the issue is not just about the numbers. Indeed, a small number of cases may still demonstrate problematic under-criminalization, and there have been examples of high profile cases in those jurisdictions where the acquittal of intoxicated defendants gave rise to considerable public disquiet.[18] There is also an associated worry of jury application (akin to a reversal of jury equity), where juries may be making inappropriate findings of subjective mens rea in circumstances of (what they may perceive as) blameworthy

[15] Discussed in S Gough, 'Surviving without Majewski?' (2000) *Criminal Law Review* 719.

[16] See, e.g., JJ Child, 'Defence of a Basic Voluntary Act Requirement in Criminal Law from Philosophies of Action' (2020) 23(4) *New Criminal Law Review* 437.

[17] We discuss this further in Chapter 11, Section 11.3.1 as part of our concluding observations, though a full investigation will have to wait for a future project.

[18] See, e.g., the case of Nadruku, a high-profile rugby league player in Australia, who in 1997 became acutely intoxicated and severely assaulted two women in a Canberra bar. Nadruku was charged with violent offences, but he was found by the court to have been so intoxicated that he was not capable of forming the intent required within the definition of the crime, and therefore he was acquitted. This outcome was (and remains) highly controversial and prompted predictable public and political criticism of a legal system that allowed conduct described in the court as 'drunken thuggery' to go unpunished. See Law Reform Committee, *Inquiry into Criminal Liability for Actions Performed in a State of Self-induced Intoxication* (Parliament of Victoria, Australia, 1999) [1.11–1.17].

incapacity.[19] Essentially, there remains a great deal of empirical uncertainty about whether and how facts indicating prior fault are treated.

Alongside these critical concerns, we are also convinced—within England & Wales at least—that the need to maintain some manner of criminalization represents a political and moral reality.[20] We have identified several examples of prior fault^{OFF} in the preceding chapters where there is a strong normative case for criminalization, where D's choices across T1–T2 demonstrate a culpable disregard for the interests of others. The intuitive appeal of prior fault^{OFF} in such cases is not simply a product of misconception, based upon the inaccurate framing of intoxication (and other prior fault^{OFF} rules) as defences to be blocked.[21] Rather, whilst recognizing the potential impact of inaccurate framing within common law jurisdictions, it is important to acknowledge that the intuitive appeal of prior fault^{OFF} is also apparent within civil law jurisdictions, which do not typically present prior fault^{OFF} rules in terms of defences.[22] In such jurisdictions, the application of prior fault^{OFF} rules are much clearer in their inaccurate claims of culpability equivalence, and thus the critique of those claims may be more readily understood; and yet, the intuitive appeal of liability has continued to protect and buttress their application.[23] Thus, our position, again, is that abolition of prior fault^{OFF} should be accompanied by the creation of a new bespoke offence.

5.2.2 Target and scope of criminalization

Accepting the case for a new bespoke offence returns us to questions of construction. How should the new bespoke offence be designed across T1–T2? And to what extent, if any, can we draw upon existing offences to assist in that construction? We begin by setting out three alternative points of focus that may be used in the construction of a new bespoke offence. We see each of these in the specific offence examples discussed in later sections of the chapter, as well as in the academic commentaries discussed in previous chapters.

The three options reflect alternative points of blame across the T1–T2 time spectrum. The first locates D's wrong principally at T1, where D acts voluntarily in creating a risk of future incapacity and/or resulting harms (e.g. when becoming intoxicated). We refer to this as a 'T1-focused offence', and it has been popular among

[19] Discussed in A Ashworth, *Principles of Criminal Law* (2nd Ed, OUP, 1995) 213.

[20] Discussed in M Shain and G Higgins, 'The Intoxication Defence and Theories of Criminal Liability: A Praxeological Approach' (1997) 24(4) *Contemporary Drug Problems* 731, 753–54.

[21] See Chapters 2–4.

[22] The German doctrine of *actio libera in causa*, e.g., which has been adopted or remodelled within much of the civil law world, provides for a quite explicit substitution of T1 mens rea states into T2.

[23] See discussion and references in A Goldberg, JJ Child, H Crombag, and D Roef, 'Prior Fault Blame in England and Wales, Germany and the Netherlands' (2021) 8(1) *Journal of International and Comparative Law* 53.

commentators who prioritize the need for culpability at a point where D retains capacity.[24] From here, any harms caused at T2 either become unnecessary for the offence (in its most extreme form), or serve only as a filter to identify cases for prosecution. The second alternative, at the other end of the spectrum, would locate D's wrong principally in the harms they cause at T2. We refer to this as a 'T2-focused offence'. Focusing on D's harms at T2 provides for a more familiar offence construction, similar to the structure of complicity for example.[25] Crucially, in view of D's lack of mens rea and/or voluntariness at T2, culpability must be derived from T1, making causality (between acts at T1 and T2) and/or foresight or intention (at T1) potentially key concerns. The third alternative is what we refer to as a 'T1–T2-focused offence'. Here we imagine an offence construction between the two alternatives, locating the wrong of the offence as a genuine combination of T1 and T2 factors. Constructing an offence in this way is arguably most difficult, in that we do not have obvious equivalent structures elsewhere within the current law.

Each alternative point of focus represents a quite distinct target for blame, which will have a direct impact on the debates in the subsections below. It is a normative choice, fundamentally, based on the identification of a potential criminal wrong. But it is one that must also take account of an uncertain scientific and factual context. For example, the precise degree of D's incapacity may be difficult to determine (and prove/evidence), even in paradigm intoxication cases where D may be arrested some considerable time after the potentially criminal event.[26] This may be problematic for any new offence, but particularly for a T1-focused offence, where the degree of incapacity (and D's associated choices) are likely to be crucial factors in determining whether the offence can apply.[27] Equally, where a causal link is required between D's conduct at T1 and their later harmful conduct whilst lacking capacity at T2, establishing such a link with any degree of empirical accuracy will be highly challenging.[28] Again, this may be problematic for any new offence, but particularly for T2-focused offences, where such links are likely to be essential. Where the offence engages with mental health disorders, we also need to be cognizant of how such disorders (and their causal/aetiological origins) are understood and/or contested within clinical and scientific domains.[29] These concerns—and others—combine to create a challenging context for *any* new bespoke offence, but it is a context within which the use of criminal law must be justifiable.

[24] See, e.g., A Ashworth, 'Intoxication and General Defences' [1980] *Criminal Law Review* 556, discussed further in Section 5.4 below.

[25] As with complicity, although D's agency is exercised at T1, the relevant harms are caused by separate conduct at T2. However, when labelling and punishing D, focus is placed on their responsibility for the T2 harms.

[26] This contrasts to other intoxication offences such as drink driving, e.g., where D is typically arrested at the time of the offence and where breath testing is less problematic.

[27] See A Lynch, 'The Scope of Intoxication' (1982) *Criminal Law Review* 139.

[28] See C Mitchell, 'The Intoxicated Offender—Refuting the Legal and Medical Myths' (1988) 11(1) *International Journal of Law and Psychiatry* 77, 78–79.

[29] See discussion in Chapter 4, Section 4.3.2.

5.2.3 Labelling and sentencing

Proposals for a new bespoke offence begin from a blank canvas regarding the core issue of criminalization, and it is right that questions in this area should remain at the front and centre of our discussion. However, associated issues—fair labelling and sentencing in particular—have represented a major target in the critique of bespoke offence proposals. In circumstances where an offence is proposed to replace conduct currently criminalized through prior fault^{OFF}, the argument has been that a single offence label and a single sentencing provision can never adequately capture the variety of conduct and harms criminalized.

It is important to qualify this criticism. Current prior fault^{OFF} rules may appear to provide for a variety of offence labels and sentencing ranges, but this is only because the current law inaccurately equates prior fault with subjective recklessness (i.e. liability for existing offences is created through a legal fiction). Labelling defendants for crimes—the elements of which they have not completed—and sentencing on that basis, creates only the illusion of precision and specificity.[30] Indeed, in terms of accuracy and fairness, it does considerable damage across the criminal law landscape.[31]

Notwithstanding this qualifier, issues such as labelling and sentencing remain vitally important for a successful bespoke offence proposal. One of the major benefits of the adoption of a *de novo* offence has been highlighted as the ability (outside current prior fault^{OFF} rules) to label and punish defendants more accurately for what they have done, and, through such accuracy, to provide greater *ex-ante* notice to potential offenders. Where this is not delivered in practice, or not seen as being deliverable, then it becomes an obvious target for criticism.[32] In this regard, it is vital that the new bespoke offence is clear about what D is being blamed for: if we are pursuing a T1-focused offence, then a singular label and sentence may be appropriate (i.e. we are blaming D for becoming dangerously incapacitated), but this is clearly not the case if we are pursuing a T2-focused offence (or a T1–T2-focused offence) where the variety of T2 harms are core elements of evaluating or calibrating the extent or scale of the criminal wrong.

[30] Described as a 'smoke-screen' in E Macdonald, 'Reckless Language and Majewski' (1986) 6(3) *Legal Studies* 239, 245.

[31] See JC Smith, 'Intoxication and the Mental Element in Crime' in P Wallington and R Merkin (eds) *Essays in Memory of FH Lawson* (Butterworths, 1986) 119, 125–26.

[32] See, e.g., P Robinson, 'A Brief Summary and Critique of Criminal Liability Rules for Intoxicated Conduct' (2018) 82(5) *Journal of Criminal Law* 381; S Gough, 'Intoxication and Criminal Liability' (1996) 112 *Law Quarterly Review* 335, 349.

5.2.4 Application and procedure

It is also important to consider how any new bespoke offence would be applied in practice by prosecutors and the courts. This is a question for *any* new criminal offence, in terms of its place within the broader catalogue of crimes, asking when and why it is likely to be applied singularly and/or in the alternative with other offences. However, it is particularly pertinent for a new bespoke offence. The potential bespoke offence is proposed to fill a specific gap within the law: where D causes harms at T2 without sufficient mens rea and/or voluntariness to be caught within existing offences, but is nevertheless thought to be deserving of criminal liability when D's conduct across T1 and T2 is considered. Current prior fault^{OFF} rules attempt to fill this gap through the fiction that D did have mens rea and/or was in fact voluntary at T2. We have argued against this fiction. But its replacement with a bespoke offence (corresponding to any of the three alternatives mentioned above) gives rise to issues concerning the process for deciding when to charge or convict individuals with such an offence in preference, or as an alternative, to other substantive offences. Charging and prosecution authorities may not know at the relevant decision-making juncture whether D will raise or contest any issue regarding their incapacity/absence of mens rea or voluntariness. Similarly, such authorities may be of the view that their *prima facie* claim that D has committed a substantive offence in the usual mode should be tested before reverting to any alternative bespoke offence.

Two main options have been considered in that context. The first is the creation of a traditional stand-alone bespoke offence (following any of the three alternatives explained above), to be charged alone or in the alternative with other offences. This option has obvious appeal in terms of familiarity. However, when we consider the potential breadth of a new bespoke offence (i.e. circumstances of impaired capacity across a range of T2 harms), and the likelihood of it being charged in the alternative where capacity impairment is in issue, this adds up to a potentially significant increase in contested and complex trials.

It is because of this concern that a second option is often preferred, which only introduces the new bespoke offence after D has been acquitted of an existing offence. The idea here is that D's liability should be tested against existing offences, without the potentially complex inclusion of a new bespoke offence in the alternative. Where D is acquitted of the lead offence, the court/jury will then be invited to consider whether D only lacked mens rea and/or voluntariness as a result of their blameworthy conduct at T1, and thus whether D should be convicted of the new bespoke offence. A mechanism of this kind is intended to make trials less complicated, as a conviction for the lead offence will mean that the court need never consider the bespoke offence alternative. However, its novelty has given rise to concerns, as has its basic workability, and as we will see in the sections that follow, such concerns have proven to be major barriers to reform.[33]

It should be acknowledged that many practical and procedural concerns are likely to be jurisdictionally specific. Some of the issues raised above, for example, will be less pronounced within civil law jurisdictions operating an inquisitorial model, where alternative charges may be worked through over time, and (unlike jury systems) findings of fact can be interrogated. Our primary jurisdiction in this study is the common law system in England & Wales, and so our discussion will focus on the potential for a new bespoke offence within that adversarial model of justice that is at present (to say the very least) stretched in terms of time and resources. In this manner, while we also explore a wider range of comparative insights, our focus remains on the potential construction of a bespoke offence for operation (in particular) within England & Wales.

5.3 Comparative insights

This section considers jurisdictions outside of England & Wales that have legislated for new bespoke offences to replace (partially or completely) the use of prior fault^{OFF} rules. Our aim here, in light of the discussion in Section 5.2, is to unpack and understand the choices that have been made in the construction of these offences, and the lessons that may be learned from them. We focus on two jurisdictions that have bespoke offences in operation, Germany and South Africa: Germany because of the long-standing and influential status of the bespoke offence, serving as a focus for policy reform debates and academic discussion more widely, and South Africa because the offence was created to fill a perceived gap, following the abolition of prior fault^{OFF} rules.[34]

[33] See G Dingwall, *Alcohol and Crime* (Routledge, 2006) 121–22.

[34] It should be highlighted that reform of this kind (i.e. creating a new bespoke offence in place of prior fault^{OFF} rules) has been discussed and endorsed by courts and commentators across a great many jurisdictions besides. This has been particularly apparent in the common law states of Canada and Australia. Re Canada, see the proposal for an intoxication offence in Law Reform Commission of Canada, *The General Part: Liability and Defences* (Working Paper 29, 1982), endorsed in the subsequent report Law Reform Commission of Canada, *Recodifying Criminal Law* (Report 31, 1988), and more recently the endorsement of the Canadian Supreme Court in *Brown* 2022 SCC 18; re Australia, see A Loughnan and S Gless, 'Understanding the Law on Intoxicated Offending' (2016) 3(2) *Journal of International and Comparative Law* 345; judicial support in *O'Connor* (1980) 54 AJLR 349, and work of State Law Commissions, such as the Victorian Law Reform Committee's Report, *Criminal Liability for Self-Induced Intoxication* (1999).

5.3.1 Germany

Section 323a of the German Criminal Code provides perhaps the best-known bespoke offence, which has existed in one form or another since 1933.[35] Like much of the German Code, it has also inspired similar provisions in some other civil law jurisdictions, including Austria and Switzerland.[36] The offence applies to those 'committing offences in a senselessly drunken state':[37]

> 323a (1) Whosoever intentionally or negligently puts himself into a drunken state by consuming alcoholic beverages or other intoxicants shall be liable to imprisonment not exceeding five years or a fine if he commits an unlawful act while in this state and may not be punished because of it because he was insane due to the intoxication or if this cannot be excluded.

In scope, the German offence is predominantly a T1-focused offence. D is criminalized for becoming 'senselessly drunk', to an extent that they would otherwise satisfy the terms of the German insanity rules. Although harms are required at T2 (i.e. 'unlawful acts'), these simply provide a filter for liability rather than the point of focus. This is clear from the offence label ('committing offences in a senselessly drunken state'), and also from the absence of a requirement for causal connection between D's conduct at T1 and T2, and/or a mens rea connection between T1 and T2. The offence is *de facto* one of strict liability in relation to T2, requiring intention or negligence as to the T1 state of intoxication only.[38]

The German offence provides a relatively simple example of a T1-focused bespoke offence, in both a positive and a negative way. It is positive in the sense of its clarity, shaped around the mischief at T1, and avoiding (as far as possible) scientific and factual uncertainties inherent in the requirements of causation and T2-focused mens rea. There remain some points of potential confusion surrounding the meaning of 'negligent intoxication', and the threshold for being 'senselessly drunk', but, although this presents certain practical difficulties, neither represents a broader theoretical challenge.

The negative aspect is largely one of scope, with the German offence engaging a much more limited field of conduct than we might want. This begins with the

[35] With drafts dating back to 1927. See F Daly, 'Intoxication and Crime: A Comparative Approach' (1978) 27 *International and Comparative Law Quarterly* 378.

[36] See Austrian Criminal Code, s287, which limits D's penalty to three years imprisonment; Swiss Criminal Code, art 263, which limits D's penalty to a fine.

[37] Translation of the German Criminal Code provided by Prof Dr Michael Bohlander for the Federal Ministry of Justice in cooperation with juris GmbH (www.juris.de). Usual caveats apply.

[38] German courts have at times interpreted the offence to require negligence at T1 towards the future risks of harm at T2, but the prevailing view is that such fault is not required. See J Herrmann, 'Causing the Conditions of One's Own Defence: The Multifaceted Approach of German Law' (1986) 3 *Brigham Young University Law Review* 747, 765–66.

T1 focus on intoxication alone, which excludes all other potential external and/or internal causes of incapacity, and is compounded further by the requirement of *extreme* intoxication alone, excluding lower thresholds of intoxication regardless of D's fault (i.e. without regard to the circumstances of D's intoxication). Even where D is caught within the bespoke offence, the label and maximum sentence of five years imprisonment provides a further limitation. Where D's harms at T2 are significant, resulting in serious injury or even death for example, it may be questioned whether the offence label and sentence are appropriate in holding D to account.[39]

Fundamentally, the question is whether something akin to the German offence would provide an acceptable response to cases currently or potentially engaged by prior fault^{OFF} rules in England & Wales. We believe that it would not, and that an approach based upon the German offence alone would be under-inclusive. Indeed, this is not its role within the German system either. Rather, alongside the section 323a offence, German law provides for a series of prior fault^{OFF} rules under the doctrine of *actio libera in causa*. The German prior fault^{OFF} rules are different from those in England & Wales, in that they substitute for missing mens rea at T2 only where D possesses mens rea in fact at T1.[40] This approach makes German prior fault^{OFF} *less* objectionable in terms of culpability equivalence than its English counterpart, but—as we set out in Chapter 2, Section 2.4—equivalence is still lacking. The result is a problematic fiction of mens rea at T2. The German experience is not therefore one of prior fault^{OFF} abolition. Rather, the section 323a offence operates as an additional option, and one that has, notably, only been followed by a minority of civil law jurisdictions.

5.3.2 South Africa

South Africa has also legislated for a bespoke offence, but this time—crucially for our purposes—the offence was created following the abolition of prior fault^{OFF} rules. South Africa had initially adopted the English approach to prior fault^{OFF}, allowing voluntary intoxication to substitute for certain missing mens rea elements at T2.[41] However, in 1981, following the Supreme Court judgment in *Chretien*,[42] prior fault^{OFF} rules were found to be 'juridically impure' and no longer applicable to South African law.[43] Abolition of prior fault^{OFF} was therefore effected by the

[39] See A Goldberg, JJ Child, H Crombag, and D Roef, 'Prior Fault Blame in England and Wales, Germany and the Netherlands' (2021) 8(1) *Journal of International and Comparative Law* 53.

[40] The *actio libera in causa* doctrine is capable to translating both intentional (including reckless) states and negligent states from T1 to T2. This leaves relatively little ground for the s323a offence.

[41] See *Fowlie v R* 1906 TS 505; *S v Johnson* 1969 (1) SA 201 (A).

[42] 1981 (1) SA 1097 (A).

[43] Ibid 1103H–1104A.

courts, and was not immediately followed by any legislative intervention creating a new bespoke offence. South Africa became a simple abolition state.

The decision in *Chretien* was met with considerable public and political criticism.[44] Familiar concerns about intoxicated impunity (i.e. in the absence of prior fault^{OFF} rules) led to a report by the South African Law Commission in 1986 which recommended the creation of a new intoxication-focused bespoke offence.[45] The offence is set out within section 1 of the Criminal Law Amendment Act 1 of 1988:

> 1(1) Any person who consumes or uses any substance which impairs his faculties to appreciate the wrongfulness of his acts or to act in accordance with that appreciation, while knowing that such substance has that effect, and who while such faculties are thus impaired commits any act prohibited by law under any penalty, but is not criminally liable because his faculties were impaired as aforesaid, shall be guilty of an offence and shall be liable on conviction to the penalty, except the death penalty, which may be imposed in respect of the commission of that act.

The South African offence (SA offence) has a clear T1 focus. D is liable on the basis of their conduct at T1, for consuming or using any substance, which impairs their faculties, resulting in a lack of awareness at T2. The T2 harm must be caused in fact, but there is no requirement of causation between T1 and T2, and there is no requirement of mens rea at T1 as to the future harm (or impairment) at T2. These elements are in common with the German offence. However, unlike the German offence, the maximum sentence for the SA offence is linked to the T2 harm, mirroring the potential T2 offence (i.e. the offence D would have committed if they had mens rea and/or were voluntary at T2).[46] Linking D's sentence to the harm at T2, with the potential for significant variation between events, suggests a construction more in line with a T2-focused offence. D is liable not simply for putting themselves in an impaired state at T1, with the T2 harm as a condition of liability, but is also liable for the type and degree of harm caused at T2.

There are several problems with this construction. As a T1-focused offence, it has the same issues as the German offence in that it applies to intoxicated fault only, and is therefore under-inclusive of other potential external and internal causes of incapacity. There is also a problem of degree. Like the German offence, there is a problematic threshold for extreme intoxication alone, set out here in terms of D's appreciation of wrongfulness.[47] There also appears to be an alternative threshold,

[44] See G Kemp, 'South Africa' in A Reed and M Bohlander (eds) *Defences* (Routledge, 2014) 289, 296–97.

[45] South African Law Commission, *Offences Committed Under the Influence of Liquor or Drugs* (Report, Project 49, 1986).

[46] With the stated exception of the death penalty. Note also that the German provision also mirrors the sentence for the potential T2 offence, but—crucially—only to a ceiling of five years imprisonment.

[47] The threshold here is not entirely clear, but appears to set a high level akin to insanity.

not apparent in the German offence, where D retains awareness of wrongdoing but fails to act in accordance with that awareness. This alternative threshold has the potential to expand the bespoke offence to include mistakes of fact at T2 (leading to absent mens rea) where D is not in a state of extreme intoxication—an interpretation that would remedy some of our concerns about potential under-inclusiveness, where D is blameworthy for their incapacity despite being in a state short of extreme intoxication—but would trigger new concerns about over-inclusiveness, where the circumstances of D's intoxication do not provide a fair basis for blame. In practice, however, it appears that extreme intoxication and/or total incapacity has been required for the new offence to be applied, suggesting a preference for the first threshold only.[48]

There are also problems with the SA offence in terms of its T2 focus, varying maximum sentences in line with the harms caused. Simply, if we are to (also) focus blame at T2, the lack of causal and/or mens rea requirements at T1 seem to be entirely inappropriate. The bespoke offence appears constructed to capture a singular fault at T1 (i.e. the choice to become acutely intoxicated), and yet extreme divergence is permitted at sentencing on the basis of T2 outcome luck. Similarly, a T2-focused offence is arguably underserved by a single offence label. For example, where the difference between intoxicated killing and property damage is already recognized as significant within one part of the offence (i.e. sentencing), it is difficult to understand why it would not be significant in terms of labelling. In effect, we have a single offence pulling in two different theoretical directions, leading to a lack of coherence.

Beyond the core offence definition in South Africa, the Criminal Law Amendment Act 1988 also provides for a novel procedural device set out in section 1(2):

> 1(2) If in any prosecution for any offence it is found that the accused is not criminally liable for the offence charged on account of the fact that his faculties referred to in subsection (1) were impaired by the consumption or use of any substance, such accused may be found guilty of a contravention of subsection (1), if the evidence proves the commission of such contravention.

This subsection allows the SA offence to apply even where it has not been argued at trial. One of our procedural concerns—set out in Section 5.2.3 above—was the added complexity of alternative charges at trial, where the new bespoke offence would have to be argued alongside existing offences whenever mens rea and/or voluntariness was uncertain. Section 1(2) of the 1988 Act seeks to avoid this by allowing an existing offence to be argued alone, and only introducing the bespoke

[48] Discussed in G Kemp et al, *Criminal Law in South Africa* (3rd Ed, OUP, 2018) 200–02.

offence where a jury is minded to acquit D of the standard offence on the basis of absent mens rea and/or voluntariness.

The provision has obvious appeal in terms of its *apparent* procedural clarity. However, the experience has been quite different in practice.[49] This is because, for the provision to work effectively, it is essential that no further argumentation is required before the jury (i.e. at the point the jury decide to acquit for the existing offence on the basis of absent T2 mens rea and/or voluntariness, owing to D's intoxication, the bespoke offence should be applied). However, although section 1(1) arguably allows for a liability threshold of this kind, it has been interpreted in practice to require a total lack of capacity in all cases. This creates a contradiction where the prosecution must prove capacity to the criminal standard for D to be convicted of the lead offence, whilst the bespoke offence requires the same prosecution to prove to a criminal standard that D had a total lack of capacity.[50] Given that the latter will not be argued for in court (i.e. unless the bespoke offence is charged in the alternative), it is extremely unlikely that section 1(2) will facilitate a conviction for the bespoke offence.[51]

5.3.3 Comparative insights conclusions

Our discussion and evaluation of the bespoke offences operating in Germany and South Africa provide several valuable points of learning for would-be reform in England & Wales, and we can see their influence on that evolving debate in Section 5.4 below. Indeed, they also provide examples for reform (both in general terms, as well as within specific provisions) that have direct influence on our own preferred formulation of a culpable incapacity offence, set out and discussed in Chapter 7.

5.4 Reform debate in England & Wales

In previous chapters, we have already discussed current prior fault^{OFF} rules in England & Wales, and the critiques arguing for reform. Our focus here narrows to explore the place of the proposal for a new bespoke offence within that wider debate. As we have said, the bespoke offence option for reform (i.e. replacing current prior fault^{OFF} rules with a bespoke offence) has been around for a long time, and has garnered the support of several commentators within England & Wales, albeit typically without much elaboration.[52] This is valuable in terms of signalling

49 Ibid.

50 See *S v September* 1996 (1) SACR 325, 328B–C; *S v Ramdass* 2017 (1) SACR 30, [33].

51 It would not have applied, e.g., on the facts of *Chretien* 1981 (1) SA 1097 (A).

52 See, e.g., AP Simester, 'Intoxication Is Never a Defence' (2009) *Criminal Law Review* 3; G Dingwall, *Alcohol and Crime* (Routledge, 2006) Ch 5; G Virgo, 'The Law Commission Consultation Paper on Intoxication and Criminal Liability' [1993] *Criminal Law Review* 415.

the direction for reform. However, of particular interest here are those commentators who have taken the idea forward with a concrete proposal. We expand on four phases of this below, highlighting the strengths and weaknesses of each in turn. Our aim is to understand why the bespoke offence option for reform has so far failed to gain greater favour within England & Wales, as well as to learn specific lessons that can inform our own proposals in Chapter 7.

5.4.1 The Butler Committee

Despite long-standing debates on the bespoke offence option,[53] the first significant attempt to craft an offence to replace prior fault^{OFF} rules in England & Wales came in 1975. The Butler Committee, as part of a more general review of 'Mentally Abnormal Offenders', recommended a new offence of 'dangerous intoxication':[54]

> [18.54] We propose that it should be an offence for a person while voluntarily intoxicated to do an act (or make an omission) that would amount to a dangerous offence if it were done or made with the requisite state of mind for such offence. The prosecution would not charge this offence in the first instance, but would charge an offence under the ordinary law. If evidence of intoxication were given at the trial for the purpose of negativing the intention or other mental element required for the offence, the jury would be directed that they may return a verdict of not guilty of that offence but guilty of the offence of dangerous intoxication if they find that the defendant did the act (or made the omission) charged but by reason of the evidence of intoxication they are not sure that at the time he had the state of mind required for the offence, and they are sure that his intoxication was voluntary.

The Butler Committee offence (BC offence) takes clear inspiration from the German offence,[55] with a T1 focus on D's fault in becoming intoxicated. Harms must result at T2 (i.e. the actus reus of a listed 'dangerous offence'), but this need not be caused by D's intoxication and/or be foreseen or intended by D at T1. This is a strict liability offence for all elements beyond D's 'voluntary' intoxication. However, unlike the German equivalent, the BC offence is not designed as a standalone offence to be charged in the alternative. Rather, echoing the SA offence, it is designed as a supplement to 'standard' offences charged at T2, to be applied only where such T2 offences fail for lack of mens rea and/or voluntariness. This

[53] See, e.g., G Williams, *The General Part* (2nd Ed, Stevens, 1961) 573–74.

[54] Butler Committee, *Report of the Committee on Mentally Abnormal Offenders* (Cmnd 6244, 1975) Ch 18, Part IV.

[55] Discussed in F Daly, 'Intoxication and Crime: A Comparative Approach' (1978) 27 *International and Comparative Law Quarterly* 378.

is an attempt for procedural gains, avoiding the complexity of multiple alternative charges, where the bespoke offence is essentially substituted in where D lacks culpability at T2 due to voluntary intoxication.

Despite its qualities, however, the BC offence is a flawed proposal. This is best illustrated in terms of its over- and under-inclusiveness. The BC offence is over-inclusive as a T1-focused offence. To find sufficient fault at T1, the German offence narrows to apply to *extreme* intoxication cases only (i.e. D is blameworthy for putting themselves in a state of gross incapacity in which harmful mistakes are more likely to follow). In contrast, the BC offence attaches to *any* degree of intoxication that evidences a lack of mens rea at T2, or a reasonable doubt as to mens rea at T2. The offence is capable of applying, therefore, to relatively low levels of intoxication, even where that intoxication may not in fact have caused the lack of mens rea, and even in the absence of other blameworthy circumstances (i.e. where D had no reason to believe that their intoxication might give rise to the risk of harm).[56] The low threshold is set here because of the procedural aim of the BC offence: that it should be capable of substitution in all cases where D denies a standard offence on the basis of intoxication. However, the procedural benefits do not justify a bespoke offence that inappropriately criminalizes in the absence of fault.

The BC offence proposal is also under-inclusive. It is under-inclusive in terms of criminalization because it again fails to apply beyond intoxication cases, leaving other potentially blameworthy causes of incapacity (both external and internal) untouched. It is also under-inclusive in terms of labelling and sentencing, at least for those who would prefer more of a T2-focused offence. This is because, although the offence is capable of applying to a great variety of T2 harms (e.g. from property damage to causing death), it results in a single offence label ('dangerous intoxication') and a single maximum sentence of just one year for a first offence.[57] Notably, it was this criticism in particular—regarding label and sentencing—that prompted the new iteration of the bespoke offence outlined by the Criminal Law Revision Committee discussed below.[58]

5.4.2 The Criminal Law Revision Committee

The Criminal Law Revision Committee (CLRC) engaged with the issue as part of its Fourteenth Report on 'Offences Against the Person' in 1980.[59] In this report, the CLRC was broadly sceptical of the bespoke offence option, highlighting that any such offence would be likely to 'create problems' of additional complexity and

[56] On degrees of intoxication and blame, see A Lynch, 'The Scope of Intoxication' (1982) *Criminal Law Review* 139.

[57] Increasing to three years for any subsequent offending.

[58] Criminal Law Revision Committee, *Offences Against the Person* (14th Report, Cmnd 7844, 1980) [261].

[59] Ibid.

delay,[60] and opted instead to recommend the reform (as opposed to the abolition) of prior fault^{OFF} rules. However, the report also set out a minority position, representing the views of leading criminal law scholars JC Smith and Glanville Williams. This minority position retained a preference for a bespoke offence approach to reform, and provided a new offence proposal (the CLRC Offence) that was endorsed by the Committee as preferable to the BC offence.[61] The proposal set out in paragraph 262 of the report is as follows:

(1) Intoxication shall be taken into account for the purpose of determining whether the person charged had formed an intention, specific or otherwise, in the absence of which he would not be guilty of the offence.
(2) Where a person is charged with an offence and he relies on evidence of voluntary intoxication, whether introduced by himself or by any other party to the case, for the purpose of showing that he was not aware of a risk where awareness of that risk is, or is part of, the mental element required for conviction of the offence, then, if:
    (a) the jury are not satisfied that he was aware of the risk, but
    (b) the jury are satisfied
        (i) that all the elements of the offence other than any mental element have been proved, and
        (ii) that the defendant would, in all the circumstances of the case, have been aware of the risk if he had not been voluntarily intoxicated, the jury shall find him not guilty of the offence charged but guilty of doing the act while in a state of voluntary intoxication.

The CLRC offence is modelled on the BC offence, applicable as a default form of liability where D lacks mens rea at T2 as a result of voluntary intoxication. But significant changes were made to remedy—at least some of—the perceived weaknesses of the BC offence.[62] In doing so however, much like the SA offence, the CLRC offence ends up as a rather odd compromise between a T1- and a T2-focused offence.

Some of our criticisms of the BC offence apply equally to the CLRC offence. It remains over-inclusive in its identification of fault at T1, applicable to any degree of voluntary intoxication that results in an absence of mens rea at T2 regardless of the circumstances. It also remains under-inclusive at T1, applicable to intoxicated fault alone. As highlighted above, changes have primarily been made in response to labelling and sentencing concerns, moving the focus of the offence towards the T2 harm. In this regard, the CLRC offence allows sentencing of the bespoke offence

[60] Ibid [264].
[61] Ibid.
[62] Usefully discussed in JC Smith, 'Intoxication and the Mental Element in Crime' in P Wallington and R Merkin (eds) *Essays in Memory of FH Lawson* (Butterworths, 1986) 119.

to track the maximum sentence of the standard offence for which D lacks mens rea and/or voluntariness, and varies the labelling of D's offence in a similar way, where D is liable for an intoxicated version of the standard offence.[63]

The problem here however—reminiscent of the SA offence—is that substantive changes have not been made to the offence to justify labelling and sentencing D on the basis of the harms caused at T2.[64] The jury must be sure that D would 'have been aware' of relevant risks if sober at T2, but this falls well short of the kind of culpability required to justify a T2-focused offence discussed earlier (e.g. foresight of future incapacity and/or harms at T1, and/or a causal relationship between D's intoxication and the harms caused).[65] It also introduces a potentially problematic counterfactual, where courts are asked to arrive at a decision about something (i.e. whether D would have been aware of a risk if sober) that may be extremely difficult in practice. We are left with an already-flawed T1-focused offence, labelling and sentencing on the basis of assumed (but not necessarily established) fault at T2.

5.4.3 The Law Commission

Following the Butler Committee and the minority view of the CLRC—and reform in South Africa—the bespoke offence option was eventually taken up by the Law Commission of England & Wales. The Commission proposed the creation of a new bespoke offence to replace prior fault^{OFF} rules in its 1993 Consultation Paper,[66] before reversing that position (opting for simple modernization of current rules) in the subsequent 1995 Report.[67] The 1993 offence proposal was set out in the following terms:[68]

(a) The offence would be committed by a person who, while 'deliberately intoxicated', caused the harm proscribed by any of the 'listed offences' . . .
(b) The listed offences are provisionally proposed to be: Homicide; Bodily harm; Criminal damage; Rape; Indecent assault; Buggery; Assaulting a constable . . . ; The offences, under the Public Order Act 1986, of (i) violent disorder; (ii) affray; and (iii) putting in fear of, or provoking, violence; Causing danger to road-users.

[63] With the exception of murder, where sentencing will track manslaughter. Criminal Law Revision Committee, *Offences Against the Person* (14th Report, Cmnd 7844, 1980) [262].
[64] It is notable that Smith would have preferred sentencing to be capped as a fraction of the primary offence: JC Smith, 'Intoxication and the Mental Element in Crime' in P Wallington and R Merkin (eds) *Essays in Memory of FH Lawson* (Butterworths, 1986) 119, 131. This change may have limited the problem, but would not have removed it.
[65] Ashworth pushes back against the CLRC argument that labelling and sentence should track the T2 harm: A Ashworth, 'Intoxication and General Defences' [1980] *Criminal Law Review* 556, 560.
[66] Law Commission, *Intoxication and Criminal Liability* (Consultation 127, 1993) Part 6.
[67] Law Commission, *Intoxication and Criminal Liability* (LC No 229, 1995).
[68] Law Commission, *Intoxication and Criminal Liability* (Consultation 127, 1993) Part 7.

(c) A person would be 'intoxicated' for the purpose of the proposed offence if he had taken anything ('an intoxicant') that caused his awareness, his understanding or his control to be substantially impaired.
(d) A person would not, however, be deliberately intoxicated unless aware when he took an intoxicant that, in the amount that he knowingly took, it would or might cause him to become intoxicated (in the sense referred to in subparagraph (c) above).
(e) ...
(f) ...
(g) It would be immaterial to liability for the proposed new offence that the defendant (i) did or did not form the mental element of the underlying listed offence; or (ii) was in a state of automatism when causing the harm proscribed by the listed offence.
(h) ...
(i) The proposed new offence could be charged alone; but, further, there should be specific provision that a defendant charged with a listed offence might, instead, be convicted of the new offence.
(j) The maximum punishment for the new offence should be less than, but proportionate to, that for the underlying listed offence.

The Law Commission's bespoke offence (LC offence) represents an evolution from its predecessors, accompanied by a much more thorough review and justification.

The LC offence is more sophisticated than any of the proposed versions of bespoke offences discussed above. Although the offence is T1 focused—identifying fault in D's decision at T1 to become intoxicated and *potentially* dangerous—unlike other versions proposed by predecessor committees, the LC offence recognizes that a T1 focus requires fault beyond simple intoxication to avoid over-inclusivity. The LC offence is therefore narrowed to 'substantial' intoxication only (more akin to our international comparators),[69] as well as requiring such intoxication to result from D's 'deliberate' choice.[70] It is also notable that, as a T1-focused offence, the LC offence is capable of stand-alone application: it represents a distinct wrong, rather than simply an alternative to be introduced where mens rea is lacking for the standard charge.[71] The LC offence is not solely T1 focused however. Conscious of criticism directed at the BC offence, and the evolution this prompted within the CLRC offence, the Commission accepts the need for the offence label and sentence to track that of the offence D might have committed at T2 had they acted with mens rea.[72]

[69] Ibid [6.49–6.51].
[70] Ibid [6.52–6.61].
[71] Ibid [6.83]. The LC offence can apply as a stand-alone offence, though it may also arise without specific reference on the indictment: Ibid [6.81–6.82].
[72] Ibid [6.42–6.47].

The Law Commission made several important strides forward with its proposal. However, it remains problematic,[73] and was, as we have noted, rejected following consultation. As a T1-focused offence, the requirement that D's intoxication be both deliberate and substantial provides a coherent point of blame, but it is one that remains potentially under-inclusive in its exclusion of non-intoxication causes (i.e. whether external or internal) and lesser degrees of intoxication that might nevertheless arise in blameworthy circumstances (i.e. where these might also result in mistake making[74]). The T2-focused elements—when labelling and sentencing—are also problematic. It is not necessarily improper to engage the harms at T2, and the distinct nature of the bespoke offence is maintained by a structured reduction of sentence from the mens rea offence equivalent.[75] However, any explicit engagement with the T2 harm when labelling and sentencing D must be justified; it must be demonstrated to be a deserving target for blame. The Commission was criticized on this basis for not requiring a mens rea and/or causal link between D's conduct at T1 and the later harms at T2.[76] The CLRC attempted to remedy a similar omission with a weaker counterfactual link (i.e. that D would have foreseen the risk of harm if sober), but the Commission rejected this as unworkable.[77] The Commission's alternative is to narrow the list of T2 harms to those most likely to be associated with extreme intoxication, making a T1–T2 link more likely perhaps, but not requiring mens rea or a causal link. Thus, in this respect, it is undoubtably a weakening of the CLRC version.

The LC offence was rejected by the Commission itself in its 1995 report, following criticism arising from the consultation process.[78] In particular, the Commission accepted concerns raised about the practical and procedural application of the offence, opting instead for recommendations that would retain and reform prior fault^{OFF} rules. The Commission has been criticized for its stance here, reverting to a substantively flawed mechanism of prior fault^{OFF} for reasons of procedural difficulty.[79] However, it serves as a stark reminder of the importance of procedural workability for *any* new bespoke offence. The LC offence raised several

[73] See, in general, G Virgo, 'The Law Commission Consultation Paper on Intoxication and Criminal Liability' [1993] *Criminal Law Review* 415.

[74] This is discussed as a potential limitation by the Commission, upon which it specifically elicited views on in consultation. Ibid [6.62–6.65].

[75] Ibid [6.29] and [6.43–6.47]. The Commission note at [6.25] that this was JC Smith's preference during work on the CLRC offence as well.

[76] See R Mackay, *Mental Condition Defences in the Criminal Law* (OUP, 1995) 172–73; S Gough, 'Intoxication and Criminal Liability' (1996) 112 *Law Quarterly Review* 335, 341–42. Cf, on the difficulty of a causation requirement, G Virgo, 'The Law Commission Consultation Paper on Intoxication and Criminal Liability' [1993] *Criminal Law Review* 415, 424.

[77] Law Commission, *Intoxication and Criminal Liability* (Consultation 127, 1993) [6.24–6.25].

[78] Law Commission, *Intoxication and Criminal Liability* (LC No 229, 1995).

[79] I.e. substantive flaws that the Law Commission highlighted in its Consultation Paper. See E Paton, 'Reformulating the Intoxication Rules' [1995] *Criminal Law Review* 382; G Dingwall, *Alcohol and Crime* (Routledge, 2006) 121; R Mackay, *Mental Condition Defences in the Criminal Law* (OUP, 1995) 177.

concerns in this regard. The meaning of key terms such as 'substantial' and 'deliberate', for example, would likely cause problems in practice.[80] In terms of procedure, the Commission also highlighted the potential complexity of an offence that could either be charged directly, or introduced where a jury is in doubt about finding mens rea for an alternative charge. As the Commission state:

> . . . since it would be perceived by defendants (however unrealistically) as a chance to be convicted of a less serious offence, it would engender both more trials and, in cases where there is a trial anyway, the raising of more issues than occurs at present . . . [T]he requirement of substantial impairment would require the police to devote more time to enquiries into the defendant's movements and his intake of intoxicants prior to the offence . . . [T]he prosecution would not know in advance whether it should include the new offence as an alternative offence on the indictment. As a result, the essential features of the case would not be before the jury at the outset, and difficulties could arise in the course of the trial over the question whether and when to add a separate count.

It has been observed, correctly in our view, that each of these concerns may be addressed without abandoning the bespoke offence approach.[81] However, they are concerns that must be carefully considered when setting out our preferred approach in Chapter 7.

5.4.4 Debates post-1995

Following the rejection of the Law Commission's proposal in 1995, there has been remarkably little progress made towards the construction of a more acceptable new bespoke offence. Even when asked to consider intoxication rules again in 2009, the Law Commission referred to the bespoke offence option as 'radical' (a characterization which in a British context effectively compels rejection), repeated its reasons for rejecting it in 1995, and went on to (again) recommend reform rather than abolition of prior fault^{OFF} rules[82]—recommendations that were themselves rejected by government.[83] Indeed, it is a point of ongoing curiosity—discussed already in Chapter 2—that attempts to clarify the application of prior fault^{OFF} rules have the effect of exposing their lack of coherence, rendering reform of this kind

[80] On the term of 'deliberate', see Law Commission, *Intoxication and Criminal Liability* (Consultation 127, 1993) [6.52–6.55]; cf G Virgo, 'The Law Commission Consultation Paper on Intoxication and Criminal Liability' [1993] *Criminal Law Review* 415, 421. On the term 'substantial', see Law Commission, *Intoxication and Criminal Liability* (Consultation 127, 1993) [6.49–6.51].

[81] See, e.g., E Paton, 'Reformulating the Intoxication Rules' [1995] *Criminal Law Review* 382, 388.

[82] Law Commission, *Intoxication and Criminal Liability* (LC No 314, 2009).

[83] See discussion of this, and a general critique of the 2009 approach, in JJ Child, 'Drink, Drugs and Law Reform: A Review of Law Commission Report No.314' [2009] *Criminal Law Review* 488.

extremely unlikely, and yet reverting us back to a current legal state in which those same incoherences remain.

Some lone voices have however continued to call for adoption of a more 'radical' approach. In 2013, Rebecca Williams argued for the adoption of a general offence,[84] structured in a similar way to inchoate liability, attaching a new form of intoxication-based liability to existing offences:[85]

> ... where he or she commits the actus reus, lacking the mens rea usually required for conviction, but only as a result of the intoxication, he or she would become liable for the new offence of 'committing [the actus reus of offence X] while intoxicated'.

Williams promotes the simplicity of her approach, with explicit reference to the concerns previously raised by the Law Commission. Her approach is conceptualized within a familiar model taken from inchoate liability;[86] constructed with the use of actus reus elements from existing offences, rather than identifying distinct harms, and allowing the label and maximum sentence for the bespoke offence to track those of existing standard offences. The construction here is much more T2 focused than we have seen before. Indeed, when looking to avoid over-inclusivity, rather than focus on D's choices at T1 (e.g. degree of intoxication), Williams instead asks what a sober reasonable person would have foreseen at T2.[87]

There is an appealing simplicity to Williams' offence. However, we do not believe that it represents an appropriate way forward. This is because, although Williams is correct that her approach accurately labels D (actus reus plus intoxication), she gives insufficient weight to concerns about whether the conduct so-labelled should in fact be criminalized. Our discussion of bespoke offences began from the finding that intoxication is not equivalent to absent mens rea and/or voluntariness (i.e. our basis for rejecting prior fault^{OFF}), a finding endorsed by Williams. However, once it is accepted that intoxication is *not* equivalent to mens rea, then the wrongs captured by a bespoke offence become quite different from existing offences, and require separate justification. We cannot reject culpability equivalence in the context of prior fault^{OFF}, and then accept it (by implication) in the construction of a bespoke offence.

The problem for Williams' approach is a general one, with every combination of actus reus and intoxication capturing a new combination of wrongs that are simply assumed (within her approach) to be deserving of criminal sanction. However, the

[84] R Williams, 'Voluntary Intoxication—A Lost Cause?' (2013) 129 *Law Quarterly Review* 264.
[85] Ibid 276.
[86] See JJ Child and A Hunt, 'Inchoate Offences' in P Caeiro et al (eds) *Elgar Encyclopaedia of Crime and Criminal Justice* (Elgar, 2023) 51.
[87] R Williams, 'Voluntary Intoxication—A Lost Cause?' (2013) 129 *Law Quarterly Review* 264, 280–82.

potential for over-criminalization is most obvious in relation to two types of offences where mens rea is central to the substantive wrong. Partially recognized by Williams, the first category of offences are inchoate offences or (more accurately) any offence including an ulterior mens rea element. As the focus of these offences is the mind of D (as opposed to a harmful actus reus), Williams acknowledges that application of the 'actus reus plus intoxication' offence may not be appropriate.[88] She suggests that a list of statutory exceptions may resolve this. However, such lists are prone to inaccuracies,[89] and her choice not to rule out theft (which includes an element of ulterior mens rea) is demonstration of exactly that risk:[90] the law does not recognize the actus reus of theft as deserving of criminalization without D's ulterior intention to permanently deprive (even where V suffers the same loss[91]), so why should it do so where D is intoxicated? There may be a case for criminalization on these facts, but this requires *separate* consideration. The second category of crimes to expose problems for the Williams offence, building on the first, is any offence where a mens rea of intention or knowledge is required (e.g. knowledge for complicity, intentional touching for sexual offences, knowledge that the victim is human for homicide, and so on).[92] Here, again, the actus reus of the offence is only deemed to be deserving of criminalization where a high level of mens rea is present, and the assumption that actus reus plus intoxication will be sufficiently blameworthy is on weak footing.[93]

These two illustrations represent the tip of a critical iceberg, and one that does not 'vanish' on recognition that D is being charged with a new intoxication offence.[94] D may be appropriately labelled by Williams' approach, but the question of appropriate criminalization remains unanswered. It is a critical lesson for any new bespoke offence. Simplicity must be valued within an inevitably complex area, and so making use of existing and readily understood concepts is a clear virtue. However, core values of legal principle and fairness must not be overlooked.

88 Ibid 284.

89 JJ Child, 'The Structure, Coherence and Limits of Inchoate Liability: The New Ulterior Element' (2013) 34(4) *Legal Studies* 537, discussing the inadequacy of statutory lists used to limit infinite inchoate liability.

90 R Williams, 'Voluntary Intoxication—A Lost Cause?' (2013) 129 *Law Quarterly Review* 264, 283.

91 Williams highlights that from 'the victim's point of view' a deprivation is theft: Ibid 279. This is true, but the criminal law is concerned with the defendant: where a sober person takes without the intention to permanently deprive there is no theft (despite the victim's deprivation), and thus, without a claim that intoxication is equivalent to such an intention, this does not justify the application of Williams' offence.

92 We have not included examples where an alternative offence (with the same actus reus) allows for a lesser mens rea (e.g. intention to kill or cause serious harm for murder). The examples given are those where intention or knowledge is required for D's conduct to be considered criminal *at all*.

93 This point is used by Horder to defend the current specific/basic intent distinction: J Horder, 'Sobering Up? The Law Commission on Criminal Intoxication' (1995) 58(4) *Modern Law Review* 534, 538–39.

94 R Williams, 'Voluntary Intoxication—A Lost Cause?' (2013) 129 *Law Quarterly Review* 264, 283. Virgo had previously discounted a model of this kind, describing it as 'absurdly wide': G Virgo, 'The Law Commission Consultation Paper on Intoxication and Criminal Liability' [1993] *Criminal Law Review* 415, 422.

5.5 Conclusion

This chapter has provided an essential context for our preferred bespoke offence, to be built upon in the following two chapters. There is a clear case in principle for a bespoke offence constructed on the concept of culpable incapacity, and for the abolition of prior fault^{OFF} rules that such an offence would enable. However, as we have discussed in this chapter, the construction of a fair and practically workable bespoke offence is not straightforward, and any proposal is likely to involve compromise.

The key now is to extract lessons that can be taken forward. Three areas warrant particular mention, and will be explored further in subsequent chapters. The first is the need for conceptual clarity in the identification of a bespoke offence mischief, along the spectrum from a T1-focused to a T2-focused offence. It is notable that most bespoke offence examples in this chapter held a predominantly T1 focus, locating fault in D's conscious decision to become incapacitated. However, the question remains whether a singular T1 focus can represent an adequate response to a range of quite different harms at T2, or whether (as we have seen) some manner of T2 variation should be built into the offence. The second area is characterized by questions of labelling and sentence, and the need for both accurately to track and describe the mischief targeted for criminalization. If the abolition of current prior fault^{OFF} rules is (at least in part) driven by problems of inappropriate labelling, it is obviously unacceptable to reintroduce such problems within a new bespoke offence. Finally, the third area is one of procedural clarity and workability, a point of major concern for almost all the bespoke offence proposals discussed in the chapter.

We set out and justify our proposal for a culpable incapacity offence in Chapter 7, with particular focus on each of the areas identified here. However, before doing so, a different kind of context is provided in Chapter 6, in terms of clinical scientific understanding and validity. Several commentators, ourselves included, have highlighted the essential role of scientific enquiry to supplement and inform the legal debates outlined in this chapter. But the reality of current legal debate has been quite different, as demonstrated in this chapter and those preceding it in Part I, where gestures to scientific and clinical understanding or workability are typically made without much, if any, empirical engagement. The next chapter seeks to remedy that gap in the debate, demonstrating how existing empirical studies and insights can (and should) feed into our bespoke offence proposal, including findings and understanding from our own empirical studies, which we designed with this specific task in mind.

6

EMPIRICAL INSIGHTS TOWARDS A PRIOR FAULT BESPOKE OFFENCE

6.1 Introduction

When discussing legal responses to mental impairment and prior fault^{OFF},[1] whether resulting from intoxication or otherwise, our normative position is inevitably shaped by a set of psychological and/or pharmacological assumptions (often referred to as 'folk psychology'). We make assumptions, for example, about the increased likelihood of mistake making when impaired, about what someone is likely to foresee when becoming impaired at T1, about their ability to control and/or desist across T1–T2, and so on. Such assumptions are informed by personal and collective experiences of impairment, and particularly so in the case of more common experiences such as alcohol intoxication. However, in the development of a potential bespoke offence, it is crucial that any assumptions can be demonstrated to be scientifically and clinically robust, and where there is scientific and/or clinical uncertainty, that uncertainty is acknowledged and accounted for within the law.

Unfortunately, when discussing the assumptions that underpin prior fault, there has been a tendency to foreground folk psychology without reference to more robust sources of scientific and clinical data.[2] We have already highlighted this criticism in previous chapters, applicable to the courts as well as within academic debate, and we have provided references to the scientific and clinical literature where appropriate. However, to engage the scientific deficit more fully, we set aside this chapter to provide some focused space for discussion.

Here, moving beyond critique of the current law, our aim is to demonstrate how empirical data can and should inform our choices in the construction of a new bespoke offence. In this manner, we refocus on several of the offence-relevant questions discussed in the previous chapter, particularly regarding the potential

[1] As introduced in Chapter 1, we are adopting the notation 'prior fault^{OFF}' and 'prior fault^{DEF}' to distinguish between prior fault rules relevant to the construction of a crime and prior fault rules relevant to the blocking of a defence.

[2] Discussed in Yaffe G, 'Intoxication, Recklessness and Negligence' (2012) 9(2) *Ohio St Journal of Criminal Law* 545, 549. See useful analysis, in the Australian context, in J Quilter and L McNamara, 'The Meaning of "Intoxication" in Australian Criminal Cases: Origins and Operation' (2018) 21(1) *New Criminal Law Review* 170.

Prior Fault Criminalization. John J Child, Adrian Hunt, and Hans S. Crombag, Oxford University Press.
 DOI: 10.1093/9780191874734.003.0007

scope for prior fault^{OFF} beyond intoxication, and the identification of culpability across T1–T2. Our reason for considering this material is that we are attempting to identify a genuine mischief deserving of criminalization, and to construct offence elements that capture it with clarity and fairness. This requires us to, first, articulate theoretically robust markers of blame—what we have characterized above as T1- and T2-focused elements—and, second, to combine those markers into a framework that is both fair and workable in practice. Fairness requires that intuitions about blame and control are tested rather than assumed, and practicality requires that legal thresholds rest on facts that are scientifically robust and, ideally, testable.

Our examination of the empirical and scientific research in this chapter is organized as follows. In Section 6.2, we provide an overview of existing relevant research on different types of incapacity, before focusing on some key conclusions which both provide a basis for critiquing certain key features of the current law on prior fault^{OFF}, as well as some suggesting overarching considerations relevant to prospective legal reform. In Section 6.3, we proceed to explain our own empirical studies which were specifically designed to inform the construction of a bespoke offence by modelling a T1–T2 intoxication scenario, and allowing us to test potential markers of blame within that specific context. In section 6.4, we draw together the main insights from the empirical work, explaining how they provide a basis for mapping a framework for the construction of our preferred bespoke offence criminalizing 'culpable incapacity', the precise details of which will then be considered in depth in Chapter 7.

6.2 Overview of empirical research on self-induced incapacity

Intoxication remains the most familiar and extensively studied example of prior fault, not only within legal scholarship, but also in psychology and the behavioural neurosciences. For this reason, the empirical research on intoxication stands as the most fruitful and instructive paradigm for exploring prior fault^{OFF} in this way, in order to illustrate how voluntary intoxication can foreseeably produce impairment and the conditions under which people act erroneously or harmfully. Within that context, alcohol has attracted more scrutiny than any other psychoactive substance due to its licit status, availability, prevalence of use, and deep social embeddedness. This together with its complex and well-documented association with offending have made it an enduring focus of inquiry across disciplines. But, as we will see in this chapter, the relevant research is not confined to alcohol intoxication, and also involves work on impairment produced by other psychoactive drugs. In addition, beyond drug-induced intoxication, there is also instructive research on other sources of incapacity, such as sleep deprivation, to which attention should be paid.

So, broadly speaking, we can say there are three different, but related, relevant areas of research to be highlighted in this context. These are research on alcohol intoxication and impairment, research on non-alcohol intoxication and impairment, and research on non-intoxicated impairment. We briefly summarize aspects of this work below, before proceeding to highlight some headline conclusions which emerge from that research.

6.2.1 Alcohol and impairment

Survey evidence shows considerable correlative associations between alcohol and violent incidents, with alcohol implicated in roughly two-fifths of violent incidents,[3] and in nearly half of those resulting in injury.[4] This suggests an effect of intoxication by alcohol not just in the odds of violent incidents, but also on their seriousness.[5]

Yet, for present purposes, the significance of intoxication lies less in this well-recognized correlation with violence, than in its role as a mechanism for mistake making. Alcohol, like most other psychoactive drugs, interferes with the cognitive and behavioural systems upon which accurate judgement and self-control depend. As we shall see, even moderate levels of intoxication, pharmacologically disrupt brain systems responsible for attentional mechanisms, decision-making, and inhibitory control processes, producing measurable increases in impulsive and erroneous responses. Additionally, experimental studies show that intoxicated participants are slower to detect hazards, more likely to misinterpret social cues, and less able to correct errors once made.[6] In social-cognitive paradigms, these effects often manifest as a narrowing of attention or what Steele and Josephs in their 1990 paper[7] called 'alcohol myopia', describing how the drinker focuses on the most immediate and salient aspects of a situation while neglecting peripheral or contextual information that would otherwise guide restraint. This same attentional narrowing can be applied to understand intoxication-related aggression,[8]

[3] Office for National Statistics, *Nature of Crime: Violence* (ONS Centre for Crime and Justice, 2024) Table 9a.

[4] Ibid Table 9b.

[5] It is this link, with not just the likelihood but also the seriousness of offending, that arguably forms the basis for alcohol's status as an aggravating factor at criminal sentencing; see, e.g., C Lightowlers, *Intoxication and Sentencing: A Review of Policy, Practice and Research* (Sentencing Academy, 2022).

[6] CA Marczinski and MT Fillmor, 'Acute Alcohol Tolerance on Subjective Intoxication and Simulated Driving Performance in Binge Drinkers' (2009) 23 *Psychology of Addictive Behaviors* 238; K Bombeke et al, 'The Effect of Alcohol and Placebo on Post-error Adjustments' (2013) 7 *Frontiers in Human Neuroscience* 3; KR Ridderinkhof et al, 'Alcohol Consumption Impairs Detection of Performance Errors in Mediofrontal Cortex' (2002) 298 *Science* 2209.

[7] C Steele and R Josephs, 'Alcohol Myopia. Its Prized and Dangerous Effects' (1990) 45 *The American Psychologist* 921.

[8] PR Giancola, AA Duke, and KZ Ritz, 'Alcohol, Violence, and the Alcohol Myopia Model: Preliminary Findings and Implications for Prevention' (2011) 36 *Addictive Behaviors* 1019.

and accounts for a wider pattern of misjudgement and error seen with intoxication: the missed warning sign, the misread threat, the overconfident decision to act when one should not, and so forth.

6.2.2 Non-alcohol intoxicated impairment

Although alcohol produces well-characterized and broadly predictable impairments in cognitive capacity, other drugs also interact with cognition and behaviour often in more varied and contingent ways. This in part is to do with the different mechanisms in the brain that alcohol as distinct from other drugs impact on, with alcohol impacting (in opposite directions) inhibitory and excitatory cellular (receptor) mechanisms ubiquitous throughout the central nervous system. And like alcohol, but in some instances more so, the effects of other drugs vary in often complex ways depending on dose, context, and the presence of underlying vulnerabilities, including mental health conditions. This complexity, common to psychoactive drugs, should not be mistaken for the absence of impairment (the incapacitating effects of these substances are real, even if less easily generalized).

Psychomotor stimulant drugs such as cocaine and amphetamines (that produce their effects principally by acting on monoamine receptor mechanisms more confined to deeper-laying areas of the forebrain) illustrate the point. At lower doses they may heighten alertness and perceived energy, and at moderate doses these effects are heightened and accompanied by hyperactivity, but at higher doses they frequently produce agitation, stereotyped behaviours, paranoia, loss of impulse control, and can even lead to psychotic break. These are states strongly associated with violent offences, but also predictive of contact with the criminal justice system for any type of criminal offence.[9] Like alcohol, stimulants also exacerbate underlying psychiatric vulnerabilities, making it difficult to separate pharmacological effects from those interactions. The result is a pattern of impairment that may be less linear than with alcohol, yet equally destructive of rational judgement and restraint.

Cannabis likewise reveals the complexities of drug-related incapacity. While, like alcohol, cannabis is often associated with relaxation or altered perception, sustained or early-onset use has been linked to an elevated risk of psychosis. And whilst cannabis is less likely to 'cause' psychosis in the general population, it can trigger or accelerate symptoms in those with genetic or prodromal (the initial stages of psychosis) vulnerabilities.[10] Here again, incapacity arises not just from

[9] S Fazel et al, 'Antipsychotics, Mood Stabilisers, and Risk of Violent Crime' (2014) 384 *Lancet* 1206; N Yee et al, 'A Meta-analysis of the Relationship Between Psychosis and Any Type of Criminal Offending, in Both Men and Women' (2020) 220 *Schizophrenia Research* 16.

[10] A Paparelli et al, 'Drug-Induced Psychosis: How to Avoid Star Gazing in Schizophrenia Research by Looking at More Obvious Sources of Light' (2011) 5 *Frontiers in Behavioral Neuroscience* <https://doi.org/10.3389/fnbeh.2011.00001>.

immediate and direct pharmacological actions, but from the drug's potential to precipitate existing cognitive disturbance.

We provide these examples to underline that although the impairments produced by psychoactive substances, especially non-alcohol drugs, are often more complex and variable than is the case with alcohol, they share many of the same features and, like alcohol, can also produce significant impairments that interact with other factors such as mental health disorders in similar ways.

6.2.3 Non-intoxicated forms of incapacity

The widespread effects of alcohol on the cognitive and behavioural function necessary for 'normal' behavioural regulation discussed above, combined with its broad availability and social acceptance, give it a central, paradigmatic place in the research. However, the significance of alcohol in the research does not lie in intoxication alone, but also because a wide body of research shows that the cognitive and behavioural impairments linked to alcohol are paralleled in other, non-intoxicated forms of incapacity relevant to our inquiry. Moderate sleep deprivation, for instance, produces deficits in motor and cognitive performance similar to those found at legally permitted blood-alcohol levels for driving.[11] Indeed, more severe (total) sleep deprivation impairs the ability to revise decisions in light of feedback, while the combination of alcohol and sleep restriction produces marked reductions in vigilant attention.[12] In short, the functional consequences of incapacity, including slowed responses, impaired updating, and diminished vigilance, emerge across conditions that share little beyond their capacity to undermine cognitive control.

More direct experimental comparisons make the parallel especially clear. Dawson and Reid,[13] for instance, were able to demonstrate that seventeen hours of wakefulness produces psychomotor performance deficits comparable to a blood alcohol concentration (BAC) of 0.05 per cent, rising to roughly 0.10 per cent after twenty-four hours without sleep. Noting that in England & Wales, the legal limit for driving is 0.08 per cent BAC (higher than in most other regions, including Scotland where the legal limit is 0.04 per cent BAC), subsequent work has confirmed that both fatigue and intoxication disrupt the same wide range of executive functions[14]—vigilance, working memory, inhibitory control, and

[11] P Whitney et al, 'Feedback Blunting: Total Sleep Deprivation Impairs Decision Making that Requires Updating Based on Feedback' (2015) 38 *Sleep* 745.

[12] J Lee et al, 'Alcohol and Sleep Restriction Combined Reduces Vigilant Attention, Whereas Sleep Restriction Alone Enhances Distractibility' (2015) 38 *Sleep* 765.

[13] D Dawson and K Reid, 'Fatigue, Alcohol and Performance Impairment' (1997) 388 *Nature* 235; but also P Maruff et al, 'Fatigue-related Impairment in the Speed, Accuracy and Variability of Psychomotor Performance: Comparison with Blood Alcohol Levels' (2005) 14 *Journal of Sleep Research* 21.

[14] Executive function refers to a set of high-level cognitive processes, including working memory, inhibitory control, and cognitive flexibility, that enable goal-directed behaviours, primarily mediated

error detection—leading to more frequent mistakes and poorer awareness of those mistakes once made. Neurobiological studies also indicate overlapping mechanisms: for instance, alcohol and sleep deprivation both appear to impair higher cognitive function through adenosine-related modulation of attention and self-control.[15]

Similarly, non-adherence to prescribed medication—estimated to affect approximately 40–50 per cent of individuals with chronic illness—is well documented.[16] In psychiatric and neurological conditions in particular, lapses in adherence can result in marked decrements in attention, inhibitory control, and error monitoring that are functionally comparable to those observed under intoxication or sleep deprivation. Analogous considerations apply to individuals with other recognized vulnerabilities, such as those with diabetes who are prone to hypoglycaemic episodes, or persons with severe stress- or trauma-related disorders who often fail to take preventive measures despite the foreseeability of deterioration. Thus—whether through failed medication adherence, condition management, or responsiveness to warning signs—the resulting deficits in control and decision-making are functionally similar and, in principle, open to attribution of blame.

6.2.4 Key Headlines from the existing research

The behavioural, psychological, and neural evidence converge on a common picture: intoxication research provides not merely a lens on alcohol-specific impairment and incapacity, but a general model for understanding how various conditions can create a similar type of incapacity. This is the case whether mental impairment is induced by alcohol, other psychoactive drugs, or other contextual non-drug factors such as lack of sleep or medication non-adherence. Each one may contribute to mistake making relevant to the criminal law, or increases the risk of doing so.

It is also the case that we are presented with a more complicated picture than existing legal doctrines and approaches seem willing to allow or contemplate, which we highlight in the subsections below: namely, that it is an error to treat intoxication as a proxy for fault (Section 6.2.4.1), that impairment is a spectrum rather than

by the prefrontal cortex. These functions allow individuals to plan, focus attention, manage tasks, and regulate impulses effectively.

[15] EM Elmenhorst et al, 'Cognitive Impairments by Alcohol and Sleep Deprivation Indicate Trait Characteristics and a Potential Role for Adenosine A(1) receptors' (2018) 115 *Proceedings of the National Academy of Sciences of the United States of America* 8009.

[16] F Kleinsinger, 'The Unmet Challenge of Medication Nonadherence' (2018) 22 *The Permanente Journal* 18.

a binary on–off state (Section 6.2.4.2), and that impairment includes progressive incapacity to self-monitor or correct errors (Section 6.2.4.3).

6.2.4.1 Treating 'intoxication' as a proxy for fault is an error

It is simply wrong to treat 'intoxication' as a proxy for all fault-based incapacity. Although alcohol provides the paradigm for scientific research and insight, and is most commonly associated with harmful behaviour, other forms of self-induced intoxication and non-intoxicated impairment can lead to the same forms of incapacity, producing the sorts of mistake making and poor judgement relevant to our prior fault^{OFF} analysis. Each involves conduct at T1 potentially leading to increased risks of harms caused by or linked to that decision-making subsequently at T2. The research therefore presents a *prima facie* case for all such causes of self-induced incapacity to be treated in like manner by the law, regardless of whether the person is drunk, intoxicated by other means, or incapacitated in a non-intoxicated sense.

From a legal perspective, the challenge lies not in establishing that such impairments exist—as indicated above they plainly do—but rather in determining whether, where, and when it is appropriate to blame people for creating a condition (whether through alcohol, other drugs, or for some other non-drug reason) which compromises their volition and/or rational capacities.

6.2.4.2 Impairment is a spectrum rather than a binary on–off state

The current law typically views incapacity as a binary state or condition, either a person possesses the requisite capacities for voluntariness and mens rea or they do not. The empirical record tells a more nuanced story, showing instead what is better described as a 'spectrum of impairment'.

Alcohol provides a useful example of this spectrum of impairment, though (again) comparable impairments also arise for other drugs and non-drug conditions.[17] Neurocognitive studies show that at low BACs, even before overt signs of intoxication or drunkenness, deficits in divided attention and executive functioning are measurable.[18] Experimental work shows complex dose-effect curves: divided attention and inhibitory control decline at modest levels—so individuals may therefore appear outwardly composed while already cognitively compromised—whereas selective attention and motor coordination deteriorate

[17] See P Philip et al, 'Fatigue, Sleep Restriction, and Performance in Automobile Drivers: A Controlled Study in a Natural Environment' (2003) 26 *Sleep* 277. Psychoactive substances display similar patterns: acute cannabis intoxication impairs working memory and temporal estimation, psychostimulants such as cocaine and amphetamines can provoke impulsivity or paranoid misperceptions, and sedatives including benzodiazepines slow psychomotor responses and blunt hazard detection. Thus, despite divergent pharmacological mechanisms, the resultant impairments, diminished inhibitory control, attentional narrowing, and degraded self-monitoring consistently align within a shared spectrum of cognitive incapacity.

[18] SA Grant, K Millar, and GN Kenny, 'Blood Alcohol Concentration and Psychomotor Effects' (2000) 85 *British Journal of Anaesthesia* 401.

typically at higher concentrations.[19] Such studies consistently show that alcohol impairs inhibitory control well before gross intoxication occurs: participants tend to act more impulsively and exhibit slower stopping latencies, reflecting a breakdown in self-regulation.[20] Neuroimaging studies associate these effects with attenuated prefrontal activation,[21] showing that intoxication weakens behavioural restraint by directly interfering with those neural systems that enable restraint. And even small 'priming' doses of alcohol have been found to increase risk-taking and premature responding, behavioural signatures of degraded judgement rather than mere motor slippage.[22] Driving simulation and vigilance studies provide a similar picture. Even moderate intoxication by alcohol slows hazard detection and delays corrective action.[23]

These studies, and a range of other evidence,[24] show that the legal perspective of incapacity/intoxication as an on–off condition or state cannot withstand the scientific evidence. Binary thresholds, between 'voluntary' and 'involuntary', 'capable' and 'incapable', obscure the fact that impairment unfolds gradually, varies across cognitive domains, and often comes with an inability to perceive its own onset. A more accurate view recognizes incapacity/intoxication as graded and cumulative.

6.2.4.3 Impairment includes progressive incapacity to self-monitor or correct errors

A particularly revealing dimension of impaired capacity is the ability to recognize and correct one's own mistakes. Error detection is central to behavioural regulation: when a person misperceives a situation or acts inappropriately, awareness of the error allows rapid correction. Alcohol undermines this process twice over by increasing the number of errors and dulling awareness that they have occurred.

[19] H Moskowitz and D Fiorentino, *A Review of the Literature on the Effects of Low Doses of Alcohol on Driving Related Skills* (US Dept of Transportation, NHTSA, Report No DOT HS 807 280, 2000); RWM Zoethout et al, 'Functional Biomarkers for the Acute Effects of Alcohol on the Central Nervous System in Healthy Volunteers' (2011) 71 *British Journal of Clinical Pharmacology* 331.

[20] AK Rose and T Duka, 'Effects of Alcohol on Inhibitory Processes' (2008) 19 *Behavioural Pharmacology* 284.

[21] BM Anderson et al, 'Functional Imaging of Cognitive Control During Acute Alcohol Intoxication' (2011) 35 *Alcoholism, Clinical and Experimental Research* 156.

[22] CA Marczinski and MT Fillmore, 'Acute Alcohol Tolerance on Subjective Intoxication and Simulated Driving Performance in Binge Drinkers' (2009) 23 *Psychology of Addictive Behaviors* 238.

[23] DA Deery and AW Love, 'The Effect of a Moderate Dose of Alcohol on the Traffic Hazard Perception Profile of Young Drink-Drivers' (1996) 91 *Addiction* 815; R West et al, 'Effect of Low and Moderate Doses of Alcohol on Driving Hazard Perception Latency and Driving Speed' (1993) 88 *Addiction* 527.

[24] See also, e.g., CE Kaestle et al, 'Perception of Intoxication in a Field Study of the Night-Time Economy: Blood Alcohol Concentration, Patron Characteristics, and Event-Level Predictors' (2018) 76 *Addictive Behaviors* 195; N Droste et al, 'Comparing Levels of Blood Alcohol Concentration and Indicators of Impairment in Nightlife Patrons' (2018) 37 Suppl 1 *Drug and Alcohol Review* S348; C Steele and R Josephs, 'Alcohol Myopia. Its Prized and Dangerous Effects' (1990) 45 *The American Psychologist* 921.

Neurophysiological studies trace this pattern to alcohol's blunting of the *error-related negativity* (ERN) signal in frontal brain regions, a neural marker normally generated within milliseconds of an error.[25] Intoxicated individuals therefore not only make more mistakes on vigilance and decision-making tasks, but are also less likely to notice and correct them. To compound the problem, alcohol dampens the emotional response to error: participants feel less discomfort or shame, weakening learning from mistakes and increasing the likelihood of repeating them.[26]

Metacognitive research reveals a parallel failure of self-evaluation. Honan et al,[27] for instance, found that intoxicated participants remained highly confident even as their performance declined, indicating a confidence–accuracy dissociation. And a similar overconfidence can appear under fatigue, where participants underestimate how far their performance has deteriorated despite clear evidence to the contrary.[28] Across these states, self-monitoring erodes in step with performance: the individual becomes both less capable and less aware of that incapacity. This deterioration of metacognition helps explain why those who have voluntarily impaired themselves may genuinely lack adequate awareness of their risk of error when acting.

It follows from this that we should be mindful of this scientific and empirical evidence when making assumptions about foresight and blame. The evidence does not support, for example, simple characterizations of intoxication as recklessness, where it is assumed that D will have foreseen specific future incapacitated errors. The causal links between error-making and incapacity are quite robust, but this is not true of D's foresight and/or awareness of error. As a result, the relevant mischief becomes more objective: it is not intoxication itself, but rather the *foreseeable creation* of a state of diminished capacity—one that materially heightens the risk of harmful or criminal error—which provides a more robust footing for the law.

6.3 Our Empirical Studies

In the preceding section, we have drawn on the extensive scientific literature, produced across countless international laboratories, to outline when and how intoxication—and other factors such as sleep deprivation—impair attention, judgement, and self-monitoring in ways that predictably increase the likelihood

[25] KR Ridderinkhof et al, 'Alcohol Consumption Impairs Detection of Performance Errors in Mediofrontal Cortex' (2002) 298 *Science* 2209.

[26] BD Bartholow et al, 'Alcohol Effects on Performance Monitoring and Adjustment: Affect Modulation and Impairment of Evaluative Cognitive Control' (2012) 121 *Journal of Abnormal Psychology* 173.

[27] CA Honan et al, 'Alcohol Intoxication Impairs Recognition of Fear and Sadness in Others and Metacognitive Awareness of Emotion Recognition Ability' (2018) 18 *Emotion* (Washington, DC) 842.

[28] HP Van Dongen et al, 'The Cumulative Cost of Additional Wakefulness: Dose-Response Effects on Neurobehavioral Functions and Sleep Physiology from Chronic Sleep Restriction and Total Sleep Deprivation' (2003) 26 *Sleep* 117.

of mistake making. Yet, much of this research employs procedures and tasks—and is often constrained by legal dosage limits and laboratory conventions—that are somewhat removed from the capacities and contexts most relevant to law. In particular, few studies examine impairments as they manifest in settings directly tied to legally significant errors: the taking of unlawful risks, the commission of offences, or mistaken acts of self-defence when no threat exists.

For these reasons, we set out to design a series of studies aimed at bringing the scientific evidence and the legal debate into closer alignment—each informing and reinforcing the other. Our studies aimed to explore this relationship more directly: to examine how intoxication gives rise to legally relevant mistakes, which types of mistakes become more likely, and where along the spectrum of impairment those mistakes begin to emerge. We also sought to test how fault might be understood empirically: whether in the foresight of impairment, foresight of mistake making, or in the failure to recognize and manage it once impaired.

6.3.1 Study overview and experimental setting

We conducted two complementary studies: one laboratory-based, one field-based, employing multiple tasks including a hazard perception and eye-tracking task, and a combined social-emotional recognition and response-intentions task. Together, these allow comparison between controlled (laboratory) and naturalistic settings, moderate and high intoxication, and different types of errors relevant to legal responsibility.

The experimental tasks were designed to investigate intoxicated mistake making, of a kind most relevant to real legal contexts. This included errors of perception, interpretation, and response, including errors that create risk or harm, misreadings of hostility or fear, and failures to disengage from conflict. Our goal was to model such errors in a setting where participants' cognitive mechanisms and subjective awareness could be measured.

6.3.1.1 Participants and screening

All participants were healthy adults aged between eighteen and thirty-five, and were mostly students at the University of Sussex.[29] As is typical for this style of experiment (and to adhere to Health & Safety and Ethical requirements), participants' prescreening excluded those who we identified as having an alcohol or other drug dependence, any psychiatric conditions, or using medications contraindicated with alcohol. Only moderate social drinkers were eligible. Participants provided written informed consent after reading an information sheet explaining the nature and risks of the study.

[29] Brighton, UK.

6.3.1.2 Alcohol administration

The laboratory study was conducted in the Human Psychopharmacology Unit at the University of Sussex. Participants were randomly assigned to one of four conditions: sober control, placebo (believing they had consumed alcohol but receiving none), moderate intoxication (target BAC ≈ 0.04 per cent), or high intoxication (≈ 0.08 per cent). Beverages were prepared and administered under double-blind conditions, meaning neither participant nor experimenter knew who received alcohol (and who did not) until after testing. This also meant that control and alcoholic drinks were presented with artificial flavour and smells to mask the taste and smell of alcohol. Actual alcohol intoxication levels (%BAC, extrapolated from measured breath alcohol level) were verified before and after testing with a calibrated breathalyser.

In our field study, participants were recruited from nightlife venues at the bars on the campus of the University of Sussex, simply by setting up our experiment equipment in a room adjacent from the main bar area, and soliciting customers who were seen drinking an alcoholic beverage. Anyone appearing to be extremely intoxicated (unsteady, incoherent, or otherwise deemed unable to participate safely) was not approached for testing. This way, BAC levels that were tested ranged widely but rarely exceeded 0.15 per cent.

6.3.1.3 Experimental setup

Our experimental tasks were computer based. In the laboratory, testing was conducted in a quiet room using a desktop computer equipped with a high-resolution eye-tracking system. In the field, equivalent tasks were presented on portable tablets and/or PC with the same eye-trackers. The eye-tracking data (measuring gaze location, duration, fixation, as well as pupil responses) provided information of where and how participants directed their attention in our hazard perception task, whether towards relevant stimuli (e.g. a pedestrian or approaching vehicle) or elsewhere in irrelevant areas.

6.3.2 Experimental tasks and key findings

Below we briefly explain the experimental tasks and outcomes. We present this work here in a form we think suited to this forum, and primarily with a legal audience in mind. Full reporting of the experiments and data will be published separately, in scientific journals.[30]

[30] P Manguele, K Nikolaou, N Sinclair-House, HS Crombag, and JJ Child, 'Empirical Insights into Acute Alcohol Intoxication, Mistake-making, and Self-Defence: Testing Problematic Criminal Law Assumptions in the Laboratory and Field' (Forthcoming).

6.3.2.1 Emotion recognition task and outcomes

In what we called the 'emotion recognition task', participants viewed a series of faces expressing the seven basic emotions famously investigated and described by psychologist Paul Ekman as being universal emotions.[31] This included happiness, sadness, fear, anger, disgust, surprise, as well as neutral—at varying intensities. The facial expressions were made using computer-generated avatars that slowly developed starting from neutral to eventually the full emotional expression. The task for participants was to, as quickly and accurately as possible, correctly identify and indicate which expression was developing by pressing a key on the computer keyboard. Once they did (also providing a measure of speed of recognition), they were asked to select the appropriate emotion label from a list. The task can thus be described as a social perception probe: testing the ability to infer others' emotional states promptly and correctly, and intended to measure the effects of intoxication on errors that are legally salient because they parallel misjudgements of consent, fear, threat, or provocation.

In line with other comparable studies,[32] we found that accuracy declined as intoxication increased, with errors clustering around affiliative emotions—especially happiness and sadness[33]—which were more often misclassified as neutral or mildly hostile. This distortion of social perception shows how intoxication can lead to misinterpretations of another's state or intentions. Taken together with findings of others, these distortions are not random, but systematic, reflecting a predictable degradation of perception of critical social cues in the interpersonal environmental context.

In legal terms, we propose that misreadings such as these could underlie mistaken beliefs about consent, distress, threat, or provocation. These lapses reflect legally significant omissions, akin to those found in negligence and endangerment offences. Importantly, they arise not from deliberate risk-taking, but from a compromised ability to perceive and respond to foreseeable danger; the type of incapacity that the law might well view as avoidable, and therefore blameworthy when attributed to earlier voluntary intoxication or other causal roots.

[31] P Ekman, ER Sorenson, and WV Friesen, 'Pan-Cultural Elements in Facial Displays of Emotion' (1969) 164 *Science* 86. See Chapter 9, Section 9.4 for further discussion.

[32] See AS Attwood and MR Munafò, 'Effects of Acute Alcohol Consumption and Processing of Emotion in Faces: Implications for Understanding Alcohol-Related Aggression' (2014) 28 *Journal of Psychopharmacology* 719; LC Craig et al, 'Effects of Acute Alcohol Consumption and Alcohol Expectancy on Processing of Perceptual Cues of Emotional Expression' (2009) 23 *Journal of Psychopharmacology* 258.

[33] Though negatively valanced, we categorize sadness here as affiliative as it is widely understood to (also) serve affiliative interpersonal functions by signalling vulnerability and eliciting support, and so distinct from threat-related emotions such as anger or fear.

6.3.2.2 Hostility response task and outcomes

On separate trials viewing similar stimuli—but now focused on either hostile or non-hostile facial expressions—participants were then asked to indicate whether they would approach or avoid the face/person they were viewing, with some facial expression being clearly hostile, and others showing neutral or a positive emotion. The task was thus intended to measure (instinctive) approach/avoidance tendencies in response to perceived threat. This design captured a different class of error, persisting in or escalating risky interactions that might be an important consideration in instances of claimed self-defence,[34] as well as situations involving criminal harassment and/or assault contexts.

Importantly, and unique in our studies, we found that these same intoxicated participants also showed reduced tendency to avoid hostile faces, and even at higher intoxication levels in our field studies, they were as likely to approach threatening as neutral stimuli, suggesting a significant change in normal self-protective behaviour. In simple terms, they were less likely to 'get out of bad situations'. These findings require further investigation in the future to better understand dose-effect relation, the reasons underlying these trends, and relations to past experiences. However, they already provide pointers to the type of escalation dynamics we see in alcohol-related violence, where intoxication-impaired individuals engage and persist in confrontations they might otherwise avoid, being more likely to maintain engagement with perceived threats, and less likely to withdraw or de-escalate. This behavioural shift might go some way to explain many real-world cases of alcohol-related violence, where conflict is misread or provocation is exaggerated.

For the law, these findings speak to mistaken self-defence, public-order offences, provocation, etc. A person who misperceives threat and responds with force may sincerely believe their actions are justified. However, when such beliefs stem from predictable impairments in perception and control, responsibility can be grounded not in the reaction itself, but in the earlier decision to compromise one's capacity for restraint. We return in Chapter 9, Section 9.4 to these findings in the context of mistaken self-defence scenarios.

6.3.2.3 Hazard perception task and outcomes

Our hazard perception study modelled perceptual and attentional errors analogous to what might be described as negligent or reckless acts. Participants viewed short video clips depicting everyday situations, some from a typical driver's perspective (akin to a hazard perception task administered when sitting the theory portion of a driving examination) and half from a pedestrian's or cyclist's viewpoint. The task was similar to those described above, but now (intoxicated)

[34] Discussed further in Chapter 9, Section 9.4.

participants were asked, as accurately and quickly as they could, to press a keyboard key as soon as a potential hazard was perceived (e.g. a pedestrian stepping from the kerb, a turning vehicle, a sudden obstruction, etc).

Simultaneously, as we collected participants' behavioural responses, eye-tracking data was recorded to capture gaze dispersion and fixation durations, allowing us to measure attentional processes and changes in vigilance under different alcohol conditions. In essence, the task aimed to simulate 'real-world blundering'[35] and/or participants' abilities to (mis)detect, (mis)identify, and (mis) respond to environmental cues to danger.

Behavioural performance was assessed using signal detection indices (discrimination sensitivity and response criterion), hit rates, false-alarm rates, mean reaction times (RTs), and RT variability.[36] In the laboratory setting, alcohol intoxication did not significantly affect any of these behavioural measures.[37] These null effects suggest that, under controlled laboratory conditions, low-to-moderate levels of intoxication were not sufficient to disrupt hazard perception performance. However, clear intoxication-related impairments emerged in the field study, with higher levels of intoxication. Discrimination sensitivity declined significantly as a function of %BAC, with participants in highest BAC groups showing the poorest ability to distinguish hazards from non-hazards. Hit rates similarly decreased with increasing intoxication, with highly intoxicated participants detecting significantly fewer hazards than those less intoxicated.[38] Taken together, the results suggest that alcohol intoxication impairs hazard perception primarily through reduced sensitivity to environmental cues signalling danger, rather than through impulsive responding or global slowing.

These lapses reflect legally significant omissions, akin to those found in negligence and endangerment offences. Importantly, again, they arise not from deliberate risk-taking but from a compromised ability to perceive and respond to foreseeable danger; the type of incapacity that the law might well view as avoidable, and therefore blameworthy when attributed to earlier voluntary intoxication or other causal root.

[35] On intoxication as 'blundering', see J Horder, 'Sobering Up? The Law Commission on Criminal Intoxication' (1995) 58 *Modern Law Review* 534.

[36] Discrimination sensitivity (denoted by d') describes how well someone can tell the difference between real dangers and safe situations. Response criterion (denoted by c) describes how cautious a person is about saying that a danger is present. Hit rate is how often someone correctly spots a real hazard, while false alarms are times when they report a hazard that was not actually there.

[37] Discrimination sensitivity, response criterion, hit rates, false-alarm rates, mean RTs, and RT variability were statistically the same across control, placebo, moderate, and high-dose groups.

[38] Importantly, false-alarm rates did not increase with intoxication, indicating that alcohol did not just cause more indiscriminate or impulsive responding. Instead, the deficits reflected a reduced capacity to correctly detect genuine hazards. In this manner, alcohol selectively disrupted perceptual sensitivity and hazard detection accuracy.

6.3.2.4 Confidence and awareness of impairment

Our findings across all experimental task data support a particular interpretation regarding foresight (T1) and contemporaneous awareness (T2). Consistent with previous work,[39] we observed that confidence rose with intoxication, even as and while performance declined. Participants told us they believed they were performing competently despite objective evidence to the contrary. However, when asked how *impaired* they felt overall, their self-assessments tracked actual impairment more closely.

This suggests a dissociation between general awareness of impairment and task-specific confidence. Many acknowledged being affected by alcohol, yet remained highly confident in their immediate judgements or responses. Indeed, the pattern demonstrates that metacognitive insight can operate on multiple levels: people may hold an abstract belief that they are impaired without integrating that awareness into moment-to-moment decision-making.

Under conditions that diminish self-monitoring such as intoxication by alcohol, drugs, or fatigue, subjective feelings of fluency can remain strong and misleading. As a result, individuals can recognize impairment in theory yet still act with undue confidence in practice. It is a gap between foresight and contemporaneous self-assurance that highlights the limits of relying on T2 awareness to regulate behaviour and to inform future T1 foresight.

6.3.2.5 From mistake to fault: Awareness as the locus of culpability

A further consistent theme across our studies was the dissociation between impairment awareness and behavioural restraint. Participants often acknowledged, in general terms, that their abilities were compromised. Yet, this awareness rarely translated into caution or reduced confidence in specific tasks.

This suggests that T1 confidence and the belief, prior to intoxication, that one can maintain control is a poor predictor of actual performance. What matters more is the awareness of impairment at T2, and the subsequent failure to adjust behaviour in light of that awareness, much in line with the earlier mentioned behavioural and physiological work on alcohol's effects on the ERN signal in the frontal regions of the brain.[40] In other words, the legally significant fault lies not in failing to predict a particular mistake, but in continuing to act as if unimpaired, even when one recognizes that impairment is forthcoming.

[39] See CA Honan et al, 'Alcohol Intoxication Impairs Recognition of Fear and Sadness in Others and Metacognitive Awareness of Emotion Recognition Ability' (2018) 18 *Emotion* (Washington, DC) 842; HP Van Dongen et al, 'The Cumulative Cost of Additional Wakefulness: Dose-response Effects on Neurobehavioral Functions and Sleep Physiology from Chronic Sleep Restriction and Total Sleep Deprivation' (2003) 26 *Sleep* 117.

[40] KR Ridderinkhof et al, 'Alcohol Consumption Impairs Detection of Performance Errors in Mediofrontal Cortex' (2002) 298 *Science* 2209.

These patterns support the rationale for a bespoke offence that grounds culpability in foreseeable incapacity and inaction, rather than the fiction of mens rea equivalence. By identifying the kinds of mistake that arise under self-induced impairment and demonstrating that individuals are often aware of their compromised state, our findings help with the process of articulating a principled and evidence-based model of T1–T2 criminalization.

6.4 Mapping the empirical research onto a pathology of 'culpable incapacity'

The empirical literature on intoxication and impairment, along with our own studies, provide a detailed map of how cognitive and behavioural control deteriorate. In this section, we summarize how such findings bear directly on the law's effort to identify reliable markers of blame for self-induced incapacity, leading into our construction of a bespoke offence of culpable incapacity in Chapter 7.

The T1–T2 distinction marks two moments in the temporal sequence of culpable incapacity. T1 referring to the decision to consume alcohol, take a psychoactive substance, or otherwise act in a way that (somewhat) predictably reduces cognitive control. T2 referring to the later moment of impaired action, when judgement and self-monitoring are already degraded. From a cognitive standpoint, these points engage distinct mechanisms: anticipatory foresight at T1, and situational awareness at T2. The key question is whether and what fault should be located for the actor's contemporaneous lack of awareness at the time of conduct (T2) in their earlier decision to enter a state of foreseeable impairment (T1). Experimental data permit a relatively precise analysis of this distinction, revealing when, along the impairment spectrum, legally relevant mistakes become more likely and why situational awareness ceases to be a dependable index of control.

While/because awareness at T2 deteriorates rapidly under intoxication/impairment, this illustrates why the law cannot sensibly ground culpability in contemporaneous insight that is absent in fact. The operative moral and legal question should be located principally at T1, when the individual still possesses capacity to foresee that their chosen conduct will compromise later decision-making and action, and in the time between T1 and T2 as capacity is degraded.

The empirical evidence we have canvassed supports this asymmetry. The ability to predict one's own impairment depends on experience, long-term memory, and social learning, whereas recognizing impairment once it has set in relies on the type of metacognitive monitoring and error-related feedback discussed earlier. However, under intoxication/cognitive impairment, the latter may deteriorate quickly, whereas the former generally remains intact at the point of voluntary consumption or other conduct leading to incapacity. The result is a type of one-way erosion of regulatory mechanisms: once foresight is exercised and impairment begins, awareness cannot recover within the same episode. Individuals knowingly engage in behaviour that foreseeably impairs cognition, but once impaired, lose the very insight required to correct it.

This framework also captures a second, deeper layer of foresight. The blameworthy choice at T1 does not rest merely on knowing that one will become impaired, but on understanding—or having reason to understand—that once impaired, one's capacity for awareness and self-correction will be compromised. The decision therefore includes a recognition of foreseeable unawareness: a voluntary creation of a state in which one's future-self will predictably lack the very insight needed to avoid mistake.

Thus, the empirical pattern points to T1 (dual) foresight capacity as the most reliable marker of blame: the capacity to anticipate (i) incapacity or the loss of inhibition or error correction, or (ii) mistake making such as heightened probability of misperceiving or misjudging risk. Across experimental paradigms, these outcomes are foreseeable, rising predictably along a measurable continuum of impairment.

The thresholds should not be seen as rigid legal cut-offs, but as empirically informed indicators of when self-impairment begins to produce a disproportionate risk of serious error. They identify a practical boundary between 'ordinary' human variation and a state of measurable unreliability. For legal purposes, such thresholds offer an evidential target for attributing fault to voluntarily entering a state while residual foresight remains intact, in which the cognitive systems for monitoring and correcting error are predictably and measurably degraded.

6.5 Conclusion

The empirical evidence reviewed in this chapter shows that intoxication produces predictable patterns of cognitive and behavioural failure. These failures occur across psychological and cognitive domains that are central to legal responsibility: perception, interpretation, inhibition, and vigilance. At modest levels of intoxication, divided attention and social perception begin to degrade; at higher levels, inhibitory control and hazard detection collapse. The resulting mistakes, misreading others' emotions, persisting in escalating encounters, and overlooking obvious risks are not random or idiosyncratic. They follow a graded, reproducible trajectory that can be mapped along the spectrum of alcohol concentration.

Crucially, these impairments are accompanied by a decline in self-monitoring. Individuals retain a reasonable level of awareness that they are impaired, yet this knowledge fails to translate into a form of adaptive restraint. Confidence and performance diverge, producing the paradoxical state in which those least capable of control feel most assured of it. This dissociation is precisely the kind of scientifically demonstrable incapacity that legal doctrine has struggled to capture.

From these findings, two principles emerge for the construction of a bespoke offence of culpable incapacity. First, blameworthiness cannot rest on contemporaneous awareness at T2: by the time legally relevant mistakes occur in circumstances of substantial impairment, the cognitive systems that sustain awareness or attention and control are already compromised. Reliance on real-time capacity would therefore invert responsibility, exempting those most impaired. Second, liability must instead attach to the earlier voluntary act at T1, and/or within the T1–T2 span, during the creation of the condition that foreseeably undermines rational self-regulation. Empirical data now and going forward allow that foreseeability to be defined with some greater precision: thresholds of impairment (e.g. the BAC range at which hazard detection collapses or error-awareness fails) can be identified as markers of foreseeable incapacity.

A scientifically informed offence would therefore criminalize not the fact of intoxication, but the foreseeable creation of a state in which legally relevant mistakes become highly probable, and awareness of those mistakes is predictably lost. It would recognize that incapacity is graded, cumulative, and often accompanied by the very inability to appreciate its presence. Embedding that insight into law would move the doctrine of prior fault^{OFF} beyond fictions of binary capacity and towards a model that aligns culpability with evidence-based thresholds of blame.

7

A NEW OFFENCE OF CULPABLE INCAPACITY

7.1 Introduction

This chapter sets out and explores our recommendations for a new bespoke offence, which we have termed 'culpable incapacity'. The proposed offence aims to capture a distinct multi-event criminal wrong, where D culpably becomes mentally impaired at T1 and causes harm at T2. The offence is designed, in turn, to allow for abolition of all current prior fault^{OFF} rules,[1] including those applicable to prior fault^{OFF} intoxication and automatism.

Our culpable incapacity offence (CI Offence) builds explicitly from the analyses and conclusions regarding prior fault^{OFF} in previous chapters. We begin, for example, with a basic acceptance of the case for criminalization within a subset of examples where D's culpable conduct at T1 leads to harms at T2 in circumstances of mental impairment, with such examples both inside and outside current prior fault^{OFF} rules. Whilst the simple abolition of prior fault^{OFF} *without replacement* is a viable policy option in theory, we do not see it as desirable. There are normative reasons in favour of limited criminalization, recognizing both the potential for culpability among those causing harms when mentally impaired, as well as the goal of harm reduction through better *ex-ante* notice regarding the markers of that culpable behaviour. There are also practical reasons for our acceptance of the case for criminalization since we do not see a viable route to simple abolition (i.e. in the current context at least, simple abolition appears politically unrealistic).[2] Our basic acceptance of the case for criminalization should not, however, be understood as endorsing current prior fault^{OFF} rules in any form. We reject the framing of prior fault^{OFF} in terms of 'defences', and the status-based focus that this has engendered (i.e. the focus on states of intoxication, automatism, and insanity). And even within these categories, we reject the essential claim that T1 prior fault is (or

[1] As introduced in Chapter 1, we are adopting the notation 'prior fault^{OFF}' and 'prior fault^{DEF}' to distinguish between prior fault rules relevant to the construction of a crime and prior fault rules relevant to the blocking of a defence.

[2] We see this reflected, e.g., across the various Law Commission projects engaging with prior fault.

Prior Fault Criminalization. John J Child, Adrian Hunt, and Hans S. Crombag, Oxford University Press.
 DOI: 10.1093/9780191874734.003.0008

can be) equivalent to missing mens rea and/or voluntariness at T2, and so we reject the essential legal fiction on which prior fault^{OFF} is constructed.

Thus, we are led to consider the potential for a new bespoke offence. The idea here is to unshackle the law from current prior fault^{OFF} mechanisms and fictions, allowing conceptual and practical space to reconsider the T1–T2 wrongs at issue. From here, a new bespoke offence can be crafted to better reflect and capture those wrongs, defining the boundaries of criminalization on its own terms. And where D commits the new offence—culpable incapacity—D may be labelled and punished on that basis, providing clarity (and honesty) in the law's communication both with D and the wider public. This latter point should be emphasized further. Current prior fault^{OFF} rules create a fiction of T2 mens rea, establishing mens rea in law despite its absence in fact, thus miscommunicating to D and the public by misrepresenting key facets of a core element of liability; and misrepresentations of this kind risk corroding trust in the system and its authority to communicate.[3]

It is possible to agree with our analysis above, and in the preceding chapters, but nevertheless reject the specific offence construction that we recommend in this chapter. Our work in Part I of this book has brought us to this point, and informs the detail of our recommendations, but the chapters also stand alone as a comprehensive rejection of prior fault^{OFF} and the equivalence thesis. In what follows, we seek to express what we consider to be a *best version* of the new bespoke offence in retributivist terms, though we readily accept that it is not the only possible version.

The chapter will be structured as follows. Section 7.2 sets out our preferred definition of the CI Offence, in the form of draft legislation. We then unpack the detail of the offence, explaining the reasoning behind its elements in Section 7.3, before discussing its potential application to different classes of defendants in Section 7.4. In Section 7.5, we explain how the new offence is intended to operate at trial. Finally, we clarify the application of supervening defences in Section 7.6, before concluding in Section 7.7.

7.2 The new offence of culpable incapacity

We set out the terms of our preferred offence construction below, in the form of draft legislation. This is done for maximum clarity, before we unpack and explain our choices in the sections that follow. The caveat is that we are not Parliamentary Counsel, and so the draft is not intended to be subjected to classic statutory canons of construction.

[3] We are grateful to Professor Roberts for this idea, discussed on the related issue of wilful ignorance.

1. Culpable incapacity

(1) A person (D) commits an offence if they intentionally or recklessly become significantly mentally impaired and/or involuntary; and
(2) whilst in that impaired or involuntary state D causes or engages in one of the following harms:
  (a) death to another person,
  (b) injury to another person,
  (c) non-consensual sexual penetration of another person,
  (d) non-consensual sexual contact with another person, or
  (e) damage or destruction of another's property, and
(3) in so doing, D was,
  (a) in a state of extreme intoxication with a dangerous drug taken voluntarily or
  (b) negligent in causing or engaging in the harm, having failed to take steps that could reasonably be expected of D in avoidance of the specific harm, where those steps were available at the time of, or shortly before, the harm was caused or engaged in.
(4) A person guilty of an offence under this clause, where the harm caused is the death of another person, is liable on conviction on indictment to imprisonment for life for 'causing death whilst culpably incapacitated'.
(5) A person guilty of an offence under this clause, where the harm caused is the injury of another person, is liable for 'causing injury whilst culpably incapacitated'—
  (a) on summary conviction to imprisonment for a term not exceeding twelve months or to a fine not exceeding the statutory maximum or both, or
  (b) on conviction on indictment to imprisonment for life.
(6) A person guilty of an offence under this clause, where the harm engaged in is the non-consensual sexual penetration of another person, is liable on conviction on indictment to imprisonment for life for 'non-consensual sexual penetration whilst culpably incapacitated'.
(7) A person guilty of an offence under this clause, where the harm engaged in is the non-consensual sexual touching of another person, is liable for 'non-consensual sexual touching whilst culpably incapacitated'—
  (a) on summary conviction to imprisonment for a term not exceeding twelve months or to a fine not exceeding the statutory maximum or both, or
  (b) on conviction on indictment to imprisonment for a term not exceeding ten years.
(8) A person guilty of an offence under this clause, where the harm caused is the destruction or damage of property, is liable for 'causing the destruction or damage of another's property whilst culpably incapacitated'—

(a) on summary conviction to imprisonment for a term not exceeding twelve months or to a fine not exceeding the statutory maximum or both, or
(b) on conviction on indictment to imprisonment for a term not exceeding ten years.

7.3 Understanding the culpable incapacity offence

Our CI Offence attempts to reflect a genuinely T1–T2 focus, in the sense discussed in Chapters 5 and 6, and to apply without causal distinction between internal and external routes to incapacity.[4] In this manner, the CI Offence is considerably more expansive than a T1-focused offence, such as that in Germany,[5] in that it seeks to engage with and blame D for the specific harms caused at T2. However, the CI Offence remains considerably narrower than a simple T2-focused negligence offence, restricting liability for T2 harms to cases in which those harms may be traced back to D's subjective choices at T1. In application, the CI Offence is to be charged and prosecuted alone or (more likely) in the alternative, in cases where D significantly lacks capacity when causing relevant harms.

The CI Offence is best understood in terms of three offence requirements, which will also be used to structure the discussion that follows within this section. These include D's conduct at T1 leading to a foreseen significant impairment, D's conduct causing or engaging in harm at T2, and D's culpability linking events at T1 and T2. We discuss each in turn, before a brief discussion of labelling and sentencing.

7.3.1 Foreseen significant impairment at T1

The CI Offence requires voluntary conduct at T1, intentionally or recklessly leading to a state of significant mental impairment and/or involuntariness. This provides a point of blame at T1, without distinguishing between internal and external causal routes.

7.3.1.1 T1 blame

The requirement of *significant* impairment marks an important point of blame at T1. It mirrors similar requirements from equivalent offences in Germany and South Africa, as well as the Law Commission's 1993 proposal, differing from proposals of the Butler Committee and Criminal Law Revision Committee that did

[4] The only exception being the 'extreme intoxication' clause within clause 1(3)(a), discussed further below.

[5] German Criminal Code, s323a.

not provide for a specific requirement of extreme or significant impairment.[6] The need for mental impairment rules out cases where D's lack of awareness at T2 is attributable to a failure to investigate (e.g. wilful ignorance[7]) or carelessness (e.g. trigger slip cases[8]). And the need to demonstrate *significant* impairment and/or incapacity narrows the CI Offence further to those cases where future mistakes and harms are more likely to be attributable to D's conduct at T1, providing a basis for linking events between T1 and T2.

The 'significant impairment' requirement is particularly important following our decoupling of the CI Offence from other existing substantive offences. Alternative bespoke offences have typically required D's intoxication/impairment to have undermined mens rea and/or legal capacity in relation to an existing substantive offence—a construction that has been employed within each of the previous English law reform proposals,[9] and mirrors the application of current prior fault^{OFF} rules. This approach—requiring impairment as a denial of mens rea—does provide a quantum threshold of sorts, in that D is only likely to lack mens rea where intoxication/impairment is significant. And so, our proposed approach—decoupling the impairment requirement from mens rea denial—means losing this threshold.

Replacing 'denial of mens rea' with a 'significant impairment' requirement is a core (and, we contend, positive) feature of the proposed CI Offence. Whilst denial of mens rea may provide a threshold of sorts, it remains uncertain in terms of causation whether and how a clinically identified cognitive or mental impairment can be shown to account for absence of a specific mens rea. The denial of mens rea threshold is also problematic for those identifying blame in D's degree of impairment, in that even quite low levels of impairment *may* lead to relevant mistakes in fact. Requiring proof of 'significant impairment' provides a single stable and consistent standard, and one that avoids problematic counterfactual enquiries into the cause of an absent mental state. It is not a panacea, and proof of significant impairment will provide challenges for courts in terms of the availability and interpretation of evidence.[10] However, it is a measure that we use elsewhere in law, and one that provides a much clearer message for the public in terms of guiding behaviour. Decoupling from mens rea denial may also improve messaging *within* the law, by creating a clear break from current prior fault^{OFF} rules and the perception of impairment as a substitution for missing fault at T2 (i.e. as opposed to a distinct point of blame).

[6] As discussed in Chapter 5, Sections 5.3 and 5.4.
[7] Discussed in Chapter 3, Section 3.5.
[8] Discussed in Section 7.4.4 below.
[9] Discussed in Chapter 5, Section 5.4.
[10] See J Quilter and L McNamara, 'The Meaning of "Intoxication" in Australian Criminal Cases: Origins and Operation' (2018) 21(1) *New Criminal Law Review* 170.

The CI Offence also requires mens rea, that D intended or was at least reckless at T1 as to becoming significantly impaired or incapacitated. The requirement here is broadly in line with that proposed by the Law Commission in 1993,[11] but marks a point of contrast with the proposals of the Butler Committee and Criminal Law Revision Committee, as well as the South African offence, where simple voluntariness in consumption is sufficient.[12] Like the Commission, we believe that subjective awareness at T1 provides an essential element of D's culpability, linking D not just to the incapacitating conduct, but to the future state of impairment itself. Indeed, where the criminal wrong is located in D putting themselves in a state of significant impairment leading to external resulting harms, D's awareness of both the quality and degree of their conduct at T1 (i.e. the 'putting') are crucial. Our empirical work provides further support for this position, suggesting a consistent self-knowledge in becoming incapacitated.[13]

Current prior fault^{OFF} intoxication rules assume D's awareness of impairment through the voluntary consumption of a 'dangerous drug'.[14] We do not see this as sufficient, with varied potential for unfairness. This includes, for example, where D has an unusual (and unforeseen) reaction to a drug, or where D's drug is supplemented or adulterated with other substances without their knowledge (e.g. where D's alcoholic drink is spiked with additional alcohol and/or other drugs such as chloral hydrate or GHB). Perhaps more obviously, subjective awareness is also crucial where the source of D's impairment is not drug-induced intoxication. As we discussed in Chapters 3 and 4, it is already generally accepted that prior fault^{OFF} outside of intoxication cases should require subjective foresight of impairment at T1, acknowledging that assumptions of foresight are more difficult to justify in circumstances of non-dangerous drugs and/or other causes of mental impairment. We believe that subjective foresight represents an essential element of culpability across all causes of T1 impairment.

7.3.1.2 Causal routes to impairment

Clause 1(1) of the CI Offence is drafted to encompass both external and internal causes of impairment without differentiation. This distinguishes the CI Offence from the bespoke offences in Germany and South Africa, as well as previous English proposals; each of which are explicitly limited to intoxication alone. Crucially, the CI Offence can also apply to causes beyond those engaged by current prior fault^{OFF} rules. We are not concerned, for example, whether an external cause

[11] The Commission captured this within its definition of 'deliberately intoxicated'. Law Commission, *Intoxication and Criminal Liability* (Consultation 127, 1993) Part VI.

[12] As discussed in Chapter 5, Sections 5.3 and 5.4. The German offence makes reference to intentionality in D's drunken state, but also holds negligence as sufficient.

[13] Discussed in Chapter 6, Sections 6.2 and 6.3.

[14] D's intoxicant taken at T1 must have been 'dangerous' in the sense that it is commonly known to lead to unpredictability or aggression. See *Lipman* [1970] 1 QB 152.

has also satisfied the terms of automatism, or whether an internal cause has resulted in insanity; in both cases, as with intoxication, the CI Offence is freed from distinct rules of this kind. Rather, the question is simply whether D was intentional or reckless in causing their state of significant mental impairment.

We believe that the absence of causal distinctions in the application of the CI Offence represents one of its major advantages. As we discussed in the previous chapters, the requirement of causal distinctions in the current law (and any intoxication-only offence) results in the law having to draw hard causal lines on often uncertain facts and science. In all-too-common circumstances of drug intoxication and mental disorder co-occurrence—including substance abuse disorders or addiction for example—it may be practically impossible to separate and weigh causal routes to impairment clinically, and yet this is exactly what the current law requires courts to do. And what is perhaps worse is that it is unclear what is gained—in legal terms—from the pretence. The false framing of prior fault^{OFF} creates the need to identify 'defences' to be blocked, but this is, as we have discussed, a conceptual mistake. Once it is recognized that prior fault^{OFF} rules are not blocking defences, but rather constructing liability, it is by no means clear why certain causal routes are foreclosed. In this manner, the causal breadth of the CI Offence enables the law to tackle areas of potential under-criminalization.

This is not to say that impairment causation is irrelevant to the proposed CI Offence, as such questions may well (indeed, are likely to) arise in the assessment of D's intentionality and foresight of impairment, and/or when addressing D's negligence in the context of clause 1(3)(b), which we discuss below. However, unlike the current law (and intoxication-only offence alternatives), the CI Offence does not apply hard causal distinctions to separate alternative doctrinal positions, and cases of complex and/or uncertain causation may be more easily accommodated.

The challenge for the CI Offence rather comes from the opposite direction. Although flawed, the current isolation of prior fault^{OFF} to proxy constructions of intoxication and automatism has been effective in *limiting* the potential over-criminalizing effects of those rules. Without such proxies in place, the CI Offence requires other elements to narrow liability and avoid over-criminalization, particularly in the context of internal causes. The first step to this is the proposed requirement for intent or recklessness in causing a state of significant mental impairment, but we recognize and discuss below that further narrowing is required across other elements of the offence.

One further point should be clarified here, regarding D's conduct at T1. Paradigm cases will involve D causing mental impairment through their own positive acts, such as voluntary drug taking. However, the CI Offence is also capable of applying where intentional or reckless incapacity is caused through D's omission to act (e.g. failure to take medication), or indirectly through the conduct of another person/actor (e.g. via hypnosis).

7.3.2 Conduct at T2 causing or engaging in relevant harms

Clause 1(2) of the CI Offence provides a list of relevant harms, including fatal and non-fatal harms against the person, sexual harms, and property damage. The offence will only be committed when D causes or engages in one of these harms, whilst significantly mentally impaired and/or involuntary. The idea is to capture a tailored set of harms that are commonly associated with states of mental impairment, both empirically and in terms of public understanding,[15] representing harms that D should be on notice about when choosing (intentionally or recklessly) to become significantly impaired. There is clear room for discussion and potential amendment here (i.e. in terms of the *precise* list), and so our choices should be taken as indicative only.

More critically, we are of the view that this method—listing certain harms—is preferable to current approaches in Germany and South Africa, as well as the previous proposals in English law, where intoxication offences are derivative (in structural terms at least) of other existing offences. For those bespoke offences, one must ask whether D's intoxication has undermined mens rea for a certain offence, and whether D has committed the *actus reus of that offence*. We contend that decoupling the CI Offence from other existing offences by way of listing harms (as opposed to the borrowing of actus reus requirements) reinforces our conception of the CI Offence as a distinct criminal mischief. Indeed, as we have seen within our critique of the alternative bespoke offences,[16] the borrowing of actus reus requirements will naturally encourage comparison between those offences, leading to criticism where there are inconsistencies in the offence labelling and sentencing, despite good reasons for inconsistency.

The listing of harms, as opposed to the borrowing of actus reus requirements, provides further benefits as well. Most importantly, the actus reus of other offences have not been created with their potential application with bespoke T1–T2 offences in mind, and so whilst they may capture a particular mischief quite effectively *in combination with their mens rea requirements*, this will not necessarily be the case when applied separately in the context of a bespoke offence. This is a particular problem for other proposals (such as Williams'[17]) that would apply an 'intoxication + actus reus' approach across all (or almost all[18]) existing offences. But even where the list is shortened (as we have) to focus on a specific range of harms, the use of existing actus reus requirements to express those harms remains problematic. Taking the Law Commission's 1993 proposals as an example, where

[15] Discussed in Law Commission, *Intoxication and Criminal Liability* (Consultation 127, 1993) [6.32–6.41].

[16] Discussed in Chapter 5, Sections 5.3 and 5.4.

[17] R Williams, 'Voluntary Intoxication—A Lost Cause?' (2013) 129 *Law Quarterly Review* 264. Discussed in Chapter 5, Section 5.4.

[18] Ibid. Williams would exclude certain specific offences.

this approach is employed, we are left with difficulties in the strict separation of actus reus elements (that D must complete) and mens rea elements (that become irrelevant), particularly for listed offences such as rape and provoking violence. Beyond this, the borrowing of actus reus elements creates an unnecessary uncertainty within the future application of the bespoke offence, where any subsequent change to the listed offence will carry over to the bespoke offence regardless of its merit in the latter context. The listing of *harms* thus provides greater control, accuracy, and stability for the CI Offence.

7.3.3 Linking T1 and T2

Having established intentional or reckless impairment at T1, and relevant harm causing or engaging at T2, the third and final requirement is to establish a link between those two events. The link is essential to justify the CI Offence's T1–T2 focus, providing conceptual coherence and establishing a basis for offence labelling and sentencing that captures the full T1–T2 transaction.

The proposed CI Offence provides this link through two separate requirements. The first has already been discussed in the preceding sections, which is the link created by subjective foresight of significant impairment/involuntariness (at T1) leading to a related and foreseeable harm (at T2). The idea is that D should have foreseen and taken precautions against the types of harm caused or engaged in at T2, such that a culpable connection may be established between those harms and D's prior choices in becoming significantly impaired. This formed the sole linking provision within the Law Commission's 1993 proposal. Beyond the Commission's approach, however, we propose a second linking provision, providing greater certainty, particularly outside of the intoxication paradigm. This second provision—located in clause 1(3) of the CI Offence—requires *either* 'extreme intoxication' or additional negligence in causing the relevant harm. We provide further detail on each in the subsections below.

In developing this approach, we have rejected several alternative constructions. We do not, for example, require subjective mens rea as to the specific harms at T2 (i.e. whether such mens rea is located at T1 or T2). We agree with critics of approaches of this kind that subjective foresight is likely to be extremely rare in practice.[19] This criticism was also supported by the findings in our own empirical studies, where foresight of underperformance in general (and specific mistakes in particular) was poor.[20] Equally, we have chosen not to include causal requirements between T1 and T2. We have done so because mechanical causation would

[19] Discussed across Chapters 2–5, in the context of how we might reform prior fault^{OFF} rules.
[20] Discussed in Chapter 6, Sections 6.2 and 6.3. This contrasted with foresight and awareness of impairment, which was generally present.

be almost impossible to prove, and the use of counterfactual tests (i.e. that D would not have caused harm but for their impairment) require too much in the way of jury speculation.[21] In this manner, our aim is to articulate a set of elements within the CI Offence that are both conceptually and practically robust.

7.3.3.1 Extreme intoxication as a special case

The first combination of provisions linking T1 and T2 applies narrowly to an important subset of cases where D causes or engages in a relevant harm following intentional or reckless significant impairment, in circumstances of extreme intoxication with a dangerous drug. This is set out in clause 1(3)(a) of the proposed CI Offence.

In this manner, whilst we would not attach blame to *all* cases of voluntary intoxication, we are of the view that extreme intoxication is a special case. It is special empirically, in terms of the increased likelihood of intoxicated mistake making,[22] and it is special in terms of culpability, through D's own likely awareness of impairment,[23] as well as broader public awareness of risks/mistakes in behaviour.[24] Thus, within this subset of cases, we do not think it necessary for the prosecution to demonstrate additional specific failures in avoidance of harm, and it is enough that D has voluntarily reached that extreme state, and caused or engaged in a relevant harm. Indeed, as we discussed in the context of Yaffe's approach to culpable intoxication,[25] states of extreme intoxication may pose particular problems when trying to identify (and prove) additional culpability elements, given D's limited ability to engage rationally when in that state. The specific catchment within clause 1(3)(a) of the proposed CI Offence avoids this potential problem. Our approach here mirrors much of the gross intoxication offence in German law.

Our construction of clause 1(3)(a) borrows terms from the current law that may be usefully refined, but (on balance) are preferred here for their familiarity to the courts. This includes reference to a 'dangerous drug', which has been interpreted by courts to reflect public awareness of risks associated with drugs such as alcohol;[26] and 'voluntariness', which includes requirements of volition and knowledge of the substance being taken.[27] The threshold for 'extreme

[21] See G Virgo, 'The Law Commission Consultation Paper on Intoxication and Criminal Liability' [1993] *Criminal Law Review* 415, 424.

[22] Discussed in Chapter 6, including supportive data from our empirical studies.

[23] Ibid.

[24] See, generally, A Lynch, 'The Scope of Intoxication' (1982) *Criminal Law Review* 139.

[25] Discussed in Chapter 2, Section 2.4. Yaffe G, 'Intoxication, Recklessness and Negligence' (2012) 9(2) *Ohio State Journal of Criminal Law* 545.

[26] See JJ Child et al, *Simester and Sullivan's Criminal Law* (8th Ed, Hart, 2022) §18.3(iii).

[27] We note—but are not convinced by—the Law Commission's preference for the term 'deliberate' in its 1993 offence proposal. See critique in G Virgo, 'The Law Commission Consultation Paper on Intoxication and Criminal Liability' [1993] *Criminal Law Review* 415.

intoxication' is intended—like its German equivalent—to be limited to states of complete loss of rational control, but sensitive to D's personal circumstances and tolerance.[28]

7.3.3.2 Negligent due to a failure to prevent harm

The alternative combination of linking provisions is designed for application to cases outside of the narrow category of extreme intoxication, and is, as far as we are aware, unique to our proposed CI Offence. It requires D to have caused or engaged in a relevant harm following intentional or reckless significant impairment, in circumstances of a negligent failure to take reasonable steps to avoid that harm. This is set out in clause 1(3)(b) of the proposed CI Offence.

This alternative combination allows the CI Offence to apply outside of extreme intoxication cases, but it prevents liability arising where D's impairment was reasonably controlled or managed. For example, where D is reckless in becoming significantly impaired from alcohol or other causes (e.g. sleep deprivation, failure to take medication, etc), but nevertheless acts reasonably in the circumstances to prevent the relevant harms (e.g. because D is at home, is in the company of friends, etc), the fact that D later causes accidental harms may not speak fairly to their culpability. In such cases, beyond the *generalized* fault established from D's choices leading to impairment at T1, we require *targeted* fault in D's specific preventive relationship with that specific harm: asking what D has done or failed to do in the course of the T1–T2 transaction, and what might reasonably have been expected of D.[29]

Three points may be usefully clarified: on the timing, standard, and target of D's negligence. On timing, negligence may be found before, during, and/or after the point of impairment at T1. We might therefore ask questions about D's choice of location, D's attempts to mitigate during/after incapacity, D's regard for the interests of others across the timeline, and so on. Negligence may be demonstrated from a single point in time, or from a series of acts/omissions across the T1–T2 transaction. At each point in time, the question is whether D has taken steps that 'could reasonably be expected . . . in avoidance'. This speaks to the standard of care required, which should be interpreted to reflect D's circumstances and characteristics. Crucially, where D's state of impairment changes across the transaction, and where D's circumstances change (e.g. whether the

[28] C Roxin and L Greco, *Strafrecht. Allgemeiner Teil* ('*Criminal Law. General Part*') (Beck, 2020) §20 Mn 10.

[29] Our approach takes inspiration from Yaffe's scheme for 'non-justified T1 intoxication', discussed in Chapter 2, Section 2.4; G Yaffe, 'Intoxication, Recklessness and Negligence' (2012) 9(2) *Ohio State Journal of Criminal Law* 545. However, unlike Yaffe, we are not attempting to provide mens rea equivalence, the approach will apply to causes outside of intoxication, and importantly, D's relevant failure can be located across the T1–T2 spectrum.

relevant harm becomes more obvious), what is reasonably open to D in avoidance will also change.

Finally, on the 'target' of D's negligence, this is limited to the actual harm arising at T2; it is *not* generalized across relevant harms. This is essential to provide a fair culpability link to the harm caused, relevant to the labelling and sentencing of D's offence. Thus, for example, where the circumstances of D's conduct give rise to an obvious risk of property damage, but a much lower risk of harm to the person, and where D causes accidental harm to a person in fact, the question of negligence in prevention should focus on the lower risk of physical harms and what (if any) precautions D should have taken/did take in relation to that risk across the transaction. The fact that D, in our example, did not take precautions against the obvious risk of property damage may speak to a general disregard for the rights of others, but it will only be indirectly relevant to the question of negligence for the harm caused.

7.3.4 Labelling and sentencing for culpable incapacity

Reflecting the T1–T2 focus of the CI Offence, the labelling and sentencing provisions—clause 1(4)–(8)—are drafted to engage with the specific wrongs committed. Thus, where D kills V at T2, for example, D is not simply labelled and punished for their choices at T1 (e.g. as we see in the German gross intoxication offence), or in reference to T2 harms alone (e.g. in the form of strict liability or negligence offences). Rather, D is labelled and punished for 'causing death whilst culpably incapacitated' (clause 1(4)). The idea is not to make claims of equivalence with other crimes, but to express the different, specific nature of the wrong committed. In this regard, whilst we have benchmarked the maximum sentence of each of the offence variations with similar categories of offences elsewhere, further specific sentencing guidelines would be needed to inform the application of sentencing within individual cases.

The ability for the law to speak honestly here, in labelling and punishing D for what they have actually done, is a core benefit of the proposed CI Offence and stands in marked contrast to fictions inherent in current mechanisms of prior fault^{OFF}. Moreover, that the offence is also capable of fairly capturing and reflecting D's conduct across T1–T2 is a benefit of the proposed CI Offence relative to the alternative bespoke offence options considered previously.[30]

[30] I.e. those considered and discussed in Chapter 5, Sections 5.3 and 5.4.

7.4 Applying the culpable incapacity offence

This section provides a series of case studies, briefly highlighting how the proposed CI Offence is intended to apply in practice. We discuss cases of extreme intoxication, non-extreme intoxication, non-intoxicated involuntariness, involuntary trigger slip cases, mental impairment short of involuntariness, mental impairment due to mental health disorder, and mixed-cause mental health impairments associated with substance use disorders.

We have designed the CI Offence as a stand-alone offence provision. In this manner, it may be charged alone, or in the alternative alongside other existing offences, whenever D causes or engages in a relevant harm in a state of significant mental impairment.

7.4.1 Intoxication (extreme)

In this case, we are assuming that D has caused or engaged in a relevant harm, in a state of extreme intoxication with a dangerous drug. Provided that D intended or was at least reckless at T1 as to becoming significantly impaired (clause 1(1)),[31] and provided D's drug taking was voluntary (clause 1(3)(a)), then D will have committed the CI Offence.

7.4.2 Intoxication (non-extreme)

As we discussed in the context of our own empirical studies, even where voluntary intoxication falls short of extreme intoxication, it may still lead to mistakes that can cause harm. In this case, clause 1(3)(a) is irrelevant, but liability for the proposed CI Offence may still be found under the more general clause 1(3)(b). Again, D must have caused or engaged in a relevant harm (clause 1(2)), whilst significantly mentally impaired having intentionally or recklessly become so impaired i(clause 1(1)); and beyond this, it must now be demonstrated that D was negligent in causing or engaging in that harm, having failed to take steps in avoidance that could reasonably have been expected of them. This final question requires the court to assess D's choices leading up to, during, and following their mental impairment. Both the clause 1(1) foresight requirements and the question of negligence in clause 1(3)(b) are designed to distinguish intoxicated mistakes that may be nonetheless reasonable in the circumstances (no liability) from unreasonable conduct rightly caught within the CI Offence.

[31] There is no additional requirement for D to have intended or foreseen the risk of 'extreme intoxication'.

7.4.3 Involuntariness (non-intoxicated)

Where D is involuntary at T2 due to causes other than intoxication, our focus is again on clause 1(3)(b) and the distinction between reasonable mistakes and unreasonable criminality. This requires relevant harms at T2 (clause 1(2)), and will then focus on D's foresight at T1 of impairment or involuntariness (clause 1(1)), and D's potential negligence across the T1–T2 transaction (clause 1(3)(b)).

7.4.4 Involuntariness (trigger slip cases)

We discussed the so-called trigger slip cases in Chapter 3, Section 3.4, where D accidentally shoots V in the course of committing another crime (e.g. when restraining V), explaining that in such circumstances whilst prior fault^{OFF} rules are not typically applied by the courts—not expressly at least—they provide the best explanation for liability. The question then, if we abolish prior fault^{OFF}, is whether the proposed CI Offence is intended to apply to such cases. The answer is that it depends on the circumstances.

In some cases, liability may appropriately be found without the proposed CI Offence, at least where D is charged with an offence that does not require an intended outcome. For example, where D causes death, it is likely that they commit gross negligence manslaughter under English law. However, where D causes non-fatal harm, for example, alternatives are more difficult to identify.[32] It is here that the CI Offence will *sometimes* be appropriate. The CI Offence is capable of application where D's trigger slip is involuntary at T2 (clause 1(1)),[33] when causing or engaging in a relevant harm (clause 1(2)), in circumstances of a negligent failure in avoidance (clause 1(3)(b)). The difficulty, in some cases at least, will be the clause 1(1) requirement that D was intentional or reckless at T1 as to their future involuntary state. Thus, the proposed CI Offence will only apply to trigger slip cases where D foresees the chance of a slip. This is likely in some cases (e.g. where D has removed the 'safety catch' on their gun), but nevertheless represents a narrowing of liability from the current law.

We considered whether the proposed CI Offence should be drafted to catch all trigger slip cases, but decided it should not. D's subjective choice at T1 provides an essential element of the T1–T2 focus of the CI Offence, set out in Section 7.3 of this chapter. Where D has no foresight of impairment or involuntariness at T1, there is insufficient basis (in our view) to blame D for anything more than their

[32] This will vary between different criminal jurisdictions of course.

[33] Note that clause 1(1) applies to both significant mental impairment *and* involuntariness. Trigger slip cases are an example of involuntariness without mental impairment.

negligent harm-causing at T2. English law recognizes negligent T2 harms as potentially criminal, but currently only in selected areas such as homicide.

7.4.5 Mental impairment short of involuntariness

Cases of impairment may be caught by the proposed CI Offence regardless of causal route (i.e. regardless of whether the cause was internal/external). Outside of the narrow category of extreme intoxication (clause 1(3)(a)), the proposed CI Offence requires intentional or reckless significant impairment (clause 1(1)), a relevant harm at T2 (clause 1(2)), and for D to have been negligent in their failure to avoid that harm (clause 1(3)(b)). Again, the offence focus is on distinguishing mistakes (where liability will not arise) from culpable incapacity. The potential application of the CI Offence in cases of all types of mental impairment short of involuntariness marks an expansion of liability from the current law.

7.4.6 Mental impairment (mental health disorder)

Having removed causal distinctions at T1, the potential for the proposed CI Offence to apply to internal causes represents another significant shift from the current law.[34] Thus, for example, whereas failure to follow medical advice or direction (e.g. failure to take medication) leading to uncontrolled harm would not give rise to the application of prior fault^{OFF} rules within the current law,[35] it may lead to liability for the proposed CI Offence. It will do so where D is intentional or reckless at T1 in becoming impaired or involuntary (clause 1(1)), causes or engages in a relevant harm at T2 (clause 1(2)), and is negligent in failing to prevent that harm (clause 1(3)(b)).

We believe there are cases where liability is appropriate in these circumstances, particularly where D's T1 choices reflect a disregard for the rights of others. However, there is also a legitimate concern—explored in Chapter 4—that liability within internal cause cases should not be applied too widely, and that we should be cognizant of the potential impact of D's disorder on any apparent markers of culpability.

This concern is taken seriously in the design of the proposed CI Offence, where two requirements, in particular, may usefully be highlighted. First, clause 1(1) is only satisfied where D is intentional or reckless as to becoming significantly impaired. Within this, reference to 'becoming impaired' is important as it rules out the potential application of the offence to continuous states of mental impairment: we

[34] We discuss internal causes of incapacity in Chapter 4.
[35] Though it may be caught within the insanity rules. Ibid.

are only concerned with cases where D anticipates a significant future deterioration of their capacity, creating a duty to mitigate. The subjective element of the test is crucial, and particularly so in cases where D's disorder manifests a belief that they are not unwell and/or that their medication will not help them. In such cases, D lacks intention or recklessness as to future impairment, and falls outside the proposed CI Offence. The second requirement relates to the design of clause 1(3)(b), and the need to prove that D negligently failed to take steps that could 'reasonably be expected of D in avoidance'. The test here is objective, but highly relative to the characteristics and circumstances of D: we ask what steps were open to D—given D's characteristics and circumstances—and whether, in this context, D was negligent in causing harm. Thus, for example, even where D is able to foresee the risk of future incapacity, if D's condition prevents them from understanding the risks associated with such incapacity, and/or recognizing and/or engaging measures of mitigation, D may remain outside the CI Offence.

7.4.7 Mental impairment (addiction/mixed causes)

Those familiar with this area will be well aware that substance use disorders or drug addiction can present unique challenges for the law, and certainly for rules (such as the proposed CI Offence) that engage with questions of incapacity and blame. First, addiction represents a paradigm of mixed causation, where D's proximal choice to become intoxicated at T1 should be understood in the context of an ongoing compulsive disorder, marked by impaired inhibitory control mechanisms, excessive psychological craving, and in the case of excessive and continuous use of drugs such as alcohol, severe physical dependence syndrome that can be lethal if untreated. Arguably, one advantage of the proposed CI Offence, relative to the current law, is that no strict causal distinction is required between intoxication and substance use disorder when identifying which legal rules should apply—a distinction that may be impossible to make with any scientific and/or clinical precision. Causation remains relevant to the proposed CI Offence, particularly when asking what steps were realistically open to D in avoidance under clause 1(3)(b). However, this is not a binary causal choice, and mixed or uncertain causal routes can be reflected in the court's reasoning.

A second challenge relates to the timing and length of the relevant period for assessing D's negligence in failing to avoid the T2 harm. Whilst D's substance use disorder may sensibly limit our expectations of their conduct (clause 1(3)(b)), particularly in terms of the simple cessation of drug taking, it may well be possible to trace liability back to a time before D became addicted and/or dependent (i.e. before substance use became compulsive and/or a form of self-medication). Thus, for example, we could blame D's initial experimentation with drugs which led to addiction, pointing to D's failure to take appropriate steps to avoid future harms (i.e. through addiction) at *this* early point.[36] However, unsurprisingly, we do not consider as appropriate such extensive retrospective tracing exercises potentially covering periods of months or indeed years. They present a range of significant practical and principled challenges, entailing as they do too many variables of potential mitigation (e.g. age and circumstances of first use) and simple biological luck (i.e. in terms of becoming addicted). It is for this reason that clause 1(3)(b) is explicitly limited to steps available 'at the time of, or shortly before, the harm caused'.

7.5 Application at trial

Beyond the articulation of a criminal wrong, any new offence must be capable of application in practice. At worst, overly complex and/or otherwise problematic offences risk exacerbating the problems they seek to address, and even at best, in a competitive legislative environment, practical problems of this kind may be sufficient to alienate potential reformers.

This was certainly the case with previous intoxication offences in English law, and particularly for the Law Commission's 1993 proposal, which was abandoned on grounds almost exclusively concerned with its practical workability.[37] The particular objections accepted by the Commission, which led it to abandon its new offence proposal, were only lightly sketched in ten paragraphs of its 1995 Report.[38] And this was, quite reasonably, criticized by commentators,[39] not least because it led the Commission back to a policy of codifying a set of prior fault^{OFF} rules that it had previously deemed unprincipled and unfair.[40]

The objections raised were essentially threefold: that the new offence would lead to more issues at trial, that it would complicate investigation and prosecution, and that it would lead to uncertainty when charging. Although these criticisms were directed at the Law Commission's specific offence proposal, they provide a useful evaluative checklist for our preferred CI Offence. We discuss each in turn.

[36] We discuss this possibility in Chapter 4, Section 4.3.2.

[37] Discussed in Chapter 5, Section 5.2.4.

[38] Law Commission, *Intoxication and Criminal Liability* (LC No 229, 1995) [5.8–5.18].

[39] E Paton, 'Reformulating the Intoxication Rules' [1995] *Criminal Law Review* 382, 387–88; R Mackay, *Mental Condition Defences in the Criminal Law* (OUP, 1995) 177; G Dingwall, *Alcohol and Crime* (Routledge, 2006) 121.

[40] Law Commission, *Intoxication and Criminal Liability* (Consultation 127, 1993). In light of our analysis in Chapters 2–6, reverting to codification of the current law is not viable: codification simply clarifies and highlights current unfairness, whilst doing little to resolve it.

7.5.1 Trial complexity

On the potential increase of issues at trial, the Commission accepted that:[41]

> . . . since it would be perceived by defendants (however unrealistically) as a chance to be convicted of a less serious offence, it would engender both more trials and, in cases where there is a trial anyway, the raising of more issues than occurs at present.

The objection is speculative and, we believe, at least partly incorrect. In cases where D is considering a guilty plea, it is logical to suggest that they are more likely to contest charges that do not accurately describe their conduct (e.g. those requiring subjective mens rea at T2 that was absent in fact), especially where a successful challenge may result in acquittal. Where D is presented with an offence that accurately describes their conduct across T1–T2, in the form of a bespoke offence, it may very well be that fewer cases will be contested. Where cases go to court, it may be that the Law Commission's bespoke offence would have lengthened trials, owing to its contingent construction upon D's acquittal for an alternative principal offence, thereby requiring a form of sequential analysis across offences. Our proposed CI Offence is very different however, and may be prosecuted without reference to any other offences.

There is truth in the observation that more or different issues would be raised at trial. But this should be neither surprising nor, we argue, unduly concerning. We are blaming D for their conduct across T1–T2, and so any sensible bespoke offence (including the proposed CI Offence) should be designed to engage with those points of blame. It is not a virtue of the current law that it saves time by assuming part of the wrong through a problematic legal fiction. Indeed, it is a dereliction of the law.[42]

[41] Law Commission, *Intoxication and Criminal Liability* (LC No 229, 1995) [5.10].

[42] We may usefully illustrate this point by highlighting one of the Law Commission's more problematic conclusions in 1995. For the Commission, it was important that the intoxication offence should attach a lesser punishment than harms caused with mens rea at T2, commenting that equal punishment 'would be objectionable in principle, because the defendant should be regarded as less blameworthy for becoming intoxicated than for intentionally or recklessly committing a defined criminal act when sober' (ibid [5.17]). We disagree with this point for the CI Offence, but it is a perfectly sensible position to defend: the intoxication offence represents a different wrong, and for the Commission this should be understood as a lesser wrong. It is therefore also logical—as the Commission does—to highlight consultee's preference for matched sentencing as a reason to abandon its intoxication offence proposal. However, having done so, it is frankly bizarre for the Commission to go on to recommend the codification of current prior fault rules: rules that also (though less precisely) locate blame at T1, that also fail to distinguish blame at sentencing, and, indeed, that label and punish D *as if* they acted with mens rea at T2.

7.5.2 Investigation and prosecution complexity

The next objection highlights the additional steps required to prove liability when investigating and prosecuting a bespoke T1–T2 offence. Reflecting views gathered during consultation, the Commission observed that:[43]

> ... since it was an essential ingredient of the offence, which the prosecution would have to prove, that the defendant's awareness, understanding or control was 'substantially impaired' through the use of an intoxicant, this would open the door to expert evidence and add to the length of trials ... the requirement of substantial impairment would [also] require the police to devote more time to enquiries into the defendant's movements and his intake of intoxicants prior to the offence.

The observations here are most likely correct, but, again, should not give rise to undue concerns. Where D's choices at T1 and impairment at T2 are directly material to the offence charged, then it will be necessary to investigate and prove these requirements at trial. This will present challenges, but they are challenges we accept in other areas of the law where prior choice and/or incapacity are at issue. We see this, for example, when applying the offence requirement of voluntariness, when assessing mental competence in the context of insanity and diminished responsibility, when scrutinizing D's prior choices and freedom to escape in the context of duress, and so on.

7.5.3 Charging uncertainty

The final objection highlighted by the Law Commission relates to charging decisions and how/when the bespoke offence should be introduced:[44]

> ... the prosecution would not know in advance whether it should include the new offence as an alternative offence on the indictment. As a result, the essential features of the case would not be before the jury at the outset, and difficulties could arise in the course of the trial over the question whether and when to add a separate count.

We agree that the concern expressed here is more problematic, and recognize the attention it has received in alternative bespoke offence debates.[45] It focuses on charging decisions, and the worry that having charged D with an offence requiring

[43] Law Commission, *Intoxication and Criminal Liability* (LC No 229, 1995) [5.11–5.12].
[44] Ibid [5.13].
[45] Discussed in Chapter 5, Section 5.2.4.

mens rea at T2, it will be difficult to introduce a quite different bespoke offence (such as the CI Offence) as an alternative mid-trial. This is not an insurmountable difficulty of course, but it contrasts with the relative consistency in messaging offered through current prior fault^{OFF} rules. In the context of prior fault^{OFF}, the prosecution are in a much more favourable position: as long as the prosecution pursue a basic intent mens rea offence, liability can be established either through a finding of mens rea on the facts, or through a mechanism of prior fault^{OFF} if mens rea is denied on evidence of voluntary intoxication or automatism. Essentially, two parallel routes are created to the same liability outcome.

Attempts to address this objection, in the context of bespoke offences, have borrowed from the structure of current rules. The idea is, where D is charged with an offence that requires mens rea at T2, and where mens rea is subsequently contested on grounds of blameworthy impairment, the bespoke offence (although not initially charged) should be capable of application on the facts. Indeed, ideally, such application should be automatic, without the need for further argumentation within the court. A mechanism of this kind has been adopted in South Africa, and has been central to many of the proposals in English law, including that of the Law Commission in 1993.[46] Achieving a workable mechanism of this kind is difficult however, and we have already criticized its operation in South Africa:[47] it involves substantive compromises to avoid the need for 'new' elements to be discussed when applying the bespoke offence, and the timing and form of the application is perhaps inevitably complicated. As we have highlighted, this was a principal criticism among consultees commenting on the Law Commission's 1993 Offence proposal.

We have *not* included a mechanism of this kind within the proposed CI Offence itself, which will apply simply as a stand-alone criminal offence. This allows us greater flexibility in the substantive construction of the offence, designed across the three elements discussed in Section 7.3, as well as to avoid the complexity of a mid-trial/post-trial intervention. We anticipate the proposed CI Offence being charged alone, or in the alternative, whenever D causes or engages in a relevant harm in circumstances of blameworthy impairment and/or involuntariness.

Where charged alone, the CI Offence will be pursued in the normal fashion. Where charged in the alternative, this will certainly add some complexity at trial. However, we maintain that this is the right approach in principle (mirroring the use of alternative charges elsewhere), and that although alternative charges of this kind may have been more difficult historically, the emergence and common use of 'routes to verdict' within complex trials provides a significant basis to ameliorate issues of complexity.

[46] Law Commission, *Intoxication and Criminal Liability* (Consultation 127, 1993).
[47] Chapter 5, Section 5.3.2.

Problems may emerge, of course, where the proposed CI Offence is not charged in circumstances where it should have been, and where a trial commences on the basis of offences that require (absent in fact) mens rea at T2. We have two responses here. The first is simply to say that charging mistakes happen, across all different kinds of offences. They are unfortunate, but will certainly not be unique to this context. Rather, and this is the second response, it is important for prosecutors to be cognizant of the scope of the offences they charge. We believe that by setting out the proposed CI Offence as a stand-alone offence, and explicitly abolishing prior fault^{OFF} rules, prosecutors will be put on clear notice that they should consider the new offence in circumstances of mental impairment.

7.6 Defences

We have not discussed the potential application of defences anywhere in Part I. Two points may be usefully clarified.

The first relates to the application of defences (properly so-called[48]) to liability derived from prior fault^{OFF}, or the proposed CI Offence. The simple point here is that defences will continue to apply in the normal way. Thus, even where D commits the CI Offence, D may be acquitted if they did so in circumstances that satisfy complete defences such as duress, necessity, and so on. For example, where D is threatened and forced to take drugs to the point of extreme intoxication, and goes on to cause non-fatal harm, D may appeal to the defence of duress.

The second point is that, when applying defences in the 'normal way', D's prior fault may be a relevant factor. For example, under the current law, whilst D may rely on a mistaken belief when claiming to have acted in self-defence, D may not do so if their mistake was attributable to voluntary intoxication.[49] This is an important issue, but logically separate from the role of intoxication (and other T1 fault) in constructing an offence.[50] We discuss the role of prior fault^{DEF} in blocking otherwise available defences in Part II.

7.7 Conclusion

This chapter has set out and justified our preferred construction of a bespoke offence, the CI Offence. The proposed CI Offence allows for the abolition of current prior fault^{OFF} rules, replacing the problematic fictions of the current law with an

[48] We have discussed the erroneous and misleading use of defence language when describing and applying prior fault rules of inculpation across the chapters in Part I. Defences properly so-called, or supervening defences, are those that apply to exculpate D who has committed all elements of an offence.
[49] Criminal Justice and Immigration Act 2008, s76.
[50] Discussed in Chapter 1, Section 1.3.1.

offence that accurately describes and punishes what D has done. Building upon alternative bespoke offence designs, the proposed CI Offence is unique in its application across T1 causes (i.e. applying beyond intoxication), and for its genuine T1–T2 focus (i.e. locating fault at T1 and T2, and requiring culpability links across that transaction). We acknowledge that certain elements of the proposed CI Offence may be subject to amendment and debate, including specifics within the list of harm elements and sentencing provisions. However, we contend that a new offence, reflecting the key methodological and substantive components outlined in this chapter would, if enacted, improve the law in England & Wales and beyond.

PART II
PRIOR FAULT AND DEFENCES

Part II engages with cases where D completes an offence (including, potentially, our recommended culpable incapacity offence), and then raises a supervening defence. We explore prior fault^{DEF} rules that apply to block such defences at T2, drawing on D's earlier blameworthy conduct at T1.

8
PRIOR FAULT BLOCKING DEFENCES

8.1 Introduction

In the chapters that follow, we discuss the use of prior fault^{DEF} rules to block the application of supervening defences.[1] Let us take self-defence as an example to illustrate what this involves. Self-defence is a complete defence where D uses necessary and reasonable force to protect against physical harm.[2] The standard operation of this defence is largely uncontroversial, since people should be permitted to defend themselves from unlawful attack without criminal liability arising. However, what if D manufactures the circumstances of that 'attack' in order to use the law of self-defence to 'justify' their preplanned use of force against V? For example, say D wants to kill V, D hands V a knife and then goads V until they (as anticipated) lash out at D, D shoots and kills V to protect themselves. In such a situation, should D be able to rely on self-defence, or should their prior behaviour be relevant to denying them the use of the defence? Sticking with self-defence, a quite different example of prior fault^{DEF} also arises where, say, D uses force against V in the mistaken belief that such force is necessary, where D's mistake is attributable to voluntary intoxication. For example, say, having consumed hallucinogenic drugs, D kills V in the mistaken belief that V is about to shoot them. Should D be able to rely on self-defence in this situation, or should their prior conduct be relevant to whether the defence ought to be available, and if so, in what way?

In each of these cases, a focus on D's conduct at T2 alone may give rise to a valid defence (i.e. shooting V in response to their attack with a knife in the first example, and killing V in the mistaken belief they are under attack in the second example). However, in each case, the circumstances of D's defence has arisen from their own prior blameworthy conduct. In the first example, V would not have attacked D at T2 but for D's goading at T1, and in the second, D would not have been mistaken in the need for defensive force at T2 but for their choice to become intoxicated at T1.

So the basic issue arising here mirrors that discussed throughout Part I of the book, asking whether the law should expand its temporal lens to include D's conduct at T1 as well as T2. However, there is a crucial conceptual distinction between

[1] As introduced in Chapter 1, we are adopting the notation 'prior fault^{OFF}' and 'prior fault^{DEF}' to distinguish between prior fault rules relevant to the construction of a crime and prior fault rules relevant to the blocking of a defence.

[2] Criminal Justice and Immigration Act 2008, s78.

Prior Fault Criminalization. John J Child, Adrian Hunt, and Hans S. Crombag, Oxford University Press.
 DOI: 10.1093/9780191874734.003.0010

the situations examined here and those discussed in Part I. Unlike those prior fault^{OFF} rules discussed in Part I, these are not circumstances where fault is required to construct the missing elements of a crime. Rather, in the situations we are dealing with here, the elements of D's offence are made out, and the question arises as to the potential for prior fault^{DEF} to engage with D's claim for exculpation. The question is whether to disapply a supervening defence that would otherwise be available.

Our objective, across the next three chapters, is to identify and articulate a set of principles through which to better understand the role of prior fault^{DEF} in blocking the availability of defences, and, having done so, to set out doctrinal rules capable of fair and consistent application in practice. We begin, in this chapter, with first principles, discussing the conceptual role of prior fault^{DEF} in general, and from here—in the chapters that follow—we narrow to evaluate specific existing rules and options for reform.

This chapter will be structured as follows. Section 8.2 discusses the identification of prior fault^{DEF} rules, exploring both the structural and normative qualities characteristic of such rules. In Section 8.3, we move to the categorization of prior fault^{DEF} rules, explaining an important distinction between two types of prior fault^{DEF} rules: namely, 'capacity-based' and 'contriving'—a separation that is reflected and explored in the chapters that follow. In Section 8.4, we discuss rules that should not be categorized as prior fault^{DEF}-based, but are indirectly affected by the existence and current interpretation of such rules.

8.2 What is prior fault^{DEF}?

As we have explained, prior fault^{DEF} rules operate in the context of supervening defences to block an otherwise exculpating rule (such as self-defence) from its application. But why does this happen, and what provides the theoretical basis for the application of prior fault^{DEF} when blocking a defence?

There is no simple answer to this question, and this difficulty provides some explanation for the inconsistency of the current legal rules that we will explore in the chapters that follow. In the context of offences, discussed in the chapters in Part I, presenting prior fault^{OFF} as a substitute for mens rea and/or voluntariness gives rise (in our view) to insurmountable challenges. However, at least those challenges were clear conceptually: thus, for the fiction of mens rea substitution to be justified, it must be possible to demonstrate a functional equivalence between D's prior fault^{OFF} at T1 and those elements missing at T2. This form of analysis is not available or necessary to explain the role of prior fault^{DEF} in limiting the availability of defences. There is no need for any legal fiction. Simply, D commits the offence, and the defence which would ordinarily be available to them is not available because of their prior conduct.

It might be thought that this simplifies matters. However, without the requirement of culpability equivalence, the identification and justification of prior fault^{DEF} in blocking defences can be rather opaque. Our opening contrived defence and intoxication examples demonstrate the potentially intuitive appeal of criminalization in certain circumstances, but we lack an obvious structural device to explain and manage the legal articulation of a prior fault^{DEF} rule. And it is from this conceptual and functional uncertainty that the current law—across jurisdictions—has developed a collection of prior fault^{DEF} rules, often criticized for their lack of consistency and (relatedly) for their lack of fairness.[3]

In the subsections that follow, we unpack the apparent intuitive appeal of prior fault^{DEF} in regulating the availability of defences. That is to say, we seek to move beyond the simple intuitively attractive conclusion that people who are to blame for 'creating' the circumstances of their claimed defence should not have that defence available to them, to identify a functional and analytical basis for prior fault^{DEF} which, at the same time, helps us to explain and/or critique the law as it currently stands. We contend that the intuitive appeal is best understood as prior fault^{DEF} operating as a 'denial of crisis', where the existence of a point of crisis or emergency would otherwise be necessary for the exculpatory power of the defence to be permitted. From here, we begin to sketch the broad structural and functional features necessary to ground the acceptable use of prior fault^{DEF} rules in this context.

8.2.1 The normative foundation for prior fault^{DEF}

To unpack the appeal of prior fault^{DEF} rules, it is useful to explore certain features of the role and construction of defences in criminal responsibility more generally. Indeed, this provides an essential basis for the analysis that follows.

Broadly speaking, supervening defences play a crucial role in the criminal law, applying as a form of safety net in circumstances of justified or excused offending.[4] We accept—on limited terms at least—that offences may sometimes apply over-inclusively. Ideally, the drafting of offences should always seek to articulate a mischief in narrow and precise terms, but the value of such detail should be weighed against our interest in providing clear and intelligible pronouncements of wrongful behaviour.[5] Criminal defences provide increased scope for the latter, facilitating simpler offence defining pronouncements with a series of bespoke (and sometimes quite flexible[6]) routes to exculpation.

[3] See, generally, P Robinson, 'Causing the Conditions of One's Own Defence' (1985) 71 *Virginia Law Review* 1.

[4] On justifications and excuses, see G Fletcher, *Rethinking Criminal Law* (OUP, 1978) Ch 10; AP Simester, *Fundamentals of Criminal Law* (OUP, 2021) Chs 17–19.

[5] Crucial in terms of fair warning and labelling. See W Wilson, 'How Criminal Defences Work' in A Reed and M Bohlander (eds) *General Defences in Criminal Law* (Hart 2014) 7.

[6] The general defence of necessity, most notably, remains largely undefined.

However, despite the necessary flexibility of specific defence constructions and rationale, it is possible to identify a set of consistent constituting features. On this point, we borrow from the work of William Wilson on the structure of defences, who, in his words, seeks to identify a 'common defence template' rather than a 'unifying rationale'.[7] For Wilson,[8]

> ... [t]he template common to all core defences is that in the face of an external prompt the actor reacted in such a way as to permit the usual inference to be blocked that he is a person of an anti-social character usually implicit in the fact that he has infringed a legal prohibition.

Within the template, the role played by the 'external prompt' is perhaps most significant: it is this prompt that changes D's normative position, providing the basis for exculpation (i.e. so long as D's acts are not excessive or unrelated). Not just any external prompt will be sufficient, however. Individuals may be driven to commit criminal acts by any number of societal, economic, and/or social factors/prompts, but allowance for these is rarely permitted or even formally encountered at the liability stage, where the narrow focus of legal review is unable and/or unwilling to engage with longer-term factors which may affect or cause people to act in ways which breach criminal law prohibitions.[9] What is vital for exculpation within orthodox criminal law analysis is the combination of understandable conduct in the context of immediate 'crisis'.[10] What is required here is not simply that we sympathize with D, or even that we might have acted similarly in their position. The identification of a 'crisis' allows us to sympathize with D, but to do so in knowledge that D's conduct was isolated and temporary, reassured that such conduct does not represent a continuing danger.[11]

Thus, this principle holds that supervening defences should apply to exculpate D where their conduct, despite constituting an offence, is excused or justified on the facts as an understandable response to a moment of 'crisis'. The model is perhaps most obvious when applied to excusatory defences (e.g. duress), providing that D should only be allowed a defence where their offending does not reveal a vicious character or wrongdoing, but rather an unlucky fate. We require that D was trapped or in crisis, and that D demonstrated an understandable (or reasonable)

[7] W Wilson, 'The Structure of Criminal Defences' (2005) *Criminal Law Review* 108, 110.

[8] Ibid 110, drawing from G Fletcher, *Rethinking Criminal Law* (OUP, 2000) 799–802.

[9] See SH Kadish, 'Excusing Crime' (1987) 75 *California Law Review* 257, 283–89.

[10] W Wilson, 'The Structure of Criminal Defences' (2005) *Criminal Law Review* 108, 110–12; 'The Filtering Role of Crisis in the Constitution of Criminal Excuses' (2004) 49(3) *Canadian Journal of Law and Jurisprudence* 387. See also J Dressler, 'Reflections on Excusing Wrongdoers' (1988) 19 *Rutgers Law Journal* 671.

[11] The notable exception to this principle arises in the context of ongoing conditions and the defence of insanity. However, the law deals with this through the special verdict, and the disposal options that this verdict allows.

human frailty—where 'there but for the grace of god go I'.[12] Although less often discussed, the requirement of 'crisis' is equally central to justificatory defences (e.g. including self-defence): D is never justified to commit an offence in general, but may be justified in circumstances of crisis, avoiding a greater evil. In each case, D is not allowed to choose to take the law into their own hands, but where choice is removed through crisis, we can accept that certain exceptions may be permitted.

Once we acknowledge the central role of 'crisis' to criminal defences, the role of prior fault^{DEF} becomes clear. We can accept people committing even very serious wrongs within crisis situations (e.g. killing in circumstances of self-defence), reassured by the fact that D had no *real* choice. However, where D has constructed that crisis themselves by their conduct at T1 (e.g. by provoking V into the attack, or choosing to become intoxicated), D changes their normative position vis-à-vis the subsequent external prompt.[13] D is no longer a victim of circumstance, rather D has chosen to put themselves in that situation, and a common-sense morality would appear to deny them a defence on that basis.[14] The task for the law is to articulate rules of prior fault^{DEF} that can identify when D has constructed the crisis that provides the basis for their defence.

8.2.2 Understanding the structure and function of prior fault^{DEF}

Even though prior fault^{DEF} rules operate quite differently than we discussed for prior fault^{OFF} rules in Part I, there remains a core family resemblance in terms of structure and function. It is because of these core features that we can talk sensibly of prior fault conceptually, rather than two entirely separate and distinct sets of rules (i.e. prior fault^{OFF} and prior fault^{DEF}). For present purposes, the identification of core features also helps us to discern which defence rules should or should not come within our discussion of prior fault^{DEF}.

In terms of common structural features, this concerns the *linking* of events between T2 (D's offence) and T1 (D's prior blameworthy conduct); and in terms of function, it is about the *use* of D's blameworthy conduct at T1 to change the application of rules at T2. We outline each in turn.

8.2.2.1 The structure of prior fault^{DEF} rules

All prior fault rules require an expansion of the laws temporal lens back from D's offence at T2 to include D's prior blameworthy acts at T1 (e.g. goading V, voluntary intoxication, etc). This marks an essential structural or descriptive feature of prior

[12] W Wilson, 'The Structure of Criminal Defences' (2005) *Criminal Law Review* 108.
[13] Usefully discussed in *Keane* [2010] EWCA Crim 2514.
[14] K Ferzan, 'Provocateurs' (2013) 7 *Criminal Law and Philosophy* 597, 605. In this case, *both* D and V are wrongdoers: ibid 615.

fault rules, common between prior fault^{DEF} rules, our focus here, and rules of prior fault^{OFF} discussed in Part I. However, it is perhaps easier to overlook this structural feature for defences, because defences already involve looking back to some point prior to D's criminal conduct at T2.

Although criminal offences are typically designed to capture confined snapshot events,[15] defences often require a broader appraisal. Whilst D may choose to offend at T2, our moral appraisal of that offending remains sensitive to D's broader or prior reasons in action, and it is appropriate for the law to accommodate this within criminal defences. Almost all jurisdictions, for example, provide some form of defence where D's offending at T2 represents a reasonable defensive response to an attack (at T1),[16] or results from coercion and/or serious threats from another (at T1),[17] etc.[18] This is not to claim that all defences are T1–T2 structured,[19] but simply to highlight that (unlike offences) many defences will necessarily engage with this wider temporal scope.

Nonetheless, we believe there *is* something distinctive in the structural construction of prior fault^{DEF} rules as a mechanism for blocking the use of a defence. This is because, although many supervening defences are constructed across T1–T2, they will not typically engage with *D's conduct at T1*. Defences will often engage with exculpating events at T1 (e.g. the threats or attack from another that prompted D's offence), but the focus in that context is to understand the crisis circumstances arising that give exculpating context to D's choices at T2. In contrast, prior fault^{DEF} rules operate differently. Prior fault^{DEF} rules apply to block a defence at T2 on the basis of D's blameworthy conduct at T1. Indeed, as we saw with our initial examples of contrived self-defence and intoxication, D's conduct here will typically arise *before* the external (potentially exculpating) prompt. In this manner, prior fault^{DEF} rules applicable to blocking defences are distinguishable from defences themselves, whilst being structurally similar to *prior fault*^{OFF} rules, in providing further expansion of the criminal lens to engage with D's earlier conduct.

8.2.2.2 The function of prior fault^{DEF} rules

On the functional level, we can tell a similar story. Essentially, whilst the external T1 prompt may create circumstances of apparent crisis, capable of exculpating D's choice to offend at T2, our normative perception of that prompt (and the conduct that follows) may be radically altered by knowledge of D's blameworthy conduct at T1. D's intentional manipulation in cases of contrived defending, or D's apparent

15 Discussed in Chapter 1, Section 1.1.

16 E.g. self-defence.

17 E.g. duress.

18 Other defences employ a similar T1–T2 structure, such as loss of control (Coroners and Justice Act 2009, s54) and the defence for slavery or trafficking victims who commit an offence (Modern Slavery Act 2015, s45).

19 E.g. incapacity defences such as insanity, e.g., will typically focus on T2 alone.

negligence in circumstances of voluntary intoxication, both cut directly at the normative root of D's exculpation.

In this manner, we may identify a functional correspondence between prior fault^{OFF} and prior fault^{DEF}, where D's blameworthy conduct at T1 is used to alter the application of legal rules at T2. However, there are also important differences. The application of prior fault^{OFF} as a substitution for missing mens rea elements, in the context of offending, creates a legal fiction that can only be justified through fault equivalence (i.e. between D's fault at T1 and the elements substituted for at T2). Having argued in Part I that such equivalence was not possible, we contended that the functional role of prior fault^{OFF} could only be achieved through a new bespoke offence, capturing D's fault at T1 without the need for equivalence.[20] This is not the case for prior fault^{DEF} and defences. In the context of defences, the function of prior fault^{DEF} is simply to block an otherwise applicable defence: there is no need for T1–T2 equivalence, but simply that D's conduct at T1 leads us to doubt the status of the crisis on which their defence is based. This is why in the chapters in Part II we focus our attention on the operation and reform of existing prior fault^{DEF} rules, and we do not consider the creation of new offences or defences.

8.3 Categories of prior fault^{DEF}

It is crucial to identify and explore the unifying features of prior fault analysis, in both structural and functional terms, in order to make sense of our broader enquiry. However, this is not to mistake prior fault for a singular doctrine, capable of expression and application through a single legal rule. Indeed, we have already highlighted the importance of rejecting singular approaches to prior fault in the distinction we have drawn between prior fault^{OFF} and prior fault^{DEF}.[21] Singular approaches assist us in mapping doctrinal and theoretical similarities.[22] However, they have also perpetuated inaccurate framing of prior fault^{OFF} rules as 'defences',[23] and the singular doctrinal solutions provided are simply inadequate as a response to the quite different challenges encountered in the articulation of rules of offending on one hand, and rules blocking defences on the other.[24]

It is on this basis that we have distinguished the category of prior fault^{DEF} from prior fault^{OFF}. But this is not the end of the story. In the context of prior fault^{OFF} rules, it was possible to identify and analyse a single conceptual route to liability,

[20] Discussed across Part I chapters.

[21] See discussion in Chapter 1, Section 1.3.1.

[22] See, e.g., P Robinson, 'Causing the Conditions of One's Own Defence' (1985) 71 *Virginia Law Review* 1; L Alexander, 'Causing the Conditions of One's Defence: A Theoretical Non-Problem' (2013) 7(3) *Criminal Law and Philosophy* 623.

[23] We discuss the inaccurate framing of prior fault^{OFF} rules, and why this matters, in Chapters 1–4.

[24] Singular approaches lack the resources to engage with prior fault^{OFF} as a form of *inculpation* rather than a blocking of *exculpation*.

based on D's conduct at T1 leading to impaired capacity and harms at T2. This is not possible for prior fault^{DEF} rules. Rather, in the context of supervening defences, prior fault^{DEF} rules appear to operate by reference to two quite distinct rationales.

The first rationale mirrors the conceptual route for prior fault^{OFF} rules, blaming D for mistake making in circumstances of self-induced impaired capacity. Here, despite impaired capacity, D still commits an offence at T2 (i.e. D completes all necessary actus reus and mens rea elements). D's mistake relates instead to the need for a defence, a mistaken belief in the circumstances of crisis that might otherwise (if D's belief were correct) give rise to an excuse or justification on the facts. Where D's mistake is honest (and perhaps reasonable[25]), such mistaken belief may still provide a normative basis for exculpation, and this is accepted within several existing defences. However, where D's mistake at T2 is attributable to their impaired capacity, and where that impairment is attributable to their blameworthy conduct at T1, rules have developed to block D's appeal to a defence. This is captured within the earlier example involving voluntary intoxication: having consumed hallucinogenic drugs, D kills V in the mistaken belief that V is about to shoot them.[26] We discuss this form of 'incapacity-based' prior fault^{DEF} in Chapter 9.

The second rationale is conceptually distinct, and does not engage with issues of impaired capacity or mistake making. Rather, when D commits an offence at T2, they do so in genuine circumstances of crisis capable of giving rise to a supervening defence. However, D's earlier conduct at T1 is important to our perception of the crisis point at T2, reducing or even extinguishing its normative exculpatory relevance. We see examples of this across a range of supervening defences, though it is notable that such rules have developed with a high degree of inconsistency. Our earlier example marks a particularly compelling end of the spectrum, where D's conduct at T1 is consciously aimed at manipulating the circumstances of crisis at T2: D wants to kill V, D hands V a knife and then goads V until they (as anticipated) lash out at D, D shoots and kills V to protect themselves.[27] The same rationale is employed, however, to justify the blocking of defences well beyond examples of this kind, including (in the context of duress) simple association with persons at T1 where D foresaw or should have foreseen the potential for threats and compulsion. We discuss this form of 'contrived defence' prior fault^{DEF} in Chapter 10.

Despite important structural and functional similarities, therefore, it remains necessary to separate these two sets of rules when considering prior fault^{DEF} and defences. We do this in the chapters that follow, both in our critique of current rules, as well as within our preferred reformulation of such rules. The

[25] We discuss the relationship between prior fault and objective requirements of this kind later in Section 8.4.
[26] See *Hatton* [2005] EWCA Crim 2951.
[27] See *Rashford* [2005] EWCA Crim 3377.

separation identified here provides a necessary basis for ensuring conceptual clarity and focus.

8.4 Objective and subjective defence requirements and prior fault^{DEF}

Objective tests, where D's conduct and/or foresight is measured against that of the reasonable person, are widespread (in varying degrees) across legal systems; and within common law systems, and certainly in England & Wales, they are particularly prevalent in the construction of supervening defences.[28] This has some significance for prior fault^{DEF} since the prevalence of objective elements means a reduction of subjective elements in the construction of supervening defences. This is important because it narrows considerably the scope for incapacity-based prior fault^{DEF} rules (e.g. intoxication rules).

Where D's defence is objectively defined, and we are judging D's conduct/foresight against that of the reasonable sober person, D's intoxicated incapacity at T2 becomes irrelevant. It is only where defences are defined subjectively, focused on D's actual awareness and capacity, that D's impairment becomes a live issue (i.e. potentially grounding D's defence); and so it is only here that D's reasons for impairment, including potential prior fault^{DEF} at T1, also become relevant.[29] This is why, in Chapter 9, we focus predominantly on self-defence, which includes a significant subjective element, as well as other subjective belief-based defences, where prior fault^{DEF} analysis is required to explain the blocking of defences.

It is important to recognize that the same narrowing is *not* relevant to contrived defences, discussed in Chapter 10. Where a defence is contrived (in the so-called schemer cases), the defendant's conduct at T2 may be both rational and reasonable when viewed in isolation, and so objectively constructed elements at T2 cannot do the work of prior fault^{DEF} blocking. This is why, in that chapter, a wider range of defences are discussed.

8.5 Conclusion

In the two chapters that follow, we explore current prior fault^{DEF} rules as they relate to incapacity and mistake making (Chapter 9) and contrived defence cases

[28] There are several reasons for this, both practical and theoretical. See AP Simester, *Fundamentals of Criminal Law* (OUP, 2021) Ch 19.

[29] Objective standards are noted by Wilson as an alternative, alongside prior fault^{DEF} rules, to prevent defences applying to those demonstrating a wider 'antisocial or dangerous disposition': W Wilson, 'How Criminal Defences Work' in A Reed and M Bohlander (eds) *General Defences in Criminal Law* (Hart 2014) 7, 14.

(Chapter 10). Within each, D's conduct at T1 causes us to reconsider the normative relevance of the crisis (or perceived crisis) at T2 that might otherwise ground their supervening defence. D's conduct at T1 is not used to substitute for missing offence elements; we are not dealing with the legal fictions encountered in the Part I chapters. However, if D's T1 conduct is to block a defence at T2, we need to understand how this is being achieved, and whether and to what extent rules of this kind may be justified.

9
INCAPACITY AND PRIOR FAULT BLOCKING DEFENCES

9.1 Introduction

This chapter interrogates prior fault^{DEF} rules that apply to block a defence where D's impaired capacity at T2 leads to a mistaken belief in the need for defensive action, and where that impairment has resulted from blameworthy conduct at T1.[1] Take our example from the previous chapter: having consumed hallucinogenic drugs, D kills V in the mistaken belief that V is about to shoot them. In this example, D has a mistaken belief in the necessity of defensive force, and commits an offence (murder) on that basis. Although self-defence is capable of application in English law where D's belief is mistaken, including cases where D's mistaken belief is unreasonably held, circumstances of prior fault^{DEF} (as in our example) will result in its effective exclusion.[2] Rather than being judged on the facts as D honestly believed them to be (i.e. even if unreasonable), the prior fault^{DEF} rule means that D will only be able to rely on the defence if a reasonable sober person would have made the same mistake.

Incapacity-based prior fault^{DEF} is the first of two categories of rules identified in Chapter 8, which can block the application of an otherwise available supervening defence. We discuss the second category—'contrived defences'—in Chapter 10.

Intuitions may differ on the appropriateness of incapacity-based prior fault^{DEF} rules, presenting a challenge regarding the basic fairness of the law. At one extreme, we might question whether prior fault^{DEF} should *ever* block the application of a defence on this basis.[3] D's conduct at T1 may be perceived as blameworthy in that D has voluntarily relinquished full capacity, but causing capacity impairment need not involve a criminal wrong at that point (e.g. most obviously, where D becomes intoxicated through alcohol), and D has not set out to manipulate the circumstances of later events. At T2, although D commits an offence, they do so with an

[1] As introduced in Chapter 1, we are adopting the notation 'prior fault^{OFF}' and 'prior fault^{DEF}' to distinguish between prior fault rules relevant to the construction of a crime and prior fault rules relevant to the blocking of a defence.

[2] This has been codified, for self-defence, within the Criminal Justice and Immigration Act 2008, s76. Discussed in Section 9.2 below.

[3] Two of the authors previously adopted this position in Q Jahangir, JJ Child, and H Crombag, 'Prior Fault and Contrived Criminal Defences: Coming to the Law with Clean Hands' (2017) 1 *Institute of Law Journal* 28. We revisit the issue in Section 9.3 below.

Prior Fault Criminalization. John J Child, Adrian Hunt, and Hans S. Crombag, Oxford University Press.
© Oxford University Press 2026. DOI: 10.1093/9780191874734.003.0011

honest belief in the need for defensive force. D is mistaken, and so the perceived 'crisis' justifying the defence may be absent in fact, but D's belief in it would otherwise provide sufficient basis for the defence to apply. Indeed, perhaps the strongest argument against this category of prior fault^{DEF} is to consider the dilemma created for D at T2: where D knows their capacity is impaired through intoxication, but honestly believes they are in immediate danger, what should the law expect of them? Should D restrain themselves from any and all defensive force, risking harm (perhaps death) on the basis that they *might* be mistaken about the threat? And if we think not, perhaps the better route is to allow D's defence, and to abolish the prior fault^{DEF} rule which would currently block it.

However, arguments in favour of abolition may be overstated, and at least two principal considerations should be weighed against them. The first is a recognition that defences, unlike offences, are more likely to hold D to an objective standard of reasonableness (as we introduced in Chapter 8, Section 8.4).[4] Allowing D to rely upon a potentially unreasonable mistake in self-defence is not typical across defences; it is very much the outlier. For most defences, if D's mistake is to have any exculpatory weight, then it must be based on reasonable grounds. This prevalence of objective elements within defences (and not so in the definition of offences) can be justified by the structural differences between offence and defence mistakes: whilst an offence-based mistake typically provides a *denial* of a *pro-tanto* wrong (i.e. D does not recognize that they are wronging at all), a defence-based mistake *involves* a *pro-tanto* wrong (i.e. D knows they are performing a criminal wrong) and so D is on notice that *good* reasons are required to act.[5] One might logically conclude from this that all defences should be defined to require reasonable grounds for mistake.[6] But they do not, and that debate is not our focus here.[7] Rather, our focus is on those defences which do allow for unreasonable mistakes, asking whether there may be additional grounds for qualifying this with consideration of prior fault^{DEF}.

The second reason to weigh against complete abolition of the prior fault^{DEF} rule is the worry that the 'baby should not be discarded with the bathwater'. There may indeed be legitimate concerns about the potential over-inclusivity of current rules, in the sense that they may unfairly block D's defence across an overly broad definition of fault. However, we have done considerable work in the first part of this

[4] Discussed in AP Simester, *Fundamentals of Criminal Law* (OUP, 2021) Ch 19.

[5] Ibid 485–89.

[6] This is the position endorsed by Simester.

[7] Even if we conclude that all defences should be defined to include a reasonableness requirement, this still begs questions about the definition of this requirement and whether—in particular—the reasonableness standard should be relative to D's actual capacity at T2. This discussion is likely to be heavily influenced by our perception of whether D's impaired capacity is itself justified or excused, returning us to the same normative questions that are our focus in prior fault debates here. We introduced this idea briefly in the previous chapter when discussing the indirect effects of prior fault^{DEF} rules (Chapter 8, Section 8.4), and we return to it in the final chapter (Chapter 11, Section 11.3.1).

book to identify non-absolute (more) reliable markers of blame at T1. So, it is not necessarily an 'all-or-nothing' choice. It is possible that comparable markers of blame at T1 could also be applied to the question of whether D's defence should be blocked because of T1 prior fault leading to their T2 conduct. Thus, the question here as regards blocking defences is whether—at a minimum—a narrow(er) more measured scheme of prior fault^{DEF} rules than is currently applied (in some cases) may be justified.

Before proceeding to that inquiry, our initial task is to investigate the current use of prior fault^{DEF} incapacity rules, where these are used to block an otherwise applicable defence. This is our focus in Section 9.2, which unpacks and critiques the use (and effect) of such rules in the current law. Having identified core problems with the current law in terms of both fairness and consistency, the chapter shifts focus to questions of reform. We consider options for reform in Section 9.3; the lessons from empirical data from psychological and neuroscientific studies, including our own, in Section 9.4; before setting out and justifying our preferred solution in Section 9.5.

9.2 Current prior fault^{DEF} incapacity rules

The current law in England & Wales leaves very little space for prior fault^{DEF} incapacity rules in the context of defences. However, this does not represent an express decision to reject such rules, or their normative justification. Rather, as highlighted already, it is simply because most defences require D's mistaken belief to be *reasonably* held for exculpatory relevance. Where reasonableness is required, the legal assessment of D's mistaken belief is transformed, and specific prior fault^{DEF} rules become unnecessary: the question is simply whether a reasonable person, *not* sharing D's impaired capacity, would have made the same mistake. Thus, where D's mistake was induced by their incapacity, the test will not be met and the defence will not be available. Specific prior fault^{DEF} rules are only relevant, therefore, in the context of defences that allow D to rely on their unreasonable subjective beliefs (i.e. those that may not be shared by the reasonable unimpaired person). Indeed, as we have said, although we talk of prior fault^{DEF} 'blocking' D's defence, what we really mean is that—in circumstances of prior fault^{DEF}—an otherwise subjective defence requirement will be transformed into an objective requirement, and D may only rely on their subjective mistake if a reasonable unimpaired person would have done similarly. This, in effect, blocks D's defence.

The discussion of prior fault^{DEF} incapacity rules, in English law, is therefore isolated to mistake making in the context of certain specific statutory defences, and—most importantly—to the general defence of self-defence. This is reflected in the examples discussed below. However, the conceptual questions arising here should not be misunderstood as particular to self-defence, or any other defence. Rather, it is particular only to the category of *mistaken* defences, where, for the defence to be available, D's mistake need not be held on objectively reasonable grounds. Although this represents a minority of defences (and particularly so outside of England & Wales[8]), it remains a significant minority, and may well expand in the future.

In the subsections that follow, we identify and evaluate the use of prior fault^{DEF} incapacity rules in the blocking of current defences in such circumstances. Our aim, in particular, is to understand how the current law defines prior fault in these contexts, and the mechanism through which a defence is blocked. We begin with paradigm cases of voluntary intoxication, before exploring rules that expand from that paradigm through proxy and/or analogy.

9.2.1 Voluntary intoxication

The first group of prior fault cases involves D becoming voluntarily intoxicated with a dangerous drug at T1, leading to a *relevant* mistake in defence at T2. As highlighted already, an unreasonable intoxicated mistake will not be relevant for objective elements within defences such as duress (i.e. where D's conduct/foresight is measured against a reasonable sober person standard).[9] However, for defences such as self-defence, where the focus is on D's subjective beliefs at T2, whether the law allows D to rely on an intoxicated mistake may be crucial to their liability. To repeat our introduction hypothetical: having consumed hallucinogenic drugs, D kills V in the mistaken belief that V is about to shoot them. The question here is whether D should be permitted to rely on their intoxicated belief, providing the basis for a defence, or whether they should be legally blocked from doing so?

9.2.1.1 Current prior fault^{DEF} intoxication rules

English law has inconsistently recognized and applied prior fault^{DEF} rules to block defences in circumstances of voluntary intoxication. For self-defence however, although prior fault^{DEF} rules have not always been recognized historically,[10] they are now firmly established within the common law.[11] Indeed, the intoxication rule is now confirmed by section 76(5) of the Criminal Justice and Immigration Act 2008, which states simply that the defence 'does not enable D to rely on any mistaken belief attributable to intoxication that was voluntarily induced'. In terms of

[8] Civil law jurisdictions, e.g., will typically define defences to require objective reasonableness.

[9] *Hasan* [2005] 2 AC 467; J Child et al, *Simester and Sullivan's Criminal Law* (8th Ed, Hart, 2022) Ch 20.

[10] Intoxicated mistakes were relevant to self-defence in older cases, such as *Marshall* (1830) 1 Lew 76; *Gamlen* (1858) 1 F&F 90; and even *Wardrope* (1960) CrimLR 770. A Ashworth, 'Reason, Logic and Criminal Liability' (1975) 91 *Law Quarterly Review* 102.

[11] *O'Grady* [1987] QB 995, *O'Connor* [1991] CrimLR 13; *Hatton* [2005] EWCA Crim 2951.

justification for the rule, the case law provides only limited insights, ranging from broad appeals to intuition,[12] to the drawing of a direct equivalence with prior fault^{OFF} intoxication rules. Regarding the latter, the basic logic seems to be that if intoxication is sufficiently wrongful to construct the elements of a crime, then D should not be able to rely on it in their appeal for a defence.[13]

Outside of self-defence, there is considerably more uncertainty about the legal status of the prior fault^{DEF} intoxication rule. Most prominent here is the 1980 case of *Jaggard v Dickinson*,[14] where the Divisional Court allowed D to rely on her intoxicated mistake of fact to establish a 'lawful excuse' defence to charges of criminal damage.[15] In this case, having been given permission by a friend to use his house as her own, D became intoxicated and forced entry (causing damage) to an identical house on the same street. D honestly believed that she was entitled to gain entry in this manner, mistakenly believing it to be her friend's house, which was held to be sufficient to satisfy the subjective defence test for lawful excuse.[16] However, particularly given the unreasonable nature of D's belief (i.e. the owners of the damaged property were at home, making clear that she should leave), it is questionable whether D should have been able to rely on a mistake so clearly induced by intoxication. This argument was considered by the court but rejected on the basis that the intoxication *offending* rule—clarified in *Majewski*—was not applicable to belief-based *defences*.

Jaggard v Dickinson has not yet been overruled, though it has attracted considerable criticism,[17] and its application has been confined largely to the statutory 'lawful excuse' defence to a prosecution for criminal damage.[18] It is not, however, the only supervening defence out-of-step with the simple proposition that D should not be able to rely on a mistake induced by voluntary intoxication. For example, as we discussed in Chapter 4, prior fault rules are not applied to insanity in English law, and this is also true where insanity is applied as a supervening defence (i.e. as an exculpatory rule, where D has completed all elements of an offence). Similarly, when applying diminished responsibility as a partial defence to murder, a state of voluntary intoxication will not necessarily undermine D's claim to the defence.[19] Despite the apparent solidity of the prior fault^{DEF} intoxication rule in the

[12] E.g. from Lord Lane: 'Reason recoils from the conclusion that in such circumstances [intoxication leading to mistaken defensive force] a defendant is entitled to leave the Court without a stain on his character.' *O'Grady* [1987] QB 995, 1000.

[13] The logic is 'basic' in the sense that equivalence between the function of the rule in offences and defences is assumed rather than demonstrated, and, of course, because (even if we want equivalence) this should beg questions about the appropriateness of intoxication rules in the offending context.

[14] [1981] QB 527.

[15] Criminal Damage Act 1971, s1.

[16] Criminal Damage Act 1971, s5(2)(a) and s5(3).

[17] See, e.g., Law Commission, *Intoxication and Criminal Liability* (LC No 314, 2009) [3.81–3.83].

[18] See, e.g., comments by Elias LJ in *Magee v CPS* [2014] EWHC 4089 [33–36].

[19] A state of acute intoxication is not recognized (legally) as a mental disorder when applying diminished responsibility, but the partial defence may still apply in circumstances of comorbidity. See J Child

context of self-defence, therefore, its application as a general rule across defences which excuse unreasonable mistakes is rather more uncertain and inconsistent. Notably, this confused picture is also apparent in several other jurisdictions.[20]

9.2.1.2 Evaluating the current law

There has been considerable criticism of the current legal position, which has typically focused on legal consistency rather than fundamental normative questions of fairness. Although consistency is important, it has too often (in our view) skewed towards technical debates about the elements of criminal offences/defences and has not (in our view) often enough resulted in normative evaluation of decisions to apply/not apply prior fault^{DEF} exclusion to certain defences.

In many cases, the goal of consistency is foregrounded in a manner that seeks to avoid engaging with questions of fairness. This applies to consistency arguments between defences, which simply present cases such as *Jaggard v Dickinson* as anomalous.[21] It also applies to consistency arguments between intoxication rules in the context of offending and defending. This view is often expressed in purely policy terms: that the same policy reasons seeking prior fault^{OFF}–based liability for offending apply with equal force to qualifying the use of defences.[22] This *may* be true, but the lack of principle underpinning current intoxication rules in the context of prior fault^{OFF} (which we discussed in Part I) makes this little more than an appeal to intuition by analogy for prior fault^{DEF},[23] and *should* trigger a principled normative evaluation in both contexts.

Connected to this appeal to intuition by analogy is the more technical claim that certain defences—including self-defence and lawful excuse—should be viewed as constituent elements of the *offences* to which they are applied, and so prior fault^{DEF} rules should apply in the same way as prior fault^{OFF} rules.[24] This has led to the suggestion that the prior fault^{DEF} rule should also map onto the distinction between basic intent offences and specific intent offences. This would mean that D's intoxicated mistake should block a defence where D is charged with a basic intent crime, but not where D is charged with a specific intent crime, and the current law is criticized by some for its apparent failure to make this distinction. Thus, for example,

et al, *Simester and Sullivan's Criminal Law* (8th Ed, Hart, 2022) Ch 10.5; D Ormerod et al, *Smith and Hogan's Criminal Law* (17th Ed, OUP, 2024) 598, calling for clarification from the Court of Appeal.

[20] See, e.g., A Goldberg, JJ Child, H Crombag, and D Roef, 'Prior Fault Blame in England and Wales, Germany and the Netherlands' (2021) 8(1) *Journal of International and Comparative Law* 53; P Robinson, 'Causing the Conditions of One's Own Defence' (1985) 71 *Virginia Law Review* 1, 10.

[21] This was the focus in Law Commission, *Intoxication and Criminal Liability* (LC No 314, 2009) [3.81–3.83].

[22] Ibid. This was also accepted by the Commission, as the principal justification for prior fault^{DEF}.

[23] And, as we discussed in Chapter 1, Section 1.3.1, a false analogy at that.

[24] See, e.g., G Dingwall, 'Intoxicated Mistakes about the Need for Self-defence' (2007) 70(1) *Modern Law Review* 127; J Spencer, 'Drunken Defence' [2006] 65 *CLJ* 267; R Mackay, 'The Taint of Intoxication' (1990) 13(1) *International Journal of Law and Psychiatry* 37.

responding to the mistaken self-defence cases of *O'Grady* and *Hatton*[25] where the blocking effect of intoxication was applied without such distinction, Dingwall states that[26]

> . . . *Hatton* is indefensible as a matter of principle. Consistency in the criminal law is a virtue. Yet, after *Hatton*, the current position is inconsistent both with the general principles regarding substantive criminal liability for intoxicated acts and with the general principle regarding genuine though objectively unreasonable mistakes in self-defence.

There is some merit in this argument, but only where intoxication is understood as a form of non-specific fault that should always result in one form of liability (basic intent offences) and not another (specific intent offences).[27]

However, as soon as we begin to interrogate what we mean by prior fault—in type and degree—distinguishing offence and defence elements becomes essential, even in the context of offences (like murder) that include an unlawfulness element within the offence definition. For the Law Commission in 2009, for example, having equated intoxication with a mens rea of recklessness, it was recognized that this provided little guidance on the correct approach to prior fault^{DEF}: self-defence and other belief-based defences are not concerned with recklessness (i.e. there is no mens rea state to be substituted for), but are instead asking whether D's existing intoxicated belief state should be accepted or blocked from legal application. And the answer to this binary question logically remains the same regardless of D's underlying offence.[28] Like the Law Commission, we agree that if prior fault^{DEF} is to play a principled role within the law, we must first understand the blocking of defences as conceptually distinct from prior fault^{OFF}.

How then should we quantify intoxicated fault in the context of a mistaken defence? This is the crucial question in our view, and one that has received insufficient attention in the current law and literature. The dominant view, represented by the Law Commission, is simply that prior fault^{DEF} intoxication should block D from relying on a mistaken belief to establish a supervening defence, on the basis that (i) D should have reasonable grounds for using force in defence,[29] (ii) objective facts are required to apply other defence elements,[30] and (iii) the approach to self-defence was endorsed by Parliament, and is right in policy terms.[31] The

[25] [1987] QB 995; [2005] EWCA Crim 2951.

[26] G Dingwall, 'Intoxicated Mistakes about the Need for Self-defence' (2007) 70 (1) *Modern Law Review* 127, 136.

[27] It is also fair to say that explanations of prior fault within the current law provide little more than this.

[28] Law Commission, *Intoxication and Criminal Liability* (LC No 314, 2009) [3.53–3.83].

[29] Ibid [3.62] and [3.66–3.71].

[30] Ibid [3.63].

[31] Ibid [3.64–3.65] and [3.72–3.73].

problem with these arguments, however, is that for the most part they are arguments in favour of objective tests (for defences) in general,[32] and therefore tell us little about the current prior fault^{DEF} intoxication rule as applied to unreasonable subjective mistakes. Thus, it may appear that, to understand why prior fault^{DEF} intoxication applies as an exception to an otherwise subjective test, we must either reject that test entirely, or we are left with the aforementioned non-specific intuitions about voluntary intoxication as (somehow) uniquely wrongful.

However, if the basis for the current approach simply involves the use of intoxication as a proxy for fault, without any differentiation as to type or degree of intoxication or context, this gives rise to fairness concerns over potential over-inclusiveness, where intoxication is used to block a belief-based defence without adequate justification. The argument is made in two ways. First, although we might concede that an intoxicated mistake is unreasonable, we might challenge the idea that it is uniquely so. We can see this in the reasoning of the Divisional Court in *Jaggard v Dickinson*, for example, where it was observed that 'a belief can be just as much honestly held if it is induced by intoxication, as if it stems from stupidity, forgetfulness or inattention'.[33] The second approach, in contrast, challenges the assumption that voluntary intoxication is always unreasonable. Particularly in the context of alcohol intoxication—which, of course, is in itself *legal*—the argument is that the law should take account of context. For example, Lynch argues that the law is 'hypocritical' where D is blocked from relying on a mistake induced by only partial intoxication,[34] and indeed Sir Brian Leveson P raised the concern, (obiter) in *Collins*, that the intoxication exclusion might be 'unduly restrictive' in the context of householder self-defence cases where D 'is not anticipating any interaction with a trespasser'.[35] In each case, the underlying concern is with the use of intoxication as a proxy for fault generally, rather than defining and identifying fault differently where such differentiation is normatively justified.[36]

There are also concerns that intoxication may be under-inclusive as a proxy for fault generally, and rather that other causes of incapacity should also apply to block belief-based defences. This may be argued in quite general terms, as we discussed in relation to the Law Commission above, where a focus on reasonableness leads to arguments against subjective tests for defences entirely. However, short of this, it may be that specific types of conduct at T1 (leading to mistakes at T2) should be identified alongside intoxication, blocking the application of a defence. Indeed, there is evidence of this tension in the current law, leading to the developments discussed below in Section 9.2.2.

[32] Indeed, the Commission make key use of an article arguing for just this [at 3.62]: AP Simester, 'Mistakes in Defence' (1992) 12(3) *Oxford Journal of Legal Studies* 295.

[33] [1981] QB 527. See also D Ormerod et al, *Smith and Hogan's Criminal Law* (17th Ed, OUP, 2024) 346.

[34] A Lynch, 'The Scope of Intoxication' (1982) *Criminal Law Review* 139, 144.

[35] [2016] EWHC 33, [30].

[36] See also J Horder, 'Sobering Up? The Law Commission on Criminal Intoxication' (1995) 58(4) *Modern Law Review* 534, 543, discussing the reasonableness of certain intoxicated reactions.

9.2.1.3 Conclusions on prior fault^{DEF} intoxication

We are left to reflect upon a prior fault^{DEF} rule that is routinely presented as robust and fair in the context of self-defence, but on analysis appears to be anything but. The rule is inconsistent in its application across different defences, it lacks a clear normative rationale in its construction (i.e. the intoxication proxy), it is over-inclusive in its potential application to 'reasonable' intoxication, and it is under-inclusive in its lack of potential application outside of that proxy. The next subsection elaborates on the last of these concerns.

9.2.2 Beyond voluntary intoxication

A potential second group of prior fault cases also involves incapacity, but this time caused by circumstances *other than* voluntary intoxication. The law here is highly uncertain. However, in theory at least, prior fault^{DEF} rules in this group would share the same basic structure and function as the intoxication rules discussed in Section 9.2.1. Thus, we are concerned with situations where supervening defences engage with D's subjective beliefs in defence (such as self-defence), where D's mistaken belief is attributable to a state of impaired capacity, and D's impairment may be traced back to blameworthy conduct at T1. In this group, D's blameworthy conduct at T1 would not be limited to voluntary intoxication and would be capable of including any other external or internal cause.

The initial headline regarding this group, however, is that there are *no* prior fault^{DEF} rules of this kind. Thus, whereas intoxication rules may apply to block subjective supervening defences, there are no further incapacity-based exclusions articulated as a matter of doctrine. Prior fault^{OFF} automatism, discussed in Chapter 3 in the context of offending, has no role in defences,[37] and internal causes of incapacity are (again) set aside from prior fault analysis.[38] Regarding the latter, there is an ongoing debate about the *potential* for prior fault insanity,[39] and we discussed this, in the context of offending, in Chapter 4. Should prior fault rules ever extend to insanity then this would also impact insanity as a supervening defence: potentially blocking the application of the defence in circumstances of prior fault^{DEF} (e.g. in cases of medication non-compliance). Currently, however, there appears little prospect of this type of reform being taken forward.[40]

[37] If D lacks voluntariness, then they cannot form a belief state necessary for a subjective defence, and so there can be no mistaken belief to block.

[38] *Beard* [1990] AC 479. Discussed in Chapter 4.

[39] See, in particular, Law Commission, *Insanity and Automatism* (Discussion Paper, 2013) Part 6.

[40] Despite this, as we also discussed in Chapter 4, Section 4.3.1, even without the explicit expansion of prior fault, the current insanity defence is capable of satisfying many of the public policy aims pursued by a prior fault$^{OFF \,\&\, DEF}$ rule (i.e. in terms of public protection from future dangerousness). Rather than an unqualified acquittal, the special verdict of 'not guilty by reason of insanity' provides the court with a number of disposal options, including compulsory treatment and/or supervision orders.

So why are we identifying non-intoxicated incapacity as a separate group (at least potentially) of prior fault^{DEF} rules? The answer is that, notwithstanding the headline position, certain inculpatory rules may be identified. These rules are not articulated within current doctrine as prior fault^{DEF} rules outside of intoxication. But therein, perhaps, lies the problem. If one accepts—as we do[41]—that T1 fault may exist *normatively* outside of intoxication, then the absence of prior fault^{DEF} rules in this space represents a problem of potential under-criminalization. The rules we discuss below are examples of courts, tacitly at least, recognizing this potential under-criminalization problem, and stretching current laws to achieve a liability outcome. The approach of the courts here is understandable, but—as we will discuss—also deeply problematic. On the one hand, the manipulation of existing rules is insufficient, in that such rules can never realistically replace the absence of a non-intoxication-based prior fault^{DEF} rule, and so the risk of under-criminalization remains. And on the other hand, the manipulation of existing rules can do very real harm to the coherence (present and future) of those rules. Such manipulation risks greater uncertainty in the law, and potential unfairness where legal rules are applied to achieve liability without normative engagement with the unique circumstances of the perceived gap being filled.

We see both problems exhibited in the current law examples discussed below. It is clear the current law is woefully ill-equipped to engage with this group of potential prior fault^{DEF} cases.

9.2.2.1 Expanding the proxy of intoxication

The first example of prior fault^{DEF} expansion comes by stretching the notion of 'intoxication' for legal purposes. 'Intoxication' has traditionally been understood as requiring a 'drug-on-board' state (i.e. where drugs are active within D's system).[42] However, English courts have been willing to extend this definition to include certain kinds of impairment *following* a drug-on-board state, and having done so, to block defences which would otherwise be available on account that D's claimed mistake was the result of 'intoxication'. This extended version of 'intoxication' was confirmed by the Court of Appeal in *Taj*,[43] which we have discussed previously (in the context of prior fault^{OFF}) in Chapter 2.

It will be recalled that *Taj* involved circumstances of mistaken self-defence. Coming upon the broken-down vehicle of V, an electrician, D became convinced (mistakenly) that V was a terrorist, intent on causing explosions in London. D attacked V, causing serious bodily harms, and was later charged with, and convicted

[41] Discussed in Chapters 3 and 4.
[42] This is still the orthodox approach outside of English law.
[43] [2018] EWCA Crim 1743.

of, attempted murder. D's appeal to mistaken self-defence was blocked by the intoxication prior fault^{DEF} rule on the basis that his mistaken belief was 'attributable to intoxication'.[44] Crucially, however, there was no evidence that D had drugs or alcohol active in his system. Rather, D was described as suffering a drug-induced psychosis, attributable to *previous* heavy and sustained drug use.[45] However, as explained previously in Chapter 2, the court focused on the definition of 'intoxication' and 'attributable to intoxication', and held that:[46]

> The fact is that medical science has advanced such that, in the modern age, the longer term *sequelae* of abusing alcohol or drugs are better known and understood; and, as in the present case, it was agreed that Taj's episode . . . was a direct result of his earlier drink and drug-taking in the previous days and weeks.

For the Court, this represented:[47]

> . . . an application of *Majewski*, rather than an extension of that decision or, at the highest, a most incremental extension.

Despite the confident language employed, the court's interpretation—even on its own terms—is attempting to thread the eye of a needle. It was a necessary step to expand the interpretation of the intoxication rules if they were to find liability in a non-drug-on-board case of this kind, but the aim was to do so without disturbing current precedent that excludes prior fault^{DEF} consideration from non-intoxication causes (including causes that can be traced back to previous drug use/abuse).[48] The court's aim, therefore, was to distinguish drug-induced psychosis as a particular kind of effect that can and should be treated as if it were a drug-on-board state, drawing on advances in scientific knowledge to support that shift.

Whilst the blameworthiness of Taj himself may be the subject of reasonable discussion (i.e. as an example of potential non-intoxicated prior fault^{DEF}), the *Taj* precedent does damage to the intoxication rules themselves, and we believe it should be reversed.[49] The problems created are both normative and practical. However, to understand them, it is first important to recognize the scientific/clinical fallacy at the core of the judgment.

[44] Criminal Justice and Immigration Act 2008, s76(5). D is not able to rely on his 'intoxicated' mistaken belief and will be judged instead on what a reasonable sober person would have believed.

[45] It is noteworthy that Taj acknowledged that he had experienced similar reactions to alcohol and/or cocaine intoxication in the past.

[46] *Taj* [2018] EWCA Crim 1743, [57].

[47] Ibid.

[48] Ibid [46–49, 57–60]. Referring to *Harris* [2013] EWCA Crim 223 and *Davis* (1881) 14 Cox CC 563 on withdrawal, and *Beard* [1920] AC 479 on addiction.

[49] JJ Child, H Crombag, and GR Sullivan, 'Defending the Delusional, the Irrational, and the Dangerous' [2020] *Criminal Law Review* 306.

The court's reliance on medical science to draw sharp lines between different alcohol or drug-related causes of psychotic delusions finds little support in basic pharmacology or neurobiology, and little support in the applied setting of the clinic. Whilst Taj's psychotic episode *could have* resulted from his earlier alcohol and/or drug use, and this was initially highlighted in the expert reports as the 'best guess' of clinicians, neither of these provide anything approximating a scientifically robust determination of cause.[50] The reality is that the symptoms for psychosis—principally delusions and hallucinations—can occur in a range of alcohol and/or drug-related conditions, including acute intoxication, withdrawal (delirium tremens), alcohol or drug-induced psychotic disorder (alcohol hallucinosis), disorders associated with alcoholism (e.g. Korsakoff's dementia[51]), etc. But they could equally indicate the presence of a comorbid mental illness caused or triggered by drug and/or alcohol use, or could be entirely separate from drug or alcohol use.[52] These (and other) alcohol and drug-related causes of psychotic symptoms are understood from the research and clinical literature as being distinct, but understanding of the precise phenomenological features and underlying neurobiological mechanisms is far from settled, making differential diagnosis to separate one from the others complex and prone to error.[53]

In light of this, the practical problems created for the law become obvious. For the *Taj* precedent to be applied, sharp causal distinctions must be drawn between psychosis caused by previous acute intoxication (caught within intoxication rules), from psychosis caused by withdrawal or longer-term sequelae resulting from historic use, and psychosis resulting from primary mental illness separate from and comorbid with drug use (outside intoxication rules).[54] This is simply not credible in practice, and *Taj* is a case-in-point. The final expert opinion report before Taj's appeal (following further treatment and observation) heavily qualifies the earlier

[50] We discuss this further in JJ Child, H Crombag, and GR Sullivan, 'Defending the Delusional, the Irrational, and the Dangerous' [2020] *Criminal Law Review* 306; 'Drunk, Dangerous and Delusional: How Legal Concept-Creep Risks Overcriminalization' (2020) 115(12) *Addiction* 2200; H Crombag, JJ Child, and R Fortson, 'Understanding the "Fault" in Prior-Fault Intoxication' in A Reed and M Bohlander (eds) *Fault* (Routledge, 2022) Ch 5.

[51] Korsakoff Syndrome is alcohol-induced persisting amnestic disorder, designated as an 'alcohol-induced major neurocognitive disorder, amnestic confabulatory type': American Medical Association's *Diagnostic and Statistical Manual* (DSM V).

[52] See, e.g., G Jordaan and R Emsley, 'Alcohol-Induced Psychotic Disorder: A Review' (2014) 29(2) *Metabolic Brain Disease* 231; J Perälä et al, 'Alcohol-Induced Psychotic Disorder and Delirium in the General Population' (2010) 197(3) *The British Journal of Psychiatry* 200; CP Engelhard et al, 'Alcohol-Induced Psychotic Disorder: A Systematic Literature Review' (2015) 57(3) *Tijdschrift voor Psychiatrie* 192.

[53] E.g. in a three-year follow-up study of 535 cases initially diagnosed as acute cannabis-induced psychosis, 44.5 per cent were later re-diagnosed as (also) having schizophrenic-spectrum disorder. M Arendt et al, 'Cannabis-Induced Psychosis and Subsequent Schizophrenia-Spectrum Disorders' (2005) 187(6) *The British Journal of Psychiatry* 510.

[54] *Taj* [2018] EWCA Crim 1743, [46–49, 57–60]. Referring to *Harris* [2013] EWCA Crim 223 and *Davis* (1881) 14 Cox CC 563 on withdrawal, and *Beard* [1920] AC 479 on addiction.

view that Taj's delusion may have been the product of drug/alcohol use, with a new diagnosis of mental illness, namely bipolar disorder (manic depression), identified as an alternative potential cause of his psychosis.[55] It is far from clear if Taj's psychosis was attributable to intoxication, and far from clear if any kind of justice was done through his conviction.

What we are left with is not a measured extension of *Majewski*, but a normative blurring of the boundaries of an already imperfect proxy for prior fault^DEF. It is also not a principled extension. If future courts are to apply *Taj*, the precedent is not to focus on questions of fault (i.e. potentially outside drug-on-board intoxication) as the court provided no normative justification for singling out the type of psychotic delusion in *Taj* from others that may be linked back to previous states of intoxication. Rather, the precedent is to refocus on the proxy of intoxication in an ever more complex and unsatisfactory manner.

9.2.2.2 Expanding by analogy

Despite the headline position (i.e. denying capacity-based prior fault^DEF rules outside of intoxication), there is also a line of authority that has been developed to block mistaken self-defence in a very similar manner where D's mistaken belief results from a non-intoxicated delusion.[56] The blocking has not been expressed in terms of prior fault^DEF, but can (again) be seen as a reaction to a lack of such rules outside of intoxication. The problems here—as we will discuss—arise both in terms of legal clarity, as well as the potential for unfairness in the absence of an articulated explanation for fault/liability (i.e. an explanation *why* the defence is blocked in these circumstances).

Applying the standard tests for self-defence, delusional mistakes (outside of intoxication) should not ordinarily undermine a claim of mistaken self-defence.[57] The first limb of the standard self-defence test is subjective and focuses on whether D genuinely believed it was necessary to use force to defend themselves. The second limb is objective to the extent that it asks whether the force used was reasonable in the circumstances D believed to exist. If applied in the usual way then, self-defence should be available to D whose delusion means they mistakenly think force is necessary, so long as they do not use more force than that belief might objectively warrant. However, in a series of cases involving deluded defendants, the courts have proceeded to block the use of self-defence by applying a different version of the second limb. Rather than asking whether D's force was proportionate to the threat they mistakenly perceived, the courts have asked whether it

[55] JJ Child, H Crombag, and GR Sullivan, 'Defending the Delusional, the Irrational, and the Dangerous' [2020] *Criminal Law Review* 306, discussing Psychiatric Report from Dr Alan Reid (25th April 2018).

[56] Ibid.

[57] Criminal Justice and Immigration Act 2008, s76.

was proportionate to the threat that existed in fact.[58] Thus, where there is no threat in fact, or the threat is significantly less than that perceived by D, their defence will likely fail on this second limb.

The effect of this adjustment to the second limb is to negate the subjective limb entirely, though the courts have been disinclined expressly to acknowledge that this is what they are doing. Instead, they speak of a qualification to the second already objective limb. We are told in *Martin*, for example, that 'in deciding whether excessive force has been used [we should not] take into account whether the defendant is suffering from some psychiatric condition';[59] in *Canns*, that 'it cannot be right that the more psychotic a defendant may be the greater his chances of acquittal';[60] and in *Oye*, that an 'insane person cannot set the standards of reasonableness as to the degree of force used by reference to his own insanity'.[61] The problem with this analysis is that it disguises rather than addresses the issue: where D makes a mistake for *any* reason (including delusions) as to the necessity of defensive force, their response will never pass the second limb of self-defence unless the reasonableness of their force is measured against the facts as they honestly believed them to be. Allowing for delusions within the first limb of the defence is therefore meaningless unless they are also countenanced in the application of the second objective limb by means of examining D's actions by reference to the threat they mistakenly perceived.[62]

The harshness of the current law has also been partly disguised by the availability of alternative defences: namely, diminished responsibility in *Martin* and *Canns*, and insanity in *Oye*. In this manner, the unavailability of self-defence can be presented as a mechanism for diverting mentally disordered individuals to what may be perceived as more appropriate bespoke defences. However, again, this is

[58] See *Martin* [2001] EWCA Crim 2245; *Canns* [2005] EWCA Crim 2264; *Oye* [2013] EWCA Crim 1725; *Taj* [2018] EWCA Crim 1743.

[59] [2001] EWCA Crim 2245, [67]. D lived in a remote farmhouse in Norfolk. He was woken by two people trying to burgle his premises, disturbed them, and then shot them as they tried to escape. One was killed and the other seriously injured. D was convicted of murder and a serious offence against the person. D's appeal was later allowed, substituting manslaughter for murder. Self-defence was not satisfied because of the excessive force used by D, but new evidence provided the basis for a partial defence of diminished responsibility.

[60] [2005] EWCA Crim 2264, [19], following *Martin*. D, while within a secure hospital ward, killed V (a male nurse) whilst suffering delusions that V was attacking and trying to rape him. D was suffering from chronic paranoid schizophrenia. D was convicted of manslaughter by way of diminished responsibility; his appeal, on the basis of self-defence, was rejected.

[61] [2013] EWCA Crim 1725, [47], following *Martin* and *Canns*. D was severely affected by delusions that police officers were agents of evil spirits out to kill him, and launched a series of attacks on officers causing serious harm. D was convicted of affray and maliciously inflicting GBH. D's appeal was later allowed, rejecting self-defence, but allowing insanity (i.e. substituting the special verdict of 'not guilty by reason of insanity').

[62] The debate here has been further confused by reference in *Martin* to the potential for a psychiatric condition to be taken into account in 'exceptional circumstances' (*Martin* [2001] EWCA Crim 2245, [67]), distracting from the more fundamental question of why it should ever be excluded. See G Dingwall, 'Intoxicated Mistakes about the Need for Self-Defence' (2007) 70(1) *Modern Law Review* 127, 131.

not sufficient. Outside of *Oye* and the narrow application of insanity rules, it is important to remember that criminal liability resulted in *Martin* and *Canns* (since diminished responsibility is only a *partial* defence). And even partial defences will not always be available, as we see in *Taj*. The court in *Taj* explained that, 'even if' D's delusion was caused by a non-insane and non-intoxicated delusion, applying the 'equally apposite' authority from *Oye* (under discussion) remains a straightforward basis for rejecting D's appeal.[63] We agree that in strict precedential terms this is the outcome of applying the rule from *Martin*, *Canns*, and *Oye*, but we do not agree that this is either appropriate or fair. This is not a case where D is diverted to a more appropriate defence,[64] but simply a case where the delusional nature of D's mistake has resulted in the blocking of his defence.

Leaving aside the technical elements of this discussion, the result is that by simple virtue of a mental disorder (with no analysis of potential associated prior fault), D is treated in the same way as he would be if he were voluntarily intoxicated at T2. This is unprincipled and should be unacceptable. And yet, for some academic commentators, if D 'cannot invoke his self-induced intoxication to support a plea of self-defence . . . then it *logically follows* that he cannot invoke his own insane delusions to do so either'.[65] But this is a false, and troublesome, equivalence. D's intoxicated mistakes are held to undermine self-defence on the basis of prior fault^{DEF}: we blame D for voluntarily consuming a dangerous drug that they should have known risked uncontrolled and/or risky behaviour. Mistakes induced by mental disorders, absent prior fault, involve none of these tokens for blaming D. Thus, if we want to remove D's defence in the latter category, it is a necessity to have a different reason for doing so, though none is currently offered.

9.3 Framing the potential for reform

The current law accepts the core premise that mistake-based defences should sometimes be blocked in circumstances of prior fault^{DEF} incapacity. However, as discussed in Section 9.2, the legal articulation of that idea is limited almost entirely to cases of voluntary intoxication and, in its current form, creates a route to liability that is both over- and under-inclusive. It is potentially over-inclusive in its application to cases of intoxication, in that it blocks D's defence regardless of the non-culpable circumstances surrounding that intoxication. Conversely, it

63 *Taj* [2018] EWCA Crim 1743, [63–64]. Cf *Press* [2013] EWCA Crim 1849, [44].

64 JJ Child and GR Sullivan, 'When Does the Insanity Defence Apply? Some Recent Cases' [2014] *Criminal Law Review* 787.

65 T Storey, 'Self-Defence: Insane Delusions and Reasonable Force' (2014) 78(1) *Journal of Criminal Law* 12, 15 (emphasis added). The criticism extends to those who would block complete defences, but substitute a partial defence: see C De Than and J Elvin, Chapter 3 and Chapter 11 in B Livings et al (eds), *Mental Condition Defences and the Criminal Justice System* (Cambridge Scholars, 2015).

is under-inclusive in its inconsistent application of the intoxication rule itself, and in its failure to account for forms of prior fault^{DEF} incapacity outside of that status. For these reasons, there is a strong case for reform. To explore this, we need to return to first principles, revisiting the premise that prior fault^{DEF} incapacity at T1 should—at least sometimes—justify blocking an otherwise valid defence at T2.

We opened this chapter by asking whether it is *ever* appropriate to apply such rules, acknowledging that intuitions may differ on even this most basic question. In previous work, some of us have come down in favour of abolishing the prior fault^{DEF} rule, arguing that[66]

> Contrary to the current law, we believe that intoxicated mistakes do not demonstrate sufficient prior fault to justify the blocking of a belief-based defence.... we believe that D's defence should only be blocked where it is contrived; where D has foreseen the relevant risks from her conduct at T1; and where she has chosen to run those risks. Where D simply makes a mistake as a result of her intoxication, no such choices have been made, and so D's prior fault is not sufficient to undermine her claim of crisis.

The view expressed in this extract is a logical response to the unfairness of the current law, but it is no longer a view we support. There are two reasons for this, which we will briefly explain below.

The first reason is empirical and will be explored further in Section 9.4. This empirical work and our own empirical study, in particular, illuminate the predictable ways in which self-induced impairment disrupts the adaptive systems through which individuals recognize emotional cues, detect threat, and regulate approach–avoidance behaviour, and therefore explain why certain mistaken-defensive beliefs arise in states of mental impairment. This work enables us to identify an empirical basis for blaming D's choices at T1—linked to D's conduct at T2—which calls for justification or excuse.[67]

The second reason why we now believe there is a basis for some prior fault^{DEF} rules relates to an increased possibility of articulating such rules in practice. This will be explored subsequently in Section 9.5. Briefly stated, we can say that following our work in the first half of this book, we are now confident that a viable legal model exists for identifying T1 fault leading to incapacity that may be applied fairly and consistently. This provides us with a basis for articulating how to reform the current law. As we will see in Section 9.5, the aim is to move away from

[66] Q Jahangir, JJ Child, and H Crombag, 'Prior Fault and Contrived Criminal Defences: Coming to the Law with Clean Hands' (2017) 1 *Institute of Law Journal* 28, Part 3.

[67] On the need for T1 justification or excuse (i.e. in conduct leading to a mistake), see AP Simester, *Fundamentals of Criminal Law* (OUP, 2021) 484–85.

voluntary intoxication as a blunt proxy for prior fault^{DEF}, and instead to consider how questions of T1 fault may be framed more appropriately by reference to the impaired perceptual and behavioural capacities on which mistaken-belief defences rely.

9.4 Empirical insights

Although we do not believe that prior fault^{DEF} rules should be limited to voluntary intoxication, as we noted in Chapter 6, paradigm cases of this kind provide a practical and useful focus for empirical investigation.[68] In Chapter 6, we also explained how our own empirical studies were set up and conducted.[69] Those studies yielded two core findings relevant to this chapter: (i) a robust link between degrees of intoxication and mistake prevalence, and (ii) that high intoxication leads specifically to mistakes relevant to defensive force. In this manner, such studies provide essential data to help us understand the connection between T1 impairment and T2 mistake making and associated harms.[70]

The empirical basis for exploring these issues arises from an overarching scientific understanding of emotions, evolution, and social interactions, and in particular the idea that emotions serve critical communicative and adaptive functions in social species. This insight traces back to Charles Darwin's *The Expression of the Emotions in Man and Animals*,[71] which framed emotional displays as evolved systems enabling organisms to signal states such as fear, aggression, appeasement, and distress. Darwin's thesis that emotional expressions have adaptive value and cross-species continuity has provided the foundation for empirical work since. In the twentieth century, Paul Ekman's seminal cross-cultural studies, which we have already mentioned in Chapter 6, further refined Darwin's thesis by demonstrating the universality of six *basic emotions* (anger, fear, happiness, sadness, disgust, and surprise) as reflected in recognizable facial expressions.[72] Ekman's work showed that these expressions are reliably identified across diverse cultures and are tightly coupled to rapid, automatic perceptual systems, thus underlining their key role

[68] We do acknowledge a gap here in the empirical literature however, which we hope to return to in future studies.

[69] See Chapter 6, Section 6.3.1.

[70] To understand the nature of this T1–T2 connection, we must look beyond general claims of 'drunkenness' and examine specifically how intoxication degrades the evolved mechanisms of social–emotional perception. If the law is to blame D for a mistake at T2 based on conduct at T1, it must be because D has voluntarily compromised the specific psychological and biological systems responsible for distinguishing safety from danger, and therefore, the justifiable need for use of defensive force.

[71] C Darwin, *The Expression of the Emotions in Man and Animals* (OUP, 1872).

[72] P Ekman, 'Universal Facial Expressions of Emotions' (1970) 8(4) *California Mental Health Research Digest* 151.

as evolved adaptations for coping with threats and opportunities in the environmental niche.[73]

Contemporary affective neuroscience has elaborated this evolutionary picture by outlining the largely automatic neural pathways linking the amygdala (the brain's threat alarm system), fusiform gyrus, superior temporal sulcus,[74] and the prefrontal cortex (the brain's executive, 'braking' system).[75] These systems are normally efficient and reliable, enabling individuals to distinguish distress from aggression, neutrality from hostility, and sincerity from threat within milliseconds. However, these mechanisms are also highly vulnerable to alcohol. A substantial body of psychological and neuroscientific evidence shows that intoxication by alcohol impairs:[76]

- accurate detection of (subtle) emotional cues,
- integration of facial musculature signals,
- sensitivity to affiliative and distress expressions,
- discrimination between neutral and hostile cues,
- approach–avoidance regulation (or protective disengagement), and
- metacognitive monitoring of one's own accuracy.

Our empirical findings, discussed below, align with this literature: intoxication produces predictable, dose-dependent distortions across these systems to compromise the perceptual and behavioural capacities on which subjective mistaken-belief defences rely.

In the subsections below, we explain the main parts of our own empirical studies examining specifically the connection between intoxication and mistaken beliefs relevant to defences. We highlight three specific areas. First, we explain the findings on impairment of emotion recognition in Section 9.4.1. Second, we focus on findings concerning responses to threats in Section 9.3.2. Third, we briefly note our findings concerning 'metacognitive distortion' (i.e. the disruption of peoples' ability to measure/monitor their own diminishing capacities and to form accurate views of their susceptibility to mistake) in Section 9.4.3.

[73] RM Nesse, 'Evolutionary Explanations of Emotions' (1990) 1(3) *Human Nature* 261.

[74] With the fusiform gyrus helping us to recognize faces, and the superior temporal sulcus involved in understanding facial movements and expressions, both these cortical regions play key roles in the perception and recognition of emotional facial expressions.

[75] T Dagleish et al, 'Affective Neuroscience: Past, Present and Future'(2009) 1 *Emotion Review* 355.

[76] IC Baltariu et al, 'The Acute Effects of Alcohol on Social Cognition: A Systematic Review of Experimental Studies' (2023) 245 *Drug and Alcohol Dependence* Article 109830; CA Honan et al, 'Alcohol Intoxication Impairs Recognition of Fear and Sadness in Others and Metacognitive Awareness of Emotion Recognition Ability' (2018) 18 *Emotion* 842; BN Sanov, L Kumar, and KG Creswell, 'A Systematic Review of the Acute Effects of Alcohol on Emotion Recognition of Facial Expressions' (2023) 28 *Addiction Biology* Article e13345.

9.4.1 Emotion recognition impairment

Across our laboratory and field studies, alcohol produced clear, dose-dependent impairments in emotion recognition. At moderate per cent blood alcohol concentration (BAC) levels, participants showed selective difficulties with sadness (laboratory) and happiness (field)—emotions which ordinarily avoid or inhibit aggression and facilitate de-escalation. Even higher intoxication levels resulted in more general declines in accuracy across all emotional categories.[77] These results align with the wider experimental literature, including some meta-analytic studies reviewed in our articles elsewhere.[78] Our results further replicate and extend this pattern.[79] Crucially, the literature on anger recognition converges on a tendency towards hostile attribution under moderate intoxication.[80] Consistent with this, our field study revealed a shift towards perceiving hostility in ambiguous or neutral faces in the highest intoxication ranges (>0.08 per cent BAC), indicating that at real-world intoxication levels, and in real-world (bar) settings, alcohol does not merely enhance anger sensitivity but erodes overall threat discrimination (i.e. the ability to tell if someone is a genuine threat or just neutral). For present purposes, this reinforces the point that mistaken, intoxicated defensive beliefs do not arise against a neutral perceptual background: intoxication predictably causes a misapprehension of hostility and potential for attack, thereby supporting the argument that the misperceived need for defensive action is connected to the defendant's prior fault^{DEF}.

[77] IC Baltariu et al, 'The Acute Effects of Alcohol on Social Cognition: A Systematic Review of Experimental Studies' (2023) 245 *Drug and Alcohol Dependence* Article 109830; BN Sanov, L Kumar, and KG Creswell, 'A Systematic Review of the Acute Effects of Alcohol on Emotion Recognition of Facial Expressions' (2023) 28 *Addiction Biology* Article e13345.

[78] P Manguele, K Nikolaou, N Sinclair-House, HS Crombag, and JJ Child, 'Empirical Insights into Acute Alcohol Intoxication, Mistake-Making, and Self-Defence: Testing Problematic Criminal Law Assumptions in the Laboratory and Field' (forthcoming). Meta-analyses combine results from numerous, select studies to identify (and statistically support) overall trends in the empirical literature, allowing stronger and more reliable conclusions to be drawn.

[79] SK Kamboj et al, 'Processing of Facial Affect in Social Drinkers: A Dose-Response Study of Alcohol Using Dynamic Emotion Expressions' (2013) 227(1) *Psychopharmacology* 31; IC Baltariu et al, 'The Acute Effects of Alcohol on Social Cognition: A Systematic Review of Experimental Studies' (2023) 245 *Drug and Alcohol Dependence* Article 109830; CA Honan et al, 'Alcohol Intoxication Impairs Recognition of Fear and Sadness in Others and Metacognitive Awareness of Emotion Recognition Ability' (2018) 18 *Emotion* 842; JN Khouja et al, 'Effects of Acute Alcohol Consumption on Emotion Recognition in Social Alcohol Drinkers' (2019) 33 *Journal of Psychopharmacology* 326.

[80] AS Attwood et al, 'Effects of Acute Alcohol Consumption on Processing of Perceptual Cues of Emotional Expression' (2009) 23 *Journal of Psychopharmacology* 23; LC Craig et al, 'Effects of Acute Alcohol Consumption and Alcohol Expectancy on Process Ing of Perceptual Cues of Emotional Expression' (2009) 23 *Journal of Psychopharmacology* 258.

9.4.2 Maladaptive threat responses

The perceptual impairments under intoxication were accompanied by systematic changes in behavioural responses to threat. Across both our studies, higher BAC levels were also associated with reduced (intended) avoidance of hostile faces and a greater likelihood of either remaining in place or, at even higher doses in the field study, approaching perceived hostility. This marked increase in approach behaviour indicates a shift away from what can be described as 'protective disengagement'. This pattern refines and strengthens existing models of intoxicated aggression: while prior research established that alcohol weakens inhibitory control and increases impulsive behaviour,[81] our results add to this by detailing how this specifically affects social–emotional approach–avoidance in response to hostility.[82] Consistent with evidence that alcohol dampens neural responses to threat,[83] we observed predictable changes in behavioural orientation.

When taken together then, our findings reveal a double impairment: intoxicated individuals are more likely both to misperceive hostility (Error 1) and to respond with escalatory behaviour (Error 2). As discussed in Chapter 6, 'alcohol myopia'–dampened prefrontal regulation leading to impaired behavioural inhibition likely contributes to this, but our data indicate that a core deficit lies in the selective degradation of (in part, emotion-specific) perceptual and behavioural mechanisms that ordinarily support safety/danger discrimination and disengagement. From a doctrinal perspective, this two-stage impairment, misreading hostility and failing to disengage from it, creates precisely the conditions in which mistaken defensive beliefs arise, supporting the application of a prior fault^{DEF} rule by demonstrating that the need for defensive force at T2 is causally linked to D's failure to avoid the perceived threat as it developed.

9.4.3 Metacognitive distortion: self-monitoring and awareness of risk of error

Lastly, and as we already discussed in some detail in Chapter 6, intoxication disrupted metacognitive monitoring across our studies. Participants in the highest BAC field ranges expressed inflated confidence despite lower accuracy, displaying

[81] PR Giancola et al, 'Men and Women, Alcohol and Aggression' (2009) 17 *Experimental and Clinical Psychopharmacology* 154; MJ Dry et al, 'Dose Related Affects of Alcohol on Cognitive Functioning' (2012) 7 *PLoS ONE* Article e50977.

[82] RC Hollett et al, 'Changes in the Relative Balance of Approach and Avoidance Inclinations to Use Alcohol Following Cue Exposure Vary in Low and High Risk Drinkers' (2017) 8 *Frontiers in Psychology* 8:8:645; JS Simons et al, 'Acute Effects of Intoxication and Arousal on Approach / Avoidance Biases toward Sexual Risk Stimuli in Heterosexual Men' (2016) 45 *Archives of Sexual Behavior* 43.

[83] CS Sripada et al, 'Effects of Alcohol on Brain Responses to Social Signals of Threat in Humans' (2011) 55 *NeuroImage* 371; LD Stafford et al, 'Alcohol and Disgust: An Intimate Relationship' (2020) 206 *Drug and Alcohol Dependence* Article 107780.

a clear confidence–accuracy dissociation (trade-off). This matters because sincerity at T2 is normatively ambiguous: a mistaken belief may be honest yet stem from impaired self-monitoring and distorted perception. And it matters for the law, because it casts doubt on approaches to prior fault^{DEF} that assume increased foresight of mistake making when impaired.

9.4.4 Empirical studies: Key findings and conclusions

Together, these findings demonstrate that the types of mistaken beliefs central to mistaken defence cases are foreseeable consequences of self-induced impairment of the systems governing emotion recognition, threat discrimination, behavioural response, and metacognition. We summarize our findings across both studies in Table 9.1, showing intoxication disrupted participants' ability to read emotions and respond adaptively to threat.

At higher BACs, individuals shifted from simple recognition errors towards riskier behavioural responses: remaining in place or even approaching hostility. Importantly, these impairments coexisted with distorted self-assessment, either overestimating impairment (laboratory) or under-estimating it (field), but in both cases, confidence decoupled from accuracy.

Our findings show that alcohol heightens both the frequency and dangerousness of mistakes while weakening awareness of risk. For psychology, this underscores alcohol's disruptive effect on emotion recognition, decision-making, and metacognition in social contexts. For law, the studies provide empirical evidence supporting the rationale for restricting mistaken self-defence claims under intoxication and other forms of incapacitation, and also demonstrate that treating intoxication as a binary condition ('sober vs intoxicated') is inadequate. Instead, a degree-based framework better reflects the dose-dependent nature of impairment and offers a more just basis for culpability assessment.

Table 9.1 Key findings

Domain	Lab Study	Field Study	Convergent Message
Emotion recognition	High BAC → more errors, esp. sadness	High BAC → more errors, esp. happiness	Alcohol impairs recognition, emotion-specific effects vary
Hostility responses	High BAC → less avoidance, more remain-in-place	High BAC → less avoidance, more approach hostility	Intoxication reduces adaptive disengagement from threat
Confidence vs performance	High BAC → aware of impairment but miscalibrated	High BAC → inflated confidence despite errors	Intoxication disrupts self-monitoring and metacognition

Note: BAC = blood alcohol concentration.

9.5 Defining prior fault^{DEF} incapacity rules

Having accepted a role for prior fault^{DEF} incapacity rules, our next challenge is to define what that role should be. In particular, how T1 prior fault^{DEF} should be defined. This is a challenge of legal theory and substantive law, but any recommendations must continue to draw from the empirical data just discussed in Section 9.4. In this regard, although our empirical studies focused on T1 intoxication, it would be wrong to interpret them as a simple endorsement of the current law. Our data suggest a robust empirical connection between T1 intoxication and relevant mistake making at T2, and this is crucial. But the connection is not linear. Rather, the circumstances of D's intoxication at T1 (most importantly, the degree of intoxication) led to significantly changed performance at T2, pushing against binary perceptions of intoxication and fault. Equally, although our studies focused on T1 intoxication, data from other labs suggest similar patterns of T2 impairment and mistake making with other forms of incapacity, such as lack of sleep.[84] Thus, again, we are encouraged to move away from binary status-based proxies for fault, refocusing on what it means to be at fault at T1 in causing one's own incapacity.

There is very little within the current literature to help shape our recommendations. One of the few exceptions has been the work of the Law Commission, although even here we see relatively little discussion beyond calls for consistency. At one time, the Commission was convinced that the legal approach to prior fault^{DEF}–intoxicated mistakes should mirror prior fault^{OFF} intoxication rules, in particular by distinguishing basic and specific intent offences.[85] We have already criticized this approach earlier in the chapter as lacking coherence,[86] and it is notable that the Commission has more recently come to a similar conclusion.[87] But having rejected this alternative, the Commission has been largely content with the current legal position. Thus, for the Commission, in 2009:[88]

> D should not be able to rely on a mistake of fact arising from self-induced intoxication in support of a defence to which D's state of mind is relevant, regardless of the nature of the fault alleged. D's mistaken belief should be taken into account only if D would have held the same belief if D had not been intoxicated.

In large part, this represents a simple restatement of the current law. However, the final sentence provides a point of interest, allowing D to rely on their mistaken

[84] D Dawson and K Reid, 'Fatigue, Alcohol and Performance Impairment' (1997) 388 *Nature* 235; P Maruff et al, 'Fatigue-related Impairment in the Speed, Accuracy and Variability of Psychomotor Performance: Comparison with Blood Alcohol Levels' (2005) 14 *Journal of Sleep Research* 21.

[85] Law Commission, *A Criminal Code for England and Wales: Report and Draft Criminal Code Bill* (Vol 2, 1989) [8.42]; *Intoxication and Criminal Liability* (LC No 229, 1995) [7.9–7.12].

[86] Section 9.2.1.2 above.

[87] Law Commission, *Intoxication and Criminal Liability* (LC No 314, 2009) [3.53–3.65].

[88] Ibid [3.53].

belief if *they* would have held the same belief if sober. This counterfactual approach is potentially more generous for D than the switch to an objective reasonable person test, allowing D to claim that—although a reasonable person may not have made the same mistake—D still would have done so even if sober. Having said that, there are of course obvious problems with an approach that requires a court to make reliable findings about individual foresight in counterfactual circumstances.[89] However, for our present purposes, it demonstrates that the Commission was at least conscious of the potential over-inclusiveness of the current prior fault^{DEF} rule.

It is perhaps the absence of a viable alternative that best explains the legal stagnation in this area, despite the problems with the current law set out in Section 9.2. And it is this absence that we seek to address here. Indeed, having done the work in the first half of this book to understand and define a better conception of T1 prior fault incapacity (i.e. in the context of prior fault^{OFF}), we believe that the same model of fault may be repurposed for application to blocking mistaken defences as well. Most importantly, it is a model that seeks to explain prior fault^{DEF} incapacity without reliance on intoxication as a proxy, addressing concerns of both over- and under-inclusivity.

9.5.1 Our recommended approach

We set out our preferred approach below in the form of draft legislation, in the clause 2 provision below.[90] This is done for maximum clarity; it is not intended to represent final legislative text.

2. Mistaken Beliefs in Defence and Culpable Incapacity

(1) This clause applies if—
  (a) there are proceedings against a person ('D') for any offence,
  (b) D was at any material time in a state of culpable incapacity, and
  (c) by way of defence, or in support of a defence, D relies on having at that time held a particular mistaken belief as to any fact.

(2) In this clause, 'culpable incapacity' requires D intentionally or recklessly to have become significantly mentally impaired and/or involuntary, making a mistake either—
  (a) through extreme intoxication with a dangerous drug taken voluntarily; or

[89] See E Paton, 'Reformulating the Intoxication Rules' [1995] *Crim LR* 382; R Mackay, 'The Taint of Intoxication' (1990) 13(1) *International Journal of Law and Psychiatry* 37.

[90] Clause number is '2' since we conceive of this clause following on from '1', which defines the offence of culpable incapacity. We borrow the basic structure of the draft provision from the Law Commission, *Intoxication and Criminal Liability* (LC No 314, 2009) 106.

(b) through negligence, having failed to take steps that could reasonably be expected of D in avoidance of the circumstances of that mistake; where those steps were available at the time of, or shortly before, the mistake was made.

(3) In application of a defence in these circumstances, D's actual belief is to be taken into account only if a reasonable person sharing D's characteristics would have held the same belief.

The approach set out in this clause borrows heavily from our previous analysis of culpable incapacity in Chapter 7, and so we do not propose to repeat a full justification of that policy here. However, the discussion in Chapter 7 analyses culpable incapacity in the context of offending only. Therefore, in repurposing the concept here (i.e. in the context of blocking defences), there are some important points of difference that require explanation.

9.5.2 Foreseen significant impairment at T1

The crucial point of blame at T1 is established through D's conduct. D must intentionally or recklessly become significantly impaired and/or involuntary: clause 2(2) in our draft provision. This mirrors the same requirement within the clause 1 culpable incapacity offence (CI Offence), set out in Chapter 7. Three aspects should be highlighted in particular.[91]

First is the need for a 'significant' impairment, as opposed to 'any' impairment, which narrows the rule to those cases where future mistakes are more likely to be attributable to D's conduct at T1 (i.e. in line with our empirical insights discussed in Section 9.4). This provides a stable and consistent standard, which avoids problematic counterfactual enquiries into whether D would have made the same mistake if sober.

The second aspect requires D to have been aware of their impairment: that D was intentional or reckless at T1 as to becoming significantly impaired. Requiring awareness of this kind allows us to blame D for their choices at T1. In doing so, we are focused on a set of choices that D makes (i.e. D's conduct at T1, intentional or reckless as to causing incapacity at T2), identified by our empirical studies as scientifically robust markers of blame.[92]

The third relates to the cause of D's impairment. As with the CI Offence, the provision here is drafted to encompass both external and internal causes of impairment without distinction. This is designed to address the potential under-inclusiveness

[91] Each one is discussed more fully in Chapter 7.

[92] As discussed in Chapter 6, Section 6.3.2 and Section 9.4 above, we did not find empirical support for the alternative focus on D's awareness of impaired *performance* or anticipated *mistake making*.

of the current law, expanding the potential for prior fault^{DEF} beyond voluntary intoxication alone, as well as to remove a set of practical difficulties identified within the current law, where courts are required to make binary distinctions between causal influences, contrary to scientific and clinical understanding. The question is simply whether D was intentional or reckless through their acts or omissions such that they brought about their state of significant mental impairment.

9.5.3 Relevant mistake at T2

The most significant point of difference between the CI Offence and the defence provision at issue here relates to D's conduct at T2. Rather than causing a certain harm at T2, here we are concerned with factual mistakes relevant to a belief-based defence: clause 2(1)(c) of the draft provision. For example, D's mistaken belief in the need for defensive force, D's mistaken belief in an owner's consent, and so on. Despite the difference in T2 conduct, however, the basic relationship between T1 and T2 remains the same. Just as we selected a range of harms associated with impaired conduct for the CI Offence, there is a similarly justifiable link between impairment and mistake making. Indeed, the causal link between D's impairment and relevant mistakes in defence was a core finding from our empirical studies.[93]

Where culpable incapacity is proven by the prosecution, the analysis of D's mistake at T2 will be transformed from a subjective to an objective test. In this manner, D's mistaken belief will only remain relevant to their defence if a reasonable person sharing D's characteristics would have held the same belief. This will apply to all defences where D's honest beliefs are relevant, including those such as insanity which are currently excluded from prior fault^{DEF} analysis.

9.5.4 Linking T1 and T2

Just as it was essential to link events at T1 and T2 for the CI Offence, the same is true for a provision that relies on a similar combination of factors to justify the blocking of a defence. This is partly achieved through our preferred definition of fault at T1, which requires D to become 'significantly impaired' with intention or foresight of that fact, going on to make a related and foreseeable mistake of fact at T2. As with the CI Offence, the idea here is that D should have foreseen and taken precautions against the types of mistakes made at T2, such that a culpable connection may be established between those mistakes and D's prior choices in becoming significantly impaired.

[93] Discussed in Section 9.4 above.

The link between T1 and T2 is completed by the requirement that D's mistake was induced either through a state of 'extreme' intoxication, or through a negligent failure to avoid the circumstances in which the mistake was made. This is set out within clause 2(2)(a)–(b) of the draft provision, and again mirrors the construction of the CI Offence. In this manner, we reflect the special status of extreme intoxication, which provides perhaps the most obvious link to mistake making at T2, as well as going beyond this, in cases where D should have taken steps available to them to avoid the circumstances of their mistake. The second alternative criterion (i.e. a negligent failure to avoid the circumstances which gave rise to the mistake) is an important limit on the use of prior fault^{DEF}, allowing for the possibility that D's impaired mistake may not have been unreasonable. This could apply, for example, in some of the hypotheticals discussed earlier,[94] such as the intoxicated householder who is unexpectedly interrupted by a trespasser. In cases of this kind, the reasonableness of D's conduct in avoiding impaired mistakes will take account of D's legitimate expectation of being alone at home.

9.5.5 Relationship with the Culpable Incapacity Offence

In this final subsection, we clarify the potential interaction between the two sets of culpable incapacity rules that we have recommended thus far. Most importantly, where D commits the CI Offence, it is necessary to understand how that same incapacity is likely to impact the potential for a defence.

Our inquiry here is quite narrow. We are not proposing the creation of any specific defences, for example, applicable to the new CI Offence. Therefore, we are only interested in the potential application of general defences, such as self-defence and insanity, where D's subjective beliefs (i.e. including mistaken beliefs) are at issue. Regarding self-defence, it will be extremely rare for this defence to arise in the context of the CI Offence: where D causes harms in a state of impaired capacity, such that this offence is charged ahead of more typical mens rea offences, it is unlikely that D will also be in a position to assert that they were acting in necessary self-defence. However, it cannot be ruled out entirely, and depends in part upon charging practices. It is also quite possible to imagine fact patterns where the defence of insanity could be raised in response to a charge of culpable incapacity: for example, where D's prior fault incapacity arises from an internal cause, such as medication non-compliance, leading D to cause harms without understanding the nature or quality of their actions.

Crucially, our proposed reformulation of the prior fault^{DEF} rule will apply in the same way to defences regardless of the underlying charge. Thus, even within

[94] At Section 9.2.1.2 above.

the limited class of cases where belief-based defences are relevant to an offence of culpable incapacity, there will be no need to adapt the elements of those defences and/or the proposed prior fault^{DEF} rule.[95] In such cases, having established that D's significant mental impairment was caused intentionally or recklessly, the jury will have to answer separate questions about the connection of this impairment to D's causing of harm (i.e. for D's offence) and D's mistake in defence (i.e. for D's defence). Where the proposed prior fault^{DEF} rule is satisfied, the defence will be 'blocked' in that the subjective test will be transformed into an objective test: clause 2(3) in our draft provision.

9.6 Conclusion

This chapter has focused on impaired mistake making in defence, but the crossover of discussion with Part I of the book should be obvious. The current law is striving for simplicity and consistency, but is doing so from a position of conceptual and normative confusion. Whilst there is broad agreement that T1 prior fault^{DEF} should affect the way we apply or block defences, fundamental questions about the definition of prior fault^{DEF} and the normative basis for that blocking are obscured through analogy with problematic prior fault^{OFF} rules, and a fixation on voluntary intoxication alone. The result, as we have discussed, is a set of prior fault^{DEF} rules that are both over-inclusive in their potential application to intoxication in reasonable circumstances, and under-inclusive in their lack of application to prior fault^{DEF} incapacity outside of intoxication.

The route to viable reform has required us to return to first principles, drawing on our conceptual and empirical work, first to establish the case for prior fault^{DEF} rules here at all, and then in the construction of those rules. In Section 9.5, we set out a mechanism for prior fault^{DEF} that is capable of fair and consistent application across all relevant defences. There will still be difficult cases of course, where factors indicating fault are complicated or obscured by comorbid conditions and/or uncertain causal paths. However, even within such cases, it is crucial that the criminal law should continue to ask the correct liability-justifying questions, focusing on whether the conditions of guilt can be proven beyond reasonable doubt. The retreat within the current law to proxies for guilt, and pronouncements of causal certainty without scientific basis, are mistakes that should finally be set aside.

[95] Note that in previous works, where we have mooted the abolition of incapacity prior fault^{DEF} rules, we found it necessary to retain such a rule where defences were raised against prior fault-based offences. This represented a significant limitation of the previous position. Q Jahangir, JJ Child, and H Crombag, 'Prior Fault and Contrived Criminal Defences: Coming to the Law with Clean Hands' (2017) 1 *Institute of Law Journal* 28, Part 3.

10
CONTRIVED DEFENCES AND PRIOR FAULT

10.1 Introduction

In this chapter, we explore the application of prior fault^{DEF} rules where D has manipulated their circumstances at T1, giving rise to a potential supervening defence at T2.[1] Various terms are used to describe such cases within the literature, but we will refer to this category of prior fault^{DEF} rules as 'contrived defences'. The example provided in Chapter 8 is one of contrived self-defence: D wants to kill V, D hands V a knife and then goads V until they (as anticipated) lash out at D, D shoots and kills V to protect themselves. If we focus narrowly on D's response to V's knife attack (T2), then it may be possible to justify D's actions in terms of reasonable self-defence.[2] However, if we allow D to rely on self-defence (i.e. if we maintain a narrow T2 event focus), the concern is that we have effectively allowed D to manipulate the circumstances in such a way that they rely on the law to kill another with impunity. Although there may be a point of crisis at T2 where D is attacked providing the foundation for potential justification in defence, if we widen our evaluative lens to include D's provocation at T1, this reveals that crisis to have been manufactured by D. Prior fault^{DEF} rules provide the legal mechanism for widening the evaluative lens in this manner, and thereby for blocking D's defence. Applying prior fault^{DEF} rules to our example then, D would not be permitted to rely on self-defence and would be guilty of murder.

The core feature of contrived defences is D's manipulation of circumstances at T1, in view of both the offence and potential defence at T2. These prior fault^{DEF} rules may therefore apply across a wide range of defences. Most common is their application to block contrived choice-based defences such as self-defence, duress, and necessity; and we focus on these examples in this chapter. D's conduct at T1 does not remove their T2 choice in such cases, but manipulates the circumstances of that choice into a potentially defence-justifying crisis. We see this in our provocation example above, and in similar examples of property destruction provided

[1] As introduced in Chapter 1, we are adopting the notation 'prior fault^{OFF}' and 'prior fault^{DEF}' to distinguish between prior fault rules relevant to the construction of a crime and prior fault rules relevant to the blocking of a defence.

[2] Criminal Justice and Immigration Act 2008, s76.

Prior Fault Criminalization. John J Child, Adrian Hunt, and Hans S. Crombag, Oxford University Press.
 DOI: 10.1093/9780191874734.003.0012

by Robinson, such as where 'an actor sets a fire that threatens a nearby town to create the conditions that will justify his using his enemy's farm as a firebreak'.[3]

Contrived defences are not limited to choice-based defences of this kind, although the facts necessary for application beyond this become increasingly unlikely in practice. It is possible to contrive the circumstances of a mistake-based defence, for example, but this would require D to manipulate the circumstances (T1) of a genuine mistake of fact at T2 (e.g. where D is intentionally hypnotized to believe that any approach from V (D's enemy) is an attempt to kill them at T1; D then uses force against V, mistakenly believing in this threat at T2). It is also possible to contrive the circumstances of an incapacity defence, such as insanity or diminished responsibility. This would apply where D manipulates an internal incapacitating condition at T1 (e.g. by not taking medication), *in order to* satisfy the elements of an incapacity defence when causing harms at T2.

In this manner, although there may be some factual overlap with the prior fault^{DEF} rules discussed in the previous chapter, prior fault^{DEF} rules relating to contrived defences are conceptually distinct. We are still concerned with D's blameworthy conduct at T1, but that concern is focused on D's manipulation of future circumstances at T2, not simply D's choice to become impaired at T1. This expands the potential scope of the rules across a broader range of supervening defences, as we have highlighted. But it also introduces new challenges, such as the conceptual framing of what it means to 'contrive' a defence, without the help of proxies like intoxication or automatism.[4]

Another crucial difference is that, when we talk of 'blocking' D's defence here, we mean it quite literally. Unlike the prior fault^{DEF} incapacity rules discussed in the previous chapter, where blocking D's defence meant changing a subjective defence element into an objective one, applying prior fault^{DEF} rules to a defence identified as contrived means simply that that defence will no longer be applicable. This is why, even in cases of factual overlap with incapacity, it is important to identify which category of prior fault^{DEF} rules is at issue. It is also why contrived defence rules raise new issues of concern, such as whether the *complete* exclusion of a contrived defence may be inappropriate where D's conduct is met with unexpected facts at T2 (e.g. a disproportionate response from V), as well as the rights of third parties to defensive intervention.

Our discussion here will follow a similar pattern to that used in the previous chapter. We begin, in Section 10.2, evaluating contrived defence rules as they operate in the current law. Following this, we look to questions of reform. We are concerned with identifying a theoretically coherent model for prior fault^{DEF} in Section 10.3, before setting out and justifying our preferred doctrinal construction of a scheme of rules in Section 10.4.

[3] P Robinson, 'Causing the Conditions of One's Own Defence' (1985) 71 *Virginia Law Review* 1, 28.

[4] We expose such proxies as 'false friends' in previous chapters, but they have allowed prior fault^{OFF} and prior fault ^{DEF} rules to function without facing up to conceptual challenges of this kind.

10.2 Current prior fault^{DEF} contriving rules

Contrived defence scenarios, such as our introductory examples, provide a compelling intuitive case for criminalization. It should therefore be little surprise that prior fault^{DEF} rules designed to block contrived defences of this kind can be identified in most jurisdictions. However, the theoretical basis for such rules remains contested and uncertain, leading to significant problems in doctrinal application. Problems include: basic fairness, in terms of when and why prior fault^{DEF} rules should apply; consistency, between different defences, and even within the application of single defences; and reform, where we see piecemeal codification and limited thoughtful engagement. We identify examples of each problem in the discussion that follows, which we divide between intentional and non-intentional contriving cases.

Our focal jurisdiction remains that of England & Wales when discussing the current law below, but it is important to highlight that the same problems are apparent across jurisdictions internationally. Much of the current published academic debate, for example, focuses on laws in the United States, where a remarkable lack of consistency can be identified between the criminal law of different states, with a minority lacking prior fault^{DEF} rules of this kind entirely.[5]

10.2.1 Intentional manipulation

The first category of contrived defence cases arises where D intentionally manipulates a situation to commit an offence with a particular defence, with the intention, thereby, of avoiding liability. To repeat our opening example: D wants to kill V, D hands V a knife and then goads V until they (as anticipated) lash out at D, D shoots and kills V in self-defence. Circumstances of intentional legal manipulation are vanishingly rare in practice, but the law in England & Wales is clear that—should they arise—D's defence will be blocked. This is the case where D culpably manufactures circumstances of self-defence,[6] as in our example, as well as other defences such as duress,[7] necessity,[8] and the partial defence of loss of control.[9] The latter is provided for in statute, where it is stated:[10]

[5] See P Robinson, 'Causing the Conditions of One's Own Defence' (1985) 71 *Virginia Law Review* 1; K Ferzan, 'Provocateurs' (2013) 7 *Criminal Law and Philosophy* 597; C Finkelstein and L Katz, 'Contrived Defenses and Deterrent Threats: Two Facets of One Problem' (2008) 5 *Ohio State Journal of Criminal Law* 479.

[6] *Rashford* [2005] EWCA Crim 3377 [19].

[7] *Hasan* [2005] 2 AC 467.

[8] This is likely through analogy with duress. It may also support Lord Denning's famous dicta about the limits of necessity in *Southwark London Borough v Williams* [1971] 2 All ER 175.

[9] Coroners and Justice Act 2009, s55(6).

[10] Ibid.

In determining whether a loss of self-control had a qualifying trigger—
(a) D's fear of serious violence is to be disregarded to the extent that it was caused by a thing which D incited to be done or said for the purpose of providing an excuse to use violence;
(b) a sense of being seriously wronged by a thing done or said is not justifiable if D incited the thing to be done or said for the purpose of providing an excuse to use violence;

...

The same rule—narrowly conceived in terms of intentional/purposive manipulation—is present across multiple jurisdictions, within both common and civil law traditions.[11]

The prior fault^{DEF} rule relating to intentional manipulation has not attracted much in the way of criticism, with broad agreement on the core normative aim of preventing defendants from consciously manipulating circumstances to exploit the law. However, uncertainty regarding the outer limits and broader implications of the rule continues to drive debate. For example, although D's defensive rights may be blocked where they *successfully* manipulate the circumstances ahead of T2, what of cases where D is not successful? If D's T1 conduct still gives rise to a defence-justifying crisis, albeit not the one intended by D, will their defensive rights be retained?

Debate here has typically focused on cases where D provokes attack from V and causes harm to V in 'self-defence', where V's response to D's provocation is disproportionate and/or unexpected.[12] And it raises several questions where the current law does not have a clear answer. For example, what of D's right to self-defence if D intentionally provokes V to hit them in order to 'justify' a fist fight, where V subsequently attacks D with a knife?[13] Relatedly, we might ask similar questions regarding third-party rights. Is X justified to intervene to protect D from attack, where D has intentionally provoked that attack from V; and what difference (if any) does it make whether X is aware of D's intentional manipulation of V or not? Facts of this kind, of course, represent subsets within an already extremely narrow class of potential cases, and so judicial engagement is very limited on how these questions might be resolved. However, their resolution remains important if we are to understand the nature of the rule, in terms of D's forfeiture of defensive

[11] See, e.g., on US law, MPC §§3.04(2)(b)(i) and 3.05(1)(a)–(b) discussed in R Segev, 'Responsibility and Justificatory Defences' (2017) 11 *Criminal Law and Philosophy* 97; on German law, J Herrmann, 'Causing the Conditions of One's Own Defence: The Multifaceted Approach of German Law' (1986) 3 *Brigham Young University Law Review* 747.

[12] The issue is not limited to self-defence, however. E.g. in the context of duress, where D manipulates X into threatening them, but X's demand is very different (and more serious) than anticipated.

[13] See *Keane* [2010] EWCA Crim 2514, which provides some useful discussion (obiter) on this issue.

rights, and so any potential reform proposal should be able to answer them.[14] We examine these matters below in Section 10.4.

10.2.2 Non-intentional contributions

The second category of contrived defence cases involves non-intentional contributions, extending the potential reach of the prior fault^{DEF}. The nature and scope of such a rule, as we will see, is considerably less certain than its intention-based equivalent. The lack of clarity here is unfortunate, particularly given that—in practice—circumstances of this kind are significantly more likely to arise. Amending the facts of our intentional manipulation paradigm, we have in mind circumstances where, for example, D goads V knowing that this *might* cause V to lash out, V attacks D, and D kills V in self-defence. The question is whether, in circumstances of recklessness or negligence such as this at T1, D's defence to murder should be blocked from application at T2.

The potential for a prior fault^{DEF} rule of this kind has typically focused on two general defences: self-defence and duress. We discuss each in turn.

10.2.2.1 Non-intentional contributions and self-defence

Some jurisdictions have developed prior fault^{DEF} rules for self-defence that are capable of application to facts beyond core intentional manipulation, but patterns of uncertainty (both conceptual and doctrinal) remain common. The picture in US law, for example, though inconsistent between states, may extend the blocking of self-defence to cases where D foresaw (or even should have foreseen) that their provocation would elicit a violent reaction from V;[15] and in German law, similar conduct may be used to qualify D's defensive rights, providing an additional limit on the force D is entitled to use in defence.[16]

At present, it is not clear whether or to what extent English law recognizes a non-intentional contribution rule in the blocking of self-defence. There is limited case law suggesting that self-defence may be unavailable where D initiated and/or went looking for an altercation.[17] But the basis for this exclusion in terms of 'prior fault^{DEF}' remains unclear, and in particular, it is unclear whether the reason for its exclusion lies in the need (at T1) for D to foresee the future offence and/or defence at T2.

[14] See, e.g., K Ferzan, 'Provocateurs' (2013) 7 *Criminal Law and Philosophy* 597.

[15] Discussed in P Robinson, 'Causing the Conditions of One's Own Defence' (1985) 71 *Virginia Law Review* 1, 3–10.

[16] Discussed in J Herrmann, 'Causing the Conditions of One's Own Defence: The Multifaceted Approach of German Law' (1986) 3 *Brigham Young University Law Review* 747, 753–55.

[17] See *Keane* [2010] EWCA Crim 2514; *Rashford* [2005] EWCA Crim 3377.

The leading authority is *Rashford*,[18] which involved a confrontation between youths, initiated by D, leading to a fight in which D killed V with a knife. D raised self-defence. The case began inauspiciously, with confusion regarding the legal implications of D's provocation to the availability of self-defence, encapsulated within a confused and contradictory direction from the lower court.[19] Even at the Court of Appeal stage, similar problems arose. The Court was obviously concerned to provide greater certainty, foregrounding the core question of justification in D's use of force (at T2), rather than questions of 'who started it' (at T1). However, to this extent, prior fault^{DEF} analysis does not feature in the Courts reasoning. Rather, on the question of justification for D's action, the Court of Appeal focused on V's reaction to D's initial confrontation, asking whether V's reaction gave rise to necessary defensive force from D.[20]

> The question whether the plea of self defence is available depends . . . on whether the retaliation [by V] is such that the accused is entitled then to defend himself. That depends upon whether the violence offered by the victim was so out of proportion to the accused's own actings as to give rise to the . . . apprehension that he was in an immediate danger from which he had no other means of escape.

The dicta in this case, endorsed by subsequent case law,[21] provides useful clarification that self-defence *is* available where D's initial aggression is met with disproportionate (i.e. unlawful) violence from V. But the precedent and dicta is limited. It is clear that D may not physically resist lawful force, and so where V is acting lawfully (i.e. acting in legitimate self-defence from D's original attack), this will never justify further force from D. But what of cases in which V is not acting lawfully?

V's force will be unlawful where D's provocation at T1 does not justify defensive force from V at all. For example, where D and V are involved in a confrontation, insulting words from D may not reasonably give rise to violence from V, but such violence may be entirely foreseeable (and foreseen by D). The legal position here is unclear, though there is some dicta suggesting that D's appeal to self-defence would be blocked, hinting at a generally applicable prior fault^{DEF} rule in such circumstances.[22] The other scenario of interest—where V's acts are not lawful—arises

[18] [2005] EWCA Crim 3377.

[19] The jury were told to dismiss self-defence if they found that D was the aggressor at T1, *and* to consider the elements of the defence as a response to V's conduct at T2. *Rashford* [2005] EWCA Crim 3377 [21–22].

[20] Ibid [19], quoting *Burns v HM Advocate* [1995] SLT 1090, 1093H. See V Higgins and D Ormerod, 'Self-Defence: Elements of Defence—Defendant Acting as Initial Aggressor' (2006) *Criminal Law Review* 546.

[21] See, e.g., *Harvey* [2009] EWCA Crim 469; *Keane* [2010] EWCA Crim 2514.

[22] E.g. Lowry LCJ in the NI case of *Browne* [1973] NI 96, 107: 'The need to act must not have been created by conduct of the accused in the immediate context of the incident which was likely *or* intended to give rise to that need' (emphasis added).

where some force may be justified, but V responds with excessive force. *Rashford* does engage here, providing useful clarification that excessive force from V may provide new justification for D in self-defence.[23] But, again, the role of D's foresight at T1 is left unclear and certainly not foregrounded. What if D realizes at T1 that their provocative acts are likely to illicit such a disproportionate response? To the extent that it has not been addressed, the answer currently is that there is no authority for excluding self-defence in these circumstances as the courts have yet to apply prior fault^{DEF} reasoning.

The recent case of *Gill* provides a useful example of current challenges in English law.[24] It involved mistaken self-defence, where D stabbed a police officer (V) executing a legal drugs-related raid of his property. It was accepted that D stabbed V not knowing that they were a police officer, but rather in belief that they were from a rival drug gang intent on causing serious injury or death to D and others inside. It was on this basis that D raised mistaken self-defence, including the additional protections afforded for self-defence of those acting in their own homes.[25] However, for the trial judge, allowing these additional protections to apply in the context of someone committing offences of this kind (i.e. drug offences), thereby making themselves more susceptible to attack, was 'a million miles away' from the intentions of Parliament.[26] Applying a prior fault^{DEF} logic, the trial judge therefore declined to direct the jury on the householder test, and directed them instead to apply the standard test for mistaken self-defence. D was convicted, and appealed on the basis that the householder test should have been applied. The Court of Appeal allowed D's appeal, holding—as if self-evident—that the householder rules should apply to everyone within the statutory criteria, and therefore treating them as not applying to D would be contrary to the rule of law.[27]

The case is interesting in several respects, but chiefly because of the prior fault^{DEF} dilemmas apparent—but not acknowledged explicitly—within the conflict. The salient facts for the lower court were that D's criminal conduct made the need for self-defence empirically more likely, and heightened his anticipation of attack, with both feeding directly into his mistaken defence. Essentially, using the language of prior fault^{DEF}, that his criminal associations at T1 created the conditions that led to his defence, and that he was reckless (and certainly negligent) in

[23] See also *Keane* [2010] EWCA Crim 2514; *Harvey* [2009] EWCA Crim 469.

[24] *Gill* [2023] EWCA Crim 259.

[25] Criminal Justice and Immigration Act 2008: Whereas in non-householder cases, the degree of force used by D is not to be regarded as having been reasonable in the circumstances as D believed them to be if it was disproportionate in those circumstances (s75(6)), for householders, the degree of force used is not regarded as having been reasonable, if it was *grossly* disproportionate in the circumstances as D believed them to be (s76(5A)).

[26] *Gill* [2023] EWCA Crim 259, [23–24].

[27] Ibid [33].

that contribution. As we will see in Section 10.2.2.2 below, prior fault^{DEF} of this kind would have been sufficient to undermine an equivalent defence of duress. And yet, the Court of Appeal, without reference to prior fault^{DEF} case law of any kind, simply held that an equivalent exclusion for self-defence was contrary to the current law. Leaving aside questions of statutory construction or case law precedent, this rather begs the obvious question as to why, as a matter of principle, this should be so for self-defence, but not, as we will see in Section 10.2.2.2 below, for duress?

In summary then, this brief survey demonstrates an inconsistent rule, both between and often within jurisdictions. A rule that courts have struggled to clarify, or even identify and articulate within the case law.

10.2.2.2 Non-intentional contributions and duress

Surprisingly, perhaps, given the lack of application within self-defence, a non-intentional contribution rule has developed to apply quite extensively in cases of duress. The rule applies where D puts themselves in a dangerous situation at T1 that is likely to lead to offences being committed at T2 in circumstances of duress (and, potentially, circumstances of necessity[28]). For example, where D voluntarily joins a criminal gang at T1, and is later threatened by gang members to commit a particular offence at T2, D's prior association provides the basis for blocking their defence. We refer to this as the 'prior-association rule'.

The prior-association rule has changed considerably over the last thirty years, expanding in application. In line with self-defence, it is likely that duress would always have been unavailable in extreme intention-based cases: for example, where D joins a criminal organization at T1 with the intention of being threatened to commit a particular offence at T2 under the guise of duress. Indeed, going beyond self-defence prior fault^{DEF} rules, it has been well established for some time that duress will not be available where D is *reckless* at T1 about being compelled to commit a certain offence at T2.[29] However, traditionally, this is as far as those blocking rules have gone. Thus, D's defence would not be blocked if they foresaw the chance of being compelled to commit a less serious offence at T1 than was actually compelled at T2,[30] or if D did not foresee the chance of compulsion even though a reasonable person would have.[31]

The association rule was recast and clarified by the House of Lords in *Hasan*.[32] In the lead judgement, Lord Bingham opted for an extremely wide view of prior

[28] There are very few necessity cases in general, and so any predictions about prior fault^{DEF} remain speculative. However, it is logical to assume that necessity will be interpreted in line with duress: A Ashworth, 'Reason, Logic and Criminal Liability' (1975) 91 *Law Quarterly Review* 102, 106.

[29] *Fitzpatrick* [1977] NI 20.

[30] *Shepard* (1987) 86 Cr App R 47; *Lewis* (1992) 96 Cr App R 412.

[31] *DPP for NI v Lynch* [1975] AC 653; *Ali* [1995] CrimLR 303.

[32] [2005] 2 AC 467.

fault^{DEF}, blocking D's defence at T2 where D (at T1) voluntarily associates with another and a reasonable person would have foreseen the risk of future compulsion. Note here the use of objective standards, and a non-specific foresight requirement. In Lord Bingham's own words:[33]

> The policy of the law must be to discourage association with known criminals, and it should be slow to excuse the criminal conduct of those who do so. If a person voluntarily becomes or remains associated with others engaged in criminal activity in a situation where he knows or ought reasonably to know that he may be the subject of compulsion by them or their associates, he cannot rely on the defence of duress to excuse any act which he is thereafter compelled to do by them.

Hasan remains the leading authority in English law,[34] expanding the association rule to apply even more widely than we see in other jurisdictions.[35] It is an authority that can be commended for clarifying the prior fault^{DEF} rule for duress on some key issues. However, it has also attracted cogent criticism.[36] Critics have highlighted the obvious inconsistency (and lack of articulated rationale) of allowing a non-intentional contribution rule to apply here but not elsewhere. But perhaps more importantly, they have also highlighted the potential for unfairness where D has a non-blameworthy reason for association at T1. Baroness Hale's minority speech in *Hasan*, for example, discussed the potential harsh effects of the rule if applied to victims of domestic abuse who may foresee future threats or compulsion from their abuser,[37] and similar observations have been made concerning drug users, or others who associate with potentially dangerous individuals, but who do not foresee specific threats. As Smith notes,[38]

> . . . it is one thing to be aware that you are likely to be beaten up if you do not pay your debts, it is another that you may be aware that you may be required under threat of violence to commit other, though unspecified crimes, if you do not.

The question arising is whether D should have a defence of duress or necessity blocked on these terms, and on what basis such blocking may be justified. We turn to these normative questions in the sections below.

33 Ibid [38].
34 See discussion in *Ali* [2008] EWCA Crim 716; *Phair* [2022] NICA 66.
35 E.g. although the US MPC also provides an expansive association rule, negligent association will only block defences to crimes of negligence: US MPC §2.09(2).
36 E.g. D Ormerod, 'Duress: Foreseeability of Risk of Being Subjected to Compulsion by Threats of Violence' (2006) *Criminal Law Review* 142.
37 *Hasan* [2005] 2 AC 467, [67–80].
38 JC Smith, 'Duress' [2000] *Criminal Law Review* 109, 111.

10.3 Theoretical models and reform

For successful reform of prior fault^{DEF} contrived defence rules, it is necessary to investigate and clarify both conceptual and doctrinal understandings. We do that here. First, in this section, we explore questions of conceptual clarity, evaluating three competing models used to explain prior fault^{DEF} rules for contrived defences—highlighting which, in our view, provides the most compelling account. We follow this, in Section 10.4, by setting out and justifying our preferred doctrinal construction for the rule.

In common with other prior fault^{DEF} rules, there is a basic intuitive appeal in blocking D from relying on a contrived defence, and particularly so in cases of intentional manipulation. Few would question the blocking of self-defence in our opening hypothetical for example, where D provokes V into attacking them for the sole reason of retaliation in manufactured circumstances of defence. However, outside of paradigm hypotheticals of this kind, intuitions may diverge, and there is a need for greater conceptual clarity to ensure fairness and consistency in the law. Contrived defence rules have the potential to apply across defence types, blocking defences where D is mistaken about a defence-justifying crisis at T2 (i.e. mistaken defences) as well as cases where that crisis—though manufactured by D—is nevertheless real. The challenge then, across defence types, is to explain why D's defence *should* be blocked in these cases. Why the T2 crisis—mistaken or real—becomes insufficient to ground D's claim of a defence?

In what follows, we explore the three bases for answering this question reflected in the academic literature. The first, and perhaps dominant approach,[39] argues that D's defence is blocked at T2 where they have *caused* the circumstances of that defence/crisis through their conduct at T1 (i.e. the 'causation approach'). The other two approaches avoid claims of causation, focusing instead on D's conduct at T1 creating a changed moral (and legal) context. D's defensive rights are either diminished by this change (i.e. the 'qualification approach') or extinguished entirely (i.e. the 'change of normative position approach'). As we shall explain, we prefer a version of the last of these three.

10.3.1 Causation approach

The first approach conceptualizes prior fault^{DEF} in causal terms, establishing liability (despite D's apparent defence at T2) on the basis that D culpably *caused* the conditions of that defence. In our example of provoked self-defence, it is D's intentional manipulation of V at T1 that creates the circumstances of defence (i.e. causes

[39] See C Finkelstein and L Katz, 'Contrived Defenses and Deterrent Threats: Two Facets of One Problem' (2008) 5 *Ohio State Journal of Criminal Law* 479.

the crisis necessary to justify defensive force). For proponents of this approach, such as Robinson, it is therefore possible to maintain both that D's conduct at T2 is justified in defence, and that D is nevertheless liable because of their conduct at T1.[40] Liability is constructed from a combination of D's acts at T1 (causing the circumstances of defence) and their mental state at T1 (typically requiring intent for the manipulation of both defence and offence at T2). In this manner, Robinson contends, D's acts at T1 are comparable to the use of an innocent agent, or even to a conspiracy with one's later self.[41]

Advocates of this approach highlight its several benefits. For example, by establishing liability at T1, and allowing D's defence at T2, we can avoid complex rules concerning the conditions for the exclusion of that defence and/or its complete or partial qualification. As Robinson explains, 'it is the nature of justified conduct that it either is or is not justified, depending on whether it causes a net societal benefit—regardless of the particular state of mind, past or present, of the actor'.[42] And thus, for Robinson, D's conduct at T2 may be justified. D is still allowed (and even encouraged) by the available defence at T2 to act in an appropriate way: to defend themselves in our example, or (more convincingly) to choose a lesser evil in circumstances of necessity.[43]

> Assume that an actor sets a fire that threatens a nearby town to create the conditions that will justify his using his enemy's farm as a firebreak. Denying a justification defence might dissuade him from undertaking such a scheme, but if it fails to dissuade him, the unavailability of the defence may reduce his incentive to set the firebreak and save the town.

When D sets the firebreak at T2, he is acting on a contrived defence, but at that moment in time, it is still the right thing to do. In this manner, for Robinson, it is D's causal conduct at T1 that grounds liability, not the quality of his defence at T2.

The causation approach also provides a useful basis for resolving more complex cases. For example, where D has not contrived at T1, or V's response to D's provocation is disproportionate, the causal chain to D's potential liability outcome may be broken. Within the causal approach, D's conduct in defence at T2 is identical, and justified/excused across case examples, but D's liability for T1 is now extinguished. There are similar benefits regarding third-party interventions. As D's defensive conduct at T2 remains justified, the causation approach is able to avoid the potentially unintuitive position where a third-party acting in the same way as D at

[40] P Robinson, 'Causing the Conditions of One's Own Defence' (1985) 71 *Virginia Law Review* 1.
[41] Ibid 30–39.
[42] Ibid 28.
[43] Ibid 28. For a similar example, see L Alexander, 'Causing the Conditions of One's Defence: A Theoretical Non-Problem' (2013) 7(3) *Criminal Law and Philosophy* 623, 623–24.

T2 would be justified where D's conduct is not,[44] and/or the unintuitive position that 'the person who has an affirmative defence is at fault in the same way as is a person who commits the same offence without a defence'.[45] Indeed, the strength of this logic led Alexander to label the whole discussion a 'theoretical non-problem', seeing the Robinson causation approach as self-evident.[46]

We do not agree, and think this goes too far, to say the very least. It is true that the causation approach has obvious advantages, as it does as a potential all-embracing explanation for all prior fault intuitions, across both prior fault^{OFF} and prior fault^{DEF}. However, just as we have rejected Robinson's approach to prior fault *in general*,[47] we highlight at least two fundamental problems with it in the specific context of contrived defences.

The first problem with the causation approach relates to the need for a causal link between D's conduct at T1 and the circumstances of defence at T2. Simply put, in the context of contrived defences, legal causation of this kind will often be absent. Although D may cause the fire in Robinson's favoured example of contrived necessity, requiring destruction of V's farm to prevent its spread, this is an example involving D as a lone agent. In many other cases, the circumstances of D's defence will rely on the conduct of another party, including our contrived self-defence hypothetical where V is provoked into attacking D.[48] In these multi-party cases, D has certainly contributed to V's conduct (D may well be complicit, where V's conduct amounts to an offence[49]), but V's free and voluntary choices in action will break any legal causal chain.[50] Thus, at best, the causation approach is only able to explain a subset of contrived defence cases where D's manipulation does not include other parties.[51]

The second problem with the causation approach, as articulated by Robinson, relates to the necessary coexistence of D's valid defence at T2 and D's liability derived from T1. Taken separately, we may understand what Robinson is trying to achieve. For Robinson, D's liability derives from T1, carrying through to the harms at T2; however, at T2 alone, he claims that D's defensive conduct remains justified or excused, incentivizing defensive action. However, we contend that this logic falters when the T1 and T2 events are taken together, recognizing

44 L Alexander, 'Causing the Conditions of One's Defence: A Theoretical Non-Problem' (2013) 7(3) *Criminal Law and Philosophy* 623, 626.

45 S Dimock, 'Actio Libera in Causa' (2013) 7 *Criminal Law and Philosophy* 549, 569.

46 L Alexander, 'Causing the Conditions of One's Defence: A Theoretical Non-Problem' (2013) 7(3) *Criminal Law and Philosophy* 623.

47 Discussed in Chapter 1, Section 1.3.1.

48 This will also be the case for contrived duress, relying on threats from a third party.

49 *Gnango* [2011] UKSC 59.

50 In English law, this rule is established in *Kennedy (No.2)* [2005] EWCA Crim 685.

51 This point is highlighted by K Ferzan, 'Provocateurs' (2013) 7 *Criminal Law and Philosophy* 597, 603; L Katz, 'Entrapment Through the Lens of the Actio Libera in Causa' (2013) 7(3) *Criminal Law and Philosophy* 587, 593; D Farrell, 'What Should We Say About Contrived "Self-Defence" Defences?' (2013) 7 *Criminal Law and Philosophy* 571, 578.

their interconnectedness. Let us return to our contrived self-defence example. Robinson's approach would recognize D's prior fault^{DEF} at T1 (i.e. when inciting V), and use this as the basis for confirming liability when D kills V at T2. However, alongside this we are also expected to view that same killing (D's use of defensive force) as justified and even incentivized by the availability of a defence at T2, even though this defence (in reality) will not prevent or qualify D's liability at all. Robinson sees the justification at T2 as an incentive for D to 'do the right thing', and yet D has already forfeited their right to the defence from their conduct at T1. So, where is the incentive?[52] Any incentive is as functionally empty as the promise of the defence: D's justified (T2) and unjustified (T1) conduct will always lead to liability.

10.3.2 Qualification approach

The 'qualification' approach to contrived defences would also allow for the potential of a valid defence at T2. A useful example of this approach has been set out by Farrell, albeit only in the context of contrived self-defence.[53]

Farrell begins from the premise that D will *always* have the *moral* right to self-defence, whether that defence is 'contrived' or not.[54] This is because, for Farrell, causing harm to protect oneself in cases of self-defence is a form of 'distributive justice', provided that the harm caused is not 'radically disproportionate' to the threat faced.[55] It is worth highlighting that Farrell's basic approach towards the concept of self-defence is influenced by deontological principles. Deontology is a normative theory which focuses on the morality of a person's choices based on the nature of their actions (inputs) as opposed to the consequences of their actions (outputs). Thus, deontological ethics are essentially non-consequentialist in nature. Farrell argues that choosing to defend oneself by causing harm to another in relevant situations is justified and that one should not be deprived of this right (even in contrived cases) since this would infringe fundamental principles of fairness and justice. Hence, according to Farrell, the focus in contrived cases should be on what justice or fairness allows, rather than the overall utility in a consequentialist sense.[56] In cases of contrived self-defence, where D's conduct

[52] Ferzan describes this position as 'rather odd'. K Ferzan, 'Provocateurs' (2013) 7 *Criminal Law and Philosophy* 597, 603. See also R Segev, 'Responsibility and Justificatory Defences' (2017) 11 *Criminal Law and Philosophy* 97, 99.

[53] D Farrell, 'What Should We Say About Contrived 'Self-Defence' Defences? (2013) 7 *Criminal Law and Philosophy* 571. This approach also gains some support from German law: J Herrmann, 'Causing the Conditions of One's Own Defence: The Multifaceted Approach of German Law' (1986) 3 *Brigham Young University Law Review* 747, 756.

[54] D Farrell, 'What Should We Say About Contrived 'Self-Defence' Defences? (2013) 7 *Criminal Law and Philosophy* 571, 572.

[55] Ibid 573.

[56] Ibid 573.

at T1 contributes to the need for defensive force at T2, Farrell distinguishes two possibilities.

In the first (standard) case, V responds to D's provocation in the manner expected, and D uses defensive force. In this case, Farrell reasons that since V uses their free will and intentionally chooses to respond to D's manipulation, it is therefore V who has created a situation where D needs to protect themselves from V's attack, thereby justifying causing V harm in defence.[57] This applies to standard cases of self-defence as well as contrived ones. The operating fact here is that V could have refrained from acting in the way they did, but voluntarily chose not to do so. It is this element of choice and free will on V's part that breaks the chain of causation from D's conduct at T1, and creates the moral right for D's defensive force.[58]

The right to self-defence therefore applies to all of the parties (D, V, and third parties) within Farrell's model, but, crucially, it is not unqualified. Rather, where D relies on a form of contrived self-defence, D's use of force at T2 will be subject to stricter standards of 'proportionality' and 'minimum harm' requirements. For Farrell, although D has the right to resist V's attack, in defending themselves, D can only perform minimum acts of self-preservation (cause no more than the 'minimum' harm required in defence).[59]

The second (non-standard) case, distinguished by Farrell, will apply where D provokes V at T1, but V's reaction is unexpectedly excessive and disproportionate. Farrell stipulates that this would be a case of shared responsibility (and not a qualified defence).[60] Thus, in cases of this kind, D will be entitled to an unqualified defence in relation to any defensive force used against V: the excessive nature of V's response effectively supersedes any original contribution from D at T1.

As an alternative to Robinson's approach discussed above, there are several attractive features to Farrell's conception. The qualified defence model allows us to avoid the potential contradiction of both criminalizing and excusing D's conduct simultaneously, it usefully highlights the independently blameworthy contributions of V in contrived self-defence, and it also allows us to recognize a limited residual right of defence (something that has a plausible moral appeal). D is to blame from their conduct at T1, and this impacts their rights in defence at T2, but D does not forfeit all rights of self-preservation against V's attack.

However, despite the merits of Farrell's approach, we remain unconvinced by it as a viable model for reform of legal rules concerning prior fault^{DEF} contrived defences. There are two principal reasons for this, one practical and one normative.

The first problem is that despite its importance to Farrell's conception, as he himself recognizes,[61] there is no clear definition of what constitutes 'minimum acts'

57 Ibid 574.
58 Ibid 577.
59 Ibid 581.
60 Ibid.
61 Ibid 581.

of self-preservation. Standard self-defence rules already require D's response to be objectively reasonable in the circumstances, meaning that self-defence will not apply where D's use of force is disproportionate.[62] It would seem, then, that Farrell somehow conceives of D's actions being judged against some lower standard than this, potentially blocking D's defence where their conduct was 'simply' proportionate. Such a threshold is likely to be very difficult to identify with any degree of precision, particularly as a jury question.[63] This creates a problem in the context of self-defence, which was Farrell's point of focus, but also beyond that if it is to operate as a more general prior fault^{DEF} rule. What, for example, does a minimum act threshold require in the context of necessity or duress? And what of contrived incapacity defences, where D—by definition—lacks control of their conduct at T2? So even if Farrrell's approach was practically implementable for contrived self-defence, which we doubt, it does not provide a useful framework for contrived defences generally.

The second problem is more fundamental for our purposes at least, as we contend that even minimum acts of self-preservation should not be *legally* justified in such contrived circumstances. Farrell may present a (generally) convincing picture of enduring moral rights to self-defence, but there is little to suggest in his arguments why this compromised moral right should also be translated into a legal right to cause harms. To allow D even a minimum legal right of defence at T2, is to legally authorize force against V in exactly the circumstances manufactured and contrived by D at T1. We contend that even this minimum right, in law, would be ill-conceived. In some cases, it may be that the minimum required acts also represent the full extent of D's plan, something that is most likely outside of the self-defence context, such as within Robinson's firebreak hypothetical. Examples of this kind provide the most obvious illustrations of potential injustice if D's minimum acts were legally justified. But even within Farrell's core self-defence examples, we do not accept the argument that legal defence rights must track residual moral rights. Farrell's analysis is expressly predicated on his objective of 'what we might be inclined to say about such cases from a moral point of view', and he expressly states his objective is not to explore 'what we should say in the law about' these cases.[64] In contrast, our task is precisely to do that. It seems perfectly plausible for us to believe that D may retain a compromised *moral* right to commit minimal harm at T2 (including through acts of self-preservation), but that D's previous conduct at T1 has changed their normative position, such that D's *legal* right to do so may be forfeited.

[62] Criminal Justice and Immigration Act 2008, s76.

[63] Existing problems identifying the reasonableness threshold in the context of so-called householder cases in England & Wales should provide ample warning of likely problems here as well. See JJ Child et al, *Simester and Sullivan's Criminal Law* (8th Ed, Hart, 2022) Ch 21.

[64] D Farrell, 'What Should We Say About Contrived 'Self-Defence' Defences? (2013) 7 *Criminal Law and Philosophy* 571, 572.

10.3.3 Change of normative position approach

Our preferred approach for conceptualizing contrived defences shares several elements with those already discussed, but in our view provides the best explanation for the application of prior fault^{DEF} rules (and, crucially, a practically viable basis for doctrinal reform). The model focuses on D's conduct and mental state at T1, asking whether those events are sufficient to undermine D's claim of justification or excuse in action at T2. This is not a question of mechanical causation (T1–T2), but one of changed normative position: is D's normative position at T2 such that the crisis in defence becomes non-justifying or non-excusing? We provide an overview of this approach here, before expanding on its doctrinal implications in Section 10.4.

The change of normative position approach ('change approach') for contrived defences is perhaps best expressed in the work of Ferzan.[65] Ferzan focuses her discussion on provocation leading to self-defence, with similar examples to our opening hypothetical. This is useful because it forces us to engage with the most difficult cases: cases where V is *not justified* in using force against D, as opposed to cases where D's aggression at T1 gives rise to legitimate defensive force. For Ferzan:[66]

> A provocateur creates the risk that another person will harm him by engaging in conduct that he knows may produce a violent response, either because it will anger the respondent or otherwise give him a reason to engage in violent conduct. Having created this risk of harm to himself, he forfeits his moral complaint when this very risk materializes. It is true that this conduct is insufficient to justify the respondent's behavior, but sometimes, there are just two wrongdoers.

In this manner, there is no separation of (at once) justified and unjustified conduct (Robinson), and no grading of rights in defence (Farrell). Rather, simply, the question is whether D's conduct at T1 is sufficient for the forfeiture of their rights in defence at T2.[67] Of course, which types of conduct and in what circumstances at T1 should be sufficient for these purposes is a complex question which requires weighty consideration and cogent reasoning. We seek to answer these questions when discussing our preferred doctrinal construction of the contrived defence prior fault^{DEF} rule in Section 10.4.

[65] K Ferzan, 'Provocateurs' (2013) 7 *Criminal Law and Philosophy* 597.

[66] Ibid 615. In Section 10.2.2, we discussed how provocation may be unhelpfully conflated with 'easier' cases of T1 aggression, allowing courts to avoid crucial prior fault^{DEF} questions.

[67] This may be alternatively described as the breach of a second-order reason not to put oneself in the crisis at T2. See C Finkelstein and L Katz, 'Contrived Defenses and Deterrent Threats: Two Facets of One Problem' (2008) 5 *Ohio State Journal of Criminal Law* 479, 502.

Before we turn to this, however, it is important to acknowledge criticism of Ferzan's approach, specifically focused on its potential scope in application. This is because, for Ferzan, the 'change approach' is presented as a particular response to provocation self-defence cases *alone*, where D is excluded from the use of defensive force to protect themselves.

The first line of critique, from authors such as Finkelstein and Katz, evaluates Ferzan's model as a potential basis for all prior fault^{OFF} and prior fault^{DEF} rules.[68] And they reject the model on that basis, highlighting its inability to explain prior fault^{OFF} cases, such as those where D does not complete the elements of an offence at T2 due to a state of intoxication-induced automatism.[69] We agree with Finkelstein and Katz on this point. The 'change approach' does not provide an appropriate model for prior fault^{OFF} analysis. However, as will be clear from our discussion throughout this book, we do not agree that the failure of the model to explain prior fault^{OFF} should be understood as any kind of reason to reject it as a model for explaining prior fault^{DEF}. Rather, as we have explained,[70] we believe that there are fundamental conceptual differences between prior fault^{OFF} and prior fault^{DEF}, such that separate models of analysis and application are required, and such that a search for an overreaching prior fault rule applying in all circumstances becomes no more than a theoretical red herring.

However, despite our rejection of the first line of critique, Ferzan's stated ambition of explaining provocation self-defence cases alone still raises a secondary potential problem of scope. This is because, where D's contrived defence involves defence of an innocent third party or their property, such as in Robinson's firebreak example, Ferzan remains open to alternative approaches that would characterize D's conduct at T2 as justified.[71] We think this is wrong; and that the change approach provides the best model for analysis across contrived defence cases (i.e. including contrived self-defence, necessity, duress, etc). There is certainly a difference between D's T2 defence of self and defence of another, in that when D is defending the rights of another—in cases such as Robinson's firebreak—we want D to act at T2 despite the contrived circumstances, and others should assist rather than prevent D in this action. However, due to D's conduct at T1, their moral status at T2 is shifted, and the basis for justification in their conduct at T2 is undermined. At T2, D is now acting to *limit* their liability, which may be permissible in isolation, but remains within the unjustified scope of the T1–T2 conduct as a whole. Indeed, in examples such as the firebreak, where third parties are present to burn the farm and create the break themselves, the most appropriate conduct may still be to restrain D from completing the same T2 conduct.

[68] Ibid.
[69] Ibid 492–94.
[70] See, in particular, Chapter 1, Section 1.3.1.
[71] K Ferzan, 'Provocateurs' (2013) 7 *Criminal Law and Philosophy* 597, 603.

10.3.4 Conclusions on models for prior fault^{DEF} contrived defences

Our preferred model for understanding contrived prior fault^{DEF} rules—change of normative position—provides an essential theoretical framework for the coherent doctrinal expression of those rules. It enables the setting aside of rules of mechanical causation, and/or the grading of defensive rights. Indeed, it brings to the fore a set of questions, related to how and in what circumstances D's normative position is changed at T1, focusing on D's conduct at T1 and D's foresight of T2 events, as well as the potential impact of subsequent events (involving D and/or others) to that normative status. These are the questions to which we now turn.

10.4 Defining prior fault^{DEF} contrived defence rules

In this section, we set out and discuss our preferred doctrinal construction for a contrived defence prior fault^{DEF} rule. There remains room within many of the doctrinal choices made for sensible policy disagreement, and we anticipate (and encourage) future debate on these issues. However, we believe that it remains useful to provide a specific recommendation of this kind. It provides a focal point for future policy debate, and crucially within the wider context of this book, it demonstrates the very different set of challenges arising from contrived defences as opposed to the other categories of prior fault.

Drawing on the discussion in Section 10.3, our preferred model is based upon the change of normative position approach. Thus, our aim is to identify reliable markers of blame at T1, such that the otherwise defence-justifying crisis at T2 loses it normative effect in respect of D's rights in defence. In doing so, the idea is to identify a reliable threshold for prior fault^{DEF} exclusion, capable of consistent application across defences.

10.4.1 Our recommended approach

We again set out our preferred approach in the form of draft legislation. This is done for maximum clarity; it is not intended to represent a final legislative text.

3. Contrived Defending

(1) Where D relies on a supervening defence, that defence is to be disregarded where D was responsible for contriving its circumstances.
(2) In determining whether D has contrived the circumstances of a defence, it must be demonstrated that–
  (a) D's conduct materially contributed to the circumstances of the defence;

(b) D intended or was reckless whether their conduct would materially contribute to the circumstances of the defence; and

(c) D foresaw the risk of their own future offending, in the context of defensive action.

(3) 'Material Contribution' is to be interpreted as significant or weighty, howsoever brought about. It will be absent where the circumstances of defence arise from the unforeseen and disproportionate misconduct of another.

10.4.2 Intent or recklessness regarding the circumstances of defence

In order to demonstrate that D's defence was contrived in some way, and that they are at fault for manufacturing the defensive crisis at T2, we believe that subjective mens rea is essential. It is not simply that D 'started it', but that they *chose* to continue with conduct that risked criminal harms in defensive circumstances.[72] The first, and arguably the most important element of this, requires D to be intentional or (at least) reckless regarding their contribution to the circumstances of defence. In our contrived self-defence example, this requires D to be at least reckless in provoking V's attack.

Despite our focus on choice, we do not agree with commentators who advocate for a narrower intention only test.[73] Intention cases may be paradigmatic, as we discussed in Section 10.2.1, but intention-based tests set an extremely high bar in terms of fault and associated evidential requirements. Indeed, in cases of duress, it is this concern that led to the development of contriving rules based on mere negligence.[74] We think this goes too far in the opposite direction, however, denying D's defence in the absence of their own contriving choice.[75]

A minimum of recklessness provides a principled and pragmatic middle ground,[76] requiring specific foresight and choice in action, in combination with an element of unreasonableness. Both aspects require some further clarification.

On the requirement of foresight, it is important to clarify exactly what kind of risk must be foreseen. For example, how precisely and accurately must D have foreseen the effects of their conduct? This was highlighted as an area of inconsistency within the current law in Section 10.2. Certain defences require specific foresight at T1 of future offence/defence details (e.g. self-defence and the loss of

[72] Ibid 615–16.

[73] See, e.g., L Alexander, 'Causing the Conditions of One's Defence: A Theoretical Non-Problem' (2013) 7(3) *Criminal Law and Philosophy* 623, 626.

[74] Discussed in Section 10.2.2.

[75] See K Ferzan, 'Provocateurs' (2013) 7 *Criminal Law and Philosophy* 597, 616.

[76] Ibid 615–21; W Wilson, 'How Criminal Defences Work' in A Reed and M Bohlander (eds) *General Defences in Criminal Law* (Hart 2014) 7, 20.

control defence), some are unclear on this point (e.g. insanity), and others require foresight of only non-specific dangers (e.g. duress). In our view, it is unnecessary and counterproductive to require D to have foreseen every detail of the events at T2, as the reality of complex criminal situations makes such foresight unlikely (and very difficult to prove). However, D's foresight must be logically connected to the circumstances of the T2 defence, such that D's choice is genuinely to risk contributing to the need for that defence (i.e. non-specific dangerous conduct and/or association would not be sufficient).

The second element of recklessness—requiring D's risk taking to be *unreasonable* on the facts[77]—is also crucial. There are many examples of wholly non-blameworthy conduct that may provoke others or contribute to the potential need for a future defence, and it is therefore important for any legal rule to be able to exclude such cases from its application. Examples mentioned in the literature include situations where D may wear 'provocative' clothing in public, or D (a black person) walks through an area known for race-related violence, when at the time each may recognize the risk of provoking attack, and the potential need for defensive action.[78] In such cases, despite D's foresight regarding the actions/reactions of others, the fact that D's conduct remains entirely reasonable on the facts means that they will not be (and should never be) considered reckless in their contribution to the circumstances giving rise to the possibility of having to rely on a potential criminal defence. D's defence will only be blocked where their conduct at T1 demonstrates the unreasonable running of a risk, for example where D goes out hoping to use defensive force as a form of vigilantism. The same logic applies to prevent the contriving rule applying to frontline police officers, for example, who are likely to foresee the risk of attack (and use of defensive force) in the context of their duties.[79]

10.4.3 Foresight of the future offence

D is required to foresee at T1 the risk of their own future offending (i.e. in circumstances of potential defence) at T2. In our contrived self-defence example, this requires D to foresee killing V. Foresight of this kind is necessary to demonstrate D's manipulation, not simply of the circumstances giving rise to defence, but of the

[77] This is a constituent element of the mens rea term in English law: *G* [2004] 1 AC 1034.

[78] P Robinson, 'Causing the Conditions of One's Own Defence' (1985) 71 *Virginia Law Review* 1, 40; J Herrmann, 'Causing the Conditions of One's Own Defence: The Multifaceted Approach of German Law' (1986) 3 *Brigham Young University Law Review* 747, 753–55; K Ferzan, 'Provocateurs' (2013) 7 *Criminal Law and Philosophy* 597, 599, 617, 621.

[79] This includes more difficult cases where D seeks out a role of this kind in order to use force against another. In each example, provided D acts (and plans to act) legitimately within their role, they will not be reckless in law. Discussed in Q Jahangir, JJ Child, and H Crombag, 'Prior Fault and Contrived Criminal Defences: Coming to the Law with Clean Hands' (2017) 1 *Institute of Law Journal* 28.

legal right to *act* in defence. This is core to the claim that D's defence is contrived, and should therefore be forfeited.

The language of foresight is used here (as opposed to recklessness) because we are discussing D's awareness of a risk in future action.[80] However, as with the previous requirement, our aim is to identify an appropriate balance in terms of culpability and breadth. On the one hand, we are not convinced of the need for an intention requirement here, or specific mens rea of the same kind required for the principal offence at T2.[81] But, on the other hand, we recognize the importance of subjective foresight to narrow the exclusionary rule appropriately. For example, where the disparity between D's expectations and reality is particularly great, it will be open for D to claim that their foresight fell outside the prior fault^{DEF} rules and they should not apply. This could be the case in duress, for example, where D joins a group of shoplifters foreseeing a chance of being coerced into other property offences, but is later coerced into committing a serious sexual offence.[82]

10.4.4 Material contribution at T1

We have included a provision requiring proof that D's conduct at T1 made a material contribution to the circumstances of defence at T2. Crucially, this is not the same as a requirement of legal or mechanical causation, which is an approach we rejected in Section 10.3.[83]

Requiring some material contribution in fact ensures that the contriving provision will not apply in purely inchoate circumstances. Varying the facts of our contrived self-defence hypothetical, for example, we do not believe that D's defence should be disregarded where their provocation has no impact at all on V's decision to attack.[84] Or, varying the facts of Robinson's firebreak hypothetical, where D's attempt to cause the initial fire is unsuccessful, but where (fortunately for D) the fire is otherwise caused by lightning. In cases of both kinds, D may be attempting

[80] See JJ Child and A Hunt, 'Beyond the Present-Fault Paradigm: Expanding Mens rea Definitions in the General Part' (2021) 42(2) *Oxford Journal of Legal Studies* 438.

[81] S Dimock, 'Actio Libera in Causa' (2013) 7 *Criminal Law and Philosophy* 549, 558. Indeed, we are sceptical of any analysis that claims D may have the same mens rea at T1 regarding events to be completed at T2: Ibid.

[82] Indeed, similar differences can arise across each of the defences (e.g. where V reacts more extremely than D anticipates to provocation, where D's mental condition has a greater than expected impact on their conduct, and so on).

[83] Despite mooting the potential for no factual link requirement at all in previous writing, we have adjusted that position within our current preferred approach. See Q Jahangir, JJ Child, and H Crombag, 'Prior Fault and Contrived Criminal Defences: Coming to the Law with Clean Hands' (2017) 1 *Institute of Law Journal* 28.

[84] A concern discussed in P Robinson, 'Prohibited Risks and Culpable Disregard or Inattentiveness: Challenge and Confusion in the Formulation of Risk-Creation Offences' (2003) 4 *Theoretical Inquiry Law* 367, 376–77.

to contrive a defence, but this is not what has happened, and so the T2 defence-justifying crisis remains genuine.

More difficult cases will involve some measure of contribution by D, in circumstances of unforeseen and disproportionate intervention from other parties. In particular, we are considering cases of provocation leading to self-defence, where the individual provoked reacts in an extreme and violent manner. Our preferred construction will allow D's self-defence where V's reaction is unforeseen and disproportionate, echoing a recognition within the current law that V's response may sometimes effectively override D's fault in attempted manipulation.[85] However, crucially, where V's response is disproportionate but not unforeseen (i.e. where D anticipates the particular reaction, however extreme) then D will not escape liability under our proposed rule.[86]

10.4.5 Consistency across supervening defences

Our draft provision is capable of applying consistently across all supervening defences. Whilst we recognize contriving as a particular example of prior fault^{DEF}, and one that requires a particular set of provisions to engage with it, we do not identify associated points of difference between defences and/or defence types.[87]

In Section 10.2, we highlighted significant differences in the application (or non-application) of a contrived defence rule across different defences within English law, an inconsistency that is equally apparent across each of our comparator jurisdictions. We do not believe that such inconsistency is borne out of principle, but rather from accidents in common law (and code-based) development. This is not to say that some degree of difference between defences would be intolerable: it may be, for example, that particular pragmatic concerns regarding group criminality may be used to broaden an exclusionary rule for duress. However, we are clear that any differences of this kind should be recognized and justified as such, as variations from a rule of general application.

There are several benefits from ensuring consistency in our theoretical approach, translated through to our recommended doctrinal provision. A final example of this, highlighted at various points across the chapter, is the potential for greater certainty in the legal rights of third-party intervenors. As we discussed in Section 10.2, the current law is far from clear on this issue, complicated by the diversity of approaches to contriving rules. One of the advantages of the change of normative position approach is the recognition that defensive rights holding is not

[85] Discussed in Section 10.2.2.

[86] Usefully discussed in L Hecht, 'Provocateurs and Their Rights to Self-Defence' (2019) 13 *Criminal Law and Philosophy* 165.

[87] We discussed the general applicability of the change of normative position approach in Section 10.3.

an either/or transaction between parties. In cases of contrived self-defence, for example, the question is not whether V *or* D has the right to defence (i.e. because it is possible that neither has such a right). Regarding third-party (X) intervention, the same insight provides useful flexibility, and encourages us to focus on X's state of mind. Where X intervenes without knowledge of D's contriving, they may do so lawfully with a relevant defence. Where X is aware of D's contriving, they may still act to limit harms (particularly where the rights threatened are not D's personal or property rights), but they should act on the basis that D has effectively forfeited their own rights to defence.

10.5 Conclusion

This chapter has engaged with a quite different form of prior fault than that discussed in the rest of the book. Rather than creating circumstances of mental impairment and mistake, contriving defences involve the specifically targeted manipulation of facts to exploit the law. Indeed, in this manner, they display perhaps the most serious form of prior fault^{DEF}. To allow the contriving of defences is effectively to allow individuals to commit offences with self-manufactured impunity.

Yet, in response, the current law provides a hotchpotch of rules, apparently undisturbed by broader theory or principle. In this chapter, we have shown how effective theorizing can bring the law to a point of potential clarity and fairness, providing our preferred doctrinal construction of a general contriving rule. It is, we would contend, an approach with potential for application across defences, ensuring the integrity of the law in a consistent and principled manner.

PART III
CONCLUSIONS

11
CONCLUSION

11.1 Introduction

Prior fault is not a single, discrete doctrine known to the current law in any meaningful sense. At best, within English law, and across jurisdictions, we can identify a loose collection of 'rules' to which that label may be applied. Typically, such rules are characterized for their pragmatic (as opposed to principled) approach to criminalization. They are rules designed to mitigate or resolve apparent problems with the narrow temporal application of criminal law. An intoxicated defendant may claim, plausibly in some cases, that they did not realize that they were harming a human, or that they honestly believed (however unreasonably) that they were defending themselves from attack. In such cases, were we simply to apply standard rules regarding non-fatal offences and/or self-defence, focused on the point of harm causing, we may well conclude that D should not be punished. This is because where D believes they are harming a non-human, they lack mens rea for a non-fatal offence against the person; and where D acts in the honest belief that defensive force against another person is required, they may rely on self-defence for any reasonable force used corresponding with that belief. Prior fault rules, as we have discussed them throughout this study, provide a mechanism for resisting such conclusions, and for stretching the lens of criminalization to include D's conduct prior to that which caused harm. In our lexicon, this prior conduct occurs at T1, but in various ways is treated as relevant to fixing D with criminal liability at T2.

Stretching the temporal lens of criminalization (across offences and defences) requires justification however. And it is here that the law, and any move towards the idea of a prior fault *doctrine*, becomes unstuck. Rather than engage in the conceptual and doctrinal heavy lifting required to understand and construct a set of principled rules, legal commentators and courts have too often retreated to the shallow, murky waters of intuition and pragmatics. Thus, specific rules have been identified and endorsed as apparent fixes, measured by their ability to reach a particular outcome on specific facts alone. In this fashion then, the proxy of voluntary intoxication becomes recognized as a flexible source of fault, the status of automatism is employed to house alternative routes to blame, and various defence labels are adjusted to produce desired policy outcomes in particular circumstances. There is a certain expediency in such rules, which has sustained their application (in some cases for more than a century), but they remain characterized by a lack of coherence, by inconsistency in application, and by the potential for unfairness. We have

Prior Fault Criminalization. John J Child, Adrian Hunt, and Hans S. Crombag, Oxford University Press.
 DOI: 10.1093/9780191874734.003.0014

explored each of the current prior fault rules in the chapters of this book, arguing that each one is unable to (and often designed to avoid having to) provide a principled basis for the expansion of criminalization.

We have identified attempts at more principled explanation, seeking to conceptualize prior fault (and examples of prior fault rules) more generally. However, across jurisdictions, such attempts have gained little traction, failing to attract a large degree of support from either academic or practitioner communities, or to offer practically viable routes to reform. In particular, attempts at principled engagement have struggled to identify the appropriate boundaries of the project.

At one end of the spectrum, Robinson and others have attempted to tether *all* prior fault rules to a singular conceptual source, applicable across offences and defences alike.[1] All-encompassing explanations of this kind have an obvious appeal, not least in the context of current unprincipled inconsistency. But, as we have shown throughout this book, they simply do not work: there are fundamental differences between prior fault^{OFF} as a constructor of absent offending, and prior fault^{DEF} as a mechanism for blocking a defence, and efforts to accommodate both within a single rule create incoherences and/or uncertainties on each side.[2] At the other end of the spectrum are those seeking reform of individual prior fault rules. A common example of this relates to 'intoxication', as the most prominent example of prior fault, which has prompted specific reviews from various Law Commissions and others.[3] The problem here, as we have discussed, is that it becomes impossible to construct coherent and principled rules through an exclusive intoxication lens: a lens which presents definitional problems in itself, and one that operates as a problematic proxy for something quite different (i.e. *legitimate* T1 blame, which may arise in cases not involving intoxication, and may not always be present in cases involving intoxication). Again, despite excellent intentions, such projects are bound to fail as an exercise in principled reform.

In this study, we have not simply pursued a middle-ground option, rather we have attempted to create a new conceptual structure for prior fault analysis: defining the role of prior fault^{OFF} in offending, and the quite different roles of prior fault^{DEF} in blocking defences.[4]

In Part I of the book, Chapters 2–5 explored how current prior fault^{OFF} rules have been used to justify the substitution of certain absent offence elements. We explored and critiqued current doctrinal distinctions between intoxication, automatism, and insanity, leading to the identification of a common conceptual

[1] P Robinson, 'Causing the Conditions of One's Own Defence' (1985) 71 *Virginia Law Review* 1; 'Imputed Criminal Liability' (1984) 93 *Yale Law Journal* 609. See also references to prior fault in A Ashworth, *Principles of Criminal Law* (2nd Ed, Clarendon Press, 1995).

[2] Our discussion of reform within each chapter typically begins with Robinson's universal approach, but—in each case—we are forced to look for alternatives beyond it.

[3] E.g. in the context of English law, Law Commission, *Intoxication and Criminal Liability* (LC No 314, 2009). See other examples discussed in Chapters 2 and 5.

[4] This fundamental distinction was first introduced in Chapter 1, Section 1.3.1, and follows through each subsequent chapter.

understanding of prior fault^{OFF} in this context. It is that singular understanding that was empirically explored in Chapter 6, leading into our recommendations for doctrinal reform in Chapter 7. Prior fault^{DEF} rules, the subject of Part II of the book, provide a set of quite different challenges. Indeed, through our exploration of the current law, not only did we find fundamental differences between prior fault^{OFF} and prior fault^{DEF} rules, but also a crucial distinction between different species of prior fault^{DEF} rules when considered in the context of blocking otherwise available defences. This distinction was introduced in Chapter 8. It involves the difference between incapacity and mistake making, on the one hand, and contrived defences, on the other, and each was fully explored in Chapters 9 and 10. By means of identification and evaluation, we have sought to clarify the conceptual divisions between existing rules, and to provide a platform for coherent principle-led doctrinal reform.

In this concluding chapter, we will identify and discuss the significance of our arguments and findings. We begin, in Section 11.2, with the most direct implications of the study, focusing on conceptual understanding of prior fault and its implications for doctrinal reform. We broaden our discussion in Section 11.3, exploring some of the indirect implications of our arguments and findings. These include the implications of our analysis on the definition of objective fault elements, as they arise in both offences and defences, as well as the implications for sentencing, including established sentencing guidelines. Finally, in Section 11.4, we broaden our discussion further to reflect on the conceptualization of criminal fault in general, exploring both conceptual and methodological insights from our study. Throughout, we highlight the importance of principled engagement with general part concepts such as prior fault, and the problems that result from a lack of such engagement (exemplified within the current law).

11.2 Implications for law reform

This section reviews the direct implications for reform arising from this study, involving the codification of prior fault rules. It is our ambition to show that a more coherent conceptual understanding of prior fault does not simply act to expose problems within the current law, but can also provide a workable basis for doctrinal reforms.

11.2.1 Reform in England & Wales

We have made recommendations for reform—including illustrative draft legislation—both for prior fault^{OFF} rules in constructing criminal liability in offending, and the two forms in which prior fault^{DEF} rules can apply to block an otherwise supervening defence. The text of these recommendations has already been set out within earlier chapters, and is repeated in a brief appendix at the end of the book for ease of reference. In this subsection, we provide some general comments, highlighting important findings from the study.

Prior fault rules are perhaps most controversial in their prior fault^{OFF} mode, functioning within the current law effectively as a substitute for missing offence fault elements (including a lack of voluntariness) to create liability. Much of our discussion of current prior fault^{OFF} rules (Chapters 2–4) is concerned with exposing the simple reality of this function across jurisdictions, despite the dominance of alternative framings within the courts and associated literature. Intoxication rules in this context, and other prior fault^{OFF} rules, are not defences and are not evidential rules, rather they represent substantive rules for the imputation of criminal responsibility. As substantive rules of imputation, they require justification, and more specifically, their function in the substitution of missing fault elements (including voluntariness) requires a justification of equivalence between the putative prior *fault* and those missing elements to ensure appropriate criminalization and fair labelling.

Our analysis exposes the lack of such justification. The current law leads to over-criminalization for intoxication and automatism, resulting in (i) the inappropriate labelling of defendants *in all cases*, where D has not completed certain offence elements and in the absence of equivalent fault, and (ii) the inappropriate criminalization of defendants *in certain cases*, where there is insufficient fault to justify liability of any kind. It also leads to under-criminalization through the non-application of prior fault^{OFF} where some form of T1–T2 criminalization might be considered appropriate, across both external (including intoxication and automatism) and internal (including insanity) conditions.

We considered a range of alternatives to the current law, including abolishing existing prior fault^{OFF} rules without replacement. Here, we noted there remained a strong intuitive appeal for criminalization in cases where D's choices across T1–T2 demonstrate a culpable disregard for the interests of others, and argued that this arises not simply as a product of misconception (i.e. based upon the inaccurate framing of intoxication and other prior fault^{OFF} rules as defences to be blocked), but rather is connected with a principled normative case for criminalization in certain cases.

Therefore, considering these difficulties, we pursued an alternative mechanism for taking account of prior fault in offending, namely abolishing current prior fault^{OFF} rules, and creating a new offence designed to capture and punish prior fault as a distinct wrong. As part of this process, we examined the range of objections which have previously persuaded policymakers and legislators to reject similar reform efforts (generally in the case of intoxication only) in the past.[5]

[5] See Chapter 5, Section 5.4.

Although we saw these objections varied depending on the proposal in question, there was a trend towards objecting to the perceived complexity and delay which it was claimed such initiatives would create. There was also, perhaps, some discernible residual discomfort at changing the claimed 'common-sense' intuitive approach of *Majewski* to meet the rigours of principled coherence, bearing in mind that it might be claimed the former delivered 'justice' of a sort in most cases anyway. Of course, the latter assertion cannot easily be evidenced since both the direct object and the indirect effect of prior fault^{OFF} rules operate to preclude the raising of the issue in many cases. However, the empirical evidence from the extant scientific literature, as well as our own studies, provides a basis for doubting the claim that injustice may occur in only a small number of cases.[6] Furthermore, as our accounts in Chapters 2–5 show, and as other commentators including the Law Commission have noted,[7] the current prior fault^{OFF} rules are themselves conceptually and technically complex, and to a large extent, as we have argued, unnecessarily so.

Nonetheless, in considering creating a new offence designed to capture and punish prior fault^{OFF} as a distinct wrong, we recognize that the cure should not be worse than the disease. With this in mind, we married our principled approach to the formulation of the substantive offence, with an eye to practical considerations concerning how any new bespoke offence would be applied by prosecutors and the courts, considering issues associated with its place within the broader catalogue of crimes, asking when and why it is likely to be applied singularly and/or in the alternative with other offences. In considering those issues, as well as our primary objective of framing the new offence, we have taken inspiration—and some substantive assistance—from others, across various jurisdictions, who have sought to construct comparable offences, as well as the evaluative literature engaging with those constructions.[8] However, our approach might be regarded as more ambitious than its antecedents, particularly in its attempt to capture (conceptually and doctrinally) an articulation of *all* prior fault in offending. Unprecedented too has been our use of neuropsychological research and empirical data, which was the focus of Chapter 6. There we employed the research and data to test the scientific validity of our underpinning assumptions. We also used this material to inform specific choices in the construction of our recommended offence. This was set out and explained in Chapter 7, and it provides some basis for establishing a model for prior fault^{OFF} rules capable of application across jurisdictions internationally.

In the case of prior fault^{DEF} rules, considered in Part II of the book, we pursued broadly similar methodology to that adopted in Part I. Thus, we began by identifying and critiquing current problematic prior fault^{DEF} rules. Again, it has been important to expose the problematic ways in which such rules are currently

[6] See Chapter 6.
[7] Law Commission, *Intoxication and Criminal Liability* (LC No 314, 2009) Ch 3.
[8] See Chapter 5, Section 5.5.

framed. This can either involve framing prior fault^{DEF} rules as defences in their own right, and/or as particular to specific defences alone, and to expose the potential for unfairness in the application of such rules, both in terms of over- and under-inclusiveness. We agree that prior fault^{DEF} has an important role to play in the (dis-)application of defences, but any viable construction and justification for those rules must reflect the legal reality. What is exposed here is fundamentally different from prior fault^{OFF} rules: we are not concerned with the potential equivalence of prior fault with culpability states, and we are not concerned with prior fault as a distinct wrong in terms of criminalization, rather we are concerned with the role of prior fault in undermining D's claim to have acted in legitimate defence. This required us to engage with theories of defence, identifying points of conflict between D's claim of defence and specific tokens of prior fault.

It is through this conceptual scoping exercise that we have been able in Chapter 8 to clearly identify and distinguish two separate routes for prior fault^{DEF} to justify the blocking of a defence. In each case, D's previous conduct (T1) effectively undermines their claim to have acted (at T2) in response to a defence-justifying crisis. The first route—discussed in Chapter 9—identifies T1 fault in a broadly similar way to that discussed in the context of prior fault^{OFF} rules. D's defensive acts at T2 are prompted by a mistaken belief in circumstances of a defence-relevant crisis (e.g. a delusional belief that force is necessary to defend against an imminent physical attack), and D's mental impairment, and thus D's mistake, can be attributed to their choices at T1 (e.g. to become voluntarily intoxicated with alcohol or other drugs). The second example of prior fault^{DEF}—discussed in Chapter 10—is quite different. This time, D is blameworthy for contriving at T1, manipulating the circumstances of an event at T2, in order to commit an offence in circumstances that might otherwise give rise to a defence. For example, where D provokes an attack from V, doing so to justify force in 'defensive' retaliation.

The reforms we recommend for prior fault^{DEF} could be achieved through the common law because (unlike prior fault^{OFF} rules) they do not represent a fundamental departure from existing rules. However, codification would offer the potential to bring much greater clarity and precision to how such rules should operate, and therefore (as was the case with prior fault^{OFF} rules) we provided a draft legislative text. Our key objectives here were: (i) to clarify what D is blamed for at T1 and how this affects their claim to a defence at T2, (ii) to do so for different types of defence, (iii) to provide for what this means for third-party rights, and (iv) to provide for situations where the circumstances turn out to be not what D anticipated.

11.2.2 Reform outside England & Wales

Our primary jurisdictional focus throughout has been England & Wales, both in terms of current law critique, as well as the drafting of reform recommendations.

However, very little of the material discussed is unique to English law. The topic of prior fault and the challenges we have engaged with are apparent across a wide range of jurisdictions, and our analyses, arguments, and recommendations also have applicability in those systems.

Indeed, despite the variety and inconsistency of prior fault rules discussed in the context of English law alone, there remains a remarkable convergence between jurisdictions. This is not to suggest that there is a principled or doctrinal convergence in the sense that exactly the same inconsistencies and incoherences exist across jurisdictions,[9] but rather that there is a basic convergence around a shared problem (i.e. the perceived *policy need* for prior fault rules) and the apparent shared inability to engage with that problem through traditional principled approaches. This is the case both across so-called common law and civil law jurisdictions, where we can identify a variety of doctrinal engagements with prior fault ideas, but it is very unlikely that any jurisdiction would stand behind its own approach as a model solution for dealing with prior fault^{OFF} or prior fault^{DEF} more generally. Indeed, regarding our parallel empirical studies exploring prior fault, the studies benefited from direct support of project partners from over ten different jurisdictions (principally through their respective Law Commission institutions).[10]

Some brief comparative examples can help here, drawing on materials discussed in previous chapters. In common law jurisdictions, it is perhaps less surprising to see points of legal conflict and confusion like those in England & Wales. However, it is notable how little progress has been made in resolving or addressing criticisms which have been directed at the relevant legal rules. We have previously highlighted Australia, for example, as a multi-jurisdictional country where we continue to see an inconsistent approach to prior fault across different Australian states.[11] Yet at the same time, policy debates have largely stagnated around a binary choice between accepting or rejecting the approach in *DPP v Majewski*.[12] So too in Canada, where despite specific rejection of prior fault^{OFF} as a substitute for voluntary action,[13] the same logic has not been applied to reject the use of prior fault^{OFF}

[9] See, e.g., P Robinson, 'Causing the Conditions of One's Own Defence' (1985) 71 *Virginia Law Review* 1; A Goldberg, JJ Child, H Crombag, and D Roef, 'Prior Fault Blame in England and Wales, Germany and the Netherlands' (2021) 8(1) *Journal of International and Comparative Law* 53.

[10] British Academy, *Understanding the 'Fault' in Prior-Fault Intoxication: A Pathway to Criminal Law Reform*, Knowledge Frontiers Project (KF3/100111, 2019). Project partnership represents an endorsement of our project, but does not—of course—necessarily represent support for any of our research conclusions or reform recommendations.

[11] E.g. the state of Victoria has abolished offence-based intoxication rules without replacement. See S Gough, 'Surviving without Majewski?' (2000) *Criminal Law Review* 719, 720–26; 'Intoxication and Criminal Liability' (1996) 112 *LQR* 335.

[12] [1977] AC 443. See *Kampeli* [1975] 2 NZLR 610 (NZ); *S v Chretien* (1981) 1 SA 1097 (SA); *O'Connor* (1980) 146 CLR 64 (Aus).

[13] Discussed in Chapter 2, Section 2.4.1.

as a constructor of mens rea states,[14] and the inaccurate language of intoxication as a 'defence' remains prevalent (i.e. obfuscating the role of prior fault^{OFF} in substituting for missing offence elements of any kind). It is also true to say that, in common law jurisdictions, the proxy understanding of prior fault in terms of intoxication is firmly entrenched.

Civil law jurisdictions provide a less direct form of comparison due to their dissimilar approach to criminal offence structures. However, despite this, there is a similar trend of prior fault rules presenting a series of knotty difficulties and/or anomalies reflected in *de jure* or *de facto* problems of incoherence and/or inconsistency. In Germany and the Netherlands, for example, despite firm constitutional preferences for principle-based codification, doctrines of prior fault remain largely uncodified and uncertain in their application.[15] Interestingly, the German prior fault^{OFF} doctrine of *actio libera in causa* has developed a more honest framing than we see elsewhere, recognizing that prior fault^{OFF} may be used to substitute for missing offence elements. There is also nothing in the specific framing of the doctrine to restrict it to intoxication cases alone, something that is also true of the Dutch equivalent *culpa in causa*. However, the *potential* for principled engagement created through better framing has not carried through to the operation of the law, where fictions of mens rea equivalence (German substitution) and a de facto focus on intoxication cases alone (across both jurisdictions) remain typical.[16] Even within the most significant point of divergence—the German gross intoxication offence—we see familiar narratives at the core, including the focus on intoxication as a proxy for fault, and the borrowing of conduct elements from more traditional offence structures.[17]

Our study therefore speaks directly to the comparable or cognate difficulties described here, providing principled analysis and reform recommendations applicable across jurisdictions. In particular, our articulation of a new 'prior fault offence' of culpable incapacity in Chapter 7 provides a bespoke special part solution to the problem of prior fault^{OFF}, and a solution that would allow for the abolition of several problematic general part mechanisms currently in use in a range of jurisdictions. Our recommendations for prior fault^{DEF} reform—in Chapters 9 and 10—would require some additional translation, bearing in mind the specific criminal law methodologies of civil law jurisdictions, many of which treat 'defences' as one

[14] See *Brown* [2022] SCC 18; P Leahy, 'Legislative Revision of Extreme Intoxication in Canada' [2022] *Criminal Law Review* 957.

[15] See A Goldberg, JJ Child, H Crombag, and D Roef, 'Prior Fault Blame in England and Wales, Germany and the Netherlands' (2021) 8(1) *Journal of International and Comparative Law* 53.

[16] Ibid. See also HU Paeffgen, 'Actio Libera in Causa und 323a StGB' [1985] *ZStW* 513; JJ Child and M van der Wolf, 'Prior Fault Insanity and Diminished Responsibility' in A Goldberg and P Manguele (eds) *Criminal Law and Prior Fault* (Hart, 2025) Ch 2.

[17] We discuss this in Chapter 5, Section 5.3.1 alongside other attempts to create something akin to a prior fault^{OFF} offence.

specific 'offence' element.[18] However, again, the conceptual analysis and recommendations remain of direct relevance.

11.3 Indirect implications

There are some areas of the criminal law in substance and process that are (or could be) influenced by prior fault rules and development, both conceptually and doctrinally. We have not examined these areas in any depth in previous chapters because, even though they may be affected by prior fault rules or analyses, they do not of themselves directly involve the application of prior fault rules in the sense we have discussed. In Section 11.4 below, we explore this in quite general terms, looking at the development of criminal fault assessments that go beyond traditional snapshot analysis (i.e. broadening the lens of the criminal law in the same way as prior fault rules). But there are also more immediate influences, where rules have developed in express connection with or alongside prior fault rules. Although still 'indirect' to the core prior fault rules themselves, we briefly discuss here how these rules may be impacted by the reforms we have recommended. We begin with a discussion of objective fault, and the definition of the 'reasonable person', before turning to the influence of the substantive prior fault rules on sentencing.

11.3.1 Defining the 'reasonable person'

Reasonable person tests are used throughout the criminal law, from the definition of negligence and objective fault in offending, through to the articulation of due diligence and reasonable responses in defending. In each case, D's conduct and/or mental state is measured against that of a 'reasonable person', providing a theoretical basis for blaming D where they fail to meet that standard.[19] Prior fault rules are not directly relevant here, in the sense that evidence of prior fault does not impact the *application* of the legal test in ways we have explored in this book. However, prior fault rules do have some indirect relevance in the construction of the test, and what we mean by a reasonable person.

A key challenge in the construction of reasonable person tests is to identify which attributes (if any) the reasonable person should be held to share with D.[20] Although inconsistent across the law, most tests will take account of D's age for example, acknowledging that it would be unfair to hold a child to the same standards

[18] I.e. as distinct from being a matter to be addressed once it has been decided D has committed the offence.

[19] See, generally, F Stark, *Culpable Carelessness* (CUP, 2016).

[20] Ibid. See also P Westen, 'Individualizing the Reasonable Person in Criminal Law' (2008) 2 *Criminal Law and Philosophy* 137.

as an adult; many will also take account of D's physical disabilities, and/or mental conditions, and so on. In each case, the idea is to hold D to a genuinely objective standard, but not to punish D unfairly for personal attributes that do not speak to their agency. This is usefully expressed by Hart in the form of two questions:[21]

(i) Did the accused fail to take those precautions which any reasonable man [*sic*] with normal capacities would in the circumstances have taken?
(ii) Could the accused, given his mental and physical capacities, have taken those precautions?

In this manner, having corrected for certain characteristics, the idea is that we may isolate only those details of an event which are legitimate targets of criminal blame (i.e. where D's failure to foresee the risk is not attributable to characteristics such as their age or disability, but rather to D's agency and wrongful choices in action). How, then, is prior fault relevant (if at all) to these issues?

The influence of prior fault logic emerges in cases where D is intoxicated at the time of the potential offence. As we have seen, alcohol and/or drug intoxication goes directly to questions of mental and physical capacity, suggesting that D should be measured against the standard of a similarly intoxicated reasonable person. However, almost universally, this is not the approach adopted; the reasonable person is held to be sober, and this is what D is measured against, thus significantly increasing the potential for liability.[22] The basic logic here is based squarely on prior fault: where D is intoxicated their incapacity is not a characteristic, such as their age, rather it is the state produced by previous blameworthy choices.

The impact of this approach is to blame D for prior conduct in much the same way as current intoxication rules. Indeed, negligence tests of this kind may be highlighted as alternatives to current intoxication rules, providing a route to blame that avoids reliance on fictions of mens rea equivalence.[23] And we have seen glimpses of this position earlier in the book. In the discussion of prior fault^{DEF} incapacity and mistake making in Chapter 9, for example, it was explained that the direct influence of prior fault^{DEF} rules was narrowed to a subset of defences that include subjective elements (in particular, self-defence). This is because, for most other defences which are defined in *objective* terms, D is already measured against a reasonable sober standard. The influence is less pronounced in the context of prior fault^{OFF}, because objective elements are much less common in the definition of 'mens rea' as an offence element. However, in the relatively short-lived period of

[21] HLA Hart, 'Negligence, Mens Rea, and Criminal Responsibility' in HLA Hart and J Gardner (eds) *Punishment and Responsibility* (OUP, 2008) 136, 154.
[22] Cf *Smith (Morgan)* [2000] UKHL 49.
[23] I.e. it has potential to avoid some of the most problematic aspects of current intoxication rules.

English law in which recklessness was defined objectively following *Caldwell*,[24] Stannard pronounced the 'demise of drunkenness', arguing that a shift to objective fault meant that the law no longer needed intoxication rules.[25] Indeed, in jurisdictions that are more accommodating of objective fault as an offence element, such as the Netherlands, a similar picture is apparent.[26]

Whether presented as an alternative to prior fault rules, or as a parallel concern, it is therefore clear how conceptions of objective fault and the reasonable person test becomes relevant to the themes of this book, and also to our critique of current approaches. In particular, we have criticized the use of 'intoxication' as a proxy for prior fault, highlighting its potential for both over-inclusive application (i.e. where D's intoxication is not unreasonable) and under-inclusive application (i.e. where D's incapacity results from other blameworthy causes), and we have argued that fault should instead be identified in D's negligent failure to take steps to avoid harms. This criticism applies equally to the 'prior fault logic' underlying the *sober* reasonable person test, and so—as with prior fault rules—should prompt us to consider potential reforms. This may be presented as a push-back against objective fault in general, to the extent that the reasonable person test would struggle to meet the critique. However, this need not be the case. Rather, it is a reason to prefer reasonable person constructions that include a variety of characteristics, going beyond those typically included in current legal tests.[27] On questions of mental capacity, it might also prompt a presumption that D is not to blame, unless the circumstances of prior fault^{OFF} can be established (i.e. following a model of culpable incapacity, and avoiding proxy devices, such as intoxication).

11.3.2 Sentencing

Sentencing people convicted of offences is in part an exercise of assessing harm and culpability by reference to all the circumstances in which the offence was committed, and this may involve considering factors leading up to the offence, as well as contextual factors which may have a bearing or impact on harm and culpability. These factors may well be similar to, or indeed the same as, those which drive prior fault rules in the substantive sense. Thus, for example, in England & Wales, it is now well established that evidence of alcohol and drug intoxication is to be considered as an aggravating factor when offending, potentially increasing

[24] [1982] AC 341. *Caldwell* was eventually overruled in the case of *G* [2003] UKHL 50, which restored the core subjective requirement for recklessness.
[25] J Stannard, 'The Demise of Drunkenness' (1982) 2 *Legal Studies* 291.
[26] Discussed in A Goldberg, JJ Child, H Crombag, and D Roef, 'Prior Fault Blame in England and Wales, Germany and the Netherlands' (2021) 8(1) *Journal of International and Comparative Law* 53.
[27] See F Stark, *Culpable Carelessness* (CUP, 2016) 247–52; AP Simester, 'A Disintegrated Theory of Culpability' in D Baker and J Horder (eds) *The Sanctity of Life and the Criminal Law* (CUP, 2013) 178; A Norrie, 'The Mysterious Case of the Reasonable Glue Sniffer' (2002) 65(4) *Modern Law Review* 538.

D's sentence.[28] Importantly, for present purposes, the aggravating status of intoxication and the language used to justify that status echo the language and intuitions of prior fault. We see this in the sentencing guidelines themselves, where voluntary intoxication is presented as an aggravating factor in terms of 'culpability' and offence 'seriousness'.[29] This tendency is also more explicitly reflected in sentencing remarks, where courts will often cite *Majewski* and other prior fault cases to *justify* the status of intoxication as an aggravating factor when sentencing. Discussing this issue in *Foy*,[30] for example, the Court of Appeal says:

> It has always been a general principle of law, on policy grounds, that self-induced intoxication ordinarily is of itself no defence: a defendant cannot defend himself by saying: 'I would never have done this had I been sober'... (see, for example, cases such as *DPP v Majewski* [1977] AC 443). The same principle extends to sentencing: voluntary intoxication cannot be advanced as a mitigating factor, indeed it ordinarily is treated by the courts as an aggravating factor.

It is clear, therefore, that prior fault intuition ('the same principle') is being carried between both liability and sentencing stage decision-making.

But is this approach correct? For us, it is important to understand (and, indeed, to question) the association between prior fault at liability and at sentencing. There is clearly *some* basis for association: if the prior fault^{OFF} rules discussed in Chapter 2 establish T1 intoxication as a legitimate source of blame relevant to D's harmful conduct at T2, then there is some logic in taking account of that blame when sentencing. However, there are also significant contrary indicators. Prior fault^{OFF} rules constructing criminal liability (as distinct from sentencing) are not concerned with T1 blame in general, but rather specifically with D placing themselves in a position that gave rise to an intoxicated mistake (i.e. resulting in absence of mens rea and/or voluntariness), where that mistake would not have occurred but for D's intoxication, and upon which D is assumed 'reckless' to the criminal standard.[31] This is not the case where intoxication is a factor in sentencing. In the vast majority of cases involving intoxication in sentencing, we are not concerned with an intoxicated mistake, but rather with a drug-induced or -impaired *choice* to offend.[32]

[28] Reflected in overarching sentencing guidelines since 2004: Sentencing Guidelines Council, *Overarching Principles: Seriousness* (2004). Current guidelines: Sentencing Council, *Sentencing Guidelines: Overarching Principles* (2019).
[29] Ibid. Discussed in C Lightowlers et al, 'Contextual Culpability: How Drinking and Social Context Impact Sentencing of Violence' (2020) 22(3) *Criminology & Criminal Justice* 442–61.
[30] *Foy* [2020] EWCA Crim 270, [73].
[31] See extended discussion in Chapter 2.
[32] C Lighthouse, *Intoxication and Sentencing* (Sentencing Academy, 2022).

In this manner, the core constituents of prior fault^{OFF} blame at liability are either missing or irrelevant at sentencing, including the causal/counterfactual link between D's intoxication and mistake, the equivalence with mens rea recklessness, and so on. There may be T1 blame in these cases, but it is not the same kind of blame. Indeed, even where it *is* the same kind of blame, where we are sentencing D within the subset of cases in which liability has been established through the intoxication rules, it is again questionable whether prior fault^{OFF} should carry through to sentencing. This is because, within this subset, D has *already* been blamed for their intoxication as an element of their offence, and so further aggravation at sentencing risks inappropriate double-counting.

The lessons from this book for sentencing, therefore, should not be understood to inform the specific content of sentencing guidelines, but rather its methodology. Key features of our methodology which should inform approaches to sentencing include: the importance of identifying particularized wrongs/aggravations (i.e. eliminating reliance on proxy or analogy), the need for specificity in discussion of different points of focus across a T1–T2 course of conduct, and sensitivity to scientific understandings (and uncertainties) in the construction of rules.

11.4 Implications for broader understandings of fault

As final points of reflection, we end with some brief remarks on the broader significance of our study in theoretical and methodological terms. In each case, we are concerned with how to make sense of multi-event offending, which is—increasingly—relevant to future debates.

11.4.1 Theoretical reflections

Prior fault creates a challenge for the law because of its structure. Typical criminal offence structures centre around a single point of conduct (act or omission), using this as an anchor point from which to assess harms (i.e. resulting from D's conduct) and culpability (i.e. D's mental state and/or awareness in action). This typical structure is beneficial for a variety of reasons, not least for its ability to narrow legal focus in a way that allows the wider criminal justice system to function. However, it is a focus that can lead to injustice, particularly in terms of under-inclusivity. In some cases, this is because the relevant wrong can only be appreciated through a wider lens that takes account of multiple conduct events: we see this in the prior fault^{OFF} and prior fault^{DEF} rules relating to mistakes and incapacity (i.e. we can only understand D's *fault* in causing harms at T2 with reference to their blameworthy choices leading to impairment between T1 and T2). In other cases, the potential for injustice is more deliberate, where D seeks to manipulate the typical single-event focus: we see this in the prior fault^{DEF} rules relating to contrived defences (i.e. we can only understand D's *fault* at T2 with reference to their blameworthy choices between T1 and T2 in creating the otherwise defence-justifying crisis).

The challenge of understanding offending and defences across multiple events, however, is neither unique to prior fault nor insurmountable. Indeed, it has become increasingly common for offences to be constructed across multiple events to capture different kinds of mischief, such as harassment and stalking,[33] controlling or coercive behaviour,[34] etc.

The real challenge for prior fault has been the refusal of courts and law reformers to *recognize* the structural challenge. Rather than present a multi-event wrong, and focus debate on how that wrong might best be captured within the law, prior fault rules have been designed and applied to create a fiction: for prior fault^{OFF}, that D has committed a single-event offence at T2, and that D's T1 conduct somehow provides for elements of the T2 offence that might otherwise appear to be absent. This fiction has been maintained through a combination of illogical reframing and obfuscations (e.g. intoxication as a defence, or an evidential rule), but can be reduced to a simple claim of equivalence between the T1 prior fault^{OFF} and the missing offence element. We have detailed several attempts at constructing such equivalence, but, in our view, it is ultimately unachievable.

The major theoretical move we have made therefore, across prior fault^{OFF} and prior fault^{DEF}, is to break away from current fictions and the flawed quest for equivalence, refocusing on understanding offending and defences across multiple events. This remains challenging. Challenging in theoretical terms, when it comes to identifying and defining both physical and mental elements without the single conduct anchor.[35] And challenging in terms of scope: identifying and justifying what span of conduct should be included, what types of harms, etc. The crucial difference between these challenges and the ones they replace is that these challenges go to the mischief for which D is actually blamed, providing principled engagement that can be debated, thereby informing the evolution of the law more generally.

11.4.2 Methodological reflections

The book is predominantly a traditional legal text, combining analytical, doctrinal, and comparative methodologies. However, given our engagement with issues of

[33] Protection from Harassment Act 1997, s2, s2A, s4, and s4A.
[34] Serious Crime Act 2015, s76.
[35] See, broadly, JJ Child, 'Wrong on Many Levels: Understanding Crimes Across and Between Events' [2024] *Criminal Law Review* 378.

mental impairment, and non-traditional assessments of fault (i.e. across events), we have also drawn upon scientific and empirical methods to help inform and test our legal analysis. Here, we provide some brief reflections on each, including the potential for future research.

11.4.2.1 Doctrinal and analytical approach

Our primary methods of legal research—doctrinal and analytical—are likely to be familiar to the reader. And the way we employed those methods also represents well-trodden ground. Essentially, we began with the identification of a problem in prior fault: a problem in terms of fairness, including the potential for inappropriate criminalization and/or labelling of offenders, and a combined problem of legal incoherence and intransigence, with over a century of jurisprudence seemingly unable to engage with that problem in any more meaningful way. Our jurisdictional focus has been on England & Wales, though a notable feature of the study has been how widely the problems are shared, across jurisdictions from both common law and civil law traditions.

There are various ways we could have approached the problems associated with prior fault, beginning at various levels of abstraction from the current law. In this book, we found it most effective to begin with the detail of the rules themselves. We wanted to understand exactly how and why the current jurisprudence has become stuck, and what barriers have emerged to prevent more principled and rational debate. This is why several of the chapters are themed around current categories of prior fault, from intoxication, automatism, and insanity, through to contrived defences. In each case, a major part of the project has been a scoping exercise, identifying and distinguishing principled arguments (normative and descriptive) from legal incoherence and fictions. We have consciously explored and tested arguments at their strongest, before concluding that the models of engagement available within the current prior fault rules were irretrievable. It was only from this point that we turned to alternative models for reform, both in the context of prior fault^{OFF} and prior fault^{DEF} rules.

The close textual and analytical approach adopted has meant compromises elsewhere. In particular, we have largely bracketed broader questions of legitimate criminalization, and this current project is certainly not one that makes claims towards any grand theory of criminalization or culpability. Rather, in accepting the potential future role of prior fault (i.e. moving to questions of reform rather than simple abolition), we have relied upon three related points: (i) that there is normative force behind certain intuitions in favour of prior fault criminalization, (ii) that, relatedly, simple abolition of prior fault rules would risk under-criminalization, and (iii) that the political reality in England & Wales (and across most other jurisdictions) makes the option of abolition of prior fault without replacement essentially untenable. These points become the basis of our pivot, from critique of the current law to the discussion of potential reforms.

Our aim has been to take readers with us on the full journey, from abolition of current rules through to specific doctrinal reform. However, one of the features of the staged approach we have adopted is that readers are free to identify points of agreement or departure without having to accept or reject our thesis as a whole. Thus, for example, whilst we hope that all readers will be convinced by our critique of the current law and the case for abandoning the current position, acceptance of this does not necessitate agreement in the case for reform *beyond* abolition, and certainly not for our specific recommendations for legislative reform. In the face of legal stagnation, this approach is aimed at generating movement, as well as facilitating the identification of areas of disagreement with which future scholarship can engage.

11.4.2.2 Scientific and empirical approach

The exploration of relevant scientific and empirical research, including our own empirical studies, has been essential to this project in two main ways. The first has been to inform our analysis and critique of the current law. The current law is constructed and maintained on the basis of a multitude of scientific understandings or 'folk psychology', including, for example, views on the effects of alcohol and other drugs, the nature of consciousness and mental impairment, the causal routes of impairment, the nature of mental disorders and comorbidity, and so on. Expert engagement with the scientific literature has allowed us to test and critique many of the assumptions made in law, exposing points of inaccuracy and uncertainty. To give just one example from the book, such engagement has been vital in demonstrating the inappropriate status of 'intoxication' as a/*the* proxy for prior fault, allowing us to expose the uncertain definitional and causal elements underlying that term.[36]

The second level of engagement has been future focused, providing valuable new input into our discussion of reforms. Where the more theoretical literature presents several options for reform, scientific and empirical insights can help identify the more robust path. We saw this, in particular, in our discussion of culpable incapacity, and the relative merits of identifying fault across T1 and T2.[37] Although several models for reform have focused on D's foresight of future mistake making as the basis for blame, our studies (in line with the wider extant scientific literature) do not support this approach: we found relevant underperformance in circumstances of (intoxicated) impairment, but we did not see this reflected in an awareness of current or future risk. Rather, we identified D's awareness of self-impairment, and D's behaviour in managing the circumstances of that incapacity (i.e. avoiding future harms), to be the more robust focus for blame.

36 See Chapter 2.
37 See Chapters 5–7.

Conducting empirical studies within the project has produced a host of challenges, not least in terms of ensuring real-world validity and scope. However, it is an area that is underserved within the current empirical literature, where studies of intoxication and cognate impairments are often not sufficiently aligned to the interests of legal study and law reform. We are happy with the progress we have made, but remain acutely aware that more is required here, with the potential to impact our reform recommendations in the future. This includes studies with even greater real-world validity and applicability, for example, using scenarios developed for and implemented in virtual reality, as well as looking beyond intoxication to test equivalent states of self-induced impairment, including those already discussed here. We will pursue this ourselves, but also hope to prompt others to do likewise, particularly in recognizing the essential role of genuine interdisciplinary collaboration from design to analysis, in promoting replication and scientific reliability.

11.5 Conclusion

This is the first long-form monograph to explore the legal conception of prior fault,[38] and has done so comprehensively across both prior fault^{OFF} and prior fault^{DEF}. Prior fault identifies a set of ideas and legal rules within the general part of the criminal law—rules that have essentially defied the dynamics of principled modernization that has marked the last century. We apply criminal blame, label, and punish offenders, all based on prior fault mechanisms built upon 'intuition' and 'policy'—terms used, apparently, to excuse unprincipled incoherence and legal fictions. The current law is indefensible, and yet comparable models of prior fault continue to operate across the world.

There has been a multitude of work engaging with the problems of prior fault, including academic and reform literature that has proven invaluable to this study. However, as we reflect upon the last century—both in terms of legal and theoretical progress—we can see a clear limitation within shorter length projects (such as journal articles and reports). With a topic as complex as prior fault, across legal and scientific planes, the literature can become stuck: focused on explaining the layers of confusion and incoherence within the current law and leaving little space for reform discussion, or abstracting to broader theoretical engagement, but then lacking the clear links back to doctrine. In each case, although such papers bring analysis and insight, it is very difficult for them to progress the debate and reform discussion in any meaningful way, risking the creation of a never-ending cycle of scholarship over time, without creating points of breakthrough.

[38] Whilst acknowledging the shorter text by M Gur-Arye, *Actio Libera in Causa in Criminal Law* (Jerusalem, 1984).

One of the primary aims of this book is to break that cycle, and to provide an analysis of prior fault that both exposes the unviable nature of the current law, as well as to plot the route to principled reform. Some of this can only—realistically—be achieved through legislation, such as reflected in our recommendations for a new offence of culpable incapacity. However, there are clear lessons for the courts as well, both in terms of containing current fictions (e.g. in the definition of 'intoxication'), as well as the common law interpretation and development of prior fault^{DEF} rules.

APPENDIX

ILLUSTRATIVE DRAFT LEGISLATION

Here we set out our recommendations for reform in illustrative draft legislative form. The caveat is that we are not parliamentary counsel, and therefore these illustrative draft clauses are not intended to be subjected to classic statutory canons of construction. The objectives sought to be achieved and rationales underlying the approaches adopted are discussed in detail as follows: Clause 1 in Chapter 7, Clause 2 in Chapter 9, and Clause 3 in Chapter 10.

Clause 1 Culpable incapacity

(1) A person (D) commits an offence if they intentionally or recklessly become significantly mentally impaired and/or involuntary; and

(2) whilst in that impaired or involuntary state D causes or engages in one of the following harms:

- (a) death to another person,
- (b) injury to another person,
- (c) non-consensual sexual penetration of another person,
- (d) non-consensual sexual contact with another person, or
- (e) damage or destruction of another's property; and

(3) in so doing, D was,

- (a) in a state of extreme intoxication with a dangerous drug taken voluntarily, or
- (b) negligent in causing or engaging in the harm, having failed to take steps that could reasonably be expected of D in avoidance of the specific harm, where those steps were available at the time of, or shortly before, the harm was caused or engaged in.

(4) A person guilty of an offence under this clause, where the harm caused is the death of another person, is liable on conviction on indictment to imprisonment for life for 'causing death whilst culpably incapacitated'.

(5) A person guilty of an offence under this clause, where the harm caused is the injury of another person, is liable for 'causing injury whilst culpably incapacitated'—

- (a) on summary conviction to imprisonment for a term not exceeding twelve months or to a fine not exceeding the statutory maximum or both, or
- (b) on conviction on indictment to imprisonment for life.

(6) A person guilty of an offence under this clause, where the harm engaged in is the non-consensual sexual penetration of another person, is liable on conviction on indictment to imprisonment for life for 'non-consensual sexual penetration whilst culpably incapacitated'.

(7) A person guilty of an offence under this clause, where the harm engaged in is the non-consensual sexual touching of another person, is liable for 'non-consensual sexual touching whilst culpably incapacitated'—

- (a) on summary conviction to imprisonment for a term not exceeding twelve months or to a fine not exceeding the statutory maximum or both, or
- (b) on conviction on indictment to imprisonment for a term not exceeding ten years.

(8) A person guilty of an offence under this clause, where the harm caused is the destruction or damage of property, is liable for 'causing the destruction or damage of another's property whilst culpably incapacitated'—
 (a) on summary conviction to imprisonment for a term not exceeding twelve months or to a fine not exceeding the statutory maximum or both, or
 (c) on conviction on indictment to imprisonment for a term not exceeding ten years.

Clause 2 Mistaken beliefs in defence and culpable incapacity

(1) This clause applies if—
 (a) there are proceedings against a person (D) for any offence,
 (b) D was at any material time in a state of culpable incapacity, and
 (c) by way of defence, or in support of a defence, D relies on having at that time held a particular mistaken belief as to any fact.
(2) In this clause, 'culpable incapacity' requires D intentionally or recklessly to have become significantly mentally impaired and/or involuntary, making a mistake either—
 (a) through extreme intoxication with a dangerous drug taken voluntarily, or
 (b) through negligence, having failed to take steps that could reasonably be expected of D in avoidance of the circumstances of that mistake, where those steps were available at the time of, or shortly before, the mistake was made.
(3) In application of a defence in these circumstances, D's actual belief is to be taken into account only if a reasonable person sharing D's characteristics would have held the same belief.

Clause 3 Contrived defending

(1) Where D relies on a supervening defence, that defence is to be disregarded where D was responsible for contriving its circumstances.
(2) In determining whether D has contrived the circumstances of a defence, it must be demonstrated that—
 (a) D's conduct materially contributed to the circumstances of the defence,
 (b) D intended or was reckless whether their conduct would materially contribute to the circumstances of the defence, and
 (c) D foresaw the risk of their own future offending, in the context of defensive action.
(3) 'Material contribution' is to be interpreted as significant or weighty, howsoever brought about. It will be absent where the circumstances of defence arise from the unforeseen and disproportionate misconduct of another.

Index

For the benefit of digital users, indexed terms that span two pages (e.g., 52–53) may, on occasion, appear on only one of those pages.

Note: names and cases are not indexed if they appear only in footnote citations